The Harris Legacy

Signed by the Author

_____

ALISTER CAMPBELL

CRU GROUP

member of Context International

www.cruadjusters.com

The Harris Legacy

Reflections on a Transformational Premier

Alister Campbell (ed.)

sh.

SUTHERLAND
HOUSE

Toronto, 2023

Sutherland House
416 Moore Ave., Suite 205
Toronto, ON M4G 1C9

Sutherland House and logo are registered
trademarks of The Sutherland House Inc.

First edition, November 2023

If you are interested in inviting one of our authors to a live event or
media appearance, please contact sranasinghe@sutherlandhousebooks.com
and visit our website at sutherlandhousebooks.com for more
information about our authors and their schedules.

To learn more about Mike Harris please visit TheHarrisLegacy.ca

We acknowledge the support of the Government of Canada.

Manufactured in China
Cover designed by Jordan Lunn

Library and Archives Canada Cataloguing in Publication
Title: The Harris legacy : reflections on a transformational premier / Alister Campbell.
Names: Campbell, Alister author
Description: Includes index.
Identifiers: Canadiana (print) 20230458297 | Canadiana (ebook) 20230458300 |
ISBN 9781990823473 (hardcover) | ISBN 9781990823480 (EPUB)
Subjects: LCSH: Harris, Mike, 1945- | LCSH: Premiers (Canada)—Ontario—Biography.
| CSH: Ontario—Politics and government—1995-2003.
Classification: LCC FC3078.1.H37 C36 2023 | DDC 971.3/04—dc23

ISBN 978-1-990823-47-3
eBook 978-1-990823-48-0

CONTRIBUTORS

Alister Campbell has served as CEO of several of Canada's larger P&C insurance companies. He has long taken a close interest in public policy in Canada and has volunteered in many municipal, provincial, and federal election campaigns. He worked as "Message Guy" in the 1995 Harris campaign, responsible for policy, speech, communications, advertising, and media.

David Frum is a staff writer at the *Atlantic* and a former speechwriter and special assistant to President George W. Bush. He is the author or co-author of ten books. In 1995, David was a columnist for the *Toronto Sun*, where he often wrote about Ontario politics.

Dr. Eugene Beaulieu is a professor in the Department of Economics at the University of Calgary and is Director of the International Economics Program at The School of Public Policy. He completed his Ph.D. at Columbia University in 1997. He has worked as an economist for the Government of Kenya and the Bank of Canada. Dr. Beaulieu is the founder of the annual Rocky Mountain Empirical Trade Conference in Banff and the Canadian International Trade Study Group.

Dr. Jack M. Mintz is the president's fellow of the School of Public Policy at the University of Calgary after serving as the Palmer Chair and founding director from 2008 to 2015. He is a regulator contributor to the *Financial Post*. Dr. Mintz became a member of the Order of Canada in 2015.

Terence Corcoran, one of Canada's leading business writers and editors, has held editorial positions with *The Gazette* in Montreal, *The Financial Times* of Canada, and *The Globe and Mail*. Since 1998, he has been a columnist with the *National Post*. Mr. Corcoran was co-author of *Public Money Private Greed*, a best-selling book on a major Canadian real estate scandal.

Will Falk has advised governments, hospitals, and innovative healthcare organizations since the 1980s. He retired in 2017 from PwC, where he ran the Canadian healthcare practice and was on the global health leadership team. A fellow at the CD Howe Institute, Women's College Hospital WIHV, and the Rotman School of Management, he writes widely on healthcare policy.

William Robson is the CEO of the C.D. Howe Institute. He has written more than 260 monographs, articles, chapters, and books on such subjects as government budgets, pensions, healthcare financing, inflation, and currency issues. He was chair of the Ontario Parent Council and a member of the Ontario Postsecondary Education Quality Assessment Board.

Sean Speer is the editor-at-large of "The Hub," a senior fellow at the Munk School of Global Affairs and the Public Policy Forum. He previously served as a senior advisor to former Canadian Prime Minister Stephen Harper.

Taylor Jackson is an experienced policy analyst and Ph.D. student in political science at the University of Toronto. He has worked with several think tanks in Canada and the United States and previously served as a senior advisor to the Ontario minister of finance.

Ginny Roth is a public affairs consultant with Crestview Strategy. She advises multinational corporations, Canadian companies, and nonprofits on government relations in Canada and is involved in politics and public policy development at all levels of government. A frequent panelist on major television and radio outlets, she contributes to "The Hub" and the *National Post*.

Howard Levitt is a labour lawyer who has appeared as lead counsel in more employment law cases in the Supreme Court of Canada and at more provincial Courts of Appeal than any lawyer in Canadian history. He writes a twice-weekly employment law column in the *Financial Post* and is the author of one of Canada's leading dismissal textbooks, *The Law of Dismissal in Canada.*

Will Stewart is a senior strategic advisor in public affairs who has driven project teams on complex files in a broad array of sectors for corporations, not-for-profits, start-ups, and member-driven associations. A speaker and strategist on public policy, he has spent much of his career in and around politics, including as chief of staff to the Ontario minister of energy.

Gordon Miller served three terms as Ontario's Environmental Commissioner, first appointed by an all-party committee of the Ontario Legislature in 1999. He previously served as a district manager for the Ontario Ministry of Environment and Energy until his role was downsized by the Harris government. He has most recently run for office on behalf of the Green Party of Canada.

Guy Giorno leads the political law practice at Fasken. He served in the premier's office of the Harris government as policy director, deputy chief of staff, and chief of staff. From 2008 to 2010, he was chief of staff to Prime Minister Stephen Harper. Now retired from partisan politics, he has been appointed as the integrity commissioner of several Ontario municipalities.

Craig McFadyen advised six Ontario premiers, including Mike Harris, on intergovernmental finance, intergovernmental policy, and international relations issues. He has been an adjunct professor at the University of Toronto and the Toronto Metropolitan University and is currently focused on issues relating to adults living with intellectual disabilities.

Hugh Segal is the Matthews Distinguished Fellow in Global Public Policy in the School of Policy Studies at Queen's University in Kingston, Canada. He was chief of staff to the Canadian prime minister, associate cabinet secretary in Ontario, and a member of the Canadian Senate. He has written books on public, foreign, and defence policy, conservative politics, and income security.

David Herle is the principal partner at a leading polling and research firm The Gandalf Group. He was a top advisor to Prime Minister Paul Martin's Liberal Party of Canada campaign co-chair for 2004 and 2006, as well as managing co-chair for Ontario Premier Kathleen Wynne's election campaigns in 2014 and 2018. He is the host of "The Herle Burly" and "Curse of Politics" podcasts.

Jaime Watt, widely regarded as Canada's leading high-stakes communications strategist, is the executive chairman of Navigator and founder of the Canadian Centre for the Purpose of the Corporation. He is the chancellor of OCAD University and a trustee of the University Health Network. He writes for the *Toronto Star* and is the author of *What I Wish I Said* (2023).

CONTENTS

INTRODUCTION

Alister Campbell

ON JUNE 8, 1995, MIKE HARRIS, after languishing in third place in public opinion polls for the five years previous and, in fact, up until the third week of the five-week writ period itself, won a landslide election to serve as Premier of Ontario. Having campaigned forcefully on *The Common Sense Revolution* (*CSR*) platform, which in content, scope, and specificity breached many political norms, he went on to defy further norms by comprehensively and firmly implementing the many policies he had advocated in the campaign. The subsequent four years in office saw dramatic reductions in government spending and levels of taxation, as well as a series of significant structural changes in the Ontario public sector. It also saw unparalleled levels of debate and public resistance. In the particularly hard-fought and bitter 1999 election, which served as a province-wide referendum on *CSR*, Premier Harris was reelected to a second majority term with an increased share of the popular vote, the first Ontario premier to achieve this feat since Mitch Hepburn in 1937.[1] He stepped down as premier midway through that second term. When asked if he had any regrets after such a whirlwind of extraordinarily dramatic changes for the province, he said only that "I wish I had done more. . . faster."

The *CSR* and the Harris era were transformational for Ontario, in terms of both public policy and politics. Today, almost 30 years after his first election victory, the mention of Premier Harris still galvanizes emotions on all sides. Indeed, decades after his terms in office ended, his name is often invoked in both federal and provincial campaigns in order to stir voter reaction. The intensity of the emotions generated can serve as an obstacle to a more balanced evaluation of the Harris "revolution."

But this look at the Harris legacy is not only retrospective. Despite the controversy surrounding so many of the wide-ranging reforms undertaken by the Harris government across so many different public policy areas, it is important to appreciate just how few of those changes have been reversed by his (largely Liberal) successors in the many years since. The City of Toronto was not unmerged. Closed hospitals were not reopened. Province-wide negotiation authority for teaching contracts was not handed back to the eighty-four Boards of Education. The old monolith of Ontario Hydro was not reconstituted. The coal-burning power plants he began to close have not reopened. The massive expansion of Ontario parkland was not reversed. Reduced welfare compensation was not reinstated. Standardized testing in Grades Three, Six, and Nine remains in place. The Oakridges Moraine is still undeveloped (as of this edition). Privatized highways (e.g., 407ETR) and nuclear plants (e.g., Bruce Power) have not been renationalized. The list goes on. And even this extraordinary list omits other profoundly meaningful accomplishments of the Harris era, including the successful balancing of a troubled province's budget, a rebalancing of the Canadian federation itself, and a burst of economic growth and job creation hard to match. The Harris government even helped make the Canada Pension Plan sustainable.

Suffice it to say that many, if not most, of the fundamental changes implemented during the Harris regime survive and define the Ontario we currently inhabit. It is not an overstatement, based on the evidence accumulated in this collection of essays, to say that we live in Mike Harris's Ontario today. And the concern that this legacy was both meaningful and perhaps unfairly maligned—or at least underappreciated—created the initial impetus for this editorial project.

There is one other important issue I want to ensure is surfaced at the beginning of this essay collection. The *CSR* and the Harris Government elected with that platform sought to confront a public policy challenge still with us today: how elected officials are to balance the costs and benefits of the public service they are entrusted with managing. As the public sector has grown as a percentage of GDP, this issue has become increasingly problematic for governments of all stripes. It was New Democratic Party (NDP) Premier Bob Rae who was first forced to grapple with Ontario's modern version of this conundrum, and his solution was the creative and nuanced Social Contract, an effort to contain costs at a time of constraint while still protecting public sector union jobs. The response of the public sector unions was tectonic, and the resulting conflict broke Rae's party in two (and probably also contributed to his personal political evolution toward the centre). It was in this period that the well-funded monopoly unions of the public sector appeared to move fully and forcefully into a permanent posture of war with whoever was in power.

The election of Harris in 1995 was completely unexpected and a particular shock to these unions and their leadership. The response was extreme, and through regional "Days of Action," two OPSEU province-wide strikes, as well as an escalating series of local, regional, and province-wide conflicts with the richly funded teachers' unions, the warring sides contributed to an environment of labour conflict with which Ontario was previously unfamiliar.

While the success of the *CSR* in 1995 caught these unions by surprise, the same cannot be said for the 1999 election, which saw organized campaigning and union-funded advertising at levels previously unparalleled. The Harris reelection, in spite of these new levels of public sector union engagement, led to an even more extreme reaction, and by the election of 2003, these unions had evolved entirely new strategies (including front groups such as the Working Families Coalition), which enabled waves of negative advertising far in excess of the combined advertising budgets of the political parties themselves and which eventually proved decisive in bringing an end to the Harris era.

The Harris legacy remains a subject of controversy today, in part at least, because these unions and so many public-sector funded think tanks and academics have exercised their monopoly power to dominate the evaluation of that legacy. But it is my view that they shouldn't be allowed to "cancel" reality. And, as this collection of essays demonstrates, the actual legacy of Mike Harris as premier of Ontario was substantial, long-lasting, and in many ways transformational. Of course, there are many lessons to be learned from this period, particularly as the lasting consequences of these past conflicts between public and private sector interests still both impact and infect the public policy debates of our day. This is precisely why I believe the publication of this retrospective—a "minority report," as one friend calls it—is both timely and appropriate.

If politicians are remembered at all in Canada, it is generally for their failings. Pierre Trudeau for the first significant run-up in Canada's public debt and the National Energy Policy, which demonized an entire region of our federation; Brian Mulroney for the Airbus Affair; Jean Chretien for the corruption scandals that concluded his long and largely successful public service career. Here in Ontario, the same is the case. McGuinty had his coal plants, and Wynne had senior staff imprisoned for trying to cover tracks on this controversial file. For Mike Harris, his legacy is undeniably associated with the names Walkerton (see Chapters 2 and 9) and Ipperwash (see the editor's note). Journalists, looking for a quick clip to summarize any politician's record, all too often default to these simplistic "memes" to describe an entire career. It is left to historians to try to achieve a more balanced perspective, achievable perhaps only with the passage of time.

This retrospective was conceived as an effort to seek a balanced view of the extraordinary shifts in the way Ontario was governed under Premier Harris. And while balanced historical evaluation appears to be somewhat out of fashion at the moment, I am convinced that enough time has now passed that such an evaluation should be possible. I also believe that such an evaluation will be beneficial, providing real insight into how the policy actions of that time can inform responses to the challenges we face as a province and country today.

It will be difficult for any engaged reader not to approach these essays "chronocentrically," by which I mean through the lens of current times. And while the Harris years concluded in this still-young century, a great deal has changed since then. For instance, social views on many topics, including LGBTQ, have evolved dramatically across the entire political spectrum. Two other quick examples come to mind. The *CSR* was written when carbon emissions were only starting to gain notice, and when interest rates were painfully high (although recent upward shifts in interest rates are providing a vivid reminder of the potentially costly consequences of excessive government debt).

A highly qualified group of seasoned and engaged observers of the Canadian public policy space has been recruited to review distinct areas of the policy landscape where the Harris "revolution" had particular impact. Some are partisan, and some are avowedly not. Some are conservatives, and some are decidedly not. Some were engaged in the politics of the time, and others barely born when the *CSR* came into being. But all of them have undertaken their task in good faith, looking at all sides of the story and articulating a balanced perspective. And all are volunteers who embarked on their work with only the pleasure of knowledge gained as compensation for their efforts.

Authors were asked to start by introducing themselves and making clear the personal perspective they brought to the inquiry. They were then tasked with outlining their understanding of the underlying motivation(s) for the specific policies or reforms in a defined policy area. Then to summarize the actual changes implemented as well as their impacts, both statistically (where appropriate) and in terms of specific stakeholder groups. Authors were asked to evaluate outcomes, both positive and negative, of the policy changes undertaken and encouraged to undertake a balanced evaluation of the net impacts, good, neutral, or bad. Finally, they were asked to summarize their considered and informed view of the Harris legacy in their defined area of focus. Authors were also free to share, from their informed perspective, any lessons which might be beneficial for those engaged in public policy review today.

It is appropriate for readers to be informed of this editor's own background and personal perspective regarding former Premier Harris and the *CSR*. I became active in politics at the University of Toronto when I first arrived on campus in 1978 and have engaged in both internal party leadership campaigns and election campaigns for decades since—as a conservative. As a volunteer, I helped Mike Harris become leader of the Progressive Conservative Party in 1990 and worked as part of his central campaign team in both 1995 and 1999. As the saying goes, "success has many fathers," and that is unmistakably true in the case of all three Harris campaigns in the 1990s, which benefited from the inspired contributions made by so many. That having been said, my name can legitimately be included in the short list of those intimately engaged in the crafting and delivery of the Harris platforms, for better or worse.

I believe this direct involvement qualifies me to comment on the formative influences on those platforms (see Chapter 1: "The Revolution's Antecedents"). But it also helps explain the deeply personal interest I have in the findings of the authors whose chapters make up this collection. I have always been deeply proud of my personal contribution to the winning campaigns of 1995 and 1999, and I am grateful for the deep friendships formed during those campaigns—friendships that have lasted a lifetime. But looking back on life and taking stock of what I have done and not (yet) done, I am curious to learn whether or not my contributions were actually a net benefit to my birth province and my country. Read along with me, and we'll find out together.

Finally, it is important to note that this editor committed, from the outset of this project, to exercise no authority over the conclusions drawn by any of these contributors. Their findings and conclusions are their own. And while I certainly do not agree with all the conclusions drawn, I am certain they will be of deep interest to any Canadian interested in properly understanding the evolution of public policy in our province and country. They are also instructive at a time when many see only intractable issues, and worry that no single individual can really make a difference. My own personal experience has taught me that it is entirely possible to make that difference. And, for those interested in seeing the very real impact a single political leader and provincial premier can have in shaping the society we share, it is a theme illustrated comprehensively in *The Harris Legacy*. I hope you enjoy reading it as much as I enjoyed the curatorial task of assembling it.

Note

1   https://en.wikipedia.org/wiki/List_of_Ontario_general_elections

FOREWORD

Lessons from a Legacy

David Frum

THERE IS SOMETHING VERY CANADIAN about the phrase "common sense revolution." Like such previous Canadian concepts as "progressive Conservatism" and "conscription if necessary, but not necessarily conscription," the phrase promises to unify opposites in search of a pragmatic balance. To outsiders, it can all seem very illogical. And yet, Canadians somehow make their unusual combinations work.

The *CSR* was built around a man as typically Canadian as the movement itself. Undramatic, self-effacing, self-controlled, Mike Harris presented himself as the kind of neighbour a homeowner would trust with the duplicate house keys. On the night of his election as premier of Ontario in 1995, he joked: "I can't imagine why anybody would want this job," as if it had somehow fallen upon him by accident. Yet inside the genial exterior was the steel will of a man who had to re-learn to walk at age thirty-five after he was confined to a wheelchair by a crippling neurological disorder.

It would not have been Harris's way to make the comparison, but in his own physical recovery he might have found a parallel to the political task that confronted his new government.

From the end of World War II to the end of the 1980s, the province of Ontario ranked as one of the happiest and luckiest places on earth. Powered by cheap and abundant hydroelectricity, joined by waterways to the great industrial cities of the American Midwest, Ontario flourished as the manufacturing powerhouse of the Canadian branch-plant economy. Political instability in the province of Quebec pushed the financial industry from Montreal to Toronto. Immigrants arrived to seize the opportunities of this booming heartland.

Then, one by one, the old formulas stopped working. In the early 1990s, Ontario tumbled into the severest recession since the 1930s. Long-established businesses never recovered. Many smaller cities and towns lost their major employers. The province found itself deeply in debt, at high rates of interest. The provincially owned hydroelectric company faced even worse financial troubles. New competition from Mexico, China, India, and beyond forced a rethink of the old economic model. The jobs of the future demanded different skills from those Ontario schools were accustomed to teach. As work shifted, so did the kind and location of the housing Ontario needed. After two failed rounds of constitutional reform, separatist sentiment intensified in the West and Quebec.

Ontario politics had long favoured continuity, moderation, muddling through. In the famous words of one of the most successful politicians of the era: "bland works."

In fact, from 1943 to 1985, a single political party governed Ontario. There was nothing unusual about this: Extreme political continuity was the rule in early postwar Canada, at both the federal and the provincial level. If it ain't broke, why fix it?

But now something *was* broke and needed fixing.

In 1985, Ontarians ended the long era of Progressive Conservative hegemony, choosing the traditional, provincial opposition Liberal Party.

Not getting the change they sought, in 1990, Ontarians voted for change again, electing the first social-democratic government in their history. In 1995, they voted for change once more, swinging back to the Progressive Conservatives. But what they chose was in fact a new, reinvented, Mike Harris-led, Conservative Party that no longer presented itself as middle of the road but as an ideologically vigorous riposte and correction of the previous hard swing to the left. Bland no longer worked.

Harris argued that Ontario had suffered a "Lost Decade" from 1985 to 1995. But Harris did not propose to return to the past. "The system is broken," he said in the introduction to the *CSR* platform. "I'm prepared to actually do something about it." But, critically, he did not vow to "Make Ontario Great Again." Instead, he embraced the future and accelerated Ontario's transition to a new kind of economy.

The changes to the Ontario economy had shifted population, wealth, and clout from towns to cities. Big cities incubated new cultural and political attitudes: culturally progressive, economically redistributive, attitudes often inimical to the cities' own success by undercutting the sources of their prosperity and the protectors of their prosperity.

The cultural divide between metropolitan and non-metropolitan that so defines twenty-first-century politics in every democracy asserted itself fiercely in the Ontario of the 1990s. Harris championed the needs of metropolitan Canada. It was Harris's government that amalgamated the little boroughs of the old, federated Toronto into one streamlined metropolitan government, enabling later generations to build even wider regional structures for the greater Toronto area. Yet even as Harris modernized metropolitan governance, he refused to surrender the values of non-metropolitan Canada: a social welfare system that expected work; effective but limited government; respect for people as individuals, not as representatives of warring collective identities.

The Harris combination of old values and new ideas proved highly contentious. Ontario politics had become rowdier anyway in the tough times of the early 1990s. The social-democratic NDP government of

1990–1995 tore itself apart from inside long before it was rejected by the voters. But even as the Harris government stabilized Ontario's rejuvenated economy, it could not quiet the political and cultural furies that have roiled modern Canadian politics.

The fury continued even after Harris departed active politics. The passions of those days still shape Ontario's collective memory and often distort the accounts of historians and policy experts.

Too many of those accounts put the emphasis on the "revolution" part of the formula and not enough on the "common sense." And this is exactly why the book you hold in your hands or scan on your handheld screen is so important.

The Harris Conservatives of the 1990s were not embarked on some ideological bender of their own devising. They always respected the hard limits of Canadian politics. Things that had been settled—the government healthcare monopoly, provincial bilingualism, quasi-national sovereignty for Indigenous peoples—they mostly left settled. Instead, they responded to immediate problems and to an electorate that had already rejected the muddle-through policies of the 1970s and 1980s. *The CSR* was both principled and pragmatic. It was principled because it was founded on deep commitments to individual initiative, to personal responsibility, and to the value of work. It was pragmatic because it applied its principles to problems everybody agreed were pressing, rather than go hunting for problems that might not be pressing in order to justify applying a principle.

Times change, and the needs change with them. Yet there are enduring lessons from the 1990s for later generations, as so well explained in the chapters of this book. Here are four that seem especially worth underscoring.

The first is that unsound public finances will sooner or later make themselves felt. The early twenty-first century saw extended periods of ultra-low interest rates, when public borrowing on a wartime scale seemed consequence-free. But the consequences lurk, and when they arrive, they force painful decisions. The moral of the story is *not* "never borrow."

The moral is to borrow with care because the reckoning will come, especially for subnational borrowers who cannot rely on a central bank to help them out.

It was a real question, in 1993, whether Canada, its provinces, and their crown corporations might default on their debts. That question was decisively rebutted over the ensuing decade, but getting there was difficult and painful, with dramatic reductions required in spending levels at federal, provincial, and municipal levels during challenging economic times. The left would disparage it as "austerity." Conservatives would argue that it worked. But all would agree it was not an experience that anyone should willingly repeat. A lesson worth keeping firmly in mind as interest rates rise and debt interest costs throughout the developed world begin to climb steadily upward once more.

A second enduring lesson is the power of clear political communication. The *CSR* specified in advance what it would seek to do. That clarity conferred a clear moral mandate for action in office. Harris won his second term despite the fierce controversies of the first because Ontarians recognized he had done what he had promised to do: not less and also not more. He wrote his own contract with the electorate, and even those parts of the electorate that might not have endorsed the terms of the contract had to acknowledge the integrity with which the contract was honoured.

A third lesson is one more urgently relevant than ever in the twenty-first century: the potential of cross-identity politics in a multiethnic society. Ontario in the 1990s was already a highly ethnically diverse place. Yet Mike Harris trusted that fiscal and economic concerns could span the ethnocultural divides that more united Ontarians than divided them. That faith was rewarded. In so many other democracies, elections function as more of a census than a choice. Some population groups vote reliably for the parties of the right; others for the parties of the left, less because they care about the issues or platforms of the right or left, more because they have been made to feel unwelcome by one or the other.

That is not the Canadian way. All the parties compete for all of the vote, sometimes successfully, and that success started with breakthroughs scored by the Harris Conservatives in the heavily ethnic Toronto suburbs in the 1990s on a platform of prosperity, public safety, and honouring achievement.

A fourth lesson is more about political style. In many countries and even to some extent in Canada, the politics of the twenty-first century has elevated the righteously angry against the cheerfully optimistic. Harris could talk tough, but he wanted to gain support and allay opposition, not excite discontent and mobilize grievance. All these years later, voters still respond to leaders who gain trust by earning it for themselves, not by fomenting distrust of everyone and everything else.

Mike Harris stepped down in 2002. His party lost power the following year and would be out for the next decade and a half.

It would return in 2018, in a time of prosperity, and face a kind of crisis unlike anything seen in a century, a global pandemic followed by a revival of global price inflation. In the interim, much has changed for parties of the right all over the world. In many places, parties of the right have espoused grievance rather than aspiration. They have sought votes by mobilizing resentments rather than by offering opportunities. They have found themselves whipsawed between their former principles, which still celebrate enterprise and markets, and their recent electorates, who fear both. Mike Harris's *CSR* reminds: It does not have to be this way.

Conservatism can be sensible, can be practical, can be decent and still be energizing and exciting. It can offer a better chance to anyone ready to invest the effort without manipulating paranoia about imaginary conspiracies or exploiting disdain against out-groups who look or sound or love or pray in a different way from the local majority.

The political legacy of a different age provides a better resource for a happier future. The common sense revolution Mike Harris led bequeaths a record to study, critique, emulate, and improve. The Harris policy revolution has proved more meaningful and enduring than that of perhaps any other Canadian provincial premier, certainly in recent times. The goal of the *CSR* under the leadership of Mike Harris was to offer more opportunity and better government to every willing citizen. That goal can still summon Canadians to politics, even as old slogans fade and old debates are forgotten.

CHAPTER 1

The Revolution's Antecedents

Alister Campbell

O PROPERLY EVALUATE THE HARRIS legacy, one must start by evaluating *The Common Sense Revolution* (*CSR*) platform that underpinned the first winning Harris election campaign in 1995. It is rare for an election platform to be remembered at all, but the *CSR* has proven to be a significant outlier in this regard. To understand the reasons for its lasting impact, one must understand its underlying motivations as well as its selected areas of focus and policy specifics. And to accomplish this, it is particularly important first to appreciate the antecedents of that revolution.

Many observers have sought to ascribe specific motives (not always charitable) to Harris himself and to the actions of his government. In fact, the impetus for the Harris policy agenda derived from multiple sources firmly rooted in a historical context. To understand the policy actions described by our contributors in the chapters to follow, it is useful to appreciate that context. In the following pages, I seek to briefly outline what I believe to be the key drivers for the Harris policy agenda in this unique period in Ontario history:

- International public policy trends, notably in the United Kingdom, the United States, and New Zealand
- Changes across the Canadian political spectrum, including the rise of "populism"
- Ontario's "Lost Decade," the actions of the Peterson/Rae governments after 1985, and their outcomes for Ontario.

Several historians (including John Ibbitson in his excellent *Promised Land*[1]) have tried to place the Harris policy platform and the driving intellectual forces underpinning it within the narrow context of "neoconservativism," suggesting that Friedrich Hayek and his defining work *Road to Serfdom* were a central influence in the platform's policy formation. While such ideas were indeed a galvanizing element for some members of the campaign team (including this editor as a young man), they were in fact only one element in a much broader context, which saw policy thinking drawing from influences across the developed world. It is overly simplistic to see the *CSR* as solely rooted in an ideologically fueled revulsion against "big government."

Undeniably, "conservative" parties worldwide drew inspiration during this period from the dramatic policy innovations of Prime Minister Margaret Thatcher in the United Kingdom after her initial election in 1979. Thatcher's efforts to revitalize the United Kingdom through a series of policy shocks intended to rebalance the public and private sectors (including through spending cuts and privatizations) had an impact (of course, not always positive) on public policy thinking worldwide. And her subsequent landslide reelections in 1983 and 1987 spoke to the political power of some of these policies. Her efforts aligned in many ways with those of President Ronald Reagan, who was elected to his first of two terms in 1980, proposing and then implementing significant cuts in marginal tax rates in the United States via the Kemp—Roth Bill of 1981. Reagan's reelection in 1984 remains among the greatest landslides (in the Electoral College) in the history of that country.

Both of these "change leaders" sought to re-galvanize major Western economies after a painful period of stagnant economic growth and high inflation ("stagflation" as it was known). But Reagan and Thatcher were not alone in seeking to address the stagnant economic performance of the Western democracies. Also influential in public policy innovation during this period were other change leaders, such as New Zealand Prime Minister David Lange and his Finance Minister Roger Douglas, first elected in 1984, who, among other things, moved to "corporatize" public services in order to both reduce the cost of delivery and improve services to citizens. These types of reforms, seeking to find more efficient and effective means of delivering public goods, were broadly discussed internationally during this period. And as in the United Kingdom and the United States, Lange's government was reelected in 1987, despite the controversial nature of some of their reforms and the adverse impacts of some of their austerity measures.

Such policy initiatives were not solely adopted by those on the "right" of the political spectrum. In 1992, President Bill Clinton was first elected US president, and he and Vice President Al Gore (they had won in part by promising to "end welfare as we know it" and include work requirements in exchange for benefits) soon began to cite the ideas of author David Osborne, whose book *Reinventing Government: How the Entrepreneurial Spirit Is Transforming the Public Sector* was published in February 1993. Clinton was also reelected with a strong majority (for America) and retired a popular president.

Clinton/Gore were not alone on the "centre-left" in adapting their thinking to the very real public policy challenges of the 1980s and 1990s, including slower economic growth and a perceived imbalance between public and private sectors, as well as the punishingly high interest costs on accumulating government debt. In the fall of 1993, the Canadian federal Liberals published their election platform (known as "the Red Book"), which included specific targets for spending reduction as well as a proposed cap on total deficits as a percentage of GDP (similar to the "Maastricht targets" established in the European Union around the same time).

The scope and scale of the "Martin cuts" implemented after their landslide election were unparalleled at the federal level, and (there is a theme here) the Chretien/Martin pairing secured reelection four times before finally being unseated (for reasons unrelated to austerity measures) in 2006.

In reality, by the time Mike Harris and his caucus began work on crafting their platform (first published as *The Common Sense Revolution* on May 4, 1994), the political "centre" had shifted. Harris and his team were in fact drawing on a broad intellectual consensus across the Western developed nations, although undoubtedly rooted on the "right" of the political spectrum, but spanning well past the centre-left, at least on some components of the overall platform. By the time of drafting, Premier Bob Rae's NDP had tried their own unique version of public spending restraint (known as the Social Contract), and both the Harris Tories and the provincial Liberals (under leader Lyn McLeod) were committed to spending reductions and targeting balanced budgets.

* * *

A second key driving influence in the evolution of public policy thinking in the run-up to the 1995 Ontario provincial election was the extraordinary way in which the Canadian political environment had shifted in the period after the reelection of Prime Minister Brian Mulroney in the famous free-trade election of 1988. Throughout Canadian history, our Western provinces have repeatedly been the source of powerful "populist" movements, including the Progressive Party of Canada, Social Credit, the Cooperative Commonwealth Federation (CCF), and Reform. Preston Manning (whose father had himself been the Social Credit Premier of Alberta) founded the Reform Party in the fall of 1987. While many policies of that new party were firmly rooted in regional grievance, they were also grounded in a broader conviction regarding the need to rebalance the Canadian federation and a strong desire to address fundamental issues of federal governance, notably spiraling federal debt.

In the landmark 1993 federal election, the favourable public response to Jean Chretien's Red Book, coupled with the parallel rise of Manning's Reform out West and Lucien Bouchard's Bloc Quebecois, saw the effective obliteration of the governing Progressive Conservative Party (reduced to a rump of two seats). Central to the rise of Reform, effectively the Chretien government's opposition after 1993 and officially after the 1997 election, was a vigorously held view that government should live within its means. As Manning said about this time, "When we started out, we couldn't even get a Liberal to even use the words cost-cutting, deficit reduction, tax reduction, debt reduction. . . . Now that's principally the program of the government."[2] The lessons of Reform's rise were firmly taken on board by the new governing Liberals and reflected (in more than just rhetoric) in the new finance minister's initial series of budgets, which saw a forceful effort to contain federal spending and bring deficits down.

These influences were not just felt in Ottawa. In an extraordinary political shift, the leadership of Alberta's governing Progressive Conservative Party transferred from "establishment" Premier Don Getty to the upstart populist and former mayor of Calgary, Ralph Klein. Getty had inherited a debt-free province when he became premier in 1985, but the severe recession of the early 1990s and a drop in prices for Alberta's oil and gas had led to average annual deficits of $2.5 billion and a total provincial debt of $11.5 billion by the time of his retirement in 1992.[3] Getty's resignation was forced, at least in part, by the strong polling results for the provincial Liberals (led by Lawrence Decore, who traveled everywhere with his famous "Debt Clock," which digitally tabulated the growth of provincial debt in real time). Klein effectively ran a "change campaign" against his own incumbent government and secured reelection for his party—but with a non-negotiable commitment to rapidly achieve a balanced budget. He did this with his famous "Alberta Advantage" program, which saw significant reductions-in-force for the Alberta public service and other significant austerity measures imposed on the education and healthcare sectors. Despite the controversies around these measures, Klein maintained substantial popular support (and was subsequently reelected in 1997 with 51 per cent of the vote, rising to 62 per cent in 2001, before falling to "only" 46 per cent in his last election in 2004). The Klein success story was unmistakably an influence on Harris and his team as they worked on policy through 1993 and into 1994.

One other political shift is worth noting at this point because it also had a substantial impact on the evolution of the revolution, and this is the shift within the Ontario Progressive Conservative Party itself. After forty-two consecutive years of political power under four different premiers, the Party fought the 1984 campaign with new leader Frank Miller but secured only a slim minority. After two months, the government was defeated in the Legislature by the joint efforts of the Liberals and NDP, bound by the "Peterson-Rae Accord." Miller resigned and was replaced by Larry Grossman. But a second costly and contentious leadership within twelve months had left the party divided, and the loss of power after so many years proved bewildering for many party loyalists. Premier Peterson called an election in 1987 and converted his slim minority into a big majority. Grossman lost his seat in that election, and the party fell to third place in the polls, where it stayed under an interim leader, effectively bankrupt. Efforts to recover proved challenging for several reasons, including continued internal divisiveness, fueled by those bent on refighting previous leadership wars. More significant perhaps was the migration of many of the party's most senior figures to Ottawa, where the opportunity to shape the newly enfranchised Progressive Conservative government of Prime Minister Brian Mulroney was significantly more attractive than volunteering the long hours required to rebuild a divided and bankrupt third-place provincial rump of a party with only sixteen seats (all outside the GTA) in the Legislature.

Among the changes introduced by the Ontario PCs during this time in the wilderness, one, the introduction of "One Member, One Vote" to replace the traditional brokered/delegated convention process for selecting a leader, had a lasting impact. This innovation, probably worthy of its own book, had a marked impact on the party's own direction. But as a "more democratic" mechanism for choosing a leader (for better and worse), it spread across Canada, spread across parties, and over time may even have had an impact on a similar shift in leadership selection processes in many other organized political institutions throughout the Western developed economies. In Ontario, this process was implemented for the first time when it finally was ready to select a new leader in 1990. The contest ended up having only two candidates, and many believe that Mike Harris' victory over Diane Cunningham would not have happened under the old delegated system. But whatever people believed about the way Harris won, there was little debate about whether Harris' victory signaled a shift in the party "centre" and that the new Ontario PCs would try to regain power in Ontario from a centre-right position materially further to the right than under predecessors such as Bill Davis.

Harris was forced to fight an election only weeks after his own leadership victory and benefited from low expectations as a result. While he was successful in firmly branding himself as "The Taxfighter," the party picked up only three additional seats, and the PCs remained firmly mired in third place in the Legislature. But Premier Peterson proved to have misjudged the political environment severely, and the 1990 election also produced the shock election of Bob Rae and his NDP to a majority government.

The Ontario Tories, perhaps because they had so recently had the opportunity to have direct input into the selection of their leader and then saw him perform capably with little preparation, proved comfortable retaining Harris as leader after the election. He was thus able to turn all his attention to the slow organizational re-building process, including a sustained and innovative policy development process. This policymaking process was in some ways a direct outcome of the new and more populist mechanism for selecting leaders. While undeniably still coordinated by the party leadership, the internal party policy development process was both new and different, including a shared "visioning exercise" known as *Vision '97*, a publication series called *New Directions*, and the formation of fourteen grassroots policy councils focused on an array of diverse policy areas. The result was a rarely experienced and hard-won party consensus on policy directions that ensured that, once the *CSR* was published and despite the controversy it engendered, the party lined up firmly behind their controversial platform. At least in part, this was a payoff for having taken the risk of moving to this very new and still untested mechanism for selecting a party leader.

The first two drivers behind the evolution of the *CSR* speak to the shifting nature of policy discourse globally and across Canada, as well as to the shifting of that discourse within the Ontario PC Party specifically. The third and final element to discuss is the extraordinary nature of the challenges that Ontario, historically the economic leader at the centre of a prosperous Canada, unexpectedly found itself facing in the aftermath of the particularly challenging recession of 1990. That recession had far more profound impacts on the psyche of Ontarians than may now be appreciated. Historically, economically powerful and diversified Ontario had gone into recessions last among Canadian provinces and then exited those recessions first, positioned to help lift the rest of the provinces out (or at least Ontarians believed this to be the case). But greater forces than the normal cycles of economic activity were at play in the 1990 downturn—in particular, a major migration of industrial production overseas, which led to a marked, and permanent, decline in industrial activity in significant parts of Ontario.

As the newly elected NDP government of Bob Rae wrestled with these challenges, it discovered itself to be in a far worse fiscal situation than it had understood. The higher embedded cost structure established during the high-spending Peterson administration kept generating more expenses even as government revenues fell. The NDP implemented three consecutive rounds of tax increases to address this, but each yielded progressively less revenue. As the NDP further increased public service spending, partly to fund NDP campaign promises to supportive sectors and partly simply to support those most adversely impacted by the downturn, the resultant mismatch between revenue and expense suddenly began to produce deficits beyond any previous imagination. Unemployment levels climbed to record levels and stayed there. Welfare caseloads climbed to the point that there were 1.3 million people supported by welfare payments in a province with barely more than 10 million in population.

Several chapters in this book (notably Professor Beaulieu's on the economic performance of Ontario before, during, and after the Harris era, as well as Terence Corcoran and Jack M. Mintz's chapter on the Harris regime's fiscal performance and Sean Speer's chapter on welfare reform) will touch on different elements of this challenging economic environment in much more detail. But this context is essential in order to properly understand the underlying drivers for the content and positioning of the Harris platforms in 1995 and 1999. And, as Thomas Courchene outlined in his landmark and award-winning study *From Heartland to North American Region State: The Social, Fiscal and Federal Evolution of Ontario*, the reforms required to tackle the challenges faced in 1995 needed to address more deeply rooted issues than simply those caused by the 1990 recession.

Courchene and Telmer outline how the Peterson/Rae Accord presaged a dramatic shift in strategic orientation for the Ontario government—what they described as a shift from an "Economic focus to a Social Agenda."[4] In this period, they argue, the historical priorities of Ontario governments, economic progress and growth, were replaced with a much greater social emphasis, with the resulting policies including new labour laws and dramatically increased welfare compensation, as well as the introduction of "American-style" employment equity/affirmative action. The Ontario PCs under Harris saw their goal as being more than simply addressing the adverse impacts of a bad recession. In fact, they saw it as their mission to do much more: to reverse the consequences of the demonstratively disastrous agenda of Peterson/Rae and bring the curtain down on what Harris called Ontario's "Lost Decade." In this interpretation, the "Harris revolution" was in fact simply intended to restore a more traditional focus on economic progress as the central objective of an effective Ontario government.

So, if the objective was a return to more traditional ways of governing Ontario, what was the political logic for marketing the platform as revolutionary? Here lies the final element in the Harris platform's contextual underpinnings. The catastrophic impacts of the 1990 recession had left Ontarians particularly eager for change. And they clearly believed that incremental adjustments would not be enough. The Harris campaign team drew deep strategic insight from political polling (as will be discussed by David Herle in his chapter on the Harris campaigns). They asked a specific polling question early in 1990 and re-polled on the same question continually thereafter: Do you think Ontario needs minor, moderate, or major change to address the challenges we face? The number in favour of major change was always a landslide and did not materially decline even as some measure of prosperity slowly returned in 1993/94 and the 1995 election date neared.[5]

Ontarians seemed to understand that the world was changing and that the province needed to move with it. They also understood that their experiments with several new parties in government had generated only painful results. So, the Ontario PCs might have reasonably expected to see a return to traditional levels of support by default. But the federal vote in 1993, which saw the federal Progressive Conservatives fall from forty-six Ontario seats held to none, had demonstrated clearly that the province was in no mood for a return to any form of political status quo and had zero appetite for half measures.

It was out of this economic and political context that Mike Harris and *CSR* were born. He offered a very clear policy agenda that manifestly and deliberately signaled major change. And he combined it with a unique leadership style, offering a strong, steady, and clearly determined potential premier who promised "to do what he said he would do" and who promised to resign if he failed, exactly what it turned out Ontario was looking for.

I have written and rewritten these paragraphs more than any other in this introductory chapter. My thinking also evolved as the authors began to share their draft chapters with me. But some elements of my own thinking have remained quite constant from the start of this project and have been entirely validated in my reading of the group's works.

First, Mike Harris was a deeply experienced Member of Provincial Parliament (MPP) with more than ten years (albeit primarily on the backbenches) in the Davis-era PC government. And as those who have worked with him or ever talked policy with him one-on-one would confirm, he was an attentive participant at Queen's Park. There were (and are, as of this writing) very few policy issues in Ontario on which he does not have a deep understanding, informed by a broad sense of all relevant stakeholder interests. And he was a student of style as well as substance, as he watched and learned from the legendary Davis-era cabinet ministers on the front benches. While his actions appeared revolutionary to some and were undoubtedly marketed in that guise, he was in fact firmly guided by his sense of how Ontario had historically been led, and his actions were fueled by a desire to restore Ontario to its "rightful" place at the centre of a strong and prosperous Canada.

Second, while evolving public-policy thinking among conservatives clearly had an impact on the policy content in the *CSR* and 1999 *Blueprint* platforms, as a general rule Harris himself was not an ideologue. He was at his core a pragmatist, and his urgency was driven not by ideology but rather by a firmly rooted sense of how far Ontario had strayed from common sense policies that he believed were demonstrably in the interests of the province.

There is of course one critical policy file where it can clearly be argued that Harris acted more from ideology than simply from a desire to return to traditional Ontario ways. I am referring here to the Harris tax cuts. As discussed above, there was a general trend toward the restoration of fiscal discipline happening across most Western jurisdictions, with spending control measures executed by parties from across the political spectrum. In Canada, Liberals in Ottawa and Conservatives in Alberta were all committed to policies we would now refer to as austerity. But Mike Harris cut taxes, too, and at the same time! There is a famous *New Yorker* cartoon that shows the lowest level of hell being reserved for politicians who promise to both cut taxes *and* balance the budget. But, perhaps uniquely, Harris really did both. Ontario's subsequent and favourable economic trajectory during the Harris era indicates to some that these aggressive and unique-to-Ontario changes in marginal tax rates were actually beneficial. History (including the next chapter of this book) will help us better understand if this was indeed the case.

It is this author's view that by far the largest single driver of the Harris revolution was the identified need to address the adverse economic consequences of Ontario's "Lost Decade." In this sense, it was truly a conservative revolution, seeking to return Ontario to a better place by restoring a more traditional bias toward economic rather than social priorities. And there is also no doubt that Harris and his team believed devoutly in the idea that lower marginal tax rates would fuel economic growth and innovation and create increased prosperity across all segments of society. Importantly, Harris was (maybe even uniquely) willing to make the difficult decisions required to ensure that these meaningful tax cuts happened within the context of a fiscally responsible, balanced budget plan.

But it is important not to lose sight of the fact that the Harris revolution came at a time of significant shifts across the Canadian political spectrum, fueled both by rising populist movements in Western Canada and also influenced by rapidly evolving public policy views across the developing world regarding the roles and costs of the public sector.

And, finally, it is also important to appreciate that the Ontario PC Party had changed itself within that shifting spectrum, primarily because the "one member, one vote" selection mechanism and the Party's grassroots policy development process allowed for a particularly cohesive campaign and enabled consistent and disciplined execution/implementation by the government once in power.

Enough now about the antecedents. It is time to start our review of what actually happened when Mike Harris became premier of Ontario in 1995!

Notes

1 *Promised Land: Inside the Harris Revolution*, Ibbotson, John
2 *The Globe and Mail*, Laghi, March 22, 2001.
3 Barrie, Doreen (2004). "Ralph Klein, 1992–". In Rennie, Bradford J. (ed.). *Alberta Premiers of the Twentieth Century*. Regina, Sask: Canadian Plains Research Centre, University of Regina. pp. 255–279. ISBN 978-0-88977-263-2.
4 *From Heartland to North American Region State*, Courchene, Thomas with Colin R. Telmer, University of Toronto Press, 1998.
5 Bradgate Group, province-wide polling—1995.

CHAPTER 2

The Economic Impacts

Eugene Beaulieu

T HE MIKE HARRIS GOVERNMENT SWEPT to power on June 8, 1995, with 45 per cent of the popular vote, winning eighty-two out of 130 seats in the Legislature. Central to its campaign success was a controversial platform branded as the *CSR*. The Progressive Conservative Party of Ontario's *CSR*, first published in May 1994, more than a year before the election, promised to "take a fresh look at government" and to "re-invent the way it works, to make it work for the people."[1] The ambitious and comprehensive *CSR* had two central "revolutionary" themes: fiscal and institutional. This chapter focuses on the fiscal revolution and seeks to evaluate its economic impacts.

The Harris Tories key messaging in the run-up to the provincial election campaign and throughout the campaign itself was that the *CSR* represented real and significant change and that the policies mandated in the *CSR* were not only necessary but feasible, and that they were not just election promises but would and could be implemented. It is hard to find another example in Canadian political history (at least, up until that point in time) where such effort was put into demonstrating the credibility of political promises. The platform projections were based on an actual econometric model. Reporters were provided with technical backgrounders, showing the basis for the fiscal and economic projections. Briefings were held to walk media through the core assumptions in the model and to contrast them directly with NDP government budget projections and Liberal campaign commitments.[2,3] On the back page of the *CSR* itself, in an appendix, the platform actually offered voters (if they read that far) a table showing year-by-year estimates for nominal growth and inflation rates and even "economic drag" (an assumption regarding adverse consequences from the implementation of the proposed spending cuts). This unusual degree of detail culminated in a dramatic bottom-line promise, perhaps the most important promise in the whole platform, made to a province still recovering from the "Great Slump" of 1900–1992: the creation of 725,000 new jobs.

I quote directly:

> The Chief Economist at Midland Walwyn, one of Canada's most respected securities firms, concludes. . . . *"This plan will work. The Mike Harris plan to cut provincial income tax rates by 30% and non-priority services spending by 20% will give Ontario a balanced budget within four years, and create more than 725,000 new jobs."*
> *— Mark Mullins, Ph.D. (Economics)*[4]

Central to a proper retrospective evaluation of the Harris legacy is a close look at the degree to which this promise was kept.

One of the other remarkable aspects of this important episode in Canadian political and economic history is that the Harris government quickly implemented almost every aspect of their election mandate. Beginning in 1995, the Mike Harris government firmly implemented dramatic fiscal policy reform as promised in the *CSR*. Other chapters in this book focus on the political and social aspects of the *CSR*, its philosophical foundations, or various policies adopted under the Harris government. This chapter focuses specifically on the economics of this dramatic shift in fiscal policy direction. The *CSR* represented an about-face in the direction of government spending and in levels of taxation and required significant structural changes in the Ontario public sector. This chapter will analyze the various economic factors that impacted the growth in spending and tax revenues over time and the change in Ontario's economic fortunes following the implementation of the *CSR*.

Although the empirical connection between government fiscal policy and economic performance is difficult to measure, it is well established, both theoretically and empirically, that fiscal policy does affect economic growth and economic prosperity. There are two challenges with this particular exercise. First is that Ontario might be a relatively large province within Canada, but it remains a "sub-national" jurisdiction. How much can changes in fiscal policy at the provincial level really impact broader economic trends? After all, there were many other factors affecting the Ontario economy in addition to the province's fiscal situation. Second, economic growth affects the fiscal outcomes of provincial finances, and provincial fiscal policy affects economic growth. Separating out which of these was responsible for what is impossible, but as we shall see, Ontario benefited from a virtuous cycle during the period of Premier Harris' terms. The primary objective of the *CSR* was to get policy right in order to lead to economic growth and prosperity and to create jobs, so it may not be unreasonable to conclude that the policies of the *CSR* had at least something to do with the marked improvement in all key economic metrics during this time.

It is also important to appreciate that Harris served two terms and that his *Blueprint* platform also had ambitious objectives that reached beyond just fiscal discipline and sought to establish a true, strategic orientation to Ontario economic policies. With this in mind, the Harris government established the Ontario Jobs and Investment Board, created to research and consult with experts and stakeholders to develop strategies on how to strengthen Ontario's economic performance in the twenty-first century. Released in March 1999, the report had five strategic goals, but the primary focus was on "getting our economic fundamentals right—including lower taxes" (p. 3). The other fundamentals of the report include less regulatory red tape, higher educational standards, and more nebulous ideas such as "greater recognition of initiative and risk-taking"—all with the goal of creating jobs and driving economic growth. When evaluating the legacy of Premier Harris, understanding his vision for the province helps us do a better job of evaluating how well he was able to execute.

This chapter seeks to present a careful economic analysis of the main fiscal components of the *CSR* and *Blueprint* platforms, examines how the policies were implemented, and then evaluates the economic impact of the fiscal "revolution." I start with an overview of the *CSR*. The chapter then presents the economic context, focusing on economic production and output and on employment and unemployment, as well as the evolving fiscal situation. At the end, I offer some concluding observations and identify topics worth further academic discussion.

* * *

The key economic priority of the newly elected Harris government was to take rapid and extreme actions to cut government spending. They saw the budget deficit as a spending crisis and set out to balance the budget by drastically cutting expenditures. The *CSR* proposed to cut "non-priority" government spending by 20 per cent. Said Minister of Finance Ernie Eves:

> Today my colleagues and I, under Premier Harris' leadership, are taking major steps to bring Ontario's spending under control. The former Government left the province with a spending crisis which is just that: a spending crisis. The deficit outlook is significantly worse than the former Government indicated in April.

> Revenues are lower. And expenditures are much higher than the former Government indicated. Today we are taking swift and decisive action to cut government spending immediately. We are cancelling programs and projects we simply cannot afford.[5]

The *CSR* focused on cutting spending <u>and</u> cutting taxes. According to the Harris government, government spending had more than doubled from 1985 to 1995. Repeated tax increases had failed to achieve required levels of revenue, and so this high and increasing level of spending drove the provincial deficit higher.

Perhaps the most truly "revolutionary" component of the *CSR* was not in fact about spending restraint. It was about cutting taxes at the same time: The *CSR* proposed to cut Ontario income tax by 30 per cent. As the Harris government kept pointing out, from 1985 to 1995, Ontario fiscal policy was characterized by continual increases in personal and business tax rates. It pointed out that Ontario had become one of the highest-taxed jurisdictions in North America. In fact, the previous Liberal and NDP governments had levied some sixty-five separate tax increases over what Harris called the "Lost Decade," and this included eleven distinct increases in personal income tax.[6] The *CSR* committed to fully balancing the provincial budget in four years. According to a representative newspaper article of the time, "Ernie Eves argued that the Harris government had little choice in implementing the *CSR* fiscal reforms as the government "was facing a deficit of $11-billion and had seen the province's debt double over five years to more than $90 billion."[7]

The Harris government moved quickly to implement the fiscal reform measures contained in the *CSR*. Courchene and Telmer (1998) provide a comprehensive and excellent analysis of the fiscal provisions contained in the *CSR* and present a careful assessment of the fiscal policies implemented in the early days of the Harris government. According to Courchene and Telmer's analysis, the Harris government actually followed through on *both* the spending cuts *and* tax cuts. The Harris government cut income taxes by 15 per cent in the first year alone.[8] The tax cuts focused on one tax, the personal income tax, and only one aspect of that tax (the marginal rate at all levels of income), which neoconservatives at the time argued had the greatest impact on employment, productivity, and investment.[9] When the Harris government took the reins of the provincial economy in 1995, the Ontario top marginal income-tax rate was the second highest in Canada at 53.2 per cent. As Mintz and Corcoran show elsewhere in this book, after the Harris tax cuts, Ontario had one of the lowest rates of Personal Income Tax (PIT) (only Alberta being lower).

With respect to spending cuts, the *CSR* plan meant a required cut to overall government spending of 11 per cent without cutting the budgets for health, education, and law enforcement. The analysis by Mark Mullins recognized that the proposed $6 billion in spending cuts would initially impose some measure of fiscal "drag" on the economy, which might even temporarily reduce employment, but argued that as the economy adjusted to the new fiscal regime, accelerated job growth would follow. Maintaining prudent conservatism, the Mullins' model did not actually project any growth-creating ("supply side") benefits from the $5 billion in tax cuts, but presumably the Harris policy team hoped there would be offsetting growth benefits from such substantial tax cuts. The *CSR* assumed ("drag" aside) that employment growth would come through normal economic growth rates, independent of any government fiscal action, as the economy rebounded from the recession. The *CSR's* published assumptions projected roughly 3 per cent real GDP growth over the plan period. According to Walkom, although the *CSR* assumed a 3 per cent real GDP growth in its fiscal projections, the projections for employment growth in the *CSR* background analysis were based on an assumed real economic growth of 4 per cent on average, annually up to the year 2000.[10]

The *CSR* clearly understood that fiscal changes and adjustments to a single tax rate would not be enough to fuel the levels of job creation they promised, and so the Harris government also proposed to deregulate the labour market and remove barriers to business and investment. Although the labour chapter in this volume takes a deep dive into the labour market provisions of the *CSR*,[11] it is worth highlighting here that the focus on removing red tape as well as other big labour market reforms was intended to increase business confidence, increase investment, and contribute to employment and economic growth. Of particular note was the Harris government's repeal of Bill 40, labour law reforms brought in under Bob Rae's NDP government.

Although the policy revolution of the *CSR* focused on spending cuts and tax cuts, the primary objective of the *CSR* was always very clearly focused on the creation of jobs with lower marginal tax rates and the elimination of annual deficits as added, but secondary, benefits. The next section examines the economic context of the economic plan for job creation and economic growth.

* * *

There are several important factors to keep in mind while considering the impact of Harris policy changes on the Ontario economy. Canada, like other industrial economies, such as the US and European countries, entered a period of deindustrialization and restructuring in the 1970s. Deindustrialization can be measured by the decline of manufacturing in total employment or total economy output shares, and this decline has been happening in Canada and other industrialized economies since the 1970s.[12] The share of manufacturing in Canada's GDP declined from over 24 per cent in the 1960s to roughly 19 per cent in the late 1980s. The relative decline of manufacturing in Canada's GDP was experienced most significantly in Ontario, Canada's manufacturing heartland.

When the Harris government took over in 1995, Canada and Ontario were still recovering from the 1990 to 1992 slump. According to Kneebone and McKenzie, the recession was more severe in Ontario than the rest of Canada.[13] At this time, Canada was also adjusting to the recently signed and ratified Canada-US Free Trade Agreement (CUSTA) in 1989 and the North American Free Trade Agreement (NAFTA) in 1994. These trade agreements meant significant economic adjustment for Ontario. Moreover, a dramatic change in the Bank of Canada policy to aggressively target low inflation rates led to a high interest rate differential with the United States and thus to an appreciation in the Canada-US exchange rate. This strong Canadian dollar (peaking in 1991) increased the relative cost of Canadian export goods, and this also had an adverse impact on the Ontario economy. Canada and other industrial economies were also experiencing a secular decline in manufacturing as the economy painfully transitioned to a more service-based economy. The secular decline in manufacturing, as a share of the Canadian economy, continued in the Harris years, with manufacturing representing only 15 per cent of Canadian GDP by 1999. Much of this transformation of the Canadian economy was centred in Ontario.

Figure 2.1 presents Ontario's real GDP per capita from 1990 to 2015. We can see that Ontario's GDP per capita was down significantly between

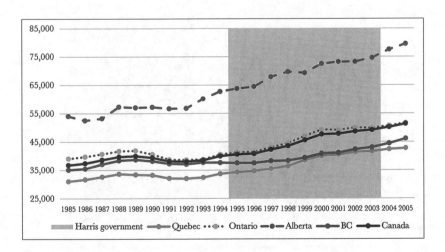

Figure 2.1 Real GDP Per Capita in Ontario, Alberta BC, and Quebec, 1985–2005 (Constant 2012 dollars)

Source: Statistics Canada. Table 36-10-0222-01 Gross domestic product, expenditure-based, provincial and territorial, annual (× 1,000,000).

1991 and 1993, as the province was hit hard by the recession and only began to grow again in 1994. Ontario's real GDP per capita reached a low (during this period) of $38,629 in 1992. The real GDP per capita in Ontario was still only $40,521 in 1994 but began to grow faster in 1995, reaching over $49,281 in 2000. Figure 2.1 also suggests that Ontario's growth in GDP per capita may have materially outperformed other major Canadian jurisdictions during the Harris era. This is confirmed in Figure 2.2, which reveals the painful underperformance of Ontario in the early 1990s but then shows consistent outperformance of Ontario in terms of GDP growth rates, particularly during the first Harris term, when the most aggressive spending cuts and tax rate reductions were being implemented.

The growth of real GDP in Ontario started increasing in 1992 at 1 per cent above 1991, climbed to 1.7 per cent in 1993, and matched Alberta's real GDP growth in 1994 at 5.6 per cent. Alberta was leading

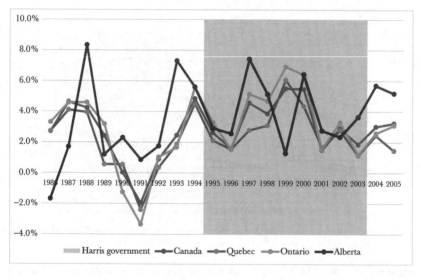

Figure 2.2   Real GDP Growth Rate (% Change from Previous Year)

Source: Author calculations based on data from Statistics Canada. Table 36-10-0222-01. Gross domestic product, expenditure-based, provincial and territorial, annual (× 1,000,000).

the country in economic growth in the late 1980s and most of the 1990s. However, after the Harris government took office in 1995, the Ontario economy experienced particularly strong economic growth, surpassing and/or matching economic growth in Alberta from 1995 to the early 2000s (when Alberta's economic growth once again separated itself from Ontario and Canadian average growth rates). It is interesting to note that Ontario's economy grew at an average annual rate of 3.7 per cent from 1995 to 1998, the first four years of the Harris government.

If we move ahead in time, strong economic growth of 6.9 per cent in 1999 increased the average annual growth from 1995 to 1999 to 4.3 per cent. Recall that the *CSR* based its fiscal projections on average economic growth of 3 per cent and its employment projections on average annual growth of 4 per cent. The conservative assumptions backing the *CSR* projections proved out to be very close to the actual growth rates experienced, with the Ontario economy in fact slightly outperforming the *CSR's* growth assumptions.

The strong economic growth performance described above is also reflected in the rapid shift in unemployment rates during the Harris era. In Figure 2.3, you can see that, from the time of Harris' first election win in June 1995 to the end of his first term, Ontario's unemployment rate fell from roughly 10 per cent to a number closer to 5 per cent. And you can also see Ontario outperforming Canada overall throughout this period. In Figure 2.4, you can see Ontario's strong relative performance relative to other major Canadian provinces, with a widening margin of outperformance (particularly relative to BC and Quebec) over the same period.

But the *CSR* made a very specific promise regarding job creation, so it is appropriate at this point to ask, was the result actually achieved? As you can see in Figure 2.5, the answer is unequivocally yes. In 1994, there were just over 5 million employed people in Ontario. The *CSR* pledged that this would increase by 725,000 within five years of taking office.

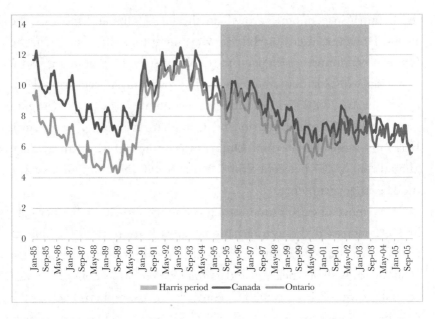

Figure 2.3 Monthly Unemployment Rates in Ontario and Canada, 1985–2005 (Seasonally Adjusted (%))

Source: Statistics Canada: Labour force characteristics by sex and detailed age group, monthly, unadjusted for seasonality (× 1,000). Table: 14-10-0017-01 (formerly CANSIM 282-0001)

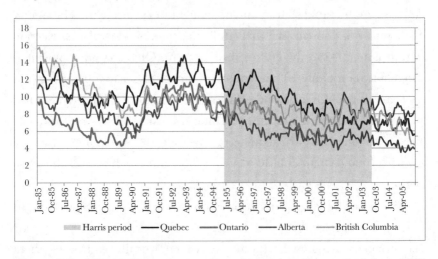

Figure 2.4 Monthly Unemployment Rates by Province (Seasonally Adjusted (%))

Source: Statistics Canada: Labour force characteristics by sex and detailed age group, monthly, unadjusted for seasonality (× 1,000). Table: 14-10-0017-01 (formerly CANSIM 282-0001)

There were 5,013,600 people employed in Ontario in 1994. If the *CSR* job creation objective was to be met, there would need to be 5,738,600 people with jobs within five years. Figure 2.5 shows total employment in Ontario from 1980 to 2010, with the red line indicating the promised number of total jobs. Employment grew in every year of the Harris government from 1995 to 2003. But the Harris *CSR* target was actually surpassed in 1999/2000, as total employment reached 5,635,300 in 1999 and 5,814,900 in 2000. The ambitious job creation objective of the *CSR* was achieved.

Buoyed by their economic (and political) success, the Harris Tories set a new and higher job creation target for the second term of their government. In the *Blueprint* platform, published before the 1999 election, Harris committed to further tax cuts and projected another 825,000 jobs over the subsequent five years.[14] The platform was written based on 1998 job numbers (when Ontario had "only" seen 540,000 jobs created).

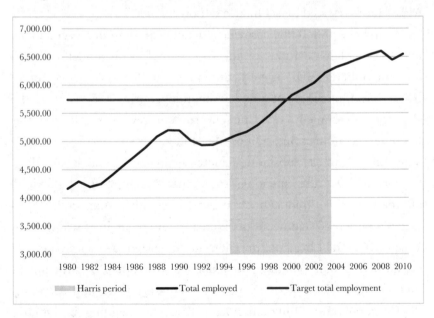

Figure 2.5   Total Employed in Ontario, 1980–2010 (× 1,000)

Source: Statistics Canada. Table 14-10-0027-01 Employment by class of worker, annual (× 1,000)
DOI: https://doi.org/10.25318/1410002701-eng

Figure 2.5 indicates that between 1999 and 2003, roughly 760,000 further new jobs were created in Ontario. So in the second term the Harris government actually fell somewhat short of their target but still outperforming Canada and any of the other major provinces in this important economic metric.

Federal government deficits became a perennial feature of federal government spending in Canada in the 1970s, and provincial government deficits increased throughout the 1980s. Ontario ran persistent government deficits starting in the mid-1980s. The fiscal situation in Ontario prior to the election of Mike Harris can only be characterized as dismal. The Corcoran and Mintz chapter in this book goes into more detail on the fiscal performance of the Liberal and NDP governments leading up to the 1995 election, but the 1985–1994 Ontario provincial budgets can be summarized as a period of successive budgets focused on tax increases and substantial increases in public spending. This is what Mike Harris referred to as Ontario's "Lost Decade."

Courchene and Telmer provide a detailed account of the economic and fiscal policy decisions of the successive Liberal (under Peterson and the Liberal–NDP accord) and then NDP governments (under Rae). The Ontario economy was booming during the years of the Peterson government, and the government revenues reflected this booming economy. But, under the Liberal–NDP accord, Premier Peterson began a substantial increase in government spending. So massive was this spending spree that even the fiscal dividend afforded by the rapid economic growth couldn't support it. Thus began a period of significant tax increases and recurring fiscal deficits. When Bob Rae became premier, he inherited a regime already committed to high spending and taxing. However, the Rae government built on these fiscal woes by further increasing taxes and spending. As Corcoran and Mintz observe, per capita spending in Ontario grew dramatically during the Peterson and Rae years by almost $1,400 ($2,156 in 1985 to $4,187 in 1994 in constant 2003 dollars).

On the government revenue side, taxes and other revenues also grew rapidly in the ten years leading up to 1995. Tax revenues increased from $2,010 per capita to $3,548 by 1995.

The NDP produced consecutive fiscal deficits throughout their time in power, and the deficits increased in size. While the fiscal books were already in rough and worsening condition, the province was particularly hard hit by the 1990–1991 recession (as described above). The Rae government raised tax rates, but tax revenues actually declined, while spending continued to increase. These successive fiscal deficits led to a tremendous increase in provincial debt. This led Courchene and Telmer to label this period "Fiscalamity and 'Fair-Shares' Federalism." Prior to Harris' election in 1995, the Ontario governments delivered five consecutive deficits of more than $10 billion. In the 1992/93 fiscal year, Ontario's deficit reached $12.4 billion, which was 4.4 per cent of Ontario's GDP at the time. This string of deficits translated into a significant rise in the ratio of net debt to GDP, from 22 per cent in 1991/92 to over 30 per cent in 1994/95. As Courchene and Telmer point out, the $60 billion increase in debt during the NDP administration is "surely a record in debt increase over a five-year span for a subnational government, anytime, anywhere."[15]

The combined impact of all the Harris fiscal policy reforms was to reverse this adverse trend. Figures 2.6, 2.7, and 2.8 present the Ontario government deficit, net debt, and net debt as a per cent of GDP from 1990 to 2005. Figure 2.6 shows the increased government deficits in Ontario, Alberta, and Quebec in the first couple years of the 1990s. However, Ontario's deficit grew much larger than these other two provinces in 1991, 1992, and 1993. The budget deficit began to be reduced in 1993 and 1994 as the Ontario economy recovered from recession, but the deficit reduction began in earnest only after 1995, when the Harris government began implementing the *CSR*. As seen in Figure 2.8, by 1999, the Harris government was able to stabilize the net debt of the province, and Ontario's net debt actually declined in 2000

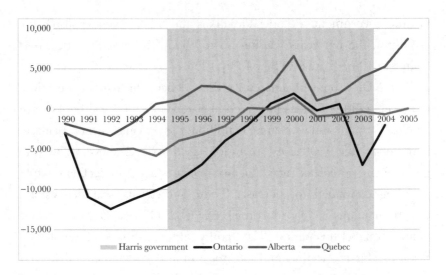

Figure 2.6   Ontario, Alberta, and Quebec Deficits, 1990–2005 ($ × 1,000,000)

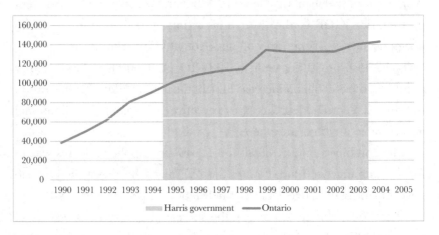

Figure 2.7   Ontario Government Net Debt

and was stable from there until the deficit budget in 2003 (Figure 2.6) and a corresponding increase in the net debt position.

In fact, the Harris government fundamentally improved Ontario's fiscal performance, and the Harris era saw the province transition from a jurisdiction with perennial budget deficits to one with perennial surplus budgets starting in 1999. Fiscal policy transformation and strong

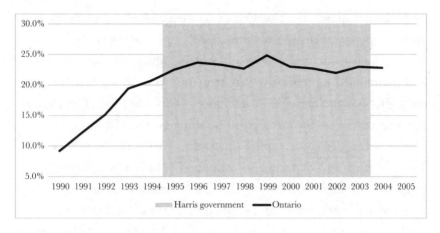

Figure 2.8 Net Debt as a Share of GDP

economic growth translated into an improved net debt position for the province starting in 1997. Provincial debt as a share of GDP declined, and so did interest costs on the debt. Ontario's fiscal performance improved in absolute terms and in comparison to other provinces.

But, as one can see in Figure 2.6, Ontario continued to run annual deficits throughout the first Harris term. And as Figure 2.7 shows, this meant that total net debt continued to climb until 1999. This raises an important question about the wisdom of the Harris tax cuts. After all, if tax rates had stayed high, wouldn't the deficit have come down faster? And wouldn't the province have then accumulated a smaller total debt burden? This remains open for debate.

McKenzie (2003) examines and compares the fiscal reforms introduced by Premier Ralph Klein in Alberta in 1993 and in Ontario by Mike Harris in 1995.[16] This is an important and useful comparison, as the fiscal reforms reflect watershed changes in the provincial fiscal environment in Canada. According to McKenzie, the Ontario and Alberta governments led the country in terms of both the timing and scope of fiscal reforms, especially with respect to tax policy. And, he argues, the tax policies of Ontario were, in fact, very successful during this period.

McKenzie points out that Ontario cut expenditures and, at the same time, cut personal income tax immediately upon taking office. Ontario's tax cuts focused on reducing taxes for low- and middle-income earners and maintained a progressive rate structure with higher marginal rates on higher-income earners. In addition to personal taxes, Ontario also reduced corporate income tax rates (although the Harris government maintained a corporate capital tax, whereas Alberta did not have this tax to begin with). Ontario also continued to offer other tax incentives targeted at specific industries and types of expenditures, such as R&D.

As we have seen, although there was very little reduction in the overall level of government debt, Ontario's debt/GDP ratio did decline due to strong economic growth and low interest rates. How much of this was due to spending restraint? And what, if anything, did pro-growth policies such as labour law reforms and tax cuts have to do with this? McKenzie (2003, p. 259) calculates that economic conditions were responsible for three quarters of the improvement in the debt/GDP ratio in Ontario during the five years following the election of the Harris government. By this analysis, only one quarter of the decline was due to discretionary fiscal policy.

Here lies the root of the public policy debate around the Harris "cuts." It is clear that simply reducing government spending (known as "austerity" in current political debates) was, in and of itself, not enough to rapidly restore Ontario to fiscal balance. Economic growth was needed as well. And while it is challenging to prove empirically, the Harris tax cuts and other labour market reforms coincide with a measurable and material turnaround in job creation and relative outperformance for Ontario relative to other major provinces and Canada as a whole. One does not have to be an all-in advocate of the Laffer curve or a card-carrying "supply side economist" to accept the evidence as indicating that it was indeed some combination of Harris spending *and* tax cuts that resulted in the strong turnaround in Ontario's overall economic performance.

One last method of establishing the degree to which Ontario's economic track record of success under Harris was attributable to luck or skill is to compare Ontario's performance in this period to neighbouring jurisdictions. Ontario's economic performance was compared to other provinces above. Next, we compare Ontario's economic performance to neighbouring US comparators, many of whom were experiencing similar economic challenges to Ontario as the deindustrialization trend swept through North America.

Figure 2.9 compares Ontario's economic growth to Ontario's neighbouring US states from 1998 to 2001. The eight Great Lake states

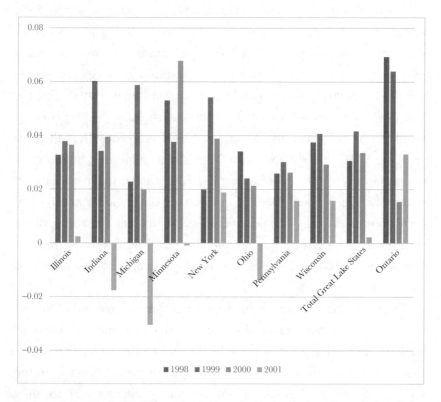

Figure 2.9 Real GDP Growth in Ontario Compared to Great Lakes States (1998–2001)

Source: Statistics Canada. Table 36-10-0222-01: Gross domestic product, expenditure-based, provincial and territorial, annual (× 1,000,000) and US Bureau of Economic Analysis, "SAGDP9N Real GDP by state 1/" (accessed Monday, February 27, 2023).

are composed of Illinois, Indiana, Michigan, Minnesota, New York, Ohio, Pennsylvania, and Wisconsin. Figure 2.9 shows economic growth for this grouping of states overall as well as presenting growth separately for each of these states. Ontario's real GDP grew 6.93 per cent from 1997 to 1998, faster than any of the Great Lakes states. Ontario's growth, as we have already seen above, was also faster than Canada, Alberta, and Quebec. At the end of Harris' first term in 1999, Ontario's real GDP grew 6.4 per cent, which was also faster growth than any of the Great Lakes states.

It is worth noting that Ontario's real GDP grew much slower in 2000, at only 1.54 per cent, when it was the slowest-growing jurisdiction in this comparison group. However, this appears to be an economic timing issue only, as Ontario was once again the fastest-growing economy in this group in 2001, growing at 3.31 per cent, while real GDP declined in four of the states (Minnesota (−0.08 per cent), Indiana (−1.76 per cent), Ohio (−1.37 per cent), and Michigan (−3.05 per cent). Over the four years from 1998 to 2001, well into Harris's second term, Ontario grew faster than any of the Great Lakes states, faster than Canada overall, and faster than Quebec and Alberta. In fact, over this period Ontario's real GDP grew on average, 4.54 per cent annually, and didn't just outperform the average. This growth rate actually represents faster growth than the fastest-growing Great Lakes states of Minnesota (3.94 per cent) and New York (3.3 per cent).

Earlier in this chapter we analyzed employment growth in Ontario and found that the Harris government reached and exceeded its goal of increasing employment by 725,000 jobs in its first term. Figure 2.10 compares the employment growth rate in Ontario to the Great Lakes states. To make the graph manageable for readers, only Illinois, Minnesota, New York, Ohio, and Wisconsin employment data are presented, along with the overall total for all eight of the Great Lakes states. The five states shown in the graph are representative of the performance of the eight states, including some of the states with

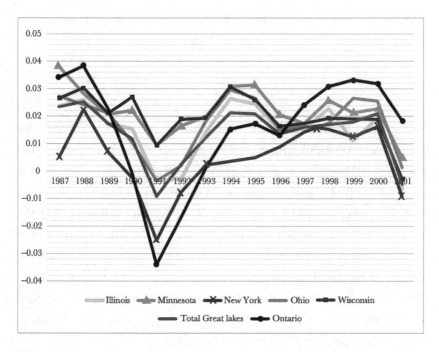

Figure 2.10   Employment Growth in Ontario and Great Lakes States, 1987–2001 (%)

Source: Statistics Canada. Table 14-10-0027-01   Employment by class of worker, annual (× 1,000) DOI: https://doi.org/10.25318/1410002701-eng and Bureau of Economic Analysis, Personal income and employment by major component. www.bea.gov/data/employment/employment-by-state

the fastest-growing employment like Minnesota and Wisconsin and some slower-growing states like New York. The overall average for the eight Great Lakes states reflects the average performance of these economies. Figure 2.10 shows that Ontario's employment growth fell more sharply from 1988 to 1991 and remained below the Great Lakes average employment growth until 1996. But the trajectory changes completely just after Harris and the *CSR*. Ontario's employment growth was higher than the Great Lakes employment growth from 1997 to 2001.

The above analysis shows Ontario's' relative underperformance in the years before Harris and significant outperformance relative both to domestic provincial peers and to US states throughout the Harris years. The implication is unmistakable: the *CSR* worked.

* * *

This chapter analyzes the economic implications of the *CSR*, focusing on the fiscal revolution that was promised prior to the 1995 election and implemented from day one of the Harris government. It points out that the platform projections were based on careful econometric analysis and that the projections and analysis were shared with the public prior to the election. The chapter provides an overview of the fiscal changes then implemented and argues that the *CSR* represented a real and significant change from the fiscal and economic status quo of the time. Most significantly, the *CSR* set forth a platform of cuts to government spending and income taxes and a bold prediction/promise that these measures would help create 725,000 new jobs in Ontario.

The chapter then analyzes various economic factors that impacted the growth in spending and tax revenues over time and the change in Ontario's economic fortunes following the implementation of the *CSR*. It acknowledges that there were many factors driving the Ontario economy in addition to the province's fiscal situation but shows that Ontario benefited from a virtuous cycle initiated during the period of Premier Harris's terms. The primary objective of the *CSR* was to get policy right in order to lead to economic growth and prosperity and to create jobs. The evidence shows that the policies of the *CSR* contributed to the marked improvement in all key economic metrics during this time. We found that improvements in the fiscal environment likely contributed to the strong economic growth over the Harris years in office and that the Harris government exceeded its pledge to create 725,000 new jobs.

Perhaps most importantly, we show that Ontario's economic performance during this challenging period was chronically worse than neighbouring provinces and US states prior to Harris and fundamentally better as the Harris reforms were implemented and began to work their way through the Ontario economy.

Unfortunately, the transformed fiscal environment and strong economic growth did not last forever. In fact, the budget was back in deficit shortly after Harris stepped down. The strong economic growth of the Harris years began to soften over the next five years, and this was before Ontario and the rest of the world were hit by the Great Recession in 2008. Manufacturing employment continued its decline, and by 2009 Ontario's manufacturing employment total had slipped to under 800,000, down from 1.1 million at its previous peak.

In this post-Harris period, Ontario once again ceased to be Canada's economic powerhouse. After 2003, Ontario's economy grew slower than the national average, and Ontario's unemployment rate has consistently been around or even above the national average ever since. Ontario's real per-capita incomes actually fell below the Canadian average in 2012 for the first time ever. Although the Harris government brought in radical fiscal policy change, and these changes coincided with strong economic growth and growth in employment, the positive changes proved to have only a short-run impact. More policy work needs to be done to establish a more positive future policy framework to rekindle Ontario's economic engine, as Harris was, at least for a time, so successfully able to do.

References

Courchene, Thomas J. and Colin R. Telmer (1998), *From Heartland to North American Region State: The Social, Fiscal and Federal Evolution of Ontario. An Interpretive Essay*, Monograph Series on Public Policy, Centre for Public Management, Faculty of Management, University of Toronto.

Eisen, Ben and Nathaniel Li, "Measuring Ontario's Regional Prosperity Gap, 2022 Update," *Fraser Research Bulletin*, February 2022, https://www.fraserinstitute.org/studies/measuring-ontarios-regional-prosperity-gap-2022-update

Fraser Institute, "Ontario Economy Falls Further behind Its Neighbours," April 19, 2022, https://www.fraserinstitute.org/blogs/ontario-economy-falls-further-behind-its-neighbou

Kneebone, Ronald and Kenneth J. McKenzie (1999), *Past (In)Discretions: Federal and Provincial Fiscal Policy in Canada*, University of Toronto Press.

Mackie, Richard, "Eves Agonized over Ontario's Cuts to Social Programs," *Globe and Mail*, May 1, 2000.

McKenzie, Kenneth J. (2003), "A Tale of Two Provinces—Tax Policy in Alberta and Ontario," in *Tax Reform in Canada: Our Path to Greater Prosperity*, Herbert G. Grubel (ed.), Fraser Institute. pp. 233–259.

Ontario Jobs and Investment Board (1999), "A Road Map to Prosperity: An Economic Plan for Jobs in the 21st Century," Ontario Jobs and Investment Board.

Ontario Ministry of Finance (1985–2002), provincial budgets, Toronto, Ontario, Ministry of Finance, http://www.archives.gov.on.ca/en/historical_documents_project/ontario_budgets_2001-1987.aspx and http://www.archives.gov.on.ca/en/historical_documents_project/ontario_budgets_2002-2016.aspx

"Ontario Fiscal Overview and Spending Cuts," Ernie Eves, Minister of Finance, July 21, 1995.

"Ontario Prosperity, Is Best of Second Best Good Enough?" Jason Clemens, Amela Karabegović, and Niels Veldhuis, Fraser Institute, 15, 2003.

Progressive Conservative Party of Ontario (1994), *The Common Sense Revolution*, Toronto: Progressive Conservative Party of Ontario

Reese, Laura A. and Gary Sands (2007), "Making the Least of Our Differences? Trends in Local *Economic* Development in *Ontario* and Michigan, 1990–2005," Canadian Public Administration 50 (1), 79–99, 2007.

"The long, slow decline of the nation's industrial heartland," *Globe and Mail*, May 30, 2014.

Petrunia, Robert and Di Matteo, Livio (2018), "The Decline of Manufacturing in Canada: Resource Curse, Productivity Malaise or Natural Evolution?," *Springer Proceedings in Business and Economics*, William H. Greene, Lynda Khalaf, Paul Makdissi, Robin C. Sickles, Michael Veall, and Marcel-Cristia (eds.), *Productivity and Inequality*, pp. 183–202, Springer.

Rowthorn, Robert and Ramaswamy, Ramana, "Deindustrialization—Its Causes and Implications," *Economic Issues*, International Monetary Fund, September, 1997, https://www.imf.org/external/pubs/ft/issues10/index.htm

Walkom, Thomas, "The Harris Government: Restoration or Revolution?" in *The Government and Politics of Ontario Fifth Edition*, Graham White (ed.), University of Toronto Press, August, 1997.

Notes

1   *The Common Sense Revolution*, Progressive Conservative Party of Ontario, 1994, p. 1.
2   I have had the opportunity to review a number of these, issued during 1994 and generally authored by Dr. Mark Mullins, at that time chief economist of Midland Walwyn.
3   *Compare the Plans*, Progressive Conservative Party of Ontario, 1994/1995.
4   *The Common Sense Revolution*, p. 1.
5   Economic Statement, July 21, 1995.
6   These are itemized in Courchene, Thomas J., and Colin R. Telmer (1998), *From Heartland to North American Region State: The Social, Fiscal and Federal Evolution of Ontario, An Interpretive Essay.*
7   Mackie, Richard (2000) "Eves Agonized over Ontario's Cuts to Social Programs," *The Globe and Mail*, Toronto. May 1, 2000. https://www.theglobeandmail.com/news/national/eves-agonized-over-ontarios-cuts-to-social-programs/article1039316/
8   Courchene and Telmer, 1998, p. 175.
9   The marginal tax rate refers to the percentage that the government takes from the next dollar of income earned by taxpayers.
10 Walkom, Thomas (2001), "The Harris Government: Restoration or Revolution?" in Graham White (ed.), *The Government and Politics of Ontario, Fifth Edition*, University of Toronto Press, p. 403, n.3 https://doi-org.ezproxy.lib.ucalgary.ca/10.3138/9781442670198

11   I encourage interested readers to take a look at Howard Levitt's detailed evaluation
      of Harris-era labour law reform elsewhere in this volume.
12   See Rodrik (2016), and Rowthorn and Ramaswamy (1997).
13   Kneebone and McKenzie (1999, p. 77).
14   *Blueprint*, Mike Harris' Plan to Keep Ontario on the Right Track, 1999.
15   Courchene, Thomas J., and Colin R. Telmer (1998), *From Heartland to North American
      Region State: The Social, Fiscal and Federal Evolution of Ontario, An Interpretive Essay*.
16   McKenzie, Kenneth J. (2003), "A Tale of Two Provinces—Tax Policy in Alberta and
      Ontario," in *Tax Reform in Canada: Our Path to Greater Prosperity*, Herbert G. Grubel
      (ed.), Fraser Institute. pp. 233–259.

CHAPTER 3

Fiscal Policy and Privatization

Terence Corcoran and Jack M. Mintz

O N JUNE 26, 2020, FORMER premier of Ontario Mike
Harris was interviewed by TVO's Steve Paikin on the twenty-
fifth anniversary of the *CSR*. For the many Ontarians who
neither lived through nor remember the policy agenda advanced in
1995, the interview provided a historical review of a revolutionary
policy. Paikin asked Harris about "what was going on in the province at
that time that made you think we needed a so-called common sense
revolution?" Harris replied:

> We had had ten years of Liberal and NDP, together and separate,
> governments and a buildup of annual deficits and a buildup of
> debt and it was our belief that this wasn't sustainable. . . . For
> example, we said we were going to cut tax rates that would
> produce more jobs and in fact more revenue for the government.
> That was counterintuitive so in that sense, it was kind of
> revolutionary.[1]

While *CSR* focused on several policy reforms, the interview certainly emphasized the important fiscal policy shifts the Mike Harris government wanted to adopt after he was elected. What was particularly innovative was a set of policies that would not only balance budgets by cutting "non-health care" spending but *also* reduce taxes.

In this chapter, we assess whether *CSR* accomplished its main fiscal policy aims. We begin with an introduction to the *CSR* and its philosophical underpinnings. We then turn to a review of the troubled fiscal situation Harris inherited from the Liberal and NDP governments that preceded him, followed by an assessment of what the Harris government actually did and did not do. We then pay particular attention to the important topic of privatization, which played a smaller role in the original *CSR* but a larger part in the critiques later. While there were some privatization successes, there were also major failures to privatize that represent a real missed opportunity to demonstrate the true benefits of privatization, a message that could have been transferred to other sectors of the economy, particularly health care. We conclude with a discussion as to whether the *CSR* platform would work in the Ontario of today.

The story is told that on Tuesday, June 13, 1995, five days after the Mike Harris Progressive Conservatives won their resounding election victory on the back of the *CSR* platform, the Harris transition team held meetings with various government officials, deputy ministers, and bureaucrats. The objectives of the meetings included building bridges with Ontario's top civil servants and making it clear where the new government intended to take the province. On that Tuesday, the team got around to Jay Kaufman, deputy minister of finance and head of the Ontario Treasury Board under Bob Rae's NDP government. During his conversations with Harris and his transition associates, Kaufman reportedly said he assumed "they weren't serious about the fiscal plan set out in the *CSR*, and inquired what they really wanted to do." By the next day, Wednesday, Kaufman had been relieved of his Finance Department position.[2]

As an experienced player in Ontario's political system, Kaufman should have known better. That Mike Harris and his Conservative election team were serious about fiscal plan issues had been forcefully and clearly laid down during the 1995 election and was emphatically outlined in the *CSR* platform, one of the most clear-eyed economic policy platforms in the history of Canadian economic policymaking. It was specific in its promises and bluntly categorical in its statement of objectives.

The *CSR* document covered many subjects, from labour reform to health care and welfare, but radical reform of the tax and spending habits of the Ontario government dominated the outline for action. The introductory note, signed by Harris, set out reductions in government taxes and spending as the driver of what the document described as the foundation for an overhaul of the Ontario political system. "Tinkering with the system will not be enough. It's time for fundamental change."[3]

The fiscal highlights were set out in bold, declaratory sentences: "This plan will cut your provincial income tax rate by 30 per cent . . . reduce non-priority government spending by 20 per cent . . . fully balance the budget in four years." That these extremely ambitious fiscal objectives set out in the *CSR* were actually achievable in the real world of the 1995 provincial government was supported only by a simple statement that preceded Mike Harris's summary. "This plan will work," said Mark Mullins, who was then chief economist at Midland Walwyn, a leading Toronto securities firm. "The Mike Harris plan to cut provincial income tax rates by 30 per cent and non-priority services spending by 20 per cent will give Ontario a balanced budget within four years and create more than 725,000 new jobs."[4]

Assessing whether Mullins' aggressive projections of achievability were in fact met by the Harris government in the years that followed his landslide election victory in 1995 is a key mission of this chapter. Our conclusion is that, in general, and in individual respects, many of the revolutionary goals were in fact achieved. But, beyond the specifics of actual tax and spending reforms, how successful was the Harris government in revolutionizing Ontario? In a 2022 interview for this project, Mullins recalled a conversation he had with Harris in the later years of the Conservative's seven years in power or perhaps just after Harris had left office. Mullins said he will never forget what Harris said: "Listen, I wish we'd gone further, and I wish we'd gone faster." And today, looking back on the period, Mullins certainly believes that the *CSR* program and the Harris terms of office were part of a successful and transformative national and international movement to reform government, a movement that, however desirable and necessary then, seems impossible to imagine today, as Canada comes to the end of the first quarter-century of a new millennium, lost again on a sea of swollen debt and amid rising spending and taxes.

* * *

It is important to appreciate that Harris was not alone in the neoliberal political arena at the time. Many books and papers have been written over the years about the Harris era in Ontario, each with different perspectives and conclusions. It is universally agreed, however, that a fundamental aspect of the rise of the Harris Conservatives was the party's role as a local player in a global phenomenon. Nationally, in Ottawa, Prime Minister Jean Chretien led Canada into a major fiscal reform period that culminated in a 1995 federal budget plan that also set the federal government on a balanced budget path. It was "the budget that changed Canada," the title of a book edited by William Watson and Jason Clemens about a federal fiscal revolution in spending that was delivered in Ottawa by Finance Minister Paul Martin four months before the Ontario election that lifted Harris into power.[5]

Substantial spending reforms implemented in the federal 1995 budget made it politically easier for Harris to implement the ideas he had been proposing for several years before Martin's historic budget.

Among other objectives, the 1995 federal budget promised to cut departmental spending by $9.5 billion over three years (equivalent to an $18 billion cut in spending in 2022 dollars). The overall objective was, in the words of the federal budget document, to "sustain growth and create jobs by addressing the long-term deterioration of the financial condition of the Government of Canada." While the political "sale" of the proposed Harris cuts might have been made easier by Martin's federal reductions, the arithmetic was made much harder as so much of the federal "savings" were in fact cuts to provincial transfers. After the Martin budget and before the 1995 provincial election, Harris released an update to his *CSR* plan, reaffirming its commitment to both spending and tax reductions, with even larger cuts than originally planned given Martin's reductions in federal transfers. Importantly, unlike the federal government's approach, the Harris plan focused not only on spending reductions but also on tax cuts. Martin was later to join the movement to reduce taxes at the start of the new millennium, when the federal government also brought out a package of personal and corporate tax reductions.

Internationally, the idea that government spending reductions and tax cuts would be the source of economic renewal was part of an economic rethink in the 1990s that has now come to be disparagingly known as "neoconservatism" but is today better understood as "neoliberalism." The differences between neoliberalism and neoconservatism are many, although the basic tenets of neoliberal ideas are clearly at the heart of the Harris fiscal revolution. In his 1997 book on the Harris government, *Promised Land: Inside the Mike Harris Revolution*,[6] journalist John Ibbitson narrowed the sources of the *CSR* down to the work of Friedrich von Hayek, whose 1944 book *The Road to Serfdom* laid out the risks faced as governments around the world replaced "the impartial discipline of the market with the intrusive hand of state intervention."[7] More broadly and politically, neoliberalism was born with the publication of Hayek's groundbreaking work.

There have been no reports that businessman-turned-politician Mike Harris ever read Hayek or other intellectual leaders of the movement to reduce the role of the state in order to allow private market players to generate growth and prosperity. However, Hayek specifically and neoliberalism more generally (as a part of neoconservativism) certainly animated some members of the political team that surrounded Harris (known, in the satirical magazine *Frank*, as Harris's "Smug Little Shits™").

We leave it to others to tell the political and ideological story behind the creation of the Harris manifesto. But, in the *CSR*'s fiscal policymaking, the role of neoliberal economic thinking was clearly evident in the work done by Mark Mullins, who built the econometric model that supported claims that less government in the form of lower taxes and reduced government spending would stimulate growth and create jobs. While Mullins was the public face of the fiscal economic strategy, these ideas had broad support that ran deep through Canadian and international economic thinking at the time. In the Harris government's first full-year budget document, which was released in May 1996, the supporting economic theory was highlighted in a section titled "Economic Policies for Jobs and Growth."[8]

In this section of the Ontario budget, Finance Minister Ernie Eves set out the underlying neoliberal thinking behind the *CSR* strategy. Under the heading "The New Economics of Government" Eves outlined a plan. "The shift toward smaller government in Ontario reflects a new understanding that letting government grow too large cuts economic growth." Expanding government involvement in the economy "leads to high spending levels and taxpayer resistance. There is now a worldwide movement to find savings in government operations and redirect resources back in the private sector." The budget document included references to seventeen high-level national and international economic papers supporting the *CSR* theme that less government and lower taxes would boost economic activity.

One was a working paper published roughly a year after the *CSR* was first drafted, in which two economists at the International Monetary Fund (IMF) argued that "most of the important social and economic gains can be achieved with a drastically lower level of public spending than what prevails today." In words that could have been ripped directly from the pages of the *CSR*, the economists called for "radical reforms" that should aim at maintaining public spending at 30 per cent of GDP. Such reform "will require much privatization of higher education and of health care. They will require the privatization of some pensions and many other changes. In this process, the role of the government will change from provider to overseer or regulator or of activities. Its role will be mainly to set the "rules of the game" in the economy."[9]

The 1996 budget document went on to cite other papers to support its theme: "The time to reshape government is now." One of those other papers, titled "The Causes of Unemployment in Canada," was a 1994 working paper from the Bank of Canada authored by Stephen S. Poloz (later to be governor of the Bank of Canada) that supported the idea that rising unemployment in Canada during the 1990s was "mainly because of a substantial rise in payroll taxation."[10]

If economic thinking and research through the early 1990s tended to support aspects of neoliberalism, the general ideological state of the media and academic universes had *not* realigned with ideas of smaller government and lower taxes. Columnists at the *Toronto Star* and in other media routinely ridiculed the neoliberal orientation on taxes and spending, especially as it became clear that the *CSR* fiscal strategy was gaining support among a population of voters increasingly disenchanted after a decade of Liberal–NDP financial governance.

Whatever the philosophical underpinning for the *CSR* economic plan, it was rooted in the belief that Ontario needed to change direction. In fact, Harris viewed his economic plan in practical terms.

In the twenty-fifth anniversary interview with Steve Paikin, Harris laid out his views as follows:

> What's changed is we've had ten years, the period we called the "Lost Decade" of some sixty-five new tax increases, massive buildup in government spending, a significant intervention by government into the marketplace and so what needs to happen now is to restore the balance that Bill Davis had throughout that period of time. We do need a correction from this politics of the past ten years. We need major change to get Ontario back on track.[11]

Ontario's "Lost Decade" began with the 1985 election, when Frank Miller, leader of the Progressive Conservatives, won only fifty-two seats, while the Liberals won forty-eight and the NDP twenty-five. The Liberals and NDP negotiated a two-year "accord," but with the NDP taking no cabinet positions. When the agreement ended in 1987, another election was held, with the Liberals under David Peterson forming a solid majority government. After a series of scandals and an early opportunistic call for an election in 1990 (which proved to be a fatal political error), the Liberals were turfed out and replaced by Bob Rae's NDP, which then formed, for the first time, a socialist majority government in Ontario.

The Peterson government raised income taxes in four of its five budgets. Following the federal government, the Liberals broadened the provincial corporate tax base, but, unlike the federal government, they actually raised corporate income tax rates. The Peterson government also increased the retail sales tax rate from 7 to 8 per cent in 1988, after a few exemptions were introduced in prior years, including food sales of less than $2. The land transfer tax was increased, as were the alcohol and tobacco taxes, and a new tax on tires was also introduced. To be fair to them, the Liberals did reduce excise taxes on a few items such as motive fuels (later increased again in 1990) as well as introducing a three-year tax holiday for mining profits and various other tax credits.

Rae promised his own fiscal revolution. To that effect, the Rae government created the Fair Tax Commission to study, among various tax reforms, a new wealth tax and a corporate minimum tax. Its name said it all: tax reform that was specifically intended to redistribute wealth, despite the deepening recession in the government's first year. The NDP hoped that public spending, especially on social assistance and a higher deficit, would shelter the economy from the recession's worst effects. As then-Finance Minister Floyd Laughren stated in the 1991 budget: "The government is convinced that allowing the deficit to rise to this level is not only justifiable but also the most responsible choice we could make."[12]

Under the NDP, income tax rates were increased in their first three budgets, and a corporate minimum tax was introduced in 1993. No wealth tax was officially adopted, but the NDP did substantially increase probate fees charged on estates. Corporate taxes were initially reduced for manufacturing, resource, and small businesses but later raised for financial institutions. Retail sales tax was broadened to include insurance premiums (that were also subject to the insurance premium tax), used vehicles, and a few other goods and services. It is worth noting that some land assets were sold off, including the provincial investment in Toronto's Skydome stadium.

In summary, successive budgets from 1985 to 1994, under both Liberal and NDP governments, were largely focused on tax increases, except for certain politically favoured activities. And, as we shall discuss next, this period also saw substantial increased public spending on health, education, welfare, and infrastructure.

Overall, real per capita Ontario spending grew dramatically during the Peterson and Rae years by almost $1,400 ($2,156 in 1985 to $4,187 in 1994) as shown in Figure 3.1 (all numbers are expressed in 2003 values). Somewhat less than half of the increased spending happened in the Liberal years of 1985–1990 (an increase of $930 per capita), with the balance ($1,101 per capita) during the four NDP years. Taxes and other

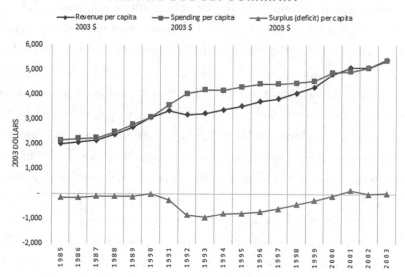

Figure 3.1 Real Per Capita Spending, Revenues, and Deficits (in 2003 Dollars) from 1985 to 2003

Source: Ontario budgets various years.

revenues also grew quickly from $2,010 per capita to $3,548 by 1995. About two-thirds of this increase occurred in the Peterson years, with the rest under the NDP government, which of course saw tax revenues diminish given the deep recession.

The NDP also introduced a host of new social programs in their first budget that contributed to the jump in real per capita spending of $450, almost half of the big increase that already incurred during the Peterson years. The new programs included a $1.1 billion Jobs Training Program and a $2.3 billion Jobs Ontario Capital Fund in 1992. Social assistance spending doubled to $4.5 billion from $2.3 billion just two years earlier (a result of Peterson's generous increases in rates and the consequences of the severe recession).

We leave it to others in this book to analyze the various economic factors that impacted the growth in spending and tax revenues over time.

However, it is useful to show how Ontario differed from the other provinces, particularly the other large ones, Alberta, British Columbia, and Quebec, in regard to government spending.

As shown in Figure 3.2, Ontario's spending rose much faster than population and prices during the Liberal and NDP years—that is, until the fiscal year 1995/96. At the beginning of the Harris mandate (1996/97 full year), Ontario cut per capita spending from $6,245 in 1995/96 to $5,880 in the first full fiscal year of its first mandate (1996/97). After the first year, per capita spending rose only slightly faster than population and prices, rising to $6,192 at the end of the first mandate (1999/2000). In the second mandate, spending per capita rose to $6,536 by the fourth year. While seen as dramatic by some observers, overall, Ontario's spending pattern closely followed British Columbia and actually moved up to Quebec's level after the fiscal year 2000/01. The biggest reduction in provincial spending actually

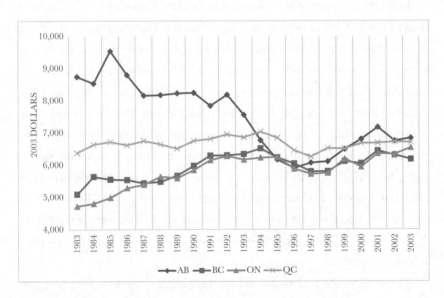

Figure 3.2   Provincial Spending Per Capita (in 2003 Dollars)

Source: Expenditure data https://www.utpjournals.press/doi/pdf/10.3138/cpp.2015-046

Population data Table: 17-10-0005-01 (formerly CANSIM 051-0001)

CPI data Table: 18-10-0005-01 (formerly CANSIM 326-0021)

occurred in Alberta as the Ralph Klein government aggressively pared down the size of government, with real per capita spending dropping from $8,179 in 1992/93 to $7,559 in just the first year. By 2003/04, per capita spending in Alberta rose above that in Ontario to $6,833 as oil and gas revenues recovered. Even so, by 2003/04, Alberta per capita spending was still well below the years prior to 1992/93 level.

Deficits in the Rae years led to a substantial build-up of public debt, with interest charges increasingly crowding out other expenditures. In 1990–1991 fiscal year, public debt charges as a share of total expenditure were 7 per cent. By the time the Harris government was elected in 1995, public debt charges rose to 13 per cent of total expenditure. Even after Harris was elected, it took some time to reduce the deficit before the budget was balanced by 2000–2001. Public debt charges peaked at 16 per cent as a share of total expenditures in 1999–2000 before finally beginning to trend downward to 11 per cent in 2003–2004.

It is critical to note that it was not just the growth in spending and deficits during "the Lost Decade" that laid the foundations for the *CSR*. It was also the extraordinary increase in personal income taxes, the largest source of revenue for the provincial government. As shown in Figure 3.3, real per capita income tax revenues (expressed in 2003 dollars) more than doubled from $478 in 1985 to $1,137 in 1994. The recession in 1991 and 1992 took a bite out of growth in progressive personal income taxes since the average tax rate falls when income drops. But the NDP government's response was to substantially hike personal income tax rates further, beginning in 1992. Despite these rate hikes, from an average Ontario rate of 17 per cent in 1991 to 22 per cent in 1994, growth in real per capita personal tax revenues stalled altogether.

The reality was that sustained tax rate increases under Peterson and Rae could not keep up with the burgeoning growth in spending. The provincial deficit grew from $3 per capita in 1990 to $934 per capita by 1993. In 1993, the Rae government sought to pivot and begin to reign

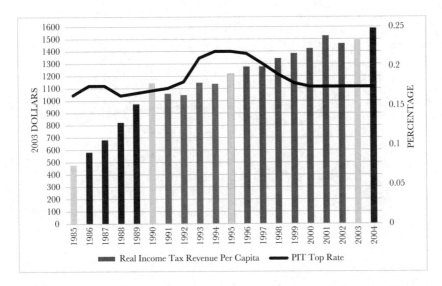

Figure 3.3   Real Per Capita Personal Income Tax Revenues, 1985–2003

Source: Various Ontario budgets.

in spiraling costs via its Social Contract, which effectively limited wage increases for the broad public sector. But this new policy came with a significant political cost, deeply alienating its voter base. In fact, spending did slow down near the end of the NDP government's term, but deficits remained high at $792 per capita in 1994. It was this chronically poor fiscal performance under both the Liberal and NDP regimes that Harris so effectively labeled the "Lost Decade" and that established the context and clear contrast with the economic plan set forth in the *CSR*.

It is also useful to understand how Ontario's personal income tax policy differed from other provinces during the Liberal and NDP years. In Figure 3.4, we show the top personal income tax rates for the four largest provinces. Except for Quebec at 33 per cent, the provincial top rates were relatively similar in 1985 (15 per cent in Alberta and British Columbia and 16 per cent in Ontario). By 1994, the top rate in Ontario reached 22 per cent (four points below Quebec and one point below British Columbia) and well above the Alberta rate of 15 points.

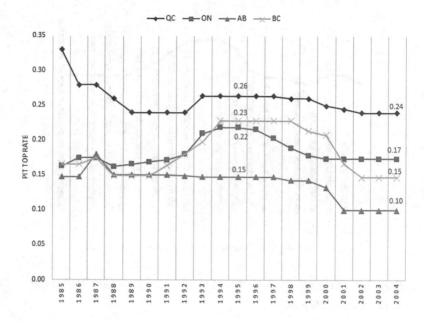

Figure 3.4 Top Personal Income Tax Rates for the Four Largest Provinces 1985–2004

Source: Canadian Tax Foundation, Provincial Finances, various years.

These differences in personal tax policy reflected both economic factors (slow growth) and, perhaps more so, the political orientation of the various governments. Alberta, which depended on skilled labour for its resource sector, elected Progressive Conservative governments throughout these years. British Columbia rotated between Social Credit and NDP governments; its tax rate hikes after 1990 were primarily in the NDP years, when Mike Harcourt was premier. The decline in the top personal income tax rate in Quebec, highest of all provinces in 1985, happened under both the Parti Quebecois (Daniel Johnson) and the Liberals (Robert Bourassa). The large difference between Ontario and Alberta opened up a competition for the personal tax base as high-income Ontarians could either move or shift income to Alberta.

Given the sharp increase in Ontario personal income tax rates after 1985, it comes as no surprise that the *CSR* paid particular attention to the personal tax system, as we further elaborate below.

* * *

The *CSR*, as laid out in the Progressive Conservative platform, had three major fiscal promises: balancing the budget by end of term (1999), cutting the personal income tax by 30 per cent, and reducing "non-priority" (i.e., except health care and policing) public spending by 20 per cent.[13] A host of major policies were promised, including welfare reform, a reduction in administrative costs, especially in education, freezing electricity rates, cutting worker compensation premiums by 5 per cent, labour law reform, childcare support for working parents, and a red-tape commission, all of which were red meat for PC supporters. A "fair-share health care levy" was also proposed, with health premiums rising with income in tranches (a proposal similar to the health levy adopted by the McGuinty government a decade later). Promises were also made to privatize surplus land and TV Ontario and, potentially, the LCBO. We leave discussion about privatization to the next section of this chapter. And specific policies in relation to health care, education, welfare (workfare), and municipal reform are covered by other chapters in this book.

With regard to its broad objectives, our assessment is that the *CSR* was largely successful in its first mandate. Although the Harris government did not in fact quite reach a fully balanced budget as promised in its first mandate, deficits (in 2003 dollars) fell from $773 per capita to $74 by the 1999/2000 fiscal year. Given the strong economy in the mid-1990s, revenues per capita actually rose even as the Harris government cut personal tax rates by a third, as promised. It also eliminated the employer education and health tax on payrolls below $400,000, also as promised. The initially proposed fair-share levy for healthcare funding was replaced by a personal income surtax. As shown in Figure 3.2, real spending levels barely budged in the first mandate, including health care. However, since healthcare spending did increase (a fact often disputed to this day) other public programs bore substantial cuts to real spending.

Most important, the Harris *CSR* promised personal tax cuts. As seen in Figure 3.4, Ontario delivered on this promise, reducing personal income tax rates before Alberta and British Columbia as well as the federal government (which began tax reductions in 2020). In this sense, Ontario was a pioneer in cutting tax rates.

While the initial *CSR* mandate focused on personal income and employer payroll taxes, it was silent with respect to corporate and sales taxation. The Harris government did little to reduce corporate income tax rates except for a small reduction in the small business rate. In fact, it imposed higher capital taxes on banks, and Finance Minister Eves was quite willing to play with corporate tax rates to support politically favoured business activities, with a host of new credits for film making, research and development, digital media, and co-op education. In this regard, the neoliberal view of keeping governments from interfering with the market seems to have been often forgotten.

Sales tax reform also was put on the back burner despite the expansion of the sales tax base under the NDP. The federal government was pushing for harmonization of the provincial sales taxes with the federal GST. Harmonization would have led to a shift from hidden sales taxes on business inputs to taxes on services, visible to voters. While serious talks took place with Ontario, the idea did not catch on (unlike in the Atlantic provinces that harmonized their sales taxes with the federal GST in 1997 after receiving a sizable transition grant to grease the wheels). Instead, the Harris government made several small adjustments to the retail sales tax, largely in the form of new exemptions or rebates.

In Table 3.1, we provide a summary list of various fiscal promises and the outcomes in the first term.

One notable issue that arose in the first mandate was Canada Pension Plan reform.[14] Amendments to CPP legislation required the agreement of the federal government and two-thirds of the provinces (i.e., seven) representing two-thirds of the population, which effectively gave Ontario a veto.

Table 3.1 Key Actions to Fulfil the *CSR*, 1996–1999

Promises	Budget 1996	Budget 1997	Budget 1998	Budget 1999	Promises Kept?
Personal tax cut of 30%	Reduction in PIT rates from 58% to 56% of federal taxes, July 1, 1996	Reduction in PIT rates from 56% to 47% July 1, 1997	Reduction in PIT rates from 47% to 40.5%, July 1 1998	Reduction in PIT rates from 40.5% to 38.5%, July 1 1998	Promise kept: Overall reduction of 33%
Cut non-priority (spending by 20%)	Elimination of job Ontario, $300 savings from spending cuts	$700 million in savings, school boards reduced by one-half, 286 billion from lower public debt charges. Reduction in capital spending by $240 million	$1035 million in savings. $460 billion from lower debt charges, capital savings of $330 million	$600 million in savings, half from health capital spending reduction	Spending kept flat (nominally between $57 and $58 billion) Health care spending rose by $2.6 billion (15%) in four years
Balancing the Budget by 1999/2000	Deficit $9.1 billion	Deficit $7.5 billion	Deficit $5.2 billion	Deficit $3.2 billion	Almost balanced at the end of the first mandate

(Contd.)

Table 3.1 (*Contd.*)

Promises	Budget 1996	Budget 1997	Budget 1998	Budget 1999	Promises Kept?
Corporate Tax	Capital tax on banks, tax credits for film and co-op education	Tax credits for R&D, animation, book publishing, graduate transition, tax on financial institution and credit union	Small business tax rate reduced from 9.5% to 9%, tax credits for digital media, sound recording, workplace accessibility, childcare	Capital tax exemption for credit unions, family farms and smaller companies	Not significant element of *CSR* promises
EHT payroll tax cut with Fair Share Health Levy	Fair share levy added to PIT surtax	Lower threshold for PIT surtax	EHT payroll tax exemption increased from $200k to $300k	EHT payroll tax exemption increased to $400k	EHT promise kept

To better fund CPP, the federal government wanted to raise payroll taxes, invest funds in the market more broadly rather than only in provincial bonds, and make some limited adjustments to benefits. Given the *CSR* focus on cutting taxes, Ontario was initially opposed to any payroll tax increase, as was Alberta. After Jim Dinning, Alberta's finance minister, agreed to a payroll tax increase, this left Ontario as the sole opponent. The federal government worked out a side deal with the province to cover other Ontario requests, which resulted in Ontario's eventual support of CPP reform. By then, the newly elected NDP government in British Columbia, supported by Saskatchewan, changed its position, proposing a significant increase in benefits to match new funding. However, those two provinces lacked the political leverage of Ontario and could not block the CPP reforms that were eventually adopted.

It was not until the second mandate that the Harris government would have the time and capacity to address other issues besides balanced budgets, personal tax reform, and reforms to spending on various programs like welfare and education. In its *Blueprint* platform for the 1999 election, the Harris government proposed a further 20 per cent cut to both personal income taxes and the provincial residential property tax. It guaranteed a 20 per cent increase in healthcare spending and increased classroom funding to match rising enrolment (but not inflation). They promised to reduce barriers to employment, including drug addiction and illiteracy. A key proposal was to create a $50 billion public/private SuperBuild Growth Fund. With budget surpluses, $2 billion in debt would be paid down.

Despite these fiscal promises, what was lacking in the 1999 *Blueprint* platform was any philosophy behind tax policy, beyond simply reducing rates. The intellectual basis for tax reform in Canada goes back to the 1967 Carter Report, which argued in favour of lower rates and broader tax bases to support both growth and fairness. These ideas became part of the neoliberal agenda in the mid-1980s, with many OECD countries, including Canada, reforming their personal and corporate taxes by reducing rates and broadening tax bases. But in 1999, the Harris *Blueprint* for their second mandate had little of this. There was no effort to reduce corporate income tax rates or other business taxes for competitiveness reasons. The idea of reducing rates and broadening the tax base, which was adopted in Alberta with its flat tax, was nowhere to be found. Neither was sales tax harmonization with the federal GST considered. These ideas would have to wait for Liberal Premier McGuinty's 2009 budget, which not only brought in sales tax harmonization but also sharply reduced the corporate income tax rate and eliminated capital taxes.

Table 3.2 provides an outline of the *Blueprint* platform's promises and whether they were met. The promised debt reduction did take place.

Table 3.2 Significant Harris Government Fiscal Promises, 2000–2004

Promises	2000	2001	2002	2003	Promises Kept?
Personal Tax Cut and Provincial Residential Property Tax Cut by 20%			PIT reduced for first two brackets 6.2% to 6.05% up to $30814 9.24% to 9.15% between $30814 and $61629 Residential property tax 20% reduction phased in	First and second rates 5.65% and 8.85% Farmland property taxed at 25% of residential rate	In part
Guaranteed Increase in Health (20%), SuperBuild Fund $20 billion	Health $22.2 billion ($20.4 billion in 1999)	Health $23.7 billion SuperBuild fund created	Health $25.9 billion	Health $27.5 billion	Health spending up 33%. SuperBuild fund created
Balancing the Budget by 2000/1 followed by debt reduction of $2 billion	Deficit $0.9 billion	Surplus $2 billion	Surplus $0.1 billion	Surplus $0.5 billion	Promise largely kept

(Contd.)

Table 3.2 (*Contd.*)

Promises	2000	2001	2002	2003	Promises Kept?
Corporate Tax: Small business tax rate cut by a half to 4%	General CIT rate reduced 15.5% to 14.5% Small business CIT rate reduced from 8 to 7% Resource and manufacturing income CIT rate reduced 13.5 to 12.5% Mining tax rate reduced 20 to 18%	General CIT rate of 14% and 12.5% as of Oct. 1 Small business CIT rate 6.5% Resource-manufacturing CIT rate 12% and 11% as of Oct. 1. Mining Tax rate 16% Tax credit for education technology	General CIT rate of 12.5% Small business CIT rate 6% Mining Tax rate 14% Capital tax rates reduced by 10%	Small business CIT rate 5.5% Resource CIT rate 12% and 11% as of Oct. 1 Mining Tax rate 12% 12 tax credits added or expanded	Small business tax rate cut by about one third

Personal income and property taxes were reduced, and healthcare funding increased (worth repeating). The *SuperBuild Fund* was created, but, using newly introduced capital budgeting, the expenditures would not reduce the surpluses or add to the deficit until capital depreciation was charged to the budget. Even though corporate tax reform was not part of the campaign proposals, the Harris government did indeed start the process with a reduction in the large corporate income tax rates, as well as the promised reduction in the small business tax rate. On the other hand, Ontario also introduced numerous new and smaller tax credits (Finance Minister Ernie Eves liked to count each tax reduction separately).

As previously seen in Figure 3.1, there was a noticeable and significant shift in fiscal policy over the period of the Harris government. After 1992, per capita real spending leveled off during the last Rae years and through the first Harris mandate. However, once the budget was finally balanced after 2000, real per capita spending picked up to match revenue growth. Perhaps Mike Harris' argument that he was just trying to return to the Davis-Era years was right after all. Viewed by the numbers, the last period of the Harris era, up until 2003, began to look more like the middle-of-the-road Ontario had traveled in earlier years.

* * *

Privatization was one of the least significant themes in the Harris government's original *CSR* platform and made no significant direct contributions to the ambitious fiscal plan. But as time has passed, privatization has loomed over the Harris political record as one of the most controversial elements of that record both for what the government did and for what it didn't do. On the negative side, it failed to unload one of its most valuable assets, the government monopoly Liquor Control Board of Ontario. Nor did it sell off TV Ontario or the Metro Toronto Convention Centre as it had promised. But, to this day, what Harris did privatize, especially the Highway 407 toll road, the province's testing laboratories, long-term care facilities, and Bruce Power, remain hot topics for critics whose aim is to tarnish the Harris record and the "neoliberal" economic principles that drove it.

As a mission statement, the original *CSR* privatization promise appears as little more than a footnote in the grand pledge to reform Ontario's economic and fiscal performance. In the final pre-election version of the *CSR*, located near the end of the twenty-one-page document, are five short sentences that illustrate its overall lack of ambition when it comes to privatization:

> We will sell off some assets, such as the LCBO and surplus government land, to the private sector. We will actively explore the sale of other assets, including TV Ontario. . . . We believe

the value of such assets is greater when being used to pay down the massive provincial debt than sitting on the government books. . . . The money we make from such asset sales will not go into the government accounts. Every penny will go directly to pay down the $80-billion provincial debt.

When it comes to actual dollars and pennies, however, the Harris government's privatization initiatives did not actually deliver much toward debt reduction. The promise to sell off "some assets" hardly ranks as a bold 1995 commitment to privatization as an overarching principle. Four years later, the 1999 *Blueprint* had whittled the privatization commitment down further in brief paragraphs focused on "Selling Things We Don't Need." The *Blueprint* nevertheless did hint at a broader objective, adding that the government was actively reviewing "everything government owns."

Over the Harris government's years in power, very little of what the government owned was privatized. In fact, based on a strict definition of the idea, almost nothing was actually sold off by the government into private hands, aside from the Province of Ontario Savings Office in 2001. This statement is true, but with two notable exceptions, which we will discuss in detail below: the Bruce Power nuclear site (notably the largest sale of its kind in the world) and the sale of the 407 Electronic Toll Road (407ETR) to a private consortium. The amount of money collected via the privatization process to reduce the provincial debt was correspondingly small. By our calculations, the total barely exceeds $4 billion, or about 0.01 per cent, of government spending over the life of the Harris government.

The following review will look at the four highest-profile transactions that are the core elements of the Harris government's privatization story. Almost three decades after the 1995 election, each continues to shadow the Harris record.

But before we get to an examination of these privatizations, which continue to fuel much political criticism of the Harris legacy, it's worth having a look at what the Harris government failed to privatize, notably the province's liquor control monopoly. In our view, failure to follow through on privatizing the government-owned television station, TV Ontario is not a significant indicator of policy failure. The station's value was minimal in 1999, and it remains of limited importance in the grand scheme of the province's political and economic structure. Failure to act on ending the Liquor Control Board of Ontario monopoly, however, is another matter and provides a useful demonstration that the Harris government's *CSR* motives were, some might say unfortunately, not totally based on deep neoliberal motives. The LCBO could have been a true privatization, a full-fledged divestiture of a government monopoly into a new open and competitive market, but it never happened.

The failure to privatize the LCBO, lamentable from a consumer and economic perspective, remains a significant lost opportunity to demonstrate the benefits of privatization. If Harris had successfully de-monopolized the alcohol market, the whole concept of privatization would have been given a major boost. Instead, the government backed away from privatization of the alcohol market, preferring instead to allow the corporation to substitute modern marketing and retail razzle-dazzle to give the false impression it was offering the public the best of all worlds.

The LCBO failure is also a demonstration of the degree to which the *CSR*'s starting principles fell short of grasping the essential benefits of private versus public ownership and control. Neoliberalism isn't exactly a fine science. The Wikipedia entry on "Neo-liberalism" is a thirty-page effort (including 400 footnote links to hundreds of warring academic papers) reflecting an economic and ideological scramble that dates back more than a century. But when the Harris government came to power, major elements of the free-market model were often overshadowed by fiscal policy objectives. With the LCBO, the Harris government veered off the neoliberal course in pursuit of standard political objectives.

In 1995, the LCBO was a government-owned and government-operated province-wide corporation that controlled liquor and wine wholesale and retail markets. Another private monopoly player, The Beer Store chain, while owned and operated by the brewing industry, was also essentially a government-sanctioned beer monopoly. The *CSR* neoliberal objective should have been to privatize the alcohol market by selling the LCBO, deregulating The Beer Store monopoly, and allowing beer sales through supermarkets and even corner stores. More importantly, dismantling the LCBO would allow other corporations to enter the alcohol retail business and provide consumers much more choice, which has been the Alberta experience. Notably, Alberta achieved a successful and deregulated approach without sacrificing provincial revenues.[15]

The neoliberal objective of privatization is to benefit consumers and enhance economic productivity through competition. Instead, the Harris government fell into the fiscal policy trap that routinely captures politicians, bureaucrats, and corporate insiders. Instead of aiming to benefit consumers, the objective soon became how to maximize the fiscal return to the government. Never mind the consumer and the market. The objective became preserving and enhancing government revenues.

Over the decades, and long after the defeat of the Harris government, any impetus toward LCBO privatization inevitably faltered with the realization that the government would lose control of a "cash cow," a risk highlighted by a succession of LCBO executives. In 2014, for example, LCBO president Bob Peter and chairman Edward Waitzer signed off on the corporation's annual report cleverly titled "20 years of growing dividends," a trend they portrayed as a great social good.

> Two decades ago, LCBO's dividend transfer to the Ontario government was $630 million. In fiscal 2013–14, LCBO transferred a new, record dividend of $1.74 billion. This latest transfer marks the twentieth consecutive dividend increase to the province. Adding up each dividend transfer over this 20-year

period equals a total of $22.5 billion. These revenues help pay for important public services, such as health care and education, that benefit all Ontario residents.

The LCBO's self-portrayal as a major supplier of do-good cash to government developed during the Harris years when it was in the executive hands of former interim Ontario PC leader and cabinet minister Andy Brandt, a shrewd political and business operator who was named CEO in 1991. Through to his retirement in 2006, Brandt transformed the LCBO into a modern retail monopoly empire by playing the role of cash dispenser to the government. The University of Winnipeg's Malcolm Bird, in his masterful 250-page thesis on the Ontario and Alberta liquor markets, captures the Brandt/LCBO modus operandi:

> Brandt's team was able to influence the LCBO's fate by ensuring that the Board was actively meeting the needs of the government in power. Under this team, the LCBO was not a passive institution. It significantly increased its remittances to the provincial treasury and it managed to accomplish this by changing consumer preferences with respect to alcohol. No longer a sinful vice of its prohibition era ethos, alcohol is today viewed as a part of healthy, middle-class lifestyle in which moderation and individual consumer responsibility—as opposed to externally imposed controls—are key hallmarks.[16]

To be fair to Brandt and his successors, the LCBO has indeed successfully turned itself into a flagship retail operation that generates growing revenues, including taxes and dividends to government. The money flow is all very welcome among the unions and statists who see government monopoly and profiteering as a social benefit. At the same time, as many have observed, by transforming itself into a slick retail giant, LCBO has won the support of consumers, even though they largely have no choice. LCBO is a market success in a market without competition. How difficult can that be?

But what would an Ontario beer, wine, and liquor market look like today if the Harris government had found a way to open the market to private and competitive forces?

Malcolm Bird sees the Harris LCBO failure to privatize as reinforcement of standard Canadian political ideas that are generally unreceptive to neoliberal principles.

> When Canadian governments attempt to embrace neoliberal-type principles, they are engaged in an attempt to fundamentally change the governing structures in this country, because neoliberalism, in its purest form, calls for the state to withdraw from involvement in all areas where its intervention is not absolutely necessary. . . . This tenet runs counter to the political, historical and institutional legacies of this country.

In Bird's view, the ability of decades of LCBO executives to maintain their control and ward off privatization provides a useful lesson to leaders in other government-controlled sectors. The ability of the LCBO to influence its fate and to successfully appeal to the needs of its political masters shows how executives and managers of agencies, hospitals, universities, and especially remaining Crown corporations can maneuver to ward off privatization. The LCBO lesson for executives is to focus on the needs of political superiors and determine, in raw practical, political terms, how the institution can help meet the political objectives.

For this reason alone, the *CSR* failure to tackle the LCBO privatization deserves a capital "F" for failure. Not only did it allow a consumer-gouging monopoly to survive as a cash machine for government, preventing the benefits of competition and market freedom. It also helped establish a state corporate control model that, to this day, influences policymaking.

One can only imagine how the continuing debate over the provision of other government services such as health care would have evolved if only the Harris "revolutionaries" had been willing to force the conversion of the LCBO into another competitor in a free-market-driven wholesale and retail sector.

* * *

In May 2020, the Walkerton water supply e-coli contamination crisis killed seven people and caused severe illness in more than 2,300 residents of the small Ontario town. Ever since, the Walkerton scandal has been a prime source of political smear campaigns against the Harris government and its neoliberal idea that privatization can deliver better products and services more efficiently.[17]

The claim that this privatization initiative created the risks that led to death and illness in Walkerton has been part of the left-liberal attack on the Harris record since the events took place, with many of the attacks coming from academics. A classic of the genre is a *Risk Management Journal* 2003 special issue titled "Regulation, Risk and Corporate Crime in a 'Globalized' Era."[18] In that issue, Queen's University sociologist Laureen Snider wrote "Captured by Neo-Liberalism: Regulation and Risk in Walkerton, Ontario." Snider concluded that the Harris government's lab privatization, based on a neoliberal "belief system that reached religious levels . . . led to the water-poisoning disaster in Walkerton."

This is a blatantly false narrative based on what can only be described as a deliberate misrepresentation of the evidence, a warped reading still often trundled out by journalists. By way of example, we cite *Toronto Star* columnist Linda McQuaig, who in 2018 claimed that "a judicial inquiry blamed cutbacks and lax oversight by Mike Harris' Conservative government for seven deaths and 2,300 illnesses from contaminated water. Shortly afterwards, Harris resigned."[19]

In reality, the privatization of Ontario's routine microbiological testing for local municipalities was not on any of the Harris government's *CSR* target lists. Instead, it was part of a plan within the Ministry of the Environment (MOE) and Bob Rae's NDP government before the 1995 election. The idea of allowing better equipped and managed private labs to take over the testing of municipal water supplies was launched in 1993 and had been approved by Rae's NDP government shortly before the election.

When the Harris team took over, the NDP's privatized labs idea fit well with the *CSR* narrative, although there was no real money to be saved in terms of debt and deficit reduction. But the principle was sound, and as already recognized by the Rae government, this was an opportunity to improve the ability to monitor municipal services for contamination. In 1996, Ontario's ministry of health sent a letter to municipalities alerting them of the decision to privatize.

It took Ontario Justice Dennis O'Connor 700 pages to complete his 2002 *Report of the Walkerton Inquiry*, but not a word of it supports the generalized smear campaign suggested above. The report, in fact, tracks a long and convoluted series of flawed water supply decisions, incompetence, dangerous water sources, and a tragic series of coincidences.

As Justice O'Connor's inquiry found, the story of the Walkerton e-coli outbreak traces back through decades of gross government incompetence. Among the sources of water for the town's 5,000 residents was Well 5, near a source of farm manure. It was a known problem for many years, yet neither the local nor provincial government officials dealt with it. The list of similar problems is endless: lack of enforcement, inspection, training; failure to monitor or chlorinate when needed; improper operating practices, including deliberate concealment of the fact that chlorination had not taken place in the weeks prior to the outbreak. None of this is in any way related to the laboratory privatization issue or can be fairly attributed to any action, or inaction, of the Harris government.

In his commission report, O'Connor makes it clear that by the mid-1990s and, specifically, in May 2000, the town's water supply and safety system was a massive hive of planning and management failure, institutional ignorance, and raw incompetence. The town's Public Utilities Commission was managed by two untrained political appointees, Stan and Frank Koebel, who routinely failed to follow proper procedures or manage the town's utilities commission.

Into this existing morass came the Harris government's decision to follow the NDP plan to privatize the testing of Ontario's water supply. Prior to the privatization, government rules required government laboratories to report adverse results to the local municipality and to the minister of environment. Under the privatized lab regime, the municipality would be notified of contamination, but not the MOE.

The day-to-day reporting of the actual results, based on the O'Connor inquiry findings, is important in assessing the false narrative regarding the lab privatization:

> May 15: Critical samples of contaminated Walkerton water were taken and sent to the private laboratory where they were tested and found to be contaminated.
>
> May 16: The samples were received by the private lab, A&L, and found to be contaminated.
>
> May 17: An employee of the private lab telephoned Walkerton's PUC manager Stan Koebel in the morning to alert him of the results. Faxed results were sent later in the day.
>
> May 18: Contaminated water was being consumed by Walkerton residents, impacting their health. Indeed, the contaminated water had been circulating through the water system for days. If the local health unit and the MOE had been advised of the contamination, boil-water alerts could have been issued immediately. But they were not. The private lab hired by the town was not obliged under the private contract to forward

the contamination results to the province's environment ministry. That job was up to Stan Koebel and the PUC and local officials, but nothing was done.

May 19: The Walkerton health unit, now aware of spreading illness in the community, asked Koebel if there was a problem with the water, and he responded that the water was "okay," despite the fact that the testing and sampling he had done was all but non-existent and despite a call from the private lab two days earlier.

May 21: After days of bungling, and with illness spreading, a boil-water advisory was finally issued. By this date, which was a Sunday, the e-coli contaminated water had already been consumed by hundreds of Walkerton residents, causing serious illness among 2,300 residents and the deaths of six people.

The claim of the anti-privatization left is that if the Harris government had not privatized the labs, the warning regarding water contamination in Walkerton would have been passed on to the province's environment ministry, which would have then issued a boil-water advisory well before the one issued on May 21. Since that did not happen, the lab's privatization is said to be responsible for the town's water disaster. Environmental lawyer and political activist Diane Saxe in 2000 revived the Walkerton privatizations scare with a classic false narrative: "It was the provincial government's hasty cancelation of the public testing labs that allowed [Walkerton] to happen and we're seeing a restitution of that model of government by this conservative government."[20]

That falsehood, regurgitated over the years by all manner of academics, politicians, and media commentators, is expressly contradicted by Judge O'Connor in his authoritative report. Here is his concluding statement on what might have happened had the private lab been required to advise the MOE, and not just Stan Koebel in Walkerton, of the contamination:

If a boil water advisory had been issued on May 19, approximately 300 to 400 illnesses would probably have been prevented, but it is very unlikely that any of the deaths would have been avoided.

It is possible that if the health unit had been notified of the adverse results on the afternoon of Wednesday May 17, it would have issued a boil water advisory before May 19. The results showed gross contamination and no doubt would have triggered an immediate response: possibly a boil water advisory, but more likely a direction to resample, flush, and maintain adequate chlorine residuals. The results of any resampling would not have been available until the following day, May 18, at the earliest. By Thursday May 18, complaints of illness had surfaced. If the health unit had been informed of those complaints and of the May 17 results, it might well have issued a boil water advisory at that point.

If a boil water advisory had been issued on May 18, between 400 and 500 illnesses would probably have been avoided. It is possible that one death might have been prevented.[21]

On the one death prevention possibility, O'Connor added in a footnote:

One of the persons who died had first experienced symptoms on May 21. Assuming a three- to four-day period of incubation, it is possible that if that person had heard of a boil water advisory on May 18 and had avoided drinking municipal water without boiling it first, he or she would have avoided infection. All the others who died had experienced symptoms before May 21, making it most unlikely that a boil water advisory on May 18 would have prevented them from becoming infected.

The story of the lab privatizations as a cause of the Walkerton disaster is false, a manufactured leftist smear that in fact misses the real story provided by the hundreds of pages of evidence that the water contamination occurred as a result of decades of government failure, political bungling, and bureaucratic mismanagement. One summary of the Walkerton affair, by the Energy Probe Research Foundation, concluded that the 2,000 illnesses and six (other sources say seven) deaths should be ascribed to massive institutional government failure over decades prior to May 2000.[22] If privatization of water services had been orchestrated decades earlier, with proper pricing, private corporate responsibility, and regulation, Walkerton might have been avoided.

* * *

The story behind the complex and controversial evolution of Ontario's electricity regime is told by Will Stewart in another chapter of this book. But one aspect of that history deserves more than a brief mention as part of the Harris privatization story. In fact, the Bruce Power Limited Partnership may be one of the least recognized privatization success stories in Canada—if not the world.

In 2001, the Harris government orchestrated a public–private partnership deal between Ontario Power Generation, a publicly owned provincial entity, and Bruce Power Limited Partnership, a private corporation. Under the terms of the deal, Bruce Power leased eight nuclear reactors on the shores of Lake Huron and contracted to operate the facilities as private, profit-making projects.

Such public–private partnerships, known as P3s, are not full-blown privatizations. But Bruce Power is a world-class example of how the P3 model successfully transferred operating control to a private enterprise that continues to deliver much of Ontario's electricity needs today at low and steady prices. Bruce Power is the largest P3 project in Canada, and the 6,430MW power stations remain the second-largest nuclear power facility in the world (after an 8,212 MW Japanese facility). Under private operation, the nuclear capacity and production have expanded, backed by tens of billions in new private investment over the years, with Bruce providing 50 per cent of the nuclear power that currently supplies Ontario with 60 per cent of its electricity needs.[23]

Bruce has often been attacked by the left, but mostly because it is nuclear rather than because it is a privatized facility. Perhaps the privatization label is less offensive since 4 per cent of the shares are owned by the Power Workers Union and 1.2 per cent by the Society of United Professionals. One of Bruce Power's major public service messages and key selling points is that it is fossil-fuel free, and so this P3 project (made possible via the Harris era transaction) has the added (and somewhat ironic) benefit of being a major contributor to Canada's prospects for a lower-carbon future.

* * *

While the Harris government's sale of Bruce Power has attracted little public attention other than occasional quiet acknowledgment that it has been a boon to electricity users, the privatization of Highway 407ETR continues to rattle Ontario politics more than two decades after the 1999 highway deal was signed. During the 2022 provincial election, Premier Doug Ford failed to support the toll road, opting instead to use it as a vote-winning policy reversal. Tolls on highways are "unfair and expensive," he said. Later he added that had he been premier in 1999, "I would not have sold it."

That's a big Progressive Conservative reversal of the neoliberal Harris era. The Ontario government's 1999 budget set the stage for Harris' sale of the 407ETR, which was ultimately branded as the "world's first" all-electric toll road, the world's longest privately owned toll road, and the world's most technologically advanced highway. In a review of projected government revenue sources for the 1999–2000 fiscal year, the budget referred to the potential for "an estimated $1,600 million from the net proceeds from the sale of Highway 407."[24]

Critics have portrayed the 1999 sale of the 407 as an economic travesty almost since the day the deal was signed. In 2000, *Globe and Mail* columnist John Ibbitson called it a desperate "cash grab," in which the government picked the winning private consortium to own and operate the highway based on a $3.1 billion price that Ibbitson said was deemed acceptable solely because it would generate the greatest short-term deficit-reduction impact for the government. In doing so, said Ibbitson, the government rejected a competing bid at a lower immediate price that would have generated more long-term benefits over the long term.[25]

Similar views were advanced by Sandford Borins, co-author of *If You Build It . . . Business, Government and Ontario's Electronic Toll Highway*, a 2004 book on the 407 that also criticized the government for essentially selling off a promising asset and highway concept at a low price. Among the book's concluding statements is the claim that it would have been better to leave the 407 in the hands of the government, as planned by Bob Rae's New Democrats, thereby giving the government greater control as well as profits. After a detailed if somewhat speculative review of the complicated history of the 407ETR sale contract process, Borins concluded that the Harris government "acted ideologically to privatize the road for a century,"[26] a decision that ended up transferring billions to the private shareholders of the 407 at the expense of motorists and taxpayers. It's an argument with a sprinkling of merit, but the scale of the merit is open to debate.

We will pass over the pre-1999 history of the 407 toll road as developed by previous Liberal and NDP governments. Facing massive deficits and growing demand for highways, the previous Liberal and NDP governments had opted for the use of tolls to directly fund the costs of construction of the 407. The highway was only partially built when the Harris government came to power, and the need to fund its future construction prompted the decision to remove the 407 debt from government books and turn future financing costs over to the private sector. As Borins puts it, the Harris government opted for a deal that achieved its immediate political objective of "producing revenue to balance the budget and fund health care," as promised in the *CSR*.

To generate that revenue, the government set up a bidding process in which private sector consortia competed for the right to operate and control the 407 toll road for an extended period of time. Initially, it was thought this might be for thirty-five years. The tolls would fund everything, from the construction to the operation of the sophisticated tolling system, including future expansion and the payment of dividends. No government debt was to be involved.

In the end, three major consortia participated in the final competition to "buy" the 407, each backed by a phalanx of bankers, consultants, and investors, including big names such as Goldman Sachs, TD Bank, CIBC, and JP Morgan. The government's side also included a line-up of top bankers and advisors, including RBC and Merrill Lynch. The winning offer of $3.1 billion came from 407 International, whose major shareholders were Cintra, a Spanish toll-highway operator, the Quebec government's Caisse de dépôt, and SNC-Lavalin, the international engineering firm from Montreal. The "sale" gave 407 International a ninety-nine-year lease on the highway and the right to charge tolls to fund the operation for the benefit of motorists and shareholders.

The length of the lease became the leading focus of controversy. A thirty-five-year lease would have been more conventional. Under full privatization theory, the best option and the one that would generate the highest sale price would have been a complete sale. The ninety-nine-year lease alternative was determined to be optimal because it would be deemed a sale for accounting purposes and would likely generate the most immediate revenue value for the government. The final $3.1 billion price covered the province's $1.5 billion in previous costs and provided a $1.6 billion net gain the government could claim as a great benefit.

In his 2001 Ontario budget, after the sale, Finance Minister Jim Flaherty hailed the transfer to private hands as a model and noted that the cash deal brought in almost twice the original estimate.

> The highway was sold for $3.1 billion to a private-sector consortium. This is an example of a privatization opportunity that SuperBuild intends to pursue in the future with other highway projects. The Ministry of Transportation and the Ontario SuperBuild Corporation will lead an inter-ministry task force to review financing options associated with the expansion of our province's 400-series highways.[27]

Neither the Harris government nor its successors fulfilled that optimistic scenario. Instead, it quickly became obvious, at least to some, that the $3.1 billion price appeared to seriously undervalue the 407 as a long-term investment. Less than three years after the 1999 deal was signed, SNC-Lavalin sold part of its share of 407 International at a price that valued the whole company at $6.3 billion, double the 1999 price. As time passed, the value of the 407 kept escalating as different investors bought and sold shares in the company. In 2019, financially troubled SNC-Lavalin sold its remaining 10 per cent stake in the 407 International for $3.25 billion to the Canada Pension Plan Investment Board (CPPIB). At that price, the 407 had a 2019 market value of more than $30 billion.

Had the government been scammed, or did the government scam taxpayers by giving billions to private operators? Neither of the above! The causes of the twenty-year price gap between 1999 and 2019 are actually the unknown risks that were assumed back in 1999. As even Borins writes in his history of the project, when the Harris government sold the highway in 1999, it "almost certainly received the highest price from the private sector it could have obtained."

Three main obstacles stood in the way of securing a higher price for the highway in 1999. One was the lack of operating data and hard numbers on the highway's revenue potential. If the government had waited a few years for traffic patterns to develop, the sale price would likely have been higher. A second risk was the highly sophisticated, but still untested, toll system. The third obstacle to a higher price was the state of the financial markets at the time, including the particularly high interest rates. For these reasons—traffic, technology, and financial market uncertainty—the $3.1 billion price paid for the 407 was the right price at the time, as we will explore in more detail later.

One of the individuals closely involved with the original 407 project was John Beck, a veteran advocate of privatization who headed a consortium that pulled out of the bidding process early on.

> "We were one of the bidders," Beck said in an interview for this chapter, "so I can tell you exactly what happened. It was a stretch to get to $3 billion because everything depends on traffic forecasts and every forecast said people will not pay to use that road if they can use the 401. Trucks for sure would not pay. In fact, for a long time after the road was built truckers boycotted it until they couldn't live with the 401 parking lot."

All forecasts, including the government's, concluded that the 407ETR would have a hard time attracting drivers who would likely resist paying $10 or $20 in order to travel across the top of the Greater Toronto Area in order to avoid the traffic-snarled alternative. As Beck sees it, the reality of 1999 was that the bidding consortia were assuming a risk. They were, he said, "gambling that traffic would show up." As we now know, in the end, motorists and truckers did "show up," a development that turned the 407 gamble into what Beck describes as "in hindsight, something that looks like the biggest giveaway of all time." But it was a "giveaway" that nobody could have confidently predicted, and certainly nobody with billions to invest foresaw as inevitable.

Another risk factor hovering over the 407 transaction during the 1999 bidding process was the state of the financial markets. Scott Carson was another of the 1999 insiders who was part of the 407 transaction. Now an emeritus professor at the Smith School of Business at Queen's University, Carson became president of the Harris government's privatization secretariat in 1998. He witnessed the entire process, and today, he agrees that the 407 became a major cash cow for the corporation's shareholders, but not because the $3.1 billion price was a political giveaway. In addition to the uncertainty over traffic numbers, Carson cites two other major risks.

First, technology: the toll road system now taken for granted by Ontario drivers did not exist in the 1990s. It is a toll road without a toll booth, a revolutionary concept. Using transponders and other computerized technology, drivers entered and exited the expressway without the need to pause or wait. In 1999, however, there was no certainty that the system would function as planned, creating a risk that caused outside investors to exercise caution before laying out hundreds of millions of dollars for a piece of the company.

Second, financial risk: a larger unknown and, in Carson's view, perhaps the most influential factor in the rising value of the 407 as an investment over time was the state of the financial markets and interest rates in 1999. When the 407 price was set during the bidding process, the Bank of Canada policy rate stood at 5 per cent. The bank rate is used to establish corporate and government interest rates, including the prime lending rate set by banks, as well as mortgage and other lending rates. When the 407 deal closed, the prime lending rate was 6.5 per cent. Within a few years, Canadian interest rates dropped dramatically. The Bank of Canada rate hit 2 per cent in 2000 and stood at 0.5 per cent in 2010. When interest rates go down, the value of cash-producing assets automatically goes up, which is part of what contributed to the increased valuations of the 407.[28]

Some rough calculations reveal how underlying financial market conditions pushed the 407 from its $3.1 billion 1999 sale price to

$9 billion in 2010 and $30 billion in 2019. One relatively simple valuation formula that takes account of the 407's earnings increase over time is to attach a long-term value to a corporation's earnings. If the 407's earnings before interest costs and taxes (EBIT) during the early years were estimated at $300 million, the estimated present value of those earnings could be calculated using interest rates at the time. With a bank prime rate of 6.5 per cent, investors might reasonably apply a risk premium of perhaps 1.5 per cent to create a discount rate of about 8 per cent. That rate would then be used to determine how much an investor would pay for shares in the 407. At 8 per cent, in 1999, the estimated annual EBIT of $300 million would be valued at approximately $3.3 billion, which in fact comes quite close to the 1999 price the government actually received.

Moving forward to 2010–2012, the 407ETR's earnings had almost doubled to about $550 million. All else being equal, nearly doubled earnings would imply a doubling of the value of the company. But interest rates were not equal. The bank rate had fallen from 5 per cent in 1999 to 1 per cent in 2012, leading to a sharp reduction in the discount rate to something closer to 3.5 per cent. At that rate, $550 million in EBIT is worth $10 billion as an investment, not far off the $9 billion value put on the 407 when Cintra Infraestructuras, S.A, the Spanish company that held 53 per cent of the 407, sold 10 per cent of its holdings to the Canada Pension Plan Investment Board (CPPIB) for $900 million (thereby implying a roughly $9 billion total valuation).

The price jump that really irks those ideologically opposed to privatization is the 2019 CPPIP purchase of another 10 per cent of the 407 for $3.25 billion, implying a total corporate value exceeding $30 billion. Linda McQuaig, in her Harris-bashing book *The Sport and Prey of Capitalists,* looked at the $30 billion value of the 407 and came up with a theme that still plays well in anti-privatization critiques: "The sheer amount of money the Harris government gave up is astonishing. Recent estimates put the value of the 407 today at a staggering $30 billion. . . . These mega-billion-dollar price tags reflect how much revenue is expected to be collected—in other words, how much Ontarians are going to pay for the privilege of driving on this road over the coming decades."[29]

How wrong is that? Let us count the ways.

First, corporate EBIT earnings had jumped to $1.2 billion in 2019 for a good reason. The rising value of the 407 in 2019 was the product of the expressway's roaring motoring success. The private sector owners of the 407ETR highway opened new lanes from 2016 to 2018 and invested in significant extensions at both ends, bringing the total capacity to 1,271 lane-kilometers, almost double the 643 lane-kilometers in 1999. With more capacity came more motorists: Average daily trips approached 400,000 in pre-COVID 2019, with total daily trips hitting an average of 2.7 million kilometers, both indicators that are more than double the traffic volumes in 1999. To suggest that the money paid by motorists is somehow immorally extracted from Ontario citizens misrepresents the role of a toll highway. Private drivers voluntarily pay the tolls. Had the 407 remained publicly owned, the highway would have had to use public taxpayer funds to reach the operating capacity of 2019. The 407, in other words, has saved taxpayers billions in construction, maintenance, and operating costs and put the costs where they belong—with motorists choosing to use the highway.

The second misunderstanding regarding the 407's $30 billion nominal value in 2019 involves another failure to grasp the importance of changes in financial markets. As in the case of earlier changes in 407 ownership, shifts in interest rates were clearly a contributor to the rising value of the 407 in the years following the sale. The 2019 purchase of 407ETR shares by the federal government's pension giant also adds another quirk. As a long-term investor, looking decades into the future to fund pension payments, the CPPIB would have a much longer investment horizon than most corporations. The pension board could borrow pre-COVID money in 2019 at 2.5 per cent. The 407's annual EBIT in

2019 was $1.25 billion. Applying a discount rate of 4 per cent to that volume of annual earnings produces a total corporate present value estimate of $31 billion.

Third, popular critics of the 407 privatization process, including Borins, portray the increase in the corporation's value as a simple matter of looking at the asset sale price while ignoring numerous underlying factors that drove up the value of the highway. But the value of the highway could still change with new developments in the future. Some of the value dynamics will likely shift dramatically in the wake of the COVID pandemic, along with rising inflation and interest rate trends that began to take hold in 2022.

In summary, the key points for evaluating the 407ETR privatization and its increasing investment value are:

- that the traffic did in fact "show up" and then expanded dramatically as the length of the highways was expanded over time from 69 kilometers to 108 kilometers and as lane capacity doubled to 1,270 kilometers;
- the electronic tolling system proved itself;
- because interest rates declined (along with inflation) and as increased usage generated increased revenues, the financial value of the profits grew—to the point where 407 International became a giant dividend machine for its shareholders.

In fact, the cash flow is now so great that the company appears to be borrowing to pay dividends, driving up the 407 International's investment value even further and giving critics and politicians another reason to criticize both the Harris government and the privatization concept. But these critics of the 407 project are mostly basking in the fake brilliance of hindsight masquerading as economic insight. The government could certainly have obtained a higher price for the highway had it somehow been able to see into the future.

A more valid alternative hypothetical scenario, however, could include imagining how future government ownership could have bungled the highway. What would have been the future of the 407ETR if the highway had remained in government hands? It is reasonable to expect endless political grandstanding over tolls and other aspects of highway transport that are favourite platforms for soundbite-hungry politicians who would rather be seen providing infrastructure at no cost to users.

It is also worth taking a moment to imagine what should have happened in the wake of the Harris government's transfer of the 407ETR to private, for-profit development. As motorists and truckers embraced the 407ETR, Ontario policymakers should have realized the immense economic and transportation policy benefits. The 407 sale could have – and, in fact, should have – become a model, a prototype, for a new economic approach to motor vehicle and highway infrastructure. Freed of government management and financing boondoggles, the privatization of major roadways promised to get the government out of major aspects of modern transportation infrastructure.

For more than two decades, the 407ETR has demonstrated that, despite the initial low-price sale to investors, major highway projects can be undertaken without loading debt burden on the government and taxpayers. Instead, the cost of highways, from debt to operations, is borne by motorists willing to pay the price and deliver profits to investors. The 407ETR should be seen for what it has become, namely a superb highway transport experience. Had the concept of privately managed toll highways been embraced and expanded instead of vilified by the left and by populist politicians, Ontarians would today be enjoying a great toll-road network and an appreciation that the road to privatization is paved with good results.

When Progressive Conservative Premier Doug Ford said, in 2022, that privatizing and tolling the 407 was a mistake, he was wrong. The mistake is Ford's failure, and everyone else's, to grasp the benefits of privatization and a toll-based funding system that relieves taxpayers of the burden of paying for other people's transport needs.

From the perspective of 2023, when mere mention of the word "privatization" creates a political storm, the *CSR* plans and the Harris government's execution deserve commendation. The LCBO was, to be sure, an abject failure driven by political expediency. But other successful privatization moves help offset that failure somewhat. By any measure, the Bruce Power private operation of the world's second-largest nuclear plant must be deemed a success, as it continues to expand and deliver low-cost clean electricity. The 407 project has also delivered what consumers want: efficient highway travel opportunity at no cost to taxpayers.

As we believe we have demonstrated, the most significant aspect of the *CSR* privatization issue is in fact the degree to which it has been subject to distortion by academics and the media. The distortions and false claims used to misrepresent the Walkerton tragedy should be seen as a political scandal in which the deaths of innocent people are used to push the false ideological message that privatization kills jobs and people. The fact that the 407ETR privatization, as late as 2022, came under attack from Premier Doug Ford suggests that political and election motives too often overcome the sound neoliberal principles and objective evidence that privatization can deliver major social and economic benefits. To paraphrase Mike Harris, if the *CSR* had taken privatization further and faster, Ontario might today enjoy more and better highways, an open alcohol market, and, most important and promising of all, a more diverse and more privatized health-care system.

* * *

The final objective of this chapter is to examine today's fiscal and economic conditions and assess the need for and the possibility of a new revolution that will bring common sense not just to Ontario again but to all of Canada and the rest of the world. Could it happen again? There are good reasons to be skeptical. No leader is currently on the horizon who can bring Mike Harris's (or Ronald Reagan's or Margaret Thatcher's) low-key credibility to a new crusade to reform government.

By the end of the 1990s, neoliberal ideas came under attack from prominent interventionists and in dozens if not hundreds of academic works written with the intention of destroying the market principles and the ideas of neoliberal thinkers such as Milton Friedman and Friedrich Hayek. One of the leaders of the attack has been Joseph Stiglitz of Columbia University. In his 2003 book, *The Roaring Nineties*, Joseph Stiglitz[30] summarized the decade as a stage-setting for economic disaster. "These market fundamentalist ideas," said Stiglitz, were advocated by the IMF, the World Bank, and the US Treasury under a "Washington Consensus" that called for minimizing the role of the state, privatization, and reduced regulation. The neoliberal consensus, argues Stiglitz, delivered a late-1990s economic expansion period that, in time, would come to a disastrous end. Some, including the authors of this chapter, would be ready to debate this grim post-mortem on such a critical time in our history. In fact, as we look around the world today and specifically at Canada, noting the rising tide of debt, deficits, government spending, and regulation and lamenting the resulting declines in business investment, productivity, and economic growth that are the products of having abandoned neoliberalism, the question needs to be asked: Is it time for another neoliberal, common sense revolution? There are many parallels between the fiscal trends today and those of the early 1990s that fueled the rise of the Harris policy initiatives that helped transform the Ontario economy.

Instead, we have governments pushing greater reliance on public provision of goods and services, rather than reducing the size of government and taxes. Deficits are okay since they are "investments" for the future. Instead of privatization, governments are using industrial policy to pursue "moonshot" technologies or reorder the economy in their political interests. Trade policy takes a back seat to "on-shoring" or "friend-shoring." Unlike the strong public support shown in the 1990s for the *CSR* with its clear aim to pare back government, voters now appear much more willing to support greater government intervention in the economy.

Canada and the world desperately need a new revolution of common economic sense based on a renewal of core neoliberal economic values. Would the *CSR* work today? It would. But nothing is inevitable. Friedman and Hayek are dead. And without the right leader to carry the message, along with broader academic and public support for the need for a renewed appreciation of neoliberal principles, the prospects seem less than hopeful. On the other hand, the fiscal and governance meltdowns now roiling Ottawa, Ontario, and all the provinces look similar to, if not worse than, the crisis Ontario faced in the mid-1990s. Perhaps the stage has been set? And all it will take is the right leadership? One can but hope.

Notes

1   https://www.youtube.com/watch?v=HQwxfWidE-U
2   David R. Cameron and Graham White, *Cycling to Saigon: The Conservative Transition in Ontario* (UBC Press, 2000), p. 105.
3   *The Common Sense Revolution*, Ontario PC Platform 1995, p. 2.
4   Ibid, p. 1
5   William Watson and Clemens, Jason (eds.), *The Budget that Changed Canada: Essays on The 25th Anniversary of the 1995 Budget*, Fraser Institute, 2020.
6   John Ibbitson, *Promised Land: Inside the Mike Harris Revolution*, (1997, Prentice Hall), p. 28.
7   Friedrich Hayek, *The Road to Serfdom*, 1944
8   1996 Ontario Budget, "Economic Policies for Jobs and Growth," pp. 81–96.
9   V. Tanzi and L. Schuknecht, "The Growth of Government and the Reform of the state in Industrial countries," (IMF Working Paper, December 1995).
10 Stephen S. Poloz, "The Causes of Unemployment in Canada" (Bank of Canada Working Paper 94–11, November 1994).
11 https://www.youtube.com/watch?v=HQwxfWidE-U
12 1991 Ontario Budget, April 29, 1991, p. 3.

13   *The Common Sense Revolution*, Fifth Printing, Post-Martin Budget, 1995.

14   We encourage interested readers to also look at Hugh Segal's chapter on Harris and federal-provincial relations later in this book for a discussion on the CPP reforms.

15   J. Mintz, "For Christmas, Ontarians Deserve Competitive Liquor Prices," *National Post*, December 16, 2022.

16   Malcolm S. Bird, "The Rise of the Liquor Control Board of Ontario and the Demise of the Alberta Liquor Control Board: Why Such Divergent Outcomes?" The School of Public Policy and Administration, Carleton University, Ottawa, Ontario Canada. 2008.

17   We would encourage interested readers to also look at Gordon Miller's Environment section on Walkerton, later in this book, for another, quite personal, perspective on this difficult chapter of the Harris legacy.

18   Laureen Snider, "Captured by Neo-Liberalism: Regulation and Risk in Walkerton, Ontario," Risk Management: An International Journal, 2003, p. 34.

19   Linda McQuaig, "The Lac Megantic tragedy . . . government oversight is still far too weak due to government deregulation," *The Toronto Star*, November 22, 2018.

20   Diane Saxe, quoted in "20 Years after Walkerton: Critics Say Ontario is Laying the Foundations of a New Water Crisis," CBC, May 19, 2020.

21   *Report of the Walkerton Inquiry, Part One*, chapter 10, "The Failure to Enact a Notification Regulation," p. 401.

22   "Energy Probe Research Foundation," written submission to the Walkerton Inquiry, August 1, 2001.

23   The Ontario Energy Report, Bruce Power, 2020. It is worth noting that Bruce Power also claims to "produce power at 30 per cent less cost than the average to produce residential power in Ontario."

24   Ontario Budget, 1999, p. 36.

25   John Ibbitson, "Cash Grab Prompted Tories' Sale of Highway 407," *The Globe and Mail*, February 21, 2000.

26   Sandford Borins, *If You Build It . . . Business, Government and Ontario's Electronic Toll Highway*, 2004.

27   Ontario Budget, 2001, "New Approaches to Infrastructure Financing," p. 168.

28   Conversation with Scott Carson, 2022.

29   Linda McQuaig, *The Sport and Prey of Capitalists*, 2019.

30   Joseph Stiglitz, *The Roaring Nineties: A New History of the World's Most Prosperous Decade"* (2003, p. 250).

CHAPTER 4

Health Care

Will Falk

HEALTH CARE WAS NOT A big part of the *CSR*. Most of the mentions were promises to not do things. They were designed to protect the Harris Conservatives from the electorate's fears of cuts to health care and from accusations of a hidden privatization agenda. Health care was specifically addressed only sparingly.

In the Introduction: "This plan guarantees full funding for health care. . ."

On Page 3 in a section entitled CUT NON-PRIORITY GOVERNMENT SPENDING: "Total spending will be reduced by 20% in three years, without touching a penny of Health Care Funding."

And on Page 7 in a section entitled Protecting priority services—health care: "We will not cut health care spending. It's far too important. And frankly, as we all get older, we are going to need it more and more. Under this plan, health care spending will be guaranteed."[1]

I was not a part of the *CSR*. I knew some of the "tiny Tories" involved in the Harris Campaigns from "across the aisle" when my Liberal party beat them (handily) in the University of Toronto model parliament in 1985. Several became lifelong friends, but they have never managed to convince me of their belief system. I remain a quiet Liberal and a progressive, albeit with math skills. My last active involvement in politics was with Prime Minister Paul Martin when I was an advisor for the 2004 first minister's meeting on health care.

My opinions on Harris's healthcare record are based upon thirty years as a management consultant and policy advisor across over 400 projects. A decade ago, as a fellow at the progressive Mowat Centre, I said positive things about Premier Harris and the Health Services Restructuring Commission (HSRC). The editor reminded me of this recently and asked me to contribute the healthcare chapter to this planned retrospective. I have (in speeches) commented on the work of the HSRC under Mike Harris, along with two other successful examples of healthcare reform in Ontario—the early Dalton McGuinty wait-times initiatives and the Deb Matthews ECFA/Bill 102/MD payment reforms. I was involved in these Liberal-era reforms as a management consultant or as an order-in-council appointed advisor. There are common elements of these three successful reforms: respect for data and expertise, thoughtful, well-organized processes, and tough-minded decision-making.

In preparing this chapter, I have had access to the files of the HSRC, press clippings from the time, the few published books on the Harris revolution, interviews with a variety of participants, and the critical commentary of several think tanks. Readers will soon learn that my work has increased my high opinion of the Harris healthcare record and particularly their firm support for the HSRC under Duncan Sinclair.

The HSRC was the centrepiece of the Harris healthcare reforms. The commission had authority to make binding decisions when it came to hospitals and to make recommendations and policy advice on other related matters. Its restructuring of Ontario's hospital system was highly successful, and it provides a model for best practice in effective central planning. Other elements of restructuring were less successful (e.g., primary care, home care, long-term care and mental health) and were recognized as such at the time (and by the commission itself at sunset). Many of these recommendations were excellent, though non-binding. In particular, the work that the HSRC did on primary care groups (REF) and aging-in-place still make for fascinating and relevant reading today.

I will also more briefly review several key policy topics outside of the HSRC purview. These include some novel work in drug benefits, capable (if unexceptional) continuations of negotiations with the Ontario Medical Association (OMA), meaningful long-term care (LTC) capacity expansion, and a few others.

The Harris health program represents exceptionally well-done central planning. This is striking and ironic because a true "revolutionary" of the "common sense" school should not believe in central planning at all.

The Harris Tories were avowed Thatcherites and Reaganites. They read and adopted[2] as guidebooks *The Road to Serfdom* and *The Constitution of Liberty* by Frederick Hayek, a Nobel Prize–winning economist who compellingly warned the British and American publics of the dangers of central planning being combined with the full power of the state (and that socialism leads to totalitarianism). The *CSR* team had read its Hayek (although I suspect most only in the *Reader's Digest* version). They presumably believed that large-scale central planning diminishes individual liberty. In a longish aside, I will try to explain this apparent paradox: how Mike Harris ended up being among the best health care central planners in Canada's history. I will also discuss and address some of the criticisms of Harris in health care.

Obviously, it is fun to tease friends who pride themselves on being free market advocates for their comprehensive use of central planning in health care. But there are important lessons here about the use of, and the limits of, planning as an allocative method. And, whether you are a progressive or a neoconservative, these deeper questions are foundational ones about what it means to have a national public health system. Harris' health care successes help explain the problems we are currently facing, a generation later, and why we are struggling to address policy areas such as aging, drug coverage, denticare, virtual care, and mental health. While good central planning still worked in the Harris era, different allocation methods and economic models may be needed in the years ahead.

* * *

The Health Services Restructuring Commission ("HSRC," "the Commission") was an independent body established by the Government in March 1996. Its role was to expedite hospital restructuring in the province, and to advise the Minister of Health on revamping other aspects of Ontario's health services system.[3]   — *HSRC Legacy Report, 1996–2000*

The Commission was very well thought-out, and structured with several key characteristics:

It had volunteer commissioners. It was chaired by Duncan Sinclair, former dean of Queen's Medical School. It had a four-year mandate with an automatic sunset. And it had lead commissioners for major urban centres who took ownership of the local report and directions when issued.

There was also a small, skilled professional staff team led by Mark Rochon (1996–1998) and Peggy Leatt (1998–2000) as CEO and David Naylor (of IC/ES) as special advisor. They had deep modeling and analytical support, including architectural and clinical analytics. They used agreed-upon methodologies for assessing current and needed bed capacities. There was 100 per cent public transparency in analytics and regular reports using clearly communicated methodologies.

Everything was published openly, and the local situation was discussed repeatedly with local newspapers.

Clear and declarative "directions" were issued under authority delegated by the minister. These directions were previewed thirty days earlier by the publication of notices of intent to issue directions. These were complete drafts with supporting analytics and, again, 100 per cent open for public discussion and comment. Also, facilitators were appointed after directions were issued to sort through the governance issues and help manage the closure of facilities and transfers of programs.

Over a period of four years, the HSRC issued directions to twenty-two communities.[4] They amalgamated several hospitals to form larger healthcare organizations and ordered the takeover of four hospitals. They directed the closure of thirty-one public hospitals, six private hospitals, and six provincial psychiatric hospitals sites. They also created a variety of provincial and regional networks and rural/northern networks.[5]

The volunteer commission ended on time, produced the well-written and readable 208-page close-out report (*Looking Back, Looking Forward*). It also published "Seven Points for Action" in March 2000, which makes remarkable (and a bit depressing) reading today as it covers topics such as primary care and long-term care that are still very much on the agenda. Several years later, it produced a book-length review published by a well-known think-tank.[6]

The commission's reports and directions make fascinating reading. For policy people of the 2020s, the HSRC language is startlingly clear. There are no flowery political promises. The press clippings and court decisions of the time are full of tough arguments on both sides of many issues. The public was involved and concerned in the debates that were happening. The commission and staff met with the editorial boards of local daily newspapers to answer any community questions.

Here are excerpts from two editorials from major daily newspapers about one year into the commission's work that illustrate how the process unfolded and how successful this transparent approach was:

The big hurt has been delivered, and now comes the time to deal with the pain. Nonetheless, what the province's restructuring commission brought forward yesterday in dealing with the cumbersome (and expensive) hospital bureaucracy in Ottawa-Carleton was not as painful as many doomsayers anticipated.

In fact, their plan verges on the brilliant. . .

It is obvious, though, that the Commission thought long and hard on what to do with Ottawa Carleton.

And to our way too thinking, it is to be congratulated for both its foresight and its compassion.

Ottawa Sun, Feb 25, 1997

[Note: The Ottawa directions closed four hospitals and ordered several amalgamations.]

Let's try to set the record straight on what Ontario's Health Services Restructuring Commission is up to. Earlier this week it ordered the closings and amalgamations that will reduce the number of hospitals in Metro Toronto to 24 from 39. . . . The first half of the mandate—downsizing the hospital sector, reducing the number of acute care beds, closing some institutions—is in good hands. The decisions the Commission has had to make are never easy ones, but it appears this far to have mostly made the right choices, in Toronto and elsewhere.

The Globe and Mail, July 25, 1997

This sense of fairness and tough choices runs through the over fifty newspaper articles I have read. There is anger and hurt and fear as well. After all, they closed forty hospitals. Many were desperately worried about job loss. But people were reassured by direct and honest communication and the commission's commitments to transparency and straightforwardness.

Direct declarative statements with no bullshit, rigorous transparent analytics and well-planned legal foundations were all keys to the success of the HSRC. I will also amplify my point about volunteer governance. Former Queens medical school dean Duncan Sinclair took no pay for his four years of work. His knowledgeable and avuncular style bred trust and was also touched by just a bit of "coolness" (his son is the bass player for The Tragically Hip). The other commissioners were a "who's who" of talented volunteers. This often proves a powerful combination in public policy.

It is important to point out here that Premier Harris and his government were able to attract this extraordinary group and had the courage to back them during some incredibly difficult decisions. This from "a golf pro from North Bay" who was often criticized for not being sophisticated enough.

It is also important to make clear that Harris had tailwinds helping. Underlying the HSRC's tough decisions was a very strong elite consensus that had existed before the Harris government took power and that provided Harris with some non-partisan backing. The basic analytical methodology used had been being developed under the Rae government and trialed by District Health Councils (DHCs). It was a workable approach, if an incredibly blunt instrument. Every DHC in the province had been asked to provide a report on acute care bed utilization and to benchmark themselves against current, and future, best-practice standards. These reports were in hand and available as the HSRC was created by the new government. In fact, Bob Rae and his team almost certainly deserve significant credit for giving the commission a running start. Whether they would want it or not I leave to the reader.

The methods and recommendations made by the HSRC ended up being accepted in a non-partisan way in practice. The McGuinty Liberals never replaced the methodologies used by the HSRC under Harris when they came into power. All three political parties knew that the analytical team was rock-solid. It is worth mentioning at this point that while similar methodologies continue to be used today, recent governments no longer publish their findings so transparently. This lack of transparency undermines effective policy development and implementation.

In its reports, the HSRC took feedback and eventually standardized the provincial methodology (available in detail in the commission references cited). Parts of this methodology are still used in many parts of the country and at research institutions in part because of the excellent personnel recruited to support the project (Naylor and team, who did great work but also populated many future organizations and consulting firms).

In each planning region, statistics for current and estimations for targeted length of stays, across a projected case mix, were used to establish a needed level of in-patient beds for the community. Often the community already had many closed beds, and because length of stay (LOS) had been declining for at least two decades, when one targeted future usage at better practice levels (75 percentile or current, whichever was lower), the needed number of beds dropped dramatically. This sounds dry and technical, but it is critical to appreciate because it gave confidence to the planning team and Commission to take bold steps.

Let me step back and give an informal history of acute care hospitals to set some context on why all this was so needed.

* * *

Hospitals were originally created as a place to isolate and comfort people, most of whom died. Before 1900, people generally only allowed themselves to be admitted if they had no other choice. Charitable orders dominated eighteenth- and nineteenth-century hospitals, as they were dedicated to alleviating suffering. This began to change with medical advances in Victorian England and in Paris that built on earlier knowledge from ancient Greek and Arabic (Islamist) physicians. Advances in infection control, hygiene and the development of early vaccines started showing that better outcomes were possible.

Surgery, anesthetics, infection control, blood transfusions, and antibiotics changed the game completely for hospitals. The two World Wars accelerated these advances, and, after WWII, hospitals had changed and become a place to go for actual treatment . . . and sometimes even for a cure! Technology adoption in health care was rampant, with new ideas, drugs, devices, and treatments increasing the range of services offered in these increasingly magical places. In Figure 4.1, you can see the impact of that trend on hospital utilization across the developed world.

Treatments and diagnostics moved from the in-patient and hospital setting and could now be offered in ambulatory settings, in physician's offices, in homes, and even virtually. Clinical teachers, under the new models developed by Flexner and Osler were committed to teaching and spreading this knowledge through formal clinical internships and residencies. Academic surgeons and physicians literally trained their next generation of competitors, who moved to community hospitals and to ambulatory centres. By the early 1990s, this trend was visible worldwide.[7]

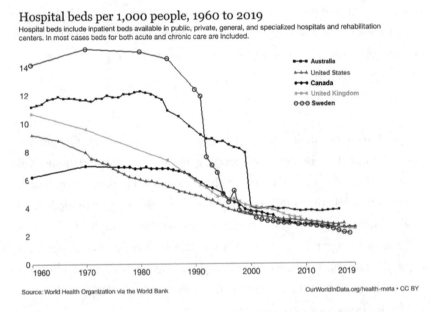

Hospital beds per 1,000 people, 1960 to 2019
Hospital beds include inpatient beds available in public, private, general, and specialized hospitals and rehabilitation centers. In most cases beds for both acute and chronic care are included.

Source: World Health Organization via the World Bank   OurWorldInData.org/health-meta · CC BY

Figure 4.1   Hospital Beds Per 1,000 People, 1960 to 2019

In Canada, we introduced public payment for hospitals in the late 1950s. Our hospital beds-per-thousand-citizens stabilized at about seven. A decline began in the 1980s, with technology diffusion, and accelerated into the 1990s. By the end of the 1990s, we had reduced the number of bed-days available in hospitals on a population basis by as much as half. And this result is mirrored, or even exceeded, in most of our closely comparable countries (e.g., the United Kingdom, Australia, Sweden, the United States). In the Bill Davis and John Robarts years, conservative politicians opened hospital, which brought new technologies to remote communities. All politicians are happy being seen to be building new things for their communities. But, by the 1990s, in-patient beds were no longer what was needed, and beds were wickedly expensive.

The numbers in Canada (above) were stark and are singled out in Figure 4.2.[8] By 1996, Ontario had already closed over 9,000 hospital beds as we benefited from the global trends described above. But *not one single hospital had been closed*. To put this in perspective, 9,000 beds is about thirty mid-size (think Windsor or Waterloo) hospitals. Observers could

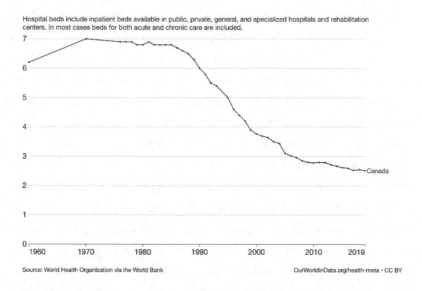

Figure 4.2 Hospital Beds Per 1,000 People, 1960 to 2019 – Canada

see by looking at the changes in practice patterns that this trend was only going to continue.

What's more, the need and function of "a bed" was changing. Patients in hospital beds were there for a shorter period of time, and they were sicker while there. An increasing number of surgeries were being moved to "same-day facilities" (e.g., cataracts) and even into doctors' offices (e.g., dental surgery). The traditional hospital facilities were often out-of-date and unsuitable and very expensive or even impossible (e.g., asbestos) to remediate. Hospitals needed to close to provide better care for patients.

Ontario policymakers realized they had a big problem. In fact, the recognition had come a few years earlier, in 1988, when Minister Elinor Caplan (in the David Peterson government) called an abrupt halt to most hospital building in the province. There was a sudden recognition that every time you build a bed in a public system *you have to pay for its operation*. While this change in the required facilities footprint was most clear in surgery, the impact of technology changes was even broader. Eventually, chemotherapy, much diagnostic imaging, endoscopy, labs, functional testing, and dialysis would all leave the in-patient hospital setting. Our system wasn't necessarily doing less stuff; it was just doing it in a different way. Governments in the pre HSRC era had underfunded hospitals when compared to inflation causing reductions in staff and traditional bed capacity often in an un-coordinated fashion. And, worse still, we had closed pieces and parts of many hospitals, because we couldn't find the courage to choose which ones to close.

The Health Services Restructuring Commission was born from a non-partisan consensus that something had to be done to reduce the number of buildings, continue to bring the number of "beds" down, and move health care to ambulatory sites, alternate levels of care, and the patient's home. This was (and is) seen as self-evidently a better model on many attributes. Whether this remains as true today, twenty-seven years later and post-COVID, it has become an arguable proposition, but in 1995, with a new government taking power, there was very broad agreement on this reality among healthcare central planners, and all three major political parties recognized that something major had to be done. The case for change was clear.

So, it's 1995 and you are a neoliberal believer in the Thatcher and Reagan revolution. You support the *CSR*, and you want to fix the Ontario healthcare system. What do you do?

Other provinces also recognized the "too-many-beds, too-many-hospitals problem." The whole country was over-bedded, and most provinces reduced beds and hospitals during the late 1980s and 1990s. Most provinces opted for some form of an exercise in governance and a technocratic solution that insulated politicians by setting up a provincial health authority or a set of regional authorities. But in discussions with Harris advisors from this period, I learned that the Harris caucus didn't much like the existing district health councils. And there was respect for independent hospital governance and the hospital boards. As one insider put it: "There was no market-based solution in the air at the time as an alternative in Ontario."

Meanwhile, in the United States, Democrat Hillary Clinton was proposing a purchaser/provider split using pseudo-market mechanisms called "health insurance purchasing cooperatives." But a market solution in Ontario would have involved multiple bankruptcies over multiple years. It was unworkable in a political reality that had already seen 9,000 beds closed but without a single hospital closure. The good thing about central planning combined with the state power is it is fast if one wants to implement massive change or modernization of an industrial process.

The solution was unexpected. Mike Harris became a great healthcare central planner. Or at least his government did.

I need to digress for a bit now about the astonishing irony of all this. This will take us into the intellectual basis of neoconservatism and the thinking of Frederick Hayek. There is a famous anecdote that during a British Conservative party policy meeting, Margaret Thatcher removed her copy of Hayek's *Constitution of Liberty* from her handbag, slammed it down on the table and declared, "This is what we believe."[9] There are numerous stories about her sitting down with Hayek and listening to him carefully. And she was not the only avid reader. In the United States, *The Road to Serfdom* was abridged for *Reader's Digest*, and 2.4 million copies were produced.

If you were a good Thatcherite/Reaganite, you would've read your Hayek and know what he wrote about central planning in *The Road to Serfdom*:

> In order to achieve their ends, the planners must create power—power over men wielded by other men—of a magnitude never before known. . . . Many socialists have the tragic illusion that by depriving private individuals of the power they possess in an individualist system and transferring this power to society, they thereby extinguish the power. What they overlook is that by concentrating the power so that it can be used in the service of a single plan, it is not merely transformed, but infinitely heightened. By uniting in the hands of some single body power formerly exercised independently by many, an amount of power is created infinitely greater than any that existed before, so much more far-reaching as almost to be different in kind.[10]

Hayek's central argument is that central planning, as an allocation methodology, cannot work without the coercive power of the state backing it up and that, in a democracy, this results in an increasingly ineffective government that then causes the rise of a "strong man" who can get things done quickly. The strongman creates an armed thuggery and an internal or external enemy before ultimately seizing power. He contended that this is what happened in both Russia (Stalin) and Germany (Hitler).

I have to admit that as a twenty-first-century Liberal and after a career in which I have done a lot of "central planning," I found Hayek's *cris de coeur* compelling. He had lived it as an Austrian Jew who fled to Britain. He identified many issues and behaviours that I have observed in large central planning initiatives. I was surprised to see George Orwell among Hayek's positive contemporaneous reviewers (1944). One can see shades of *Animal Farm* in The *Road to Serfdom*.[11]

Hayek's thesis in *The Constitution of Liberty* (which Thatcher thumped) is that freedom is the cornerstone of progress and innovation. It was written after WWII and is less alarmed about the possible rise of the totalitarian strong man. It is also more thoughtful about why planning is self-limiting and reduces innovation. He argues that no central planner could ever be so omniscient as to see all possible paths. "[T]he case for individual freedom rests chiefly upon the recognition of the inevitable ignorance of all of us concerning a great many of the factors on which the achievement of our ends and welfare depends."

So, how can it be that the Harris revolutionaries who clearly believed these things could establish one of the best healthcare central planning processes in our country's history (my opinion)? At the very least, the irony is striking. There is a paradox here that is worth exploring and understanding better.

As neoconservative revolutionaries, the *CSR*'ers "should" have chosen an allocative method that would allow for freedom of choice for citizens to pick healthcare providers and for healthcare providers to adapt and change to meet the changing needs of the population. Such an approach was used by Thatcher in the United Kingdom and proposed by Democrat Bill Clinton in the United States.

Instead, in 1995, the Harris government imposed a highly coercive, expert regime. The HRSC central planners closed over forty beloved institutions. More than 20,000 workers had their jobs disrupted.[12] Healthcare operational funding was reduced overall, and big chunks of hospital budgets were reallocated into other sectors. There were protests. There were court cases (only one having any success). There was huge media coverage and outrage.

No one would argue that restructuring was easy. But most of the informed people that I have spoken with in research for this chapter agree that it was absolutely needed. And it was well done. These opinions cross party lines, and, even on the left, the most serious criticisms have been about labour dislocation and the handling of union issues.[13]

I have reviewed the commission's reports, court decisions, directions, and other papers (made available to me by Mark Rochon) and press clippings from the time, as well as *Riding the Third Rail: The Story of Ontario's Health Services Restructuring Commission, 1996–2000,* by Duncan Sinclair, Mark Rochon, and Peggy Leatt. I have read the available political books from the time. I have supplemented my own knowledge of the Ontario healthcare system with discussions with people who were involved and affected. I have also read the available *post hoc* criticisms.

I have identified ten attributes that helped make restructuring work. Some were tightly planned; some were accidents of history and some were a combination of the two.

1. Agreement on need: The NDP had commissioned the district health council reports that formed the basic case for change. Global changes in acute care were clear. There was a strong, expert consensus. At least some members of Rae's health leadership helped set favourable conditions. The new government quickly recognized that change was required of a massive nature.

2. Independent and arm's-length: This scale of change could not have easily occurred within the usual political environment. Decisions would always be evaluated through a political lens, but when it created the HSRC as an arm's-length agency it recognized that it needed to operate independently. Premier Harris and his government largely respected this distance in the early years of the HSRC and as regards hospital restructuring.

3. Volunteer governance and a clear time-limited mandate: No commissioner received payment for work. The commission was closed by legislation on March 31, 2000. This early sunset meant that the HSRC never became a self-interested, independent bureaucracy. They were seen as committed and smart but not permanent.[14]

4. Serious legal expertise in drafting legislation/regulation and in litigation: Reading the court opinions was probably my biggest "aha" moment while preparing this chapter. I have heard Rochon make this point, but I had not really understood it until I read the court submissions and the decisions.[15] John Laskin and team were a major source of strength for the HSRC.

5. Excellent analytics and communications: The analyses are clear and clean. They were defensible and understandable even to lay people. I have already quoted the *Globe* and the *Ottawa Sun* as examples of the kind of support. Rochon has told me that they met at least twice with the editorial boards of all major daily newspapers in the province. The messages, designed by an excellent communication team under the leadership of Bruce McLellan, were straightforward, transparent, and honest. They included paid ads and TV clips.

6. Clarity of language in directions and other communications: This clarity is genuinely shocking to people accustomed to the usual political bafflegab that comes out of political and bureaucratic circles in the 2020s. As described earlier, the HSRC, usually with one or two HSRC members acting as the lead commissioner(s), would preview directions about a month before final publication by releasing an intention to issue a directive. They received public comment and then issued the final directive on its own. The minister was usually briefed *one day before release*.[16] As a representative example, the people of Sudbury must have wondered what had happened to the nice Tory party of Bill Davis

when they read the directive to the Sudbury regional hospital corporation on April 30, 1997, which said (in part):

"1. Implement a plan to consolidate all acute hospital services on the Ramsay site and to close the Paris and Regent sites no later than April 30, 1999.

2. Transfer from the Paris and Regent sites all acute, chronic and rehabilitation a hospital programs operated on the sites to the Ramsay site.

3. Implement a plan to achieve the infatuate acute services interim target of 697 patient days/1000 population by April 30, 1998, and the utilization target of 540 patient days/1000 population by April 30, 1999. . ."

Readers of this chapter familiar with healthcare systems and population health management will appreciate how incredibly draconian is the very dry statement regarding a one-year reduction of 157 patient days/1,000 population.

7. Support from the premier and minister: These reforms were incredibly tough stuff, however needed. And particularly tough to implement given the looming date for the next election. Indeed, it took a revolutionary mindset to believe in the process and to see it through. One had to make an argument that the ends justify the means.[17] Think Lenin. Think Robespierre. But also think Hamilton federalism or John A. MacDonald and the railway. What is really impressive about how the Harris team handled this is that they were ruthlessly transparent. Often, the political class tries to deliver good news and to sugar coat announcements. Harris and his health ministers during restructuring (Jim Wilson, David Johnson, and Liz Witmer) seem to have understood that this was not going to work while closing forty hospitals. They shared all the data and trusted the commission. They stayed at

arm's-length deliberately and thereby showed courage. "The Minister used to cross the street if they saw me walking near Queen's Park," quipped one commissioner.

This trust-in-your-people ethos and transparency-in-your-communication-ethic is consistent with what I saw in the two subsequent successful Liberal-era health reforms: the McGuinty first-term implementation of wait-time reforms, family health teams, and local health integration networks, and Deb Matthews' *Excellent Care for All Act*, Ontario Medical Association negotiations, and Bill 102 for drug policy. Again, these leaders spoke honestly about difficult topics. In this way, it could even be argued that Harris demonstrated a best practice in achieving healthcare reform subsequently adopted by his Liberal successors. What is certain is that some excellent analytical leaders started or furthered their careers on the commission's staff team; many are still working within the system for change and quality improvement.

8. Willingness of the core bureaucracy to not block: I suspect that the Ministry of Health was a little bit in awe of what the HSRC was attempting. The (relatively) new deputy minister was seen as (relatively) friendly to Harris, and she and her predecessor had commissioned the DHC reports. Certainly, key players such as Rochon, Sinclair, and others knew the bureaucracy well; there were multiple informal connections. While the hospital restructuring component of the reforms benefited from bureaucratic acceptance, the commission wished for more support for some of its later recommendations outside of hospital downsizing and felt that they did not get it. Overall, I am impressed that there was not more game playing.

One interesting tidbit is that the HSRC had a "principals only" rule for all meetings. No subordinate replacements could be sent by the ministry or other officials.

9. "Facilitation" strategy, an intentional misnomer: After each directive and report was delivered, a regional facilitator was appointed. When one thinks of facilitation, one usually thinks of nice hand-holding group processes in which people are coaxed toward solutions. This was not that. Very tough-minded and independent-minded men and women were appointed to facilitate regional agreement. The (lead) facilitator had the right to issue their own directive and use the full power of the commission (and hence the minister) under legislation. The team of Graham Scott and Maureen Quigley did five facilitations (including Sudbury). Scott was Bill Davis' deputy minister of health and the CEO of McMillan Binch (later McMillans) for almost two decades. Other facilitators included Michael Decter, who had been Rae's deputy minister of health and Ed Broadbent's executive assistant, and Alan Hudson, the famed neurosurgeon, who was later the CEO of the Toronto General Hospital and created the University Health Network. Each of Scott/Quigley, Decter, and Hudson are accomplished respected and visionary leaders of teams. While I am less familiar with some of the other facilitators involved in the process, I recognize one future Liberal cabinet minister and several respected jurists on the list.

These people were not selected for their facilitation skills, but neither were they chosen because they were acolytes of the *CSR*.

10. Willingness to admit limits: In an understated but clear way, the commission admitted failure in several key areas. They did so without much blame or handwringing, although there was a palpable anger at their inability to finish the job of moving toward a less institutional and more community-based health system, one that would meet the needs of the populations that they serve rather than serve the elite interests that control it. They also explicitly recognized the limits of their analytical methods and approaches to issues in areas such as mental health

and aging supports. This is a good thing given how blunt these tools were.

As they shuttered their volunteer commission, its leaders documented the key challenges that they saw for the future. Their *Looking Back, Looking Forward* report from March 2000 still reads as a contemporary analysis today. They also used the analytical resources available to undertake research that clearly informed subsequent MOH policy initiatives undertaken in the later Harris/Eves years and under McGuinty. For example, the McGuinty family health teams owe much to the commission's work on primary care groups and other conservative era policy work.[18]

My Harris grade for hospital restructuring? No doubts. Strong implementation of the correctly thought-out policy: A

* * *

The Harris healthcare record, when you look beyond Restructuring, is fairly typical of most governments in Canada in the past three decades. Overall, without including the excellent work done in hospital restructuring, I would grade them as only a B or B+ government on health policy:

- they negotiated with their doctors' union and had only limited success;
- they tried to control spending while dealing with an aging population;[19]
- they recognized that they needed more long-term-care beds and built 25,000 (which is more than anyone else has);
- they implemented rational changes to the Ontario Drug Benefit program that introduced some user fees (accepted by later governments) and introduced some competition;

- they created some limited market-based interventions in cancer services (expanded under McGuinty) and community care services (curtailed by McGuinty) by introducing purchaser/ provider splits;
- they introduced public/private partnerships into new hospital constructions, a good idea that was curtailed by election politics in 2003 and then later revived as Infrastructure Ontario.

I will review each of these briefly and provide a high-level report card grade. I will also consider whether there was any particular ideological approach evident in the approach taken by the Harris government in each key area.

The first Harris health minister, Jim Wilson, attempted to introduce some needed market forces into the doctor's fee schedule in the first Harris-era negotiation. The government proposed regional supplements and targeted fees for new physicians, for example. It also challenged the OMA's representation rights and attempted to have a discussion about malpractice expenses. Unfortunately, a comment made to a reporter by a minister's staffer appeared to have breached the privacy of a particular physician. The newspapers played "gotcha" politics with the minister and the government retreated and negotiated the usual centrally planned fee-for-service agreement and preserved "rep rights" for the OMA. No Hayek here. Some serious irony for insiders, though. The newspaper that embarrassed the minister at the time led the freedom-of-information charge twenty years later to have the same information made public about all physicians.

Physician payment was a big, missed opportunity if you were really Hayekians. Fee schedules are massively anti-competitive and restrict who can provide services and offer prices in ways that any self-respecting neoconservative would consider unwarranted. The idea of a massive every-four-year settlement of all fee codes, for all providers, in all parts of the province should make even the most committed Marxist squirm.

Yet it continues in most parts of the country, as if it is a normal way of doing things. It is an innovation killer.

My Harris grade? Good effort. Middling results. C+

Given what the HSRC was doing and the legacy of the Rae regime's Social Contract, it is hardly surprising that the ministry did not undertake separate major cost reduction programs at the time. Nor were they expected to, because the *CSR* had famously "sealed the envelope" and guaranteed total healthcare spending would not be cut. Rather, it appears that they were attempting to create a stable, ongoing funding model through the joint planning and priorities committee, DHCs, and other vehicles that would pick up after restructuring. Just implementing the orders coming across from the commission and following up on the major investments was clearly important. There was no attempt here to introduce market-based methods. In fact, it was McGuinty and Matthews who introduced prospective payments through the quality-based programs (QBP) and health-based allocation model (HBAM) program.

There is some fuzziness in the record about who was responsible for which cuts to which spending envelopes. This is hardly surprising given the complexities of having two side-by-side operational entities, one of which is de novo, with the full powers of the minister of health. In my discussions I have found that members of the HSRC team are skeptical of the government's claims to be budget neutral on healthcare spending while core members of the *CSR* team around Harris point out that it was their vision that drove hospital reductions and that they invested the saved capital in Longterm Care (LTC) and acute care facilities to enable it. There is probably no one right answer to this question, although I would give credit to Mr. Harris for supporting his people (the HSRC) and the commission credit for making tough decisions.

My Harris grade? This one has to be judged on pass/fail as the main work was at the HSRC. Pass.

Later HSRC reports are full of handwringing on the topic of aging in place. By 2000, it was clear that restructuring was only going to accomplish part of its mandate. More specifically, the shift to community-based services was not going to be completed in its four-year mandate. It is remarkable that Sinclair et al. criticize themselves for not moving quickly enough and not issuing clear enough directions (particularly in human resource areas). Most observers were, of course, left breathless from the commission's pace of change. Similarly, the commission cites its own naïveté as a major problem saying, "The commission has to accept full responsibility for its naivety, its failure to consider the reality of the political calendar and the amount of work it could reasonably achieve in the time available."

Here are Sinclair et al. five years after the HSRC:

> The commission was also successful in persuading the government to put money derived from its reduction of the hospital envelope into long-term care and home care. The total investment of $2 billion was decided on arbitrarily and was slow in coming, but it has helped to shift the focus from hospital-based to community-based care. To give credit where credit is due, the shift to out-of-hospital care was one of the declared intentions of Premier Harris's "common sense revolution." While it would have been preferable for the government to strike a different balance between long-term care "beds" and "places," substantial reinvestments were made—and in capital construction in hospitals as well. . .[20]

The Harris team claims 25,000 long-term care beds were funded and created. Sinclair et al. put the figure for the HSRC period at 20,000. In either case, it is the most of any government before or since. The big criticism seems to be that the money for building was given to private operators. This criticism is an example of fuzzy thinking by progressives.

Municipalities must run one home each and few run more; expanding municipal homes is fraught with difficulty. Not-for-profit (NFP) operators can only grow very slowly. LTC financing is based on access to capital; it is often based upon land appreciation and the ability for capital markets to price it. This source of investment is available to NFPs only imperfectly and in the very long term. Yes, religious organizations have made it work over the centuries, but that model does not allow for the kind of rapid accessing of capital markets to build new housing for high-needs seniors quickly. For governments to self-finance, this would be very expensive and a poor use of public sector capital. These beds cost a quarter million dollars each (in a 2021 estimate).

Does private LTC qualify as Hayek inspired? Decidedly not. Highly regulated and constrained LTC is the opposite of open choice for seniors. Twenty years later this is very clear, and even progressives today are becoming more Hayekesque in their rhetoric about aging in the right place.

My Harris grade? Decent job for the time and place. Missed opportunity to be more innovative. B+

Ontario drug benefit reforms appear to have begun during the Rae government and continued into the Harris years. There is no available official history, so I have reconstructed some of this by speaking with colleagues who were officials during this period. By 1996, it had become clear that drugs were going to continue to grow as a part of healthcare costs and that a mixed public/private model of financing was needed. Several historical anomalies around what was paid for needed to be cleaned up, and an income test was introduced. Prior to this point some high-cost drugs were covered, some were covered when delivered in a hospital, and some weren't covered at all.

The reforms were pretty good, and I will split the credit among the ministers, deputy ministers, and premiers of the Rae and early Harris years. An Ontario drug benefit information system was set up with high availability adjudication on some really cool technology (HP Non-stop) by GreenShield under the leadership on the drug programs branch. The income test (4 per cent of total household income) was established. Importantly, co-pays were introduced in the dispensing but not the drug price costs. There was early work on generic substitution and work on the formulary that was built upon by McGuinty. These smallish co-pays allowed for free dispensing competition to take place.[21]

This area did include some market-based thinking. This was done of necessity because it was clear at the time (as it is today) that 100 per cent public pharmacare was, and is, beyond the fiscal capacity of any government. Once one reaches this conclusion, the question of who pays first versus second dollar and how to build in price competition and consumer satisfaction become questions. These questions are not present in a 100 per cent covered system (e.g., fee-for-service medicine for physical MD visits).

My Harris grade? Surprisingly innovative policy work. A−

Market reforms were introduced into cancer care and home care through purchaser/provider split models in the later Harris/Eves years with Cancer Care Ontario (CCO) and Community Care Access Centre (CCAS). As mentioned earlier, Hillary Clinton had brought these models forward along with her partner-in-reform, Ira Magaziner. Made infamous and ultimately defeated by the "Harry and Louise" television ads, these reform initiatives in the mid-1990s were market-based thinking from Clinton-Era Democrats. As sectoral models in Ontario, they worked well, until subjected to political attack. McGuinty continued the CCO model for radiation and surgical oncology and expanded it under the leadership of Dr. Alan Hudson (the same Hudson who was an HSRC facilitator). CCO operates the same way from within Ontario health even today and no-one admits that it is a market mechanism or talks about it much. Unfortunately for the CCACs, in 2003, one of the century-old home care companies went to Premier McGuinty's first health minister and simply had the process stopped. This was a naive move and has been the source of policy problems ever since.

My Harris grade? These market reforms were limited but useful experiments. A− and C+.[22]

New capital for hospitals was desperately needed and made very difficult to fund because of public sector accounting rules in Ontario. Public–private partnerships were an answer that had been tried worldwide. It worked well in Ontario, in my opinion. Unfortunately, it became a campaign issue in 2003 ("privatizing health care"), and a senior Liberal who was soon to be finance minister made a commitment to shut down PPP. This was a bad mistake and very naive. Sorbara, McGuinty, and the team spent years trying to walk this back and created Infrastructure Ontario and alternate financing partnerships (AFPs) as ways to not do PPP. Real silliness. Clearly, public/private partnerships deserve to be part of any government's toolkit. Studies show that the 100 per cent government control of any major project doesn't work.[23]

To summarize this brief review of other policy areas, there were indeed some limited market-based reforms introduced in health care during the Harris era. However, the privatization attacks routinely made seem largely unsupported or crassly political or both. The Liberals often later regretted their partisan election time attacks as they were forced to make practical policy decisions within fiscal constraints.

In many policy areas, the Harris health ministry was aligned with, or followed in the footsteps of, the later Rae ministry. The elite consensus that I made reference and others have described in many discussions with former officials continued through the later Rae years (e.g., Social Contract) into Harris and from Harris into the McGuinty years. Michael Decter (Rae's health deputy minister) praised the work of the commission in a foreword that he wrote for *Riding the Third Rail*[24] and later McGuinty programs like family health teams, the wait-times initiative, CCAC and CCO restructuring, and even Infrastructure Ontario all owe intellectual debts to either HSRC or Harris or both. Some of McGuinty's wait-times initiatives were also supported by former *CSR* team member Tony Clement when he was federal health minister. The HSRC was the nexus for this agreement and has been the engine that has powered much policy thinking across party lines and brought more rigorous analytical approaches to the management of Ontario's health care system. During the Ford period, much of that rigour has been lost (in part due to Covid) and must now be regained.

My overall Harris grade, including the A for HSRC? An A−. Mike Harris did a good job in health care.

No sensible person enjoys restructuring complex systems. It is ghastly work that costs one sleep. Doing it well is really hard. This is true in any industry, but I believe it is particularly true in a mission-driven industry like health care. Bringing hard-nosed economic calculations into a place of caring is seen as mean-spirited. Even when almost ten thousand beds had been closed, decision-makers still shrank from closing a single hospital. The Rae New Democrats rolled back negotiated contracts by 5 per cent, but still didn't close hospitals. By contrast, Harris closed over forty hospitals. Very tough stuff.

Today "Harris Health Care Cuts" (HHCC) is taken as a shibboleth. A Google search finds various people accused of HHCC. Premier Ford is accused of HHCC, and yet his true problem (in his first term) was his lack of coherence and tough-mindedness. This is the very antithesis of Premier Harris in health care.

A second critique of Premier Harris is that he wanted to privatize health care. I hope that I have shown in the above analyses and commentaries that this is simply untrue. If anything, Mike Harris was a model central planner.

One particularly silly ad hominem version of this argument is that Harris was feathering his own nest by building all those long-term-care beds as premier so that he could (ten years later) serve on the board of an LTC company. This is bullshit (I struggle to find a more accurate descriptor). Most of the premiers and prime ministers that I have known could be subjected to a similar one. Our men and women in public service deserve to be able to continue to contribute after their public lives are completed. McGuinty, Peterson, Rae, and Davis have all done so honourably and also in positions where they contribute to areas that were under their prior jurisdiction.

Why do the critics of Harris hate him so much? He seems a nice enough fellow. And is, and was, clearly well intentioned. Yet the blind and impassioned hatred comes through. Thoughtful groups that would never descend to ad hominem attacks in other areas seem to lose their judgment and restraint when it comes to Mike Harris and health care. They literally start talking about his "hula hoops" comment more than twenty years after the guy left office. (On the subject of health care and hospital layoffs in 1997, Harris said: "Just as hula hoops went out and those workers had to have a factory and a company that would manufacture something else that's in, it's the same for government.")

My conclusion is that it has to do with job loss and job insecurity. Thousands lost their jobs, and tens of thousands had their roles change during restructuring. On a human level these care workers and many others lived with uncertainty through this period. It may well have started with the Social Contract pre-Harris. For a period of more than five years, workers who felt that they had a lifetime agreement with society felt unmoored and threatened. People who self-select into life of service to others and a vocation of caring do so because of their values; my experience has been that many do not do well with the kind of uncertainty that other professional types thrive on. They experienced a lot of uncertainty under Mr. Harris. They resented it and hate him. Personally. This is a completely understandable reaction to a very difficult situation.

Twenty years later most of the Canadian groups writing on the Harris years either repeat the HHCC shibboleth or are silently accepting. The Canadian Centre for Policy Alternatives did a twenty-year post summary of the Harris years ominously called: "The Long Shadow of Mike Harris." You can judge the dark corporatist cover and the two facile pages on health care for yourself by following the URL provided.[25]

There is literally no other comment on the entire "Harris Health Care Cuts" in this professionally produced review of the Harris regime by one of its most fervent academic critics. They apparently have nothing of substance to say on the topic. Just Hula Hoops.

Michael Decter, in his foreword to *Riding the Third Rail*, makes my favourite criticism of Harris when he says that the Harris government left the job half done. He paraphrases Sinclair, Rochon, and Leatt as follows:

> The authors are clear that the Ontario government retained—through the powers of the purse—ultimate approval power. They are also direct and honest about the 'deep frustration' of working with a government that failed to move decisively on the larger health service issues. Their recommendations on hospital restructuring were implemented, but those requiring government decisions to invest in community-based services were routinely ignored.

I think this criticism is fair and correct. The community investments that were recommended still await government action twenty-five years and several governments later. Few, other than a policy expert as tough-minded as Michael Decter, could get away with dinging Mike Harris for not moving decisively. It is a measure of how far-sighted the HSRC was under Sinclair's leadership that the same policy imperatives on primary care, health information technology, supporting aging (and others) remain into the third decade of the twenty-first century. Indeed, Sinclair as chair of the HSRC said on several occasions that if he had his druthers, the restructuring of primary care would be their top priority.

One more ridiculous and particularly unfair criticism is made in the post-Covid world and needs to be addressed. It runs like this: "Mike Harris cut hospital capacity and that is why we are having a bed shortage post-Covid." As if the hospitals closed twenty-five years ago would still be architecturally useful and as if there haven't been six intervening elections.

The folks that make this criticism also ignore that if there was an HSRC-like method still used today, then there would be more hospital beds. Particularly in the 905-region around the GTA.

The current system of funding allocation by our health ministry is (in my opinion) intentionally not transparent. Analytical documents in the ministry's possession are not published; there are no editorial board meetings. The system obfuscates bed shortages that are as well known to experts as the over-bedded situation was in 1995. We actually are now seeing the kind of bureaucratic capture of central planning elites that Hayek predicts in his writings. Frankly, I do not understand why there isn't a revolt in Brampton and York region. But it is not Mike Harris' fault, and it is silly polemics to say so.

* * *

It is ironic that Mike Harris is accused of being a free market advocate in health care while overseeing one of the best central planning processes in Canadian history. It's further ironic that he is labeled as a great privatizer. Frustratingly, the ironies obfuscate a really important debate about when we should use free consumer input as opposed to expert opinion to allocate public and private resources to health care. The naiveté in the political discussions in our country on this topic has been disgraceful. And this continues to be the case to this day.

The Harris team did a good job as central planners because they were tough-minded and evidence-driven at a time when there existed solid elite consensus. They took the proposed solution and implemented it. In areas where there was less of a consensus they did less well. As did other governments.

Areas like mental health and aging in place have been hugely challenging for central planners, and for policymakers generally, for exactly the reasons that Hayek identified. Social determinants of health are recognized as important by all parties, but central planners systematically deny the ability of consumers to use public funds to pay for these important things. We often constrain the mixing of public and private spending arbitrarily, or in the name of quality and appropriateness. A more consumer-oriented model for aging is clearly needed. Similarly, we talk about the need for wellness and investments in health, but we constrain the public from using their own dollars to purchase these. It appears to me that innovation in healthcare policy will almost certainly require an embrace of some of Hayek's free market ideas and a corresponding reduction in the role of central planning, as we move forward with meaningful healthcare reforms in the 2020s.

Fee schedules exemplify interest group capture of the means of production. As Hayek predicts, these set prices and regulatorily constrained supply have resulted in a continued reduction of both competition and innovation. Midwives, nurse practitioners, physiotherapists, pharmacists, and many others are prevented from competing on access, quality, cost, and provider satisfaction. And, ironically, this blocking of competition is done in the name of those quadruple aims.

But fee-for-service pricing is just the most obvious part of a very large regulatory iceberg. Our health care system has developed in such a way that we pay set prices for an increasingly limited set of services. In the main, these are for access to doctors and acute care hospitals; in other words, they are for physical care of the sick a la 1970. This is not the case for mid-level providers, not for drugs, not for virtual care, not for wellness, nor for many things that consumers would choose if they could. The set-price model often favours those with non-financial power and position—insiders and those with friends in health care. The vulnerable, poor, remote and indigenous populations have constrained access. Again and again, we see different choices that would be made by vulnerable groups being disallowed by mainstream rules that are culturally dominant. Allocative models that allow true choice are not permitted; we make "appropriate" decisions and impose our values as planners. This often makes the system less equitable in the name of keeping it public.

What is shocking is that today's conservatives (and Liberals?) still don't recognize the legitimate role of consumer choice in our public health-care system. Constrained choice regimes are the norm. These regimes reduce quality and drive-up prices (as Hayek would predict). This in spite of the success that CCO had with purchaser/provider splits and the later McGuinty success with wait-times spending and quality-based programs. Wait times in Ontario dropped dramatically under this model.[26] This represents a powerful example of how the use of market signals can materially enhance the quality of public health care.

Today's challenges in health care are increasingly the result of mixed public/private payment models in which central planning allocations make less and less sense. And in which rules-based central planning results in bureaucratic producer-dominated systems. Pharmacare, denticare, mental health, ageing in place, virtual care, and team-based care all require different allocative decisions than those are available through public fee schedules—precisely because these are very difficult for central planning models to accommodate. Even if those central planners are as good as Mike Harris was.

Notes

1   *The Common Sense Revolution*, 1994 (p. 2, 3 and 7).

2   Ibbitson, *Promised Land*, p. 28.

3   Looking Back, Looking Forward; The Ontario Health Services Restructuring Commission (1996—2000), March 2020 p.iii.

4   Bound black volumes 3–13 of HSRC documents (1996–2000). Private collection of M. Rochon. These volumes also include related advice to minister and other key geographic artifacts.

5   For those interested in a complete history, I recommend two sources: *Riding the Third Rail by Sinclair et al.* as well as *Looking Back Looking Forward* a legacy report issued at the end of the mandate in March 2000.

6   *Riding the Third Rail, 2005 by Sinclair et al. published by IRPP.*

7   Our World in Data, retrieved by the author.

8   Our World in Data, retrieved by the author.

9   https://www.sothebys.com/en/articles/this-is-what-we-believe-margaret-thatcher-and-f-a-hayek

10   *The Road to Serfdom (condensed), p. 40 1944* Frederich A. Hayek. I quote from the *Reader's Digest* version.

11   George Orwell wrote a review of Road to Serfdom in *The Observer* on April 9, 1944:

> By bringing the whole of life under the control of the State, Socialism necessarily gives power to an inner ring of bureaucrats, who in almost every case will be men who want power for its own sake and will stick at nothing in order to retain it. Britain, he says, is now going the same road as Germany, with the left-wing intelligentsia in the van and the Tory Party a good second. The only salvation lies in returning to an unplanned economy, free competition, and emphasis on liberty rather than on security. In the negative part of Professor Hayek's thesis there is a great deal of truth. It cannot be said too often— at any rate, it is not being said nearly often enough—that collectivism is not inherently democratic.

Strong stuff from an avowed socialist and supporter of the Labour Party. Orwell in 1944 had lived through the Spanish Civil War as a POUM supporter in which he and others were betrayed by the Stalinists. *Animal Farm* was published on August 17, 1945.

12   Ministry of Health figure, provided to the author by M. Rochon.

13   Particularly terrible were some of the ones published twenty years after the fact, who substituted "Hula Hoop" quotes and ad hominem attacks for substantive arguments (see Section 4 "What do the critics of Harris Health care policies actually say?").

14   This actually is a bit Hayekesque.

15   Volume 1: *Mandate & Legislation.* Court Decisions Black bound HSRC reports Volume 1. Courtesy of M. Rochon.

16   I was reminded of the "Directory" Period in the French Revolution, as Directors were sent out from Revolutionary Paris to parts of France to implement the Revolution.

17   Such an argument will be familiar to anyone who has lived through corporate bankruptcies or major corporate restructuring. I have done several and hope never to have to do another.

18   I have not included labour adjustment among the key success factors that I have mentioned. I have left this out in part because there is a lot of noise about this and less clarity and in part because it is an issue broader than just health care, and so I will leave it to better-informed co-authors.

19   For interested readers, I would encourage you to also refer to the chapter on the Harris fiscal record which shows that overall healthcare spending did actually increase over both the first and second terms of the Harris era.

20   *Riding the Third Rail,* p. 221.

21   Most of this section is based upon discussions with ministry officials whom I know. Interestingly, this early reform seems to have been important later to the Deb Matthews Bill 102 reforms.

22   This section is again based upon discussions with former ministry officials. In this case, supplemented by my own experience and direct knowledge.

23   This section is again based upon discussions with former MoH officials. There was an excellent "walk it back" report done early in the McGuinty years by a committee chaired by Decter (I led the consulting team but can't find a copy of the report in any archive).

24   Sinclair et al. pp. xix–xx.

25   https://policyalternatives.ca/publications/reports/onpolicy-long-shadow-mike-harris

26   Fraser Institute, *Waiting Your Turn 2014 report*, https://www.fraserinstitute.org/sites/default/files/waiting-your-turn-2014.pdf. *Page 44 Graph 13 shows surgical wait times dropped from 8.7 weeks in 2004/5 to 5.8 weeks in 2008/9.*

CHAPTER 5

An Education Report Card

William Robson

EDUCATION WAS A HUGE AREA of focus, change, and controversy under Ontario's Progressive Conservative (PC) governments from 1995 to 2003.[1] It had a prominent place in the PCs' positioning going into the 1995 election. The entire second volume in the PCs' 1992 New Directions series dealt with education and it got more space in *the CSR* campaign platform than any other topic.[2]

In office, Premier Mike Harris's government moved fast and disruptively. The cover of John Ibbitson's 1997 book on the Mike Harris "revolution" featured picketing teachers. The PCs' legacy in elementary and secondary education (ESE) is particularly notable and remains hotly disputed. Their actions in postsecondary education (PSE) generated less conflict, but also reshaped the sector in important ways.

Fans and foes agree that education should figure prominently in assessing of the premierships of Mike Harris and Ernie Eves. Notwithstanding the controversies at the time and many negative commentaries afterwards, my overall assessment is actually quite high. I award a grade of A–overall, with improvements in the quality of instruction of elementary and secondary school students, evolution toward a more diverse and dynamic post-secondary-education system and overall savings for taxpayers being key considerations behind the A−range grade. Whether those improvements could have occurred with less conflict and ill feeling afterwards is a key theme of my review and a question for education policymakers in the 2020s and beyond.

The editor encouraged contributors to this volume to alert readers to personal views and experiences that might affect their chapters. My main alert relates to elementary and secondary education (ESE). In the early 1990s, I volunteered with groups, mainly the Organization for Quality Education and the Ontario Coalition for Education Reform (OCER),[3] whose members thought Ontario's publicly funded schools were failing many students and should be more accountable for their performance. My writings and other activities likely inspired the new PC government to appoint me chair of the Ontario Parent Council in 1996, putting me close to much of the action in ESE over the next three years. My main engagement with PSE was as a member of Ontario's Postsecondary Education Quality Assessment Board (PEQAB) from its inception in 2000 until after the PCs' terms in government ended. PEQAB gave an inside view of the advent of degree programs in community colleges and the prospective establishment of new institutions, but less exposure to other PSE issues. PSE has less weight in my assessment, perhaps because my lesser involvement gives me less to say, but mainly because I see the PCs' commitments and actions in ESE as more consequential.

A report-card format seems a natural approach to assessing performance in education, so I use letter grades in each area to build up to an overall grade. The grades reflect two types of criteria.

One type, alignment, relates to correspondence between commitments and actions. The PCs made many education-related commitments before the 1995 election, particularly in New Directions, Volume 2 (OPCC 1992, hereafter *NDV2*) and the *CSR*, and their 1999 election platform

Blueprint also highlighted many education-related issues. Marking alignment between commitments and actions involves judgment within a narrower range than, say, the wisdom of a policy. In the case of actions, such as centralizing the education property tax, that had no matching commitment, I award no grade—no bonus or penalty for not including something in the platform.

The second type, impact, relates to the wisdom of a commitment or action and the quality of the results. Impact grades can differ from alignment grades. For example, if I think the government broke a bad promise or improvised well, I would mark higher on impact than alignment. Those grades involve a wider range of judgment, and more scope for readers to disagree.

When both types of criteria apply, I award one grade for alignment and one for impact. The overall grade is the average of the two. In areas where no commitments existed, the grade on impact is the only grade.

Overall, this approach yields a positive report card, better than most critics of the Harris government at the time would award and likely better than many observers of later events in Ontario education and politics would propose.

For alignment in ESE, I award the PCs an A−, scoring the Harris government particularly well on the salient issues of curriculum and reporting of student achievement. The alignment grade for PSE is somewhat lower: B+. The PCs made fewer commitments there and improvised more in response to long-standing tensions between academic and institutional autonomy on one side, and accountability for public funds on the other.

For impact, the PCs would have earned an A in ESE for the improvements in student achievement following their reforms, but the centralization of the system, relatively weak action on testing and teacher professionalism, and the intense conflicts with teachers and other opponents lower the grade to B+. In PSE, the PCs navigated the tensions well, and the blend of institutional autonomy, responsiveness at the margin to policy imperatives, and the greater diversity of institutions and programs that resulted merits an A− for impact.

Because the averaged percentages yielding both the A− grades and the B+ grades were relatively high, the average works out to A− for both types of criteria, and A− overall.[4] An A−range grade may raise eyebrows, even those of supporters of the Ontario PCs between 1995 and 2003. Critics vilified the Harris and Eves governments at the time and continue to vilify them now. Controversies over education surely contributed to the 2003 defeat of the Eves government by the overtly teacher-friendly Liberals under Dalton McGuinty.

A key question my account leaves open is whether the changes I see as positive with respect to instruction, student achievement and increased flexibility in the PSE system would have been less controversial and more durable without the spending restraint. They might have been. Money was an obvious and natural point of contention with unions and supporters of public education. As chair of the Ontario Parent Council, I urged government officials to spend more money to ease the transitions several times. But that speculation takes us into a world that did not exist in the 1990s and may never exist.

Without the confluence of concern about education quality and fiscal pressures, the political coalition and the will to act that produced such improvements as the ESE curriculum or the expanded scope of colleges might never have existed. Nor was the combination as obviously toxic as the critics make out. The PCs under Mike Harris won an impressive victory again in 1999 with a platform that emphasized continuity with respect to both education and fiscal policy. While the elementary and secondary teachers' unions became noticeably more militant during the PCs' terms in government, the circumstances of the time may just have accelerated a trend that was occurring anyway.

It would be nice to improve instruction and accountability in education while garnering praise from educators and voters who treat spending as a measure of benevolence. The tendencies for advocates of content and accountability to support budget surpluses and lower taxes, and for opponents of content and accountability to support more spending, may force a choice, however—a challenge for future policymakers in Ontario and elsewhere.

* * *

In ESE, the core focus of NDV2 and the *CSR* was what students were learning or not learning. While tensions over governance and the level and distribution of funding mattered, these documents channeled much discontent about how poorly Ontario's schools were imparting knowledge and skills. They contained many commitments on curriculum, pedagogy, testing and reporting, all of which were areas of intense activity under the PC governments. Funding and governance got less platform space, and the PCs improvised more in those areas once in government.

One backdrop to the tensions over ESE in the early 1990s is the decades-long transition from public education characterized by local finance, governance, and employer-employee relations, to a system with fewer, larger school boards, and collective bargaining with teacher federations that had become politically powerful industrial unions. Many trustees and taxpayer groups felt that school boards had become expensive and remote from their constituents, and weak, or entirely co-opted, in dealing with the unions.

Another financial problem was long-standing unhappiness about differing fiscal capacity among school boards. Different tax bases produced different levels of funding per student, a frequent focus of criticism, which the Royal Commission on Learning (RCOL), established by the NDP government in mid-1993, had urged the province to fix.

Perhaps the greatest contributor to discontent by the early 1990s was the withdrawal of the provincial government from quality assessment after it abolished high-school exit exams in the late 1960s.

Although the RCOL was less keen on testing than the advocates for content and accountability who made representations to it, it did recommend standardized tests under an independent agency. Plans for what became the Education Quality and Accountability Office (EQAO) were already under way under the NDP.

The Common Curriculum, Grades 1 to 9 issued under the NDP in 1993 became a lightning rod for critics of the province's retreat from content and measurement in ESE. The OCER released a scathing report with an overall grade of D- on publicly funded education in Ontario shortly afterwards (OCER 1994). That report complained that little information about student achievement in Ontario was available and what information was available suggested that it was poor. The International Assessment of Educational Progress in 1991, for example, had shown Canada as an international laggard, with Ontario finishing third-last among Canadian provinces in science and dead last in math. The OCER report also expressed widely held concerns about young peoples' work readiness and socialization upon graduation from Ontario's under-performing system.

In addition to a vague curriculum and no testing, the OCER criticized "child-centred" rather than "teacher-directed" pedagogy and the practice of moving students up to the next grade even if they had not mastered the material. The report complained about secretiveness, both with respect to student achievement and money. Those complaints prefigured the report's recommendations—among them a specific, sequential curriculum, teacher-directed instruction, testing and reporting of test results. On finance and governance, it advocated more autonomy for publicly funded schools, more competition within the publicly funded system, and between it and independent schools, and more power for trustees.

Many ESE-related commitments in NDV2 and the *CSR* reflected these discontents. With respect to content—what to teach—NDV2 advocated more emphasis on content, more informative reporting, including province-wide tests, and better report cards. It mentioned a mandatory math and science senior credit for high-school graduation and more emphasis on technology.

With respect to delivery—how to teach—NDV2 advocated a less child-centred approach in general and made many specific proposals. It promised to increase instruction days from 185 to 190. It promised to reduce the normal high-school program from five years to four. Rather than de-streaming high school (putting students with different abilities into the same program) as the NDP proposed to do by 1993, it promised delay and mooted cancelation.

Other pedagogical elements in NDV2 included bringing private-sector experts into the classroom, improving teacher performance through one-year classroom apprenticeships and testing teachers before initial certification and subsequent re-certification. NDV2 also focused on reducing costs. In addition to the shorter high-school program, it promised to keep junior kindergarten optional, rather than mandating it as the NDP planned for 1994. It talked about eliminating duplication among publicly funded school systems, fewer school boards, "value-for-money" audits, and using public–private partnerships for capital projects. NDV2 mentioned increased autonomy for schools with increased roles for parents and community leaders. It contained hints, but no commitments, about vouchers and funding of denominational and other independent schools.

The *CSR* was shorter. It devoted a substantial share of its pages to education, but made fewer specific commitments. It promised the core curriculum and standardized tests at all levels. It also mentioned changes to delivery: more school days, four years for high school, and reverting to optional junior kindergarten. It did not mention de-streaming and said little about pedagogy.

Being largely focused on fiscal frugality, the *CSR* emphasized governance and funding. It promised fewer school boards and hinted at changes of responsibility and remuneration, presumably less and lower, for trustees. It committed to "classroom-based budgeting" that would protect teaching, while cutting spending on consultants, bureaucracies and administration.

The *CSR* reiterated pledges to make schools more autonomous, with increased roles for parents and local communities. It said nothing about vouchers or funding for independent schools.

Once in office, the PC government moved fast on the content of instruction. An immediate project was replacing the NDP's Common Curriculum with new documents for Grades 1 through 8. Education Minister John Snobelen's office drove the process with senior policy advisor Craig Rix playing a lead role in early meetings with representatives from the Ontario Parent Council, teachers, outside experts, and officials. In those meetings, parent and teacher representatives tended to push for subject-specific content and clear learning expectations, while ministry officials tended to oppose them.[5]

The commitment to a four-year high-school program added urgency. Students would need to enter Grade 9 better prepared, and fast. The language and math documents appeared in June 1997; those for science and technology in March 1998. They were an immediate success. Teacher union leaders condemned them at first, then went quiet, as they discovered many of their members liked the richer content.

Haste was not the only challenge for the high-school curriculum. The *CSR*'s non-mention of de-streaming likely reflected the contentiousness of streaming across the political spectrum. The greatest sensitivity related to the least academically advanced of the then-existing three streams: the "basic" stream where, not surprisingly, many of the students who most needed good instruction in earlier grades, but did not get it, ended up.

The government decided to drop the basic stream and also decided to make the two remaining streams, "academic" and "applied," similar enough that students could switch between them: the same content, delivered at different levels. Delivering content suitable for students then in the basic stream, while also enriching the overall curriculum to get five years into four with the promised mandatory math and science credits, was a tall order. The first document on high-school reform released in 1996 got a rough reception and the government delayed implementation from 1998 to 1999. The new Grade 9 curriculum only appeared in the summer of 1999, so some materials were not ready for the start of school in September.

Notwithstanding raggedness on the high school side, the PCs delivered well on their curriculum commitments. Furthermore, notwithstanding the reaction and later fads in educational politics, the Ontario curriculum has not reverted to the content vacuum that made the Common Curriculum an object of derision. For that reason, I supplement my high mark for alignment between commitments and actions in this area with the observation that the changes proved durable. I award an A+ for alignment, and an A for impact, for an A+ overall.

The Harris government left junior kindergarten optional. As just noted, it proceeded with the transition to a four-year high-school program. It did not completely de-stream high-school, although the switchable two-stream program arguably went most of the way there. It increased instructional days in the school year and reduced provincially funded professional development days.

The new curriculum documents were content-heavy and pedagogy-light. Their more specific and sequential content, reinforced by new report cards and by tests as described in the next sections, must have tipped classroom practice toward more teacher-directed instruction.

The focus on curriculum reform and other pressures elaborated later in this chapter absorbed time and energy the government would have needed to deliver on their other commitments, such as the technology, co-op and apprenticeship programs. Overall, in my view, the government's actions with respect to delivery of instruction aligned well enough with its commitments to justify B+ on alignment.

What about impact: the wisdom and results? The spread of institutional childcare since the 1990s makes ending mandatory junior kindergarten look retrograde today, but evidence of the impact of earlier childcare on the kids themselves is mixed (Baker et al., 2019), so I am inclined to be neutral. The partial de-streaming and shorter high-school program are also open to debate, but there, too, there is no likely and compelling counterfactual. So, my overall mark on the impact criteria is B+, yielding an overall grade of B+.

NDV2's commitment to report cards with marks and descriptive information by subject at the elementary level also got early action. This was a major focus of the Ontario Parent's Council, with two main points at issue.

One was whether report cards should contain one mark and a single descriptive field for major areas of study, such as mathematics, or several marks and complementary descriptive fields for strands within the area, such as number sense, calculation, and so on. The other was whether report cards should use letter grades or percentages or employ a less granular four-point scale; "much below the standard," "approaching the standard," "at the standard," and "above the standard." My sense is that most parents and many, if not most, teachers favoured the more specific options, while many ministry officials leaned the other way. The discussion went at least as far as the then-deputy minister, Veronica Lacey, and likely to the minister's office as well, with the more specific and granular options carrying the day.

On alignment with commitments, I award the government an A on report cards. I also think the more detailed subject breakdowns and more granular grading are helpful for parents and students and, notwithstanding the work involved in preparing them, helpful for teachers as well, and so I award an A for impact as well, making my overall grade in this area an A.

On teaching, the *CSR* did not explicitly reiterate *NDV2*'s commitments about private-sector experts, apprenticeships, evaluation of teachers, and recognition of excellence. But the government was active on this front from the beginning.

A key development, not prefigured in either document, was the creation of a new Ontario College of Teachers (OCT) in 1996. The OCT was another recommendation of the RCOL on which the NDP had made a start. Its mandate included both professional conduct, previously mainly left to the unions, and qualification, previously a responsibility of the ministry.

On conduct, the OCT was a clear step forward, shortening the backlog of disciplinary cases that had built up under the previous system. On qualification, the story was mixed. Critics such as the OCER felt that the OCT was not set up to be sufficiently demanding. Its first run at standards-of-practice focused on accreditation of faculties of education. When all the existing faculties passed, critics of pedagogy in Ontario argued that the standards were obviously too weak. When it came to standards for teacher certification and recertification, the OCT simply bogged down. The *Blueprint* platform in 1999 committed to testing teachers for certification and recertification, apparently a commitment that resonated with the public, and the reelected government moved to legislate in these areas.

The Stability and Excellence in Education Act in June 2001 mandated a five-year recertification cycle. While the government abandoned its commitment to a recertification test, requiring instead a minimum number of professional development courses, the *Quality in the Classroom Act* in December 2001 required beginning teachers to pass a standardized test, which became a requirement of certification in 2003.

I discuss the important and contentious *Education Quality Improvement Act* (Bill 160) of 1997 at length under funding and governance below, but one of its provisions worth a mention here removed principals from the teacher unions. The unions and other critics decried that as violating collective bargaining, a stratagem to narrow the definition of classroom funding, and a step toward hiring non-teachers to run schools. My take is that it made sense: principals should be managers. Early drafts of Bill 160 would have loosened the hold of the unions even more, envisioning an end to the closed shop and allowing non-certificated teachers in subjects such as arts and physical education (Anderson and Ben Jafaar, 2003), but the final legislation left those provisions out.

The PCs' record on teaching shows good correspondence between commitments and actions. Certification and standards of practice did not exist before Mike Harris became premier, and did exist afterwards. On alignment, I award A−. On impact, the College of Teachers did not start strong and the reelected government reacted to address this. With confrontations between the governments and the unions so central to many unflattering accounts of the Harris years, it is worth noting that taking principals and vice-principals out of the unions was one move among many that never got reversed. The mixed record there yields a grade of B on impact, for an overall grade of B+.

With respect to testing, the EQAO, originally initiated under the NDP government, formally launched in 1996. It administered the first tests of reading, writing, and math in Grade 3 in the 1996–1997 school year, the first tests of those same subjects in Grade 6 in 1998–1999, and the first test of math in Grade 9 in 2000–2001. Its first literacy test required for high-school graduation occurred in 2002 (EQAO, 2013).

The pre-1995 head start on the EQAO helped the PCs move fast, but meant that its approach reflected many predilections of stakeholders who dislike testing. The tests were literacy and numeracy tests; they involved no subject-specific content, such as asking students to say when confederation occurred, name the planets in the solar system, or identify the atoms in a water molecule. Moreover, instead of the specific short-answer questions many testing advocates prefer, the designers leaned toward constructed responses, which are more cumbersome to administer and mark.

Although the EQAO was billed as testing all students, consistent with the PCs' commitments, exemptions and incomplete tests have been common, with rates in some school boards so high as to raise doubts about validity and comparability. The 1999 *Blueprint* reiterated a commitment to testing, which would allow tracking of progress year-by-year, with identification of good and bad teachers. That did not happen. And although most testing advocates wanted the results published in a format that would allow identification of good and bad classes, schools and school boards, would-be researchers cannot access machine-readable data, and the organization of the EQAO's reports inhibits comparisons of schools and boards.

A final key point of contrast is between advocates for "testing that matters" and advocates for "testing that does not matter." Only the high-school literacy test was a requirement for graduation. Although the mandatory math and science senior credit for high-school graduation should logically have had an associated high-stakes test, it did not. All the other tests were oriented toward statistical reporting, with no specific consequences for students, teachers or anyone else—an approach that is less effective in spurring improvement (Cowley and MacPherson, 2022).

In assessing the Harris/Eves governments' record on testing, three considerations lower the high mark that would otherwise make sense on alignment. One is that the move toward the type of testing that actually occurred was already under way before the 1995 election. A second is that most readers of their commitments would have anticipated testing on content, not just literacy and numeracy. The third is that they committed to testing in every year, which did not occur. With those demerits, I think a grade of B+ is fair on that criterion.

On impact, the EQAO's tests would have done more for accountability and improvement if they had been simpler and their results had been more accessible.[6] The inaccessibility of the results to researchers and the public, and their administrative burden, undermined the constituency for the tests, making them vulnerable to obstruction (teachers refused to administer them in some later years) and cancelation.[7] My assessment on that front is B, for an overall grade of B.

Education is about learning first and foremost: critics of Ontario's schools, and the PC campaign documents, complained that Ontario's students were not learning enough. As the critics also complained, almost no measurement of students' knowledge and skills was occurring before 1995, which frustrates definitive judgments about changes after 1995.

The EQAO's first tests of primary and junior students were in the 1997/98 school year. The students writing those and other early EQAO tests had received little or no instruction under the new curriculum and little exposure to other changes that occurred under the PCs. So the abilities of those students mostly or entirely reflect the pre-1995 environment. The share of students achieving at levels 3 and 4 at both ages in reading, writing and math rose quite steadily over the first decade of EQAO tests (Figure 5.1). While the tests may have gotten easier, the improvement over the decade is large and the later decline of writing scores for junior students and math scores for both junior and senior students later casts doubt on the idea that "dumbing down" was a continuing, system-wide, problem.

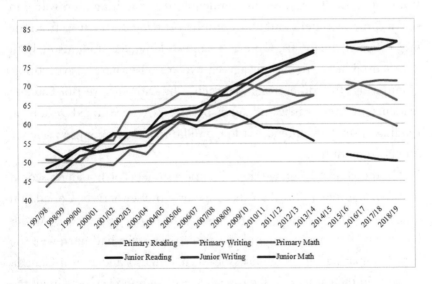

Figure 5.1   Students at Levels 3 and 4 in EQAO Tests, Per Cent

Source: EQAO.

The School Achievement Indicators Program (SAIP) administered consistent tests to thirteen-year-old and sixteen-year-old students across Canada at intervals between 1993 and 2004. Those also allows comparisons of years before the PCs took office, or early in their tenure, with those later, with later years, using the rest of Canada as a benchmark. The SAIP results also support the notion that Ontario students improved.

Table 5.1 shows the shares of students achieving at levels 3 and 4 on the tests administered closest to 1995 and on the latest year the tests were administered. The numbers in the light gray shaded squares compare students in Ontario's English-language schools and French-language schools to the Canadian average for each.[8] The numbers in the dark gray shaded squares compare the differences between Ontario students and the Canadian average in the earlier tests to the differences between them in the later tests.

Ontario's English-language students of both ages scored marginally better than their age-equivalents elsewhere in Canada in the tests from the mid-1990s in reading, much better in writing, and worse in science, math content and math problem-solving. In the tests from the late 1990s to the 2000s, Ontario's English-language students of both ages scored better than their age-equivalents elsewhere in everything. Comparing the differences between Ontario and rest-of-Canada students in the earlier and later periods, we see mixed results in reading, a small decline in writing, and large improvements in science and both math tests.[9]

On the French-language side, Ontario's students of both ages scored worse in the mid-1990s than their age group elsewhere in Canada on everything. In the tests from the late 1990s to the 2000s, the thirteen-year-olds had essentially caught up, and the sixteen-year-olds had narrowed the gap. Comparing the differences between Ontario and rest-of-Canada students in the earlier and later periods, we see improvements in all the relative scores of Ontario French-language students.

Table 5.1 Students Achieving Levels 3 and 4 in SAIP Tests, Ontario and Rest of Canada, per cent

| | Both Languages | | English-Language | | | | French-Language | | | |
| | Rest of Canada | | Ontario | | Ontario minus Rest of Canada | | Ontario | | Ontario minus Rest of Canada | |
	13-year-olds	16-year-olds	13-year-olds	16-year-olds	13-year-olds	16-year-olds	13-year-olds	16-year-olds	13-year-olds	16-year-olds
Earlier										
Reading 1994	41	68	44	69	3	1	38	61	−2	−6
Writing 1994	55	74	66	81	12	7	24	47	−31	−28
Science 1996	70	68	67	65	−3	−3	57	51	−13	−17
Math Content 1997	49	38	45	33	−4	−5	43	28	−6	−10
Math Problem Solving 1997	58	58	50	52	−8	−6	52	49	−6	−9
Later										
Reading 1998	37	65	38	72	2	7	36	65	−1	0
Writing 2002	77	55	85	59	8	4	80	45	3	−10
Science 2004	64	82	72	88	8	7	63	74	0	−8
Math Content 2001	57	47	63	51	7	3	56	42	0	−5
Math Problem Solving 2001	61	44	69	47	8	3	69	39	8	−5

(Contd.)

Table 5.1 (*Contd.*)

| | Both Languages | | English-Language | | | | French-Language | | | |
| | Rest of Canada | | Ontario | | Ontario minus Rest of Canada | | Ontario | | Ontario minus Rest of Canada | |
	13-year-olds	16-year-olds	13-year-olds	16-year-olds	13-year-olds	16-year-olds	13-year-olds	16-year-olds	13-year-olds	16-year-olds
Differences										
Reading 1998	-4	-3	-5	3	-1	6	-3	4	1	7
Writing 2002	22	-19	19	-22	-3	-3	56	-2	34	17
Science 2004	-7	14	4	24	11	10	6	22	13	8
Math Content 2001	8	10	18	18	10	8	13	14	6	4
Math Problem Solving 2001	3	-14	19	-6	16	9	17	-10	14	4

Source: Council of Ministers of Education, Canada, SAIP reports.

The more recent EQAO scores suggest that some gains Ontario students made during and after the PCs' time in office have lasted. Not all: the first-attempt pass rate on the Grade 10 literacy test was in the mid-80s in the late 2000s and declined to the low 80s a decade later (Johnson, 2019). In the junior grades, math scores have fallen notably since the late 2000s, reversing the gains after the curriculum reforms. But the latest results from the 2019 round of the SAIP's successor, the Pan-Canadian Assessment Program of students in Grade 8, showed Ontario students performing well on a national scale. The 2018 results of the OECD's Programme for International Student Assessment show Ontario fifteen-year-olds scoring very high on a world scale in reading, and high in both math and science.

The available indicators of achievement then, point quite uniformly toward improvement after the mid-1990s with evidence of decline occurring in the years after the PCs left office. On that basis, I award A+ for alignment and the same score for impact, for an A+ overall.

* * *

Fiscal frugality was central to the PCs' commitments and to their actions once in government. Reducing "non-classroom spending," in part by reducing duplication at the board level, featured in NDV2 and the *CSR*. But the upheaval in education funding and governance in the late 1990s far exceeded what those documents prefigured.

As Ibbitson (1997, 227–240) relates, the government wanted to reduce transfers to the broader public sector, including school boards. The PCs had made commitments to steer funds toward the classroom and away from activities such as preparation time, administration and consultants, but they had few levers to do that. Their campaign documents had not addressed unhappiness about uneven fiscal capacity among school boards. Province-wide pooling of education-related property taxes, however, would not only allow "leveling-up" of less fiscally robust school boards, but "leveling-down" of more fiscally robust boards, which could save money. These imperatives led to a major governance change. The province took over education-related property taxes, centralized education funding, and transferred power over many aspects of education delivery away from school boards.

These changes provoked intense confrontation with the teacher unions. Although centralized funding could have led to more autonomy at the school level, nothing of the sort occurred, and a late, promised move to a voucher-like system to fund students at independent schools did not survive the end of the PCs' time in office.

The imperative to lower spending triggered an initial cut to operating grants for school boards toward the end of the 1995/96 school year. The government intended boards to cut spending on administration and areas such as prep time less connected to classroom instruction. But most boards reacted with threatened or actual layoffs, program cuts, and property taxes hikes. That reaction set the stage for *Education Quality Improvement Act* (EQIA) of December 1997, the widely vilified Bill 160.

The EQIA was about more than money, but money was at its heart. Critically, it established a new province-wide funding formula, mostly determined on a per-pupil basis, with fewer components than the pre-existing transfer formula.

An essential feature of the new formula was more equal per-student funding across boards. That increased revenues for Catholic and French-language boards, and reduced them for many English-language public boards. The losers reacted furiously.[10] Despite the government's improvisation of three-year transition funding to cushion the blow, conflict with the unions escalated, and the 1998/99 school year featured withdrawals of extra-curricular activities, lockouts and strikes. People for Education, an activist group of parents often aligned with the teacher unions, staged a highly effective "green ribbon campaign" and published reports documenting the funding cuts and their impact.

Further re-jigging followed. The *Education Accountability Act* of 2000 redefined instructional time and class sizes. In addition to ad hoc adjustments to the funding formula, the government commissioned a task force, led by Mordechai Rozanski, to review it. Among the recommendations in the task force's 2002 report were updated benchmarks and a longer phase-in, which led to further adjustments, including extra money for remote and smaller boards and schools. Friction over funding and disputes with the unions were chronic through to the 2003 election and were undoubtedly a key factor in the PCs' loss to the Liberals.

In assessing this part of the PCs' record, it would help to have numbers showing whether the changes saved money by cutting overheads. The available numbers (Figure 5.2) suggest that the changes did save money overall, reducing per-student spending in real (inflation-adjusted) terms (Panel A) and bringing it more in line with per-student spending elsewhere in Canada (Panel B) between the mid-1990s and the early 2000s.

As for the composition of spending, school board expenditures compiled by Statistics Canada show a downward trend in administration's share of operating expenditures of Ontario school boards between the early 1990s and the early 2000s, setting aside the uptick in its share during the labour disruptions of 1997 (Figure 5.3). The share of teacher salaries and instructional supplies, the two categories that seem most closely related to instruction, also falls over the period, notably so if one includes the plunge during the disruptions of 1997. In the rest of Canada, administration's share also fell, though less, and the share of teacher salaries and instruction supplies, which was lower than in Ontario throughout the period, was more stable.

What do these numbers say about the PCs' commitments to focus spending on the classroom? On the positive side, they show a decline in the share of administration in Ontario school boards' operating expenses to the 7–8 per cent range typical of other provinces and territories. On the negative side, they show a decline in the share for teacher salaries and

Panel A

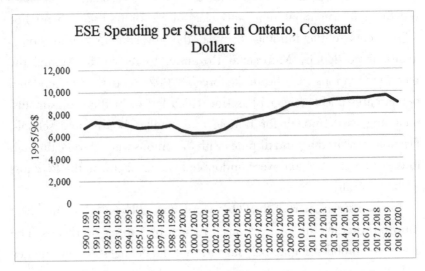

Panel B

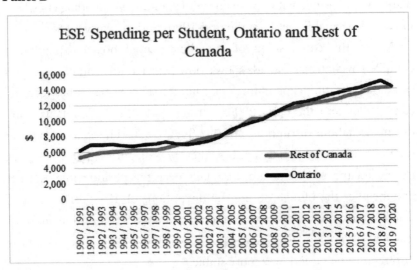

Figure 5.2 Per-Student Spending in Ontario in Real Terms and Compared to Rest of Canada

Sources: Author's calculations based on expenditure data from Statistics Canada Table 37-10-0066-01, enrolment data from Statistics Canada Catalogue 81-210, Table 37-10-0007-01, and Ontario Ministry of Education "Quick Facts," various years, and consumer price index data from Statistics Canada Table 18-10-0004-01.

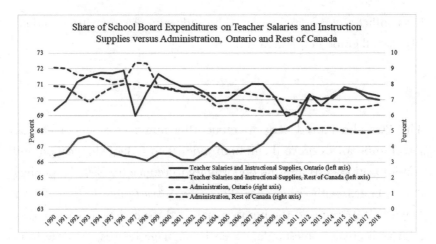

Figure 5.3 Share of School Board Expenditures on Teacher Salaries and Instruction Supplies versus Administration, Ontario and Rest of Canada

Source: Author's calculations based on data from Statistics Canada Table 37-10-0065-01.

instructional supplies. A hard marker would note the adverse movement of both measures during the disruptions of 1997 and 1998.

Before giving a letter grade, two points seem relevant. Measures of student achievement improved during this period, so whatever the impact of the funding changes, other improvements offset anything deleterious. Also, and remarkable in view of the intense criticisms at the time, the Harris funding formula has proven durable. An unsympathetic review of the changes twenty years after the PCs' 1995 election complained that the formula had "not been fundamentally changed, nor even reviewed, since the Conservatives left office" (Mackenzie, 2015, p. 14).

On alignment, I award B−. The PCs saved money as they promised, but their approach to financing differed greatly from what their platform prefigured, and the composition of school-board expenditures shows no clear tilt away from non-classroom spending. On impact, I award B+. The province-wide, per-student formula addressed long-standing tensions and resembles what has happened in most other provinces and many jurisdictions abroad. If not done on-the-fly, it could have sparked less conflict and required fewer ad hoc adjustments and extra spending. My overall grade in this area is B.

* * *

The PCs also moved early to reduce the number of school boards. Fiscal imperatives drove them, both a desire to reduce duplication and administration costs and the opportunity to reduce transfers by pooling poorer boards with richer ones. The *Fewer School Boards Act* (Bill 104) of January 1997 reduced the number of boards from 129 to seventy-two, even as it created freestanding French language boards, separate from their public and Catholic counterparts.

The act also cut the number of trustees per board and capped their salaries at $5,000 per year, a pay cut of about seven-eighths for trustees in the highest-paying boards. The EQIA, which followed at the end of 1997, gave the province power to set class size, preparation time, and the length of the school year, items previously under the control of school boards and often negotiated with the unions.

A concrete test of the province's will to exert its new powers over school boards' finances and operations came in 2002 when the Toronto, Ottawa and Hamilton District School Boards defied the province's prohibition on adopting budgets with deficits. The government appointed auditors to design balanced budgets, and when the boards balked at the changes, appointed supervisors to oversee their finances and operations.

In assessing the PCs' record in this area, a reasonably high alignment grade seems fair. Rightly or wrongly, fewer school boards and lower trustee salaries did coincide with reducing administrative costs in the popular mind. I award A−.

I take a dimmer view on impact. There is no convincing evidence in this instance, or more generally, that amalgamating local governments reduces costs; indeed, leveling-up of compensation and other contracts tends to increase them. The data on expenditures do not show a shift toward teacher salaries and instructional supplies. Reducing trustee salaries runs counter to improving trustee quality. My judgment is that it made running for trustee especially unattractive for people whose campaigns would not get in-kind support from education worker unions. Erosion of local governance is a trend in modern democracies, but its seeming inevitability does not make it desirable. On that criterion, I award C. Overall, my grade on school boards is thus B.

Part of the NDP government's response to the recommendations from its RCOL was Policy/Program Memorandum 122, issued in April 1995, which mandated school councils made up of parents, teachers, the school principal, and community members. Although the RCOL had recommended governance powers for school councils, the NDP had little enthusiasm for that idea and although the PC campaign documents talked about greater autonomy for schools, they showed equally little enthusiasm for school-based governance after their election.

The EQIA legislated school councils and lobbying by the Ontario Parent Council and others removed the term "advisory" from the original bill. Actual responsibility and accountability at the school level would have run against the centralizing trend, however. A major factor in the government's reluctance to deliver on school autonomy must have been the widespread, and highly visible in the case of People for Education's Green Ribbon campaign, community-level opposition to its policies.

In this area, the PCs do not deserve a high grade for alignment. The Education Improvement Commission, co-chaired by former Toronto School Board Chair, Ann Vanstone, and former NDP education minister, Dave Cooke, which the government appointed in 1997 to advise on the transition to the new governance system, recommended more school-based reporting of a variety of academic and nonacademic outcomes. But the PCs were no respecters of subsidiarity in general, and certainly not in education. I award C- on that criterion.

My assessment with respect to impact is no better. Per-student funding from the province and regular assessment could have set the stage for more local autonomy in budgeting and delivery. Taking principals out of the teacher unions was consistent with greater school-level autonomy. The 1999 *Blueprint* talked about a role for a school's "parent council" in working with principals of underperforming schools to turn things around, but the wrong terminology in this commitment was a harbinger of neglect after the PCs' reelection. Could an alternative approach that gave school councils more actual work to do have led to more accountability, specialization among schools, and parental choice? We do not know, but I think the overall direction warrants a grade of D, for an overall D+ in this area.

* * *

A much more powerful spur to school-based autonomy and parental choice is per-student subsidies to independent schools, as other Canadian provinces outside the Atlantic region and many European school systems provide. Notwithstanding hints about funding of denominational and other private schools in *NDV2*, the 1999 *Blueprint* said nothing about this, and the passing of the Equity in Education Tax Credit in 2001 came as a surprise to supporters and opponents of independent school funding alike. This legislation created a voucher-like system through a tax credit equal to 50 per cent of tuition up to a maximum of $3,500 per child after a five-year phase-in.

Objections from unions and others, predicting loss of students and revenue from the publicly funded system, and objections from people suspicious of religious schools, led the government to delay the phase-in after the initial year. Although subsequent legislation under Minister of Finance Janet Ecker in 2003 would have restored the credit to its original schedule (Anderson and Ben Jafaar, 2003), the McGuinty Liberals campaigned on a promise to cancel it retroactively, and it died with their election in 2003.

Since neither the *CSR* in 1995 nor the *Blueprint* in 1999 said anything about supporting students attending independent schools, no grade on alignment makes sense in this area. As for impact, subsidies for independent schools make them accessible to lower-income students and likely mitigate the correlation between student background and achievement in jurisdictions that provide them (Robson and Hepburn, 2002). The initiative deserves a high mark on that criterion, and I award A rather than A+ only because it came so late. An earlier start would have built a stronger constituency and might have made it durable. Since only impact figures in my total grade in this area, the total grade is also A.

To summarize, my assessment of the PCs' record in ESE in terms of alignment of actions to commitments is A− and my assessment of impact is B+. The curriculum and reforms regarding testing and reporting were consistent with the PC platforms, and notwithstanding problems with the EQAO's tests and the OCT's certification, rising student achievement during the late 1990s and early 2000s justifies many A-range grades. The record in governance and funding is less impressive. Centralization of taxation and funding were neither anticipated in the platform nor elegantly implemented, which inflamed opposition and may have reduced the savings otherwise available. The tax credit for independent school tuition, however great its promise—and I think its promise was great—did not survive the PC governments, leaving a legacy of a more centralized system, with feebler boards, negligible school autonomy, and entrenched producer groups. My Bs, Cs and one D on governance and funding lower the score in that area to B−. The overall grade in E&S education works out to B+.

* * *

While concerns about student achievement in ESE in the early 1990s were acute, discontents in post-secondary education were more chronic and less salient with the public. The PCs' 1995 campaign documents said much less about PSE. Although *NDV2* discussed research, accountability, specialization among institutions, and fewer restrictions on private degree-granting, the *CSR* contained only one column of text on PSE, dealing with cost reductions through cuts to administration, partial deregulation of tuition, and income-contingent student loans. A key implicit commitment from cutting secondary school to four years was providing spaces for the resulting double cohort of graduates seeking PSE. The 1999 *Blueprint* said more about enhancing PSE funding, including student support, accountability and connection to the job market. None of the documents prefigured major changes to Ontario's PSE system. The erosion of the historical separation between colleges and universities and a larger expansion of degree-granting authority and institutional diversity than prefigured in the campaign makes the PCs' record in PSE a relatively "quiet" revolution.

The three main tensions in PSE in the early 1990s were long-standing ones. The first related to access versus cost. The second was about the separate missions of the universities and the Colleges of Applied Arts and Technology (CAATs). The third was between the principles of academic autonomy and accountability.

The issue of access and cost was critical because PSE had moved from a pursuit of a minority to a pursuit of the majority of the population over the course of just two generations in Ontario. Successive governments had committed to providing spaces for all comers—the "access" aspect of what Trick (2006) described as the "access and equality paradigm" for PSE in Ontario. Potential students and their families want low-cost access to PSE instruction and credentials while taxpayers and finance ministers, on their side, impose budget constraints. Since PSE is voluntary and much of its benefit, especially in professional programs, accrues to students themselves, tuition should logically pay some of the cost of instruction. Since how much depends on program and other circumstances, including financial capacity of students and their families, tuition is never settled. Notwithstanding expanding enrolment in both universities and CAATs before the mid-1990s, restrictions on degree-granting—CAATs offered only diplomas and certificates and the seventeen privately funded institutions with degree-granting authority offered mainly religious degrees (Shanahan et al. 2014)—meant that the most sought-after baccalaureate credential was not available in proportion to demand.

The tension over the distinct roles of universities and CAATs had existed since the establishment of the CAATs in the 1960s. The vision for the CAATs at inception was that they would be equal in status to universities, but provide practical and professional instruction for students who would graduate into non-academic work. The PSE system was binary, with no formal transfer of credits between CAATs and universities, which became increasingly awkward over time as the number of students moving, or wishing to move, between them grew. A 1993 report commissioned by the NDP government, "No Dead Ends: Report of the Task Force on Advanced Training to the Minister of Education and Training," recommended more links among universities and CAATs, including credit transfer between the two types of institutions (Shanahan et al., 2014).

The third long-standing tension is perennial: between the principles of autonomy for academics and academic institutions and accountability for use of public funds. This tension plays out within institutions, between academics and administrators and, in the system, between leaders of institutions and various stakeholders.[11] Academics want freedom to instruct and research as they see fit. High on the list of constituents whose interests the provincial government is motivated to represent are students and their parents, which obliges it to pay at least some attention to quality of instruction. At the time, unlike many other provinces and many countries, Ontario had no quality assurance body outside the authority of the institutions themselves. Finally, the provincial government also represents the interests of taxpayers and others who want public support of PSE to pay social and economic benefits through research and human capital formation.

Historically, the government of Ontario's approach to the universities was quite deferential. Publicly funded universities required a charter from the Legislature, but the province did not approve courses and programs, nor systematically monitor outcomes. Universities, being autonomous, sought and largely received equal treatment from the provincial government, notwithstanding differences in their sizes, research capacity and other attributes—the "equality" aspect of Trick's "access and equality" paradigm. Enrolment largely determined funding, and the principle that instructors should be faculty who also undertake research – which is expensive and of debatable value to students, at least at the undergraduate level – was entrenched among universities.[12]

When troubles at some universities prompted the NDP government to appoint a task force, it went to the Ontario Council on University Affairs (OCUA), the long-standing advisory body representing universities, for suggestions. Its report, University Accountability: A Strengthened Framework (OCUA 1993b) promoted self-regulation. It advocated more accountability through the boards of universities themselves. It also advocated a quality-vetting agency within the OCUA, which would have vetted undergraduate programs, complementing the Ontario Council on Graduate Studies, which already vetted potential new graduate programs. The universities, defensive of their autonomy, disliked this proposal, and it went nowhere.

As for levering funding for social and economic goals, the NDP government, like the Liberal government before it, had shrunk the share of university funding linked to enrolment, and boosted the shares linked to programs in science and technology and to access for under-represented groups (Axelrod 2008). But the principle of equal treatment of institutions and per-student funding persisted (Trick 2006; Clark et all 2009) and efforts to coordinate or direct university programs from Queen's Park met with fierce resistance and came to nothing (Royce 1998).

The relative lightness of the PCs' commitments on PSE reflects the chronic, rather than acute, nature of these tensions. Unlike ESE, PSE presented no public crisis likely to determine the outcome of an election.

With respect to funding, cost and access, *NDV2* devoted attention to the need for tuition to replace public funding, notably in professional programs. It committed to let fees rise to 25 per cent of operating costs, while addressing access by requiring a share of new revenue to fund scholarships and bursaries, as well as proposing an expanded student loan program with income-contingent repayment. The *CSR* covered the same territory in its one column of text on PSE. It committed to reduce funding, with a reference to cuts in administrative costs, to partially deregulate tuition, and to provide income-contingent student loans.

Although neither *NDV2* nor the *CSR* made an explicit commitment under the PSE heading related to the shorter high-school program in the ESE part of the platform, that key plank carried with it an implied commitment: ensure that graduates in the double cohort who wanted spaces in PSE institutions would find them.

With respect to tension over the binary system of CAATs and universities, *NDV2* said nothing directly about credit transfers. It prefigured greater diversity among institutions, promising more specialization by colleges and universities in specific fields and fewer restrictions on private degree-granting universities. On autonomy and accountability, *NDV2* mentioned promoting private-sector investment in research, value-for-money audits of PSE institutions and their endowments, and training consultation centres at CAATs. None of these issues was politically salient enough to merit inclusion in the *CSR*. By the time of the 1999 *Blueprint*, however, the PCs were ready to tackle the binary system, committing to "take down the bureaucratic barriers" that prevented joint university/college programs and degrees.

As it did in ESE, the Harris government cut PSE operating grants shortly after taking office. Provincial transfers to postsecondary institutions fell from $3.4 billion in the 1995/96 year to $2.6 billion in

1996/97 and 1997/98. Although the province stepped up support for research with the Ontario Research and Development Challenge Fund in 1997, the Access to Opportunities Program to increase enrolment in science and engineering in 1998, and the Ontario Innovation Trust in 1999, transfers remained below their 1995/96 level until the advent of the double cohort in 2003/04 (Figure 5.4). Over the entire period from 1995/96 to 2003/04, provincial transfers rose at a compound annual rate of only 2 per cent in nominal terms, half the rate recorded by similar transfers in the rest of the country. Operating grants per full-time equivalent student to both universities and colleges in real terms were well below their 1995 levels through to 2003 (Clark et al. 2000).

The PCs delivered on a straightforward part of their PSE program: reducing provincial grants. No data exist on the degree to which universities and colleges, or the PSE system more generally, reduced administrative expenses over this period, and the proposed audits of institutions did not occur, so a judgment about alignment is not possible

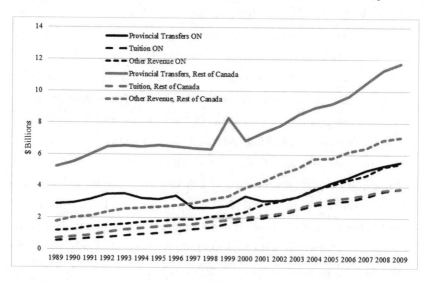

Figure 5.4 University and College Revenue by Type, Ontario and Rest of Canada

Source: Author's calculations from Statistics Canada, Table: 10-10-0045-01.

for that aspect of the program. Overall, a cautious grade of B+ seems appropriate on alignment.

With respect to impact, advocates for PSE naturally thought it unwise. For my evaluation, three considerations merit emphasis. First, provincial transfers were already smaller, as a share of sector revenue, in Ontario than in other parts of Canada. Second, major dependence on government funding is inconsistent with institutional autonomy. Third, the sector appears, as elaborated below, not just to have survived, but to have thrived during this period. On balance, I think a grade of A− is appropriate on impact, which yields an overall grade of A− with respect to funding.

The PCs also delivered on their promise to deregulate tuition for graduate and some professional programs. The first-degree programs affected included commerce, dentistry, law, medicine, optometry, pharmacy, and veterinary medicine, as well as engineering and computer science at universities participating in the Access to Opportunities Program, although not the largest professional programs of teaching and nursing (Trick 2005).

Tuition revenue of Ontario's PSE institutions climbed at a compound annual rate of 12 per cent between 1995/96 and 2002/03. This pace is consistent with the PCs' commitment to let tuition rise—it outpaced the 8 per cent pace of university and college tuition revenue increases in the rest of Canada. Perhaps surprisingly, it is not that big a break from the early 1990s under Rae's NDP, when tuition revenue rose at a similar pace. Over the period when the double cohort was entering PSE, the government capped tuition fee increases at 2 per cent for most programs (Shanahan et al., 2014), but rising enrolment continued to drive healthy revenue increases.

With respect to student support, the government tightened access to its Ontario Student Assistance Program (OSAP, an acronym some students of my generation translated as the "Ontario Stereo Acquisition Program"). Establishing a provincial income-contingent loan repayment scheme would have required cooperation with the federal government, which was not immediately forthcoming (Ibbitson 1997, 282–283). Instead, the province emphasized need-based support with matching grants, and required universities and colleges to set aside 30 per cent of tuition increases for bursaries. Further initiatives to support students were the $600 million Ontario Student Opportunity Trust Fund created in 1997, an enhanced Work Study Program in 2000, Aim for the Top tuition scholarships in 2001, and an increase in the number and value of Ontario Graduate Scholarships (Trick, 2005; Shanahan et al., 2014). Frustratingly, data on both beneficiaries and amounts of student loans are too messy to allow reliable generalizations about what happened.[13]

In assessing the PC record with respect to tuition and offsetting increases in student support, the failure to implement income-contingent student loans is a notable fail. In other respects, the PCs delivered: they partially deregulated tuition, and created new supports intended to focus student aid on those with less means to pay it. In the wake of the changes, tuition became more important as a source of revenue, especially in professional programs, a trend that continued in later years. On alignment, I award A− in this area, and on impact, I award A, for an overall grade of A−.

The PCs appear to have delivered on their implicit commitment to ensure PSE spaces for the double cohort. Tweaks to funding to encourage expansion in undergraduate enrolment and the Superbuild Program's support of capital projects gave the sector resources such that 2003's ratio of admissions to applications was in line with prior years (Anderson and Ben Jafaar 2003).

Headcounts in PSE are not straightforward. Even without the complication of the double cohort, inconsistent reporting among institutions, other changes in enrolment—full- versus part-time, among different types of institutions, and among programs—may create bumps and dips in the data (Figure 5.5).[14] The state of the economy also affects enrolment; the recession of the early 1990s boosted PSE enrolment in both Ontario and the rest of Canada (Clark et al. 2009) and the

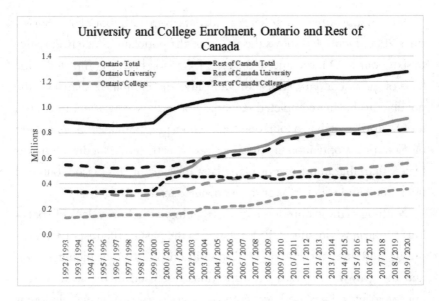

Figure 5.5 University and College Enrolment, Ontario and Rest of Canada

Source: Author's calculations from data in Statistics Canada Table 37-10-0018-01.

recovery likely flattened it in the mid-1990s. On their face, however, the available data support a success story about access. Between the 1995/96 and 2003/04 academic years, enrolment in the sector as a whole rose 31 per cent in Ontario versus 22 per cent in the rest of Canada. Enrolment in Ontario universities rose 25 per cent (versus 13 per cent in the rest of Canada) and enrolment in Ontario colleges rose 44 per cent (versus 36 per cent in the rest of Canada).

A compelling high-level measure of PSE access is the share of the population with a degree or other postsecondary certificate. Census data show the share of Ontario's population having completed a postsecondary education program rose from the early 1990s to the mid-2000s. The 1991 census showed the share with college certificates or diplomas at 12 per cent, the share with a university degree at 13 per cent, and the share having completed any program at 37 per cent. The 2006 census showed these shares at 18 per cent, 20 per cent and 51 per cent (Shanahan et al. 2014).

We can supplement these figures with data from the Labour Force Survey since 2000. Figure 5.6 shows the shares of the populations age twenty-five to sixty-four in Ontario and in the rest of Canada having completed some kind of postsecondary education, and also the combined shares of the populations having completed secondary or tertiary education, to control for Ontario's switch to a four-year high-school program in 2003. The share of Ontario's population in that age range with tertiary education was higher than that in the rest of Canada at the start of this period, bumped up in 2003 and widened over the following decade.

Nothing in these numbers suggests that higher tuition or lack of spaces hurt Ontarians' pursuit of PSE relative to the past or the rest of Canada during and after the Harris PCs' time in office. Overall, higher tuition and the growing diversity of institutions discussed in the next section appear to have increased access to postsecondary certificates, diplomas and degrees.

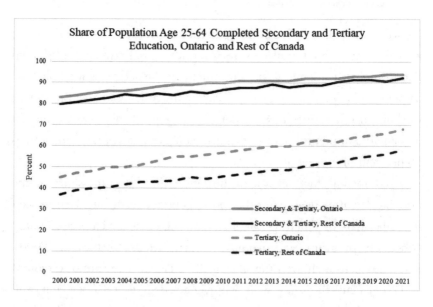

Figure 5.6 Share of Population Age 25–64 Completed Secondary and Tertiary Education, Ontario and Rest of Canada

Source: Author's calculations from Statistics Canada, Tables 37-10-0130-01 and 17-10-0060-01.

Although the PCs made no explicit commitments on access, their implicit commitments to create sufficient spaces seem strong enough to justify an alignment grade of B+. For impact, they deserve A in this area. The overall grade is A−.

* * *

The PCs' first major move with respect to institutional diversity in PSE was the *Choice and Excellence Act* in 2000. That act expanded degree-granting authority to CAATs, created the option for CAATs to become universities, and established procedures for publicly funded and private institutions outside Ontario to establish operations in the province.

In 2001, the government announced plans for the University of Ontario Institute of Technology (UOIT), Ontario's first new university in almost forty years. The UOIT was initially a partnership with Durham College, with the two institutions coordinating curriculum in technologically oriented programs.

Although the PCs lost power before they could proclaim the 2002 Ontario Colleges of Applied Art and Technology (OCAAT) act, which envisioned further expansion of the CAATs and their ability to confer degrees, the Liberal government under Dalton McGuinty went on to proclaim the legislation. By the end of the 2010s, eleven out-of-province public and private institutions, and nineteen in-province public and private institutions, were offering degree programs. A critical legacy of the PCs is the erosion of Ontario traditional binary PSE system, a rare revolution in a sector that has usually evolved slowly.

In this area, the PCs' actions aligned well with their commitments, and I award A on alignment. With respect to impact, an argument against the PC program would be that the original vision of CAATs and their certificates as equal in status to universities was a worthy one. The erosion of the binary system meant that the CAATs and their certificates would lose status, and they would seek to become universities and grant similar degrees, as has happened. But it is not clear what preferable course of action was available, since the forces for a more integrated system would not have abated. On balance, I think B+ makes sense on impact. The overall mark on system flexibility is A−.

PEQAB is a creation of the *Choice and Excellence Act* that deserves separate discussion. It formalized the processes by which institutions, other than existing universities, could grant degrees, and by which new PSE institutions, whose students would qualify for student support, could operate in Ontario. PEQAB's recommendations on both must go to the minister for approval.

A formal body advising the minister on degree programs was new in Ontario. It could have gotten off to a rough start because the government announced its intention to approve twelve new CAAT degree programs before applications had reached PEQAB. If too few applications had made appropriately strong cases for the proposed degrees, or shown high enough standards for their proposed curriculum and faculty, PEQAB would not have recommended twelve for consent. As it turned out, twelve applications were clearly above the rest, and a potential early test of the government's commitment to the new quality regime never occurred.

An independent quality-assessment agency of this type was not part of the PC education platform, so I award no mark on alignment here. With respect to impact, PEQAB filled a hole without infringing the autonomy of existing universities. Hoping my membership in its early days does not disqualify me from offering an opinion, I would say the quality of PEQAB's work has been high. It survived an initially skeptical successor Liberal government, and inspired imitation outside Ontario. On that basis, I award an A on impact, which is the overall grade in this area.

Quality and student achievement, so salient in ESE, had little profile in PSE. *NDV2* and the *CSR* said nothing about quality of PSE instruction. The government responded to criticisms in the 1996 report of the provincial auditor about lack of objectives for universities by announcing that the Ministry of Education and Training would collect and publish data on graduation rates, post-graduation employment rates and student-loan defaults by postsecondary institutions. It tweaked the funding formula to reward better outcomes on these measures, but criticisms of the formula and pushback from the institutions blunted the impact on actual dollars received (Trick 2005). Other than that, I know of no initiatives in that area by the PCs during their 1995–1999 term.

Establishment of the PEQAB in 2000 was a step toward provincial oversight of program quality, but as just noted, it covered no pre-existing universities. The universities continued in a self-governing mode, with their own programs for quality assurance at the undergraduate and graduate levels. The OCAAT act created an oversight body, the Ontario Colleges Quality Assurance Service, to examine credentials and programs. That too is in the self-governing tradition.

Assigning any mark in the area of quality of instruction separate from the PEQAB may appear a stretch. Because the PCs made no commitments in the area, I award no mark on alignment. The diversity of learning outcomes in PSE is markedly different from ESE, which has a workable consensus about what students should know and be able to do before leaving school. It is nevertheless disconcerting that so little information about the quality of instruction and other aspects of student experience in Ontario PSE is available to students, parents, and taxpayers (Clark et al., 2009; Usher, 2022a and 2022b). For that reason, I assign B on impact, which yields an overall B in this area.

When it comes to balancing academic autonomy with accountability for use of public funds more generally, the PCs committed to value-for-money audits of universities. They did not move on that once in office. Instead, they built on the previous government's thinking about steering PSE through funding incentives. The opening step was publishing key performance indicators such as graduation rates, graduate employment rates and student loan default rates for CAATs and universities in 1999. In the 2000/01 academic year, the government attached funding related to indicators of accessibility and performance, the first instance of this type of conditional funding in Canada (Shanahan et al., 2014). Although durability does not prove that a policy is wise, it is notable that the McGuinty Liberals continued and expanded this approach, adding indicators related to retention and graduate satisfaction, and making funding more responsive to performance on those indicators.

The PCs did commit to obtaining more private-sector money for research, a second area where governments seek to influence academic activity to align with other economic and social goals. The PCs supported Ontario institutions in their efforts to secure federal and private funds, with matching grants through the Ontario Research and Development Challenge Fund, and supported research through the Ontario Innovation Trust. Both these programs resulted in larger grants to larger more research-intensive universities such as Toronto, McMaster and Queen's (Trick 2006).

Assigning a mark in this area is easier than in instruction because the PCs did make firm commitments. They did not follow through on value-for-money audits. But they did support institutions' efforts to secure private funds. So, a grade of B− seems fair on alignment. When it comes to impact, the continuity of the incentive funding for PSE institutions with what the NDP had done before and what the Liberals did afterwards is notable. Universities' formal devotion to the relatively expensive model of teaching undergraduates with faculty pursuing research did not change. The PCs attempted to steer at the margin rather than centralizing control over PSE programs and institutions. The evidence on access and completion of postsecondary education cited earlier incline me to A− for impact in this area. The average comes out to B.

In PSE, the relative lightness of campaign commitments on the PCs' part leaves some blanks in the alignment criteria. The average of the grades I award in that category: B+ on funding, cost and access, A on system structure, and B− on autonomy and accountability, average to B+.

On impact, the wisdom of the government's commitments and actions, and the quality of results, assessments will differ with an assessor's views about the private versus the social benefits of PSE, the province's light touch with respect to instruction quality, the merits of the old binary system, and the appropriate degree of accountability for public money spent on PSE. Averaging across those areas, I come up with A−, a grade that reflects success with the financial parts of the program and the continued rise in tertiary credentials among Ontario's population. The average grade for PSE generally comes to A−.

* * *

Where does this assessment come out overall, and what can we learn from it?

My overall assessment of the PC governments' record in education is positive. For alignment, correspondence between commitments and actions, I award A− in ESE and B+ in PSE. For impact, wisdom, and quality of results, I award B+ in ESE and A− in PSE. The average across both types of criteria comes out to B+ for ESE and A− for PSE. Because the averages tended toward the top of the bands, the overall grades for alignment and impact are A−, which is the grade for the entire report card (Table 5.2).

In drawing lessons about politics generally, and about tackling such contentious areas as curriculum, testing, and accountability of educators, or cutting spending, my positive assessment of the Harris and Eves governments contrasts sharply with widely held views that the PCs' education policies were bad and/or doomed the PCs to electoral defeat in 2003. An obvious rejoinder, worth repeating because critics of Mike Harris usually skip over it, is that the PCs won a second majority in 1999 on a platform that promised more of the same in both education and fiscal policy. Nevertheless, because money was so central to the confrontation with unions and other people who worked in and supported public

Table 5.2 Report Card on PCs' Record in Education

	Alignment	Impact	Overall
Elementary and Secondary			
Curriculum			
What	A+	A	A+
How	B+	B+	B+
Overall	*A*	*A–*	*A–*
Assessment and Accountability			
Report Cards	A	A	A
Quality/Professionalism of Teachers	A–	B	B+
Testing of Students	B+	B	B
Student Achievement	A+	A+	A+
Overall	*A*	*A–*	*A–*
Governance and Funding			
Taxation and Funding Formula	B–	B+	B
School Boards	A–	C	B
School Councils	C–	D	D+
Funding for Independent Schools	NA	A	A
Overall	*B–*	*B–*	*B–*
Grade Elementary and Secondary	A–	B+	B+
Post-Secondary			
Funding, Cost and Access			
Funding	B+	A–	A–
Tuition and Student Support	A–	A	A–
Access	B+	A	A–
Overall	*B+*	*A*	*A–*
Structure of System			
System Flexibility	A	B+	A–
PEQAB	NA	A	A
Overall	*A*	*A–*	*A–*

(Contd.)

Table 5.2 (*Contd.*)

	Alignment	Impact	Overall
Autonomy and Accountability			
Quality of Instruction	NA	B	B
Autonomy versus Accountability	B−	A−	B
Overall	*B−*	*B+*	*B*
Grade Post-Secondary	B+	A−	A−
Overall Grade	A−	A−	A−

education, it is natural to wonder if an A-range report card would seem less peculiar if the PCs had not pursued their education and fiscal goals at the same time.

Ideally, a government intent on improving student outcomes would have spooned out financial sugar to help the quality and accountability medicine go down. As a practical matter, however, fiscal pressure may provide crucial impetus without which resolute action on other fronts does not happen.

The vehement opposition of many stakeholders, notably the teacher unions, suggests that something particularly jarring happened after the mid-1990s. But militant teacher unions are not unusual in Canada or in other countries, and it is more than plausible that fights over instructional quality and accountability on the one hand and over money on the other would have played out similarly over the following quarter century even if Mike Harris had never been premier. The PCs' commitment to save money was no less central to the 1995 and 1999 platforms than student achievement, and their delivering on that commitment is material in my strong overall grade. Since those savings occurred along with major and mostly durable improvements in student achievement and opportunities in postsecondary education, I think the PC governments of the late 1990s and early 2000s in Ontario deserve high marks for their education policies.

References

Anderson, Stephen E. and Sonia Ben Jaafar (2003). "Policy Trends in Ontario Education: 1990–2003." ICEC Working Paper #1. Toronto: Ontario Institute for Studies in Education of the University of Toronto. September.

Axelrod, Paul (2008) "Public Policy in Ontario Higher Education: From Frost to Harris," in Fisher, Donald and Adrienne S. Chan, eds., *The Exchange University: Corporatization of Academic Culture*. Vancouver: UBC Press.

Baker, Michael, Jonathan Gruber and Kevin Milligan (2019). "The Long-Run Impacts of a Universal Child Care Program," American Economic Journal: Economic Policy, Vol. 11, No. 3. August.

Clark, I.D., G. Moran, M.L. Skolnik, and D. Trick (2009). *Academic Transformation: The Forces Reshaping Higher Education in Ontario*. Montreal and Kingston: Queen's Policy Studies Series, McGill-Queen's University Press.

Coalition for Education Reform (1994). *Could Do Better: What's Wrong with Public Education in Ontario and How to Fix It*. Toronto.

Council of Ministers of Education, Canada (CMEC) (2019). *Measuring up: Canadian Results of the OECD PISA 2018 Study—The Performance of Canadian 15-Year-Olds in Reading, Mathematics, and Science*. Toronto.

Cowley, Peter, and Paige MacPherson (2022). *Testing Canadian K-12 Students—Regional Variability, Room for Improvement: A Cross-Canada Comparison of K-12 Provincial Assessment Programs*. Fraser Institute.

Education Quality and Accountability Office (EQAO) (2013). EQAO: Ontario's Provincial Assessment Program: Its History and Influence. Toronto: Queen's Printer for Ontario.

Ibbotson, John (1997). *Promised Land: Inside the Mike Harris Revolution*. Prentice Hall Canada.

Johnson, David (2019). "Resources and outcomes at Ontario secondary schools: 2005–06 to 2017–18." C.D. Howe Institute Intelligence Memo. May 17.

Mackenzie, Hugh (2015). "The Long Shadow." Ontario Policy Magazine. Canadian Centre for Policy Alternatives.

Ontario Coalition for Education Reform (OCER) (1999). *Could Still Do Better: Improving Public Education in Ontario.* Toronto.

Ontario Progressive Conservative Caucus (OPCC) (1992). *New Directions Volume Two: A Blueprint for Learning in Ontario.* Toronto, October.

Progressive Conservative Party of Ontario (PCPO1) (1995). *The Common Sense Revolution* (7th Printing). Toronto.

Progressive Conservative Party of Ontario (PCPO2) (1999). *Blueprint: Mike Harris's Plan to Keep Ontario on the Right Track.* Toronto.

Robson, William, and Claudia R. Hepburn (2002). *Learning from Success: What Americans Can Learn from School Choice in Canada.* Milton and Rose D. Friedman Foundation and the Fraser Institute. Indianapolis and Vancouver.

Royce, Diane (1998). "University System Coordination and Planning in Ontario, 1945 to 1996." Thesis submitted in conformity with the requirements for the Degree of Doctor of Education, Ontario Institute for Studies in Education of the University of Toronto.

Shanahan, Theresa, Glen Jones, Donald Fisher and Kjell Rubenson (2014). "Contradictory Trends on PSE Policy in Ontario." In Donald Fisher, Kjell Rubenson, Theresa Shanahan and Claude Trottier, eds., *The Development of Postsecondary Education Systems in Canada: A Comparison between British Columbia, Ontario, and Quebec,* 1980–2010. McGill-Queen's University Press.

Trick, David (2005). "Continuity, Retrenchment and Renewal: The Politics of Government-University Relations in Ontario, 1985–2002." Thesis submitted in conformity with the requirements for the degree of Doctor of Philosophy, Graduate Department of Political Science, University of Toronto.

Trick, David (2006). "Continuity, Retrenchment and Renewal in Public Policy: The Case of Government-University Relations in Ontario, 1985–2003." Paper prepared for the annual conference of the

Canadian Political Science Association, York University, Toronto, June 3.

Usher, Alex (2022a). "Enhancing Quality." Higher Education Strategy Associates. February 24.

Usher, Alex (2022b). "The Fracturing of Global Rankings." Higher Education Strategy Associates. May 19.

Usher, Alex (2022c). "The Long Strange History of Loan Remission Policies." Higher Education Strategy Associates. September 8.

Notes

1   The views presented here are personal, and the education-related activities referred to in this chapter were carried out in a personal capacity, not as a representative of any organization. I thank editor Alister Campbell for encouragement and criticisms, David Johnson of Wilfrid Laurier University for his assistance in assembling and interpreting EQAO data, Pamela Best, Karen Griffith, Andrija Popovic and Robert Roussel of Statistics Canada for help with data on ESE and PSE enrolment and finances, and David Trick and Alex Usher for advice and materials on PSE. Notwithstanding all this help, errors may remain—responsibility for them and for the views expressed here is mine.

2   About two of the fifteen substantive pages in the *CSR*.

3   I was a principal author of two assessments of ESE in Ontario published by the OCER (OCER 1994; OCER 1999), which I draw on in that part of this chapter.

4   I use a standard scale for letter grades relative to percentages: A+ for 90 per cent or above, A for 85–89 per cent, A– for 80–84 per cent, B+ for 77–79 per cent, B for 73–76 per cent, B– for 70–72 per cent, C+ for 67–69 per cent, C for 63–66 per cent, C– for 60–62 per cent, D+ for 57–59 per cent, D for 53–56 per cent, D– for 50–52 per cent and F for less than 50 per cent. I convert letter grades for each criterion to percentages using the mid-point of the relevant scale and convert the averages in each area back to letter grades for the summaries in each area and overall. This approach sometimes means that one grade of A– and another of B+, for example, will produce an average of A– or B+, depending on the rounding.

5   During episodes such as the struggle to get punctuation into the language curriculum, or the incorporation of the classification of living things into the science curriculum, I learned to check agreed changes against subsequent drafts line by line. I even took calls at home from members of the writing teams who feared that openly pushing for content and sequential learning in the documents would hurt their careers.

6   Professor David Johnson of Wilfrid Laurier University has published several studies of school- and board-level achievement using EQAO data for the C.D. Howe Institute. His work in the area was almost stymied at the outset when the EQAO balked at releasing school-level data and slowed by his discovering numerous errors in the data, such as all students at a mixed school being coded as one sex. Lack of transparency hides such errors and encourages superficial use of the data—simple ranking of schools by average scores, for example—that feed criticisms of testing.

7   At the time of writing, no assessment of the impact of school closures during the COVID-19 pandemic in Ontario has occurred, even though reams of data and analysis, with some alarming findings about the impact of closures on students from less academically supportive backgrounds, have come out of the United States and European countries. Testing in Ontario has not yielded timely results during an episode when the province most needed them.

8   The Canadian average is the average of each province (languages considered separately where applicable) and territory, each jurisdiction/language treated as one unit. Nunavut came into existence in 1999, so I omit it.

9   The 1998 reading tests is not a satisfactory comparison, since the new program was barely in place. Unfortunately, the SAIP ended before the reading test planned for the early 2000s happened.

10   Anderson and Ben Jafaar (2003) provide a detailed account of this period, an account I draw on heavily in this section.

11   Alexrod (2008) frames this tension differently, referring to perceived economic utility as both a justification for PSE support in the minds of much of the public and politicians, and a threat to academic integrity and autonomy. His Marxist lens adds liveliness to his account of the relations between the university sector and the Ontario government during the post-war period. Royce (1998) documents the interactions between the sector and the government with more sympathy to the case for government coordination. I rely on both sources in this section.

12   Clark et al. (2009) note the absence of convincing evidence that conducting research correlates with effective instruction and also observe that the growing importance of contract instructors shows the limits of the ideal when it comes to actual practice.

13   Trick (2006) presents data showing a surge and later decline in beneficiaries in the mid-1990s, but a surge and later decline in dollar amounts in the late 1990s. Usher (2022c) notes that changes in remissions policies, federal programs, and accounting distort the numbers.

14   Statistics Canada's data for the period are administrative data from PSE institutions based on enrolment in programs, which means that students enrolled in more than one program would get counted more than once.

CHAPTER 6

From Welfare to Workfare

The Transformation of Social Assistance

"412,000 off the dole is one of my proudest accomplishments as premier of this province." —Premier Mike Harris, 1999[1]

ENRICHED BENEFITS, RISING COSTS AMID a deep and prolonged recession, and more than 1.3 million Ontarians on welfare. Those were the realities for Mike Harris and the Progressive Conservative Party when they won a landslide election on June 8, 1995.

Welfare reform[2] was a crucial part of the party's agenda well before the 1995 campaign. Nearly two years earlier, Harris and the Progressive Conservatives held a major press conference where they profiled an Ontario woman who claimed she was leaving her job to take advantage of highly generous social assistance benefits. It was a powerful message and a clever idea to personify the growing problems inherent in the province's welfare system and ultimately establish a popular case for reform.

There was just one problem: It turned out her claims were not vetted, and her calculations were well off, creating an embarrassing gaffe for the Progressive Conservatives and a temporary setback for the cause of welfare reform.

Yet, over the long term, the Harris government marched forward with significant reforms to Ontario's costly and unperforming social assistance system. It proved to be one of the biggest and most controversial parts of the premier's governing record.

In the party's policy manifesto, the *CSR*, the Progressive Conservatives promised to cut social assistance benefits, which were high relative to other Canadian provinces, to bring in work or work training requirements for welfare recipients, and to enhance welfare verification (including verifying applicants' income and other financial assets).

Once in power, the Harris government lived up to these promises. In 1997, the government launched a complete transformation of the province's social assistance system, including creating new programs aimed at helping people get back to work and establishing a more generous stream of social assistance for Ontarians with disabilities. The totality of these changes restored the principle of social assistance as a temporary financial stopgap for people who fell out of employment rather than a long-term income substitution for paid employment.

It is worth pointing out that despite the controversy surrounding these changes, then and since, the basic structure of the Harris government's reforms is still mostly in place in Ontario nearly twenty-five years later, including benefit levels that have not shifted materially since.[3]

At the time, much of the attention was paid to the budgetary impetus for reform. The Ontario government was running large fiscal deficits, and social assistance spending represented more than 10 per cent of total provincial expenditures. Yet the historical record tells us that Harris and the Progressive Conservatives were not merely motivated by fiscal considerations. Aligned with a burgeoning conservative (and sometimes bi-partisan) movement on both sides of the border, they saw an essential connection between work and human dignity. Accounts show the premier, in particular, was motivated by the idea that work provides people with a sense of purpose and self-worth that was a crucial precondition for meaningful, dignified relationships between individuals, families, and communities.[4]

The changes made by the Harris government were significant by any measure. Benefits were cut by over 20 per cent within months of the Progressive Conservatives assuming office, although social assistance rates still remained above other Canadian provinces.[5] By the end of the Harris "revolutionaries'" time in government in 2003, the number of welfare beneficiaries in Ontario had fallen by more than 600,000 and annual spending on social assistance was down by nearly $2 billion.

These results are often presented as a major success by Harris and others who were involved in his government. While there are questions about how much of these changes resulted from the Harris government's policies and how much from improved macroeconomic conditions, the government's actions undoubtedly played an important role.

These changes were not without controversy. While many Ontarians supported their spirit of the reforms and even their specifics, detractors were fierce in casting the government as callous and cruel. Welfare reform was, in other words, a major accomplishment for the Harris government as a well as a major source of antipathy toward Harris and his party that persists to this day.

What has been missing in the public policy literature is a broad critical evaluation of the Harris government's intentions, how they were manifested in welfare reforms, and the economic and social outcomes. This chapter aims to provide such an evaluation and will proceed in three sections:

- The first section will provide the context for the difficult situation that the Harris government inherited. It will give a historical overview of the development of social assistance policy, analyze the growth in social assistance caseloads, evaluate the economic and fiscal conditions that preceded the government, and discuss the intellectual ethos within which the Harris government conceived of its reforms.

- The second section will discuss the policy changes made by the government and critically evaluate how much of the reductions in welfare caseloads and costs can be attributed to its reforms versus broader economic factors.

- The final section will discuss the legacy of the Harris government and examine how Ontario's social assistance system has changed in subsequent years.

The impetus for the Harris government's *CSR* and the changes that the government would implement to Ontario's social assistance policy cannot be assessed without understanding four trends that began in the decade prior to the 1995 provincial election. These trends set the stage and arguably demonstrate the need for a new policy direction on social assistance.

The four trends were (1) an expansion of eligibility criteria and benefits by the previous Liberal and New Democratic governments that contributed to a swelling of the province's welfare rolls, (2) a deep and sustained recession beginning in 1990 that massively expanded demand for social assistance benefits, (3) a deteriorating provincial fiscal situation and changes to federal cost sharing for social assistance programs, and (4) a shift in the intellectual climate regarding the purpose and design of social assistance programs in Canada, the United States, and elsewhere.

The 1980s saw the beginning of a reorientation in the character of Ontario's welfare programs. If previous iterations of Ontario social assistance had a narrow focus on "deservingness" to determine who ought to receive support (e.g., mothers), the 1980s saw a shift toward a focus on "employability" and a greater connection between social assistance and more active labour market policies.[6] Social assistance, in other words, became a social safety net that was broadly available to those Ontarians who found themselves out of work. It was supposed to be a temporary stopgap, but, due to a combination of poor policy choices and deteriorating economic conditions, welfare became a long-term substitute for paid work for a growing number of people in the province.

The focus on strengthening the connection between social assistance and employability can be seen in the 1988 *Transitions* report produced by the province's Social Assistance Review Committee.[7] As McMaster University political scientist Peter Graefe explains, the report aimed to strike a balance between workfare, which was gaining momentum in the United States, and an expansion of social rights to include adequate benefits, childcare, transportation, training, and, ultimately, a right to work, among others.[8] One way of achieving this balance was through "opportunity planning," whereby social assistance recipients were encouraged to transition back into the labour force or provided opportunities to develop new skills that reflected labour market demands.

A major justification for the Social Assistance Review Committee's recommendation of a greater connection between the labour market and social assistance was a recognition that, while most people on social assistance indicated that they would prefer to be working and not receiving government assistance, the structure of the social assistance system in Ontario was actively discouraging work and creating a form of dependence.[9] Social assistance recipients would have their benefits reduced, or curtailed altogether, if they worked more than a specified number of hours in a given week or month, creating an active barrier for beneficiaries to pursue self-reliance.

Upon the release of the *Transitions* report, Ontario's then Liberal government, led by David Peterson, faced bureaucratic constraints in its ability to realize the "opportunity planning" vision on a large scale. Instead, the government's approach to social assistance essentially favoured benefit enhancement.[10] When the subsequent NDP government, led by Bob Rae, was elected in 1990, there was an even greater focus on raising recipient benefits and boosting eligibility more generally.[11] A notable example of this tendency was when the Rae government enacted a child benefit in order to honour its commitment to expand social welfare programs.[12]

In response to these expansionary trends in social assistance, Mike Harris laid out a critique of Ontario welfare policy in a speech to the legislature in favour of an opposition motion on welfare reform in November 1994:

The fact is that the current system is an unmitigated disaster, one of the worst in the world—one of the worst for the taxpayers, one of the worst for creating a cycle of dependency, one of the worst for abuse and fraud, one of the easiest systems to rip off, if that's the goal of some people, but most importantly, a system with a horrendous cost to the taxpayers, seven or eight times the cost of just 12 years ago, that is actually, with all those dollars, doing a worse job today than it did just 12 years ago. . .

In fact, the system that was inherited by the current administration in 1990 was out of control. The lack of controls, the lack of empowerment of our professional social workers, who neither this administration nor the current one will even—we're the last province in Canada to recognize, empower and register as a profession social work, which is another disgrace: the very professionals themselves, the experts who came forward, the will and the desire from business, from all three political parties throughout that period of 1985 to 1990 for reform, and not one step was taken. . .

As a result, not only have taxpayers been ripped off, not only have we contributed to a loss of work ethic; the massive loss of pride, of hope, of opportunity for some one million Ontarians is the real tragedy in doing nothing. Doing nothing, sitting there pretending to analyse, pretending to have compassion, making all the statements and doing nothing, is absolutely the worst possible thing that can be done.[13]

This policy status quo became unsustainable in the face of the recession that began in 1990, which caused an explosion of social assistance caseloads and costs. Growing concerns about rising budgetary deficits and the need for spending control eventually led to policy efforts to establish greater connections between social assistance and the labour market. The result was that, while there was a growing political recognition that reform was needed, little substantive reform to social assistance would occur until after the Progressive Conservative Party's election.

In 1990, Canada entered a deep recession that lasted several years and dramatically increased the number of Ontarians receiving social assistance benefits. This was largely a result of the downturn in the business cycle and the accompanying spike in unemployment, but also, to some degree, of the expansion of eligibility and the enrichment of benefits outlined above. The end result was a significant expansion in the province's welfare rolls; in fact, the number of social assistance beneficiaries in Ontario more than doubled from 1989 to 1994, when social assistance caseloads peaked.[14] This point cannot be overstated: In a mere five years, the number of welfare beneficiaries in Ontario increased from just under 575,000 to over 1.3 million.

To put this in perspective, at the height of the province's social assistance demands in 1994, more than 14 per cent of the under-sixty-four-old population were social assistance recipients[15] (Figure 6.1).[16] As will be discussed below, the massive expansion in the number of Ontarians on social assistance led to a significant growth in the cost of social assistance provision at a time when government revenues were depressed by the poor economy. The combination of the expanded welfare rolls and their rising fiscal costs would serve as a key framing for the Harris government's push to reform the province's social assistance programs.

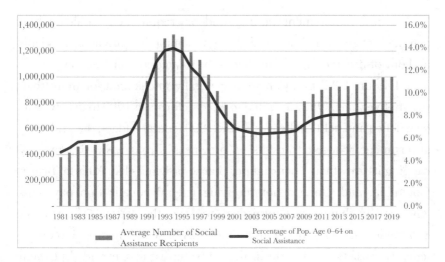

Figure 6.1 Number of Social Assistance Recipients in Ontario, 1981–2019[17]

Source: Government of Ontario (2022); Statistics Canada (2021); author calculations.

* * *

Beginning in 1966, the federal government had established the Canada Assistance Plan (CAP) to provide dollar-for-dollar funding to provinces for the provision of social assistance programs.[18] The CAP placed three substantive requirements on provinces as a condition to receive the funding.

The first was that there had to be a needs-test for the provision of benefits. While provinces had the broad ability to determine eligibility for general support and the level of benefits, they were required under the CAP to test applicant need by taking into account both income and access to assets and other forms of external support. If an individual met the requirements set out by the province, he or she could not be denied social assistance payments.

The second was that no individual could be denied benefits for refusing to take part in a work program.[19] This meant that provincial social assistance schemes could not require as a condition of eligibility that social assistance recipients work or pursue work.

The third requirement was that residency requirements could not be a condition of social assistance eligibility, meaning that provincial residents and out-of-province applicants had to be treated in a similar way.

While the CAP program went generally unchanged for more than twenty-five years, Ottawa started to enact reforms in 1990 to deal with its own deficit and debt challenges. In the 1990 federal budget, the Mulroney government reduced transfers to provinces through the program by capping its growth at 5 per cent per year to provinces like Alberta, British Columbia, and Ontario not receiving federal equalization payments The policy change was projected to save the federal government $75 million in 1990/91.[20] This limit on CAP's spending growth reduced federal transfers to Ontario in the 1991/92 fiscal year and kept them below 1990/91 levels until 1994/95 (Figure 6.2).

The timing was bad for Ontario. As discussed above, the reduction in federal transfers came at a time when the number of social assistance beneficiaries was rapidly expanding because of the persistent and deep

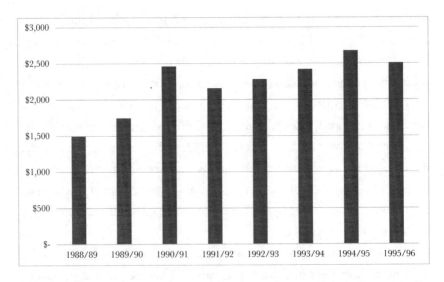

Figure 6.2 Ontario Government Revenue from CAP, 1988/89–1995/96 ($ Millions)

Source: Ontario Public Accounts, 1988/89–1995/96.

recession that had begun in 1990. The federal cuts placed considerable financial pressure on the Ontario government, which was also seeing total revenues fall and the size of its budgetary deficits rising. When the recession finally began to wane in 1994, the Ontario government was spending $6.7 billion in social assistance (12 per cent of total expenses) and had been running annual budgetary deficits of over $10 billion in each of the previous four years.

The federal government dealt Ontario another fiscal blow with the introduction of its 1995 budget. As Ottawa continued its efforts to consolidate its finances and reduce its budgetary deficits, it undertook a wide-ranging program review that resulted in the decision to end the CAP (and the Established Programs Financing (EPF) program), which would be replaced with the new Canada Health and Social Transfer (CHST) block-grant.[21]

The fiscal impact of this change would be a net reduction in transfers to the provinces. From 1995/96 to 1996/97, for instance, the shift from the CAP/EPF model to the CHST reduced federal transfers by approximately $2.8 billion (Figure 6.4). The reductions in federal transfers from the CAP/EPF baseline persisted well into the future, which added to Ontario's fiscal pressures and made the ballooning social assistance program increasingly unsustainable.[22]

However, for governments with intentions to reform social assistance programs, the shift to the block-grant CHST came with a significant upside—in particular, the removal of standards requirements, save for the residency requirement within the CAP.[23] The removal of CAP's restrictions on "workfare" would enable the new Ontario government to make many of the social assistance design changes it desired without jeopardizing federal funding. Furthermore, the removal of cost-sharing allowed the provinces to fully capture any savings from reducing expenditures on social assistance, thereby adding to the fiscal incentives for reform.

Beyond rising concerns about the number of beneficiaries of social assistance and its overall fiscal costs, there was also a shifting intellectual

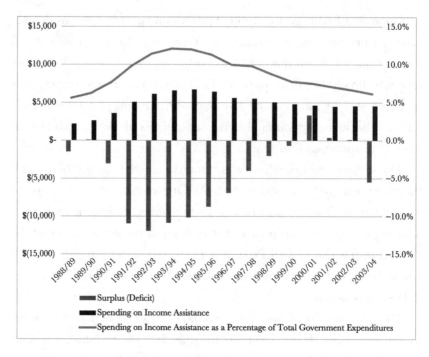

Figure 6.3 Ontario Government Spending on Income Assistance and Fiscal
Balance, 1988/89–2002/03 ($ Millions)

Source: Ontario Public Accounts, 1988/89–2003/04.

tide within conservatism in the years prior to the *CSR* about the moral
costs of government dependency. Indeed, conservatives were increasingly
concerned with the connection between work, human dignity, and the
nature of a meaningful life, and, in turn, began to set out normative
objections to a social welfare policy that disincentivized paid employment.
A quotation from a Fraser Institute publication that evaluated Ontario's
welfare system aptly sums up the concern that many conservatives were
articulating at the time:

> Work helps define us as individuals. Employment is not just a means
> of subsistence; it gives us a sense of community and of contributing.
> Work provides opportunities to socialize and structures our lives.

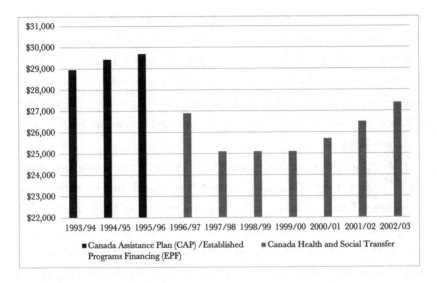

Figure 6.4 Federal Health and Social Transfers to the Provinces, 1993/94–2002/03 ($ Millions)

Source: Government of Canada (1995); Government of Canada (1996)

Work provides an important model for children, who learn to value work from their parents' example. Employment allows members of society to contribute through taxes to services we consider important that would not otherwise be available. The absence of work affects us socially, economically, psychologically, emotionally, and physically. Work is intrinsically rewarding, inherently valued, and should be encouraged by every possible means: there are incalculable human and financial costs associated with its alternative. Prolonged unemployment leads to apathy and pessimism. Recipients begin to believe that they are incapable of finding employment and so they stop looking. They become comfortable and begin 'settling in' with the notion of others providing for them.[24]

In this way, social assistance and potential dependency on government support were viewed through a normative lens as well as a fiscal one. These ideas, which mainly found their origins in a combination of neoconservative social science and Catholic social thought, became a major intellectual catalyst for the push for workfare programs aimed at connecting individuals on social assistance either to new jobs or to training programs. Put differently, conservative policy thinking across the Anglosphere was increasingly reflective of the old proverb: "If you give a man a fish, you feed him for a day. If you teach a man to fish, you feed him for a lifetime."

It is important to emphasize here that these sentiments were not just an intellectual veneer to conceal a conservative impulse to kick undeserving recipients off welfare. Many conservatives, including, for instance, 1988 US presidential candidate Jack Kemp, were genuinely committed to helping those in need get a leg up. But their key insight was that the best means were not through expansive government support programs that discouraged work, but through targeted efforts to connect individuals directly to new work or provide support for retraining.

The ideational shift for conservatives was not, as mentioned, limited to Canada. American conservatives also came to emphasize the value of dignity and work as core conservative principles and began enacting them through policymaking.[25] Experimentation with workfare programs began at the state level under the Reagan administration. They then found expression at the federal level with the bipartisan passage of the *Personal Responsibility and Work Opportunity Reconciliation Act,* which was signed into law by President Clinton in 1996. This federal welfare reform in the United States had similarities with the subsequent changes enacted by the Harris government, though Clinton's was arguably even more radical, including, for instance, a five-year lifetime limit on receiving assistance, among several other changes.[26]

While conservative intellectual thinking in Canada and elsewhere on social assistance had shifted toward a greater focus on workfare, growing concerns about state dependency and the rising share of the working-age population on welfare extended across other parts of the political spectrum. Both the *Transitions* report and even the Rae government in its later stages recognized the need to strengthen the link between welfare recipients and the labour market.

Harris frequently talked about these issues as he built the case for reform. In a November 1994 speech to the Legislature, for instance, the then-official opposition leader spoke of the ill effects of a "cycle of dependency," including "the loss of work ethic; the massive loss of pride, of hope, of opportunity for some one million Ontarians is the real tragedy in doing nothing."[27] This speech is notable precisely because the fiscal case for reform was demonstratively subordinate to the normative arguments in favour of supporting paid work as a source of meaning, purpose, and dignity.

In summer 1993, against the backdrop of significant growth in the number of recipients and fiscal costs of social assistance, Harris and the Progressive Conservatives engaged in an infamous bit of political theatre that would set the tone for their eventual policy reforms aimed at cutting social assistance benefits and getting the Ontarians receiving those benefits back to work. That August, Harris held a press conference where he introduced Ontarians to Helle Hulgaard, a single mother of two school-aged children. The Ontario civil servant earning $41,000 claimed that, after doing the math, she would only make $20 less a month on welfare and was therefore quitting her job to collect benefits.[28]

It was a powerful expression of the argument that the province's social assistance system had abandoned its core mission of serving as a basic safety net for those transitioning in and out of the labour force and was increasingly becoming a rational alternative to work for too many Ontarians. Harris used Hulgaard as an indictment of the system, arguing that "people make more money to stay home than it does to work" and that it "takes the heart out of good people who want to work and pay their way."[29] At the same time, he defended Hulgaard herself:

Many people might call Helle Hulgaard lazy: She's able-bodied and intelligent, she should be working. That would be a mistake.

Helle wants to work. But who can blame her for seizing the chance to make the same or more money while caring for her children at home?[30]

The problem is that Hulgaard's arithmetic was incorrect, and Harris' staff had failed to vet her claims in full. Media quickly found social welfare experts who calculated that by leaving her job and collecting social assistance, Hulgaard would have netted several hundred dollars less a month relative to her employment income in Ontario's civil service. After some days of further analysis, the Tories were able to publish a corrected version, which confirmed that Hulgaard's conclusion was correct even if her math was wrong. But by then it was far too late. What seemed like a strong salvo across the bow of Ontario's social assistance system instead became a damaging gaffe for the Progressive Conservatives. The experience nevertheless exemplified what *Globe and Mail* columnist John Ibbitson called the "messianic zeal" that the Harris government would bring to welfare reform once in power.[31]

* * *

Social assistance reform was a major part of the Progressive Conservative Party's 1995 election platform, the *CSR*. The plan focused on reducing taxes, creating jobs, and cutting government spending, of which social assistance reform figured prominently. In particular, the platform stated that a Progressive Conservative government would:

open up new opportunities and restore hope for people by breaking the cycle of dependency. That will be the goal of our welfare reform. The best social assistance program ever created is a real job, and this plan will generate hundreds of thousands of those. In the meantime, we must move to control costs and help people return to the workforce.[32]

The party's platform went on to explain that "while we can no longer afford the growing costs of the welfare system, we can keep benefits above the national average, and give recipients a chance to earn more money at part-time jobs."[33] However, their focus was not just on cutting people off welfare to find fiscal savings. The policy platform and accompanying communications reflected the intellectual ethos of the broader Anglo-American conservative movement, which emphasized a deep connection between work and human dignity.

The Progressive Conservatives specified three areas of reform. The first was the establishment of workfare and learnfare programs. With the ending of the federal cost-sharing CAP program and its requirements, Ontario could now tie welfare to work. The platform therefore committed to requiring all able-bodied recipients of social assistance (excluding single parents of young children) to either work or participate in retraining as a condition of receiving benefit payments. While the Progressive Conservatives did not claim that this condition would produce immediate cost-savings, they argued that work-based conditions would reduce recidivism and thus cut costs down the road.

The second proposed area of reform was to address welfare fraud and overpayments. The Progressive Conservatives estimated that welfare fraud had cost the province $247 million since 1990. They promised that a "province-wide computer system, coupled with a strictly enforced program of photo-identification for all welfare recipients, will be at the centre of this effort."

Finally, the third area of reform was to reduce welfare benefits. The Progressive Conservatives contended that Ontario had the most generous welfare benefits in North America and that this was partly to blame for the province's burgeoning caseload. It was proposed that welfare benefits would be set at 10 per cent above the national average for all other provinces, with an estimated cost savings of $1 billion. In addition, it was proposed that while welfare payments would be reduced, an incoming Harris-led government would remove restrictions on the number of hours that a welfare recipient could work without losing his or her benefits. It was not just the Progressive Conservatives who saw these restrictions as discouraging work and perpetuating welfare dependence either. Similar concerns were raised in the 1988 Transitions report as well as in a growing body of literature on the costs and consequences of welfarism.

After being elected in a landslide in June 1995, the incoming Harris government wasted little time in enacting spending reductions, including its initial reforms to the social assistance system. In July 1995, Finance Minister Ernie Eves introduced a Fiscal Overview and Spending Cuts statement to implement immediate spending cuts and deficit reduction measures.[34]

At this time, the province's deficit was projected to reach $10.6 billion. Social assistance was not only a major expenditure at $6.7 billion, but the welfare caseloads remained persistently high at 1.3 million Ontarians. In line with its campaign promise, the new government announced a 21.6 per cent reduction in social assistance rates effective October 1, with expected savings of $469 million in 1995/96 and $938 million in 1996/97.[35] The government also announced new measures to tighten eligibility and fraud.

The rate cuts were contentious, to say the least. From 1994 to 1996, real annual social assistance rates fell from $10,788 to $8,256, a drop of over $2,500 (see Table 6.1). Protests were immediate, and the cuts were even unsuccessfully challenged in court as a violation of the Canadian Charter of Rights and Freedoms.[36]

The typical criticism of the government was that it was financing spending cuts and its "revolution" on the backs of poor Ontarians.[37] It was typical, for instance, for the media to report that the benefit cuts would mean that "people won't be able to afford to live. They'll have to go to food banks for food. And they'll wind up in the worst possible housing, or they'll be homeless altogether."[38] Some of the most vociferous critics even went as far as to argue that Ontarians would die due to the government's reductions to welfare rates.[39]

Table 6.1 Social Assistance Rates in Ontario, 1989–2003 (2005 Dollars)

	1989	1994	1996	2000	2003	Percentage Change	
						1989–1994	1994–2003
Single employable	9,048	10,788	8,256	7,674	7,120	19.2	−34.0
Single parent, one child	17,756	21,233	16,582	15,468	14,493	19.6	−31.7
Couple, two children	23,280	28,013	21,917	20,478	19,236	20.3	−31.3
Disabled person	13,019	14,830	14,257	13,223	12,252	13.9	−17.4

Source: Kneebone and White (2009).

Despite the negative reaction to the rate cuts, the government would not stray from its commitments, based in part on the view that the majority of Ontarians supported reforms that tied welfare to work.[40] To this end, the Harris government introduced Bill 142, *The Social Assistance Reform Act,* in 1997. The act completely redesigned Ontario's social assistance system in a fashion that remains in place to this day. Principally, the government created two streams of social assistance—Ontario Works and the Ontario Disability Support Program, both of which came into effect in 1998.[41]

The two programs had separate political and policy purposes. The Ontario Disability Support Program provided more generous benefits for disabled Ontarians and enabled the Progressive Conservatives to keep their promise of maintaining assistance for persons with disabilities. Ontario Works fulfilled the promise of introducing work conditions for able-bodied welfare recipients. Under Ontario Works, there were various pathways to encourage work, including referral to placement agencies, job training (excluding universities), involvement in community projects through employment with non-profit agencies and community groups, and support in starting their own business.[42] If recipients failed to abide by these work requirements, their benefits could be stripped.

Meanwhile, in 1997, the Harris government had introduced new administrative procedures designed to enhance verification and control fraud. In practice, the administrative changes, which included a multi-step verification process, served as an additional measure to reduce social assistance through what some scholars have called "bureaucratic disentitlement," where the application process is so onerous as to discourage marginal applicants.[43]

By the 1999 election, the number of Ontario's welfare recipients had been significantly reduced, and spending on social assistance had fallen by more than $1.5 billion from its 1994/95 peak. In a reelection event at SkyDome in Toronto, Premier Harris described the reduction in welfare recipients as "one of my proudest accomplishments as premier thus far."[44] He also observed that the number of people that had come off the province's welfare rolls since 1995 was enough to fill SkyDome seven times over. It was a powerful metaphor of how far the province had come in just four years.

By this point, the major changes to the social assistance system that the Progressive Conservative government would enact were by and large complete. The measures in the 1999 platform were generally more marginal, with the exception of a mandatory drug treatment for welfare beneficiaries, training for case workers that focused on getting people back to work, expanding workfare programs, and introducing a zero-tolerance policy for welfare fraud that would result in a permanent ban from receiving support.[45] Most of these incremental promises would be enacted upon the government's reelection.

* * *

The Harris government's reforms to Ontario's social assistance system were profound and long-lasting. As promised, the number of beneficiaries and level of spending did fall. From the 1994 peak to the end of the Harris government's full tenure in 2003, the number of welfare recipients fell from over 1.3 million Ontarians to under 700,000 (Figure 6.1). Government spending on social assistance similarly fell from a 1994/95 high of $6.7 billion to approximately $4.6 billion in 2002/03 (Figure 6.3).

Yet while the former government claims credit for getting people off social assistance, there is an empirical question about the extent to which the reduction in welfare caseloads was due to policy reforms and how much was the result of broader improvements in economic conditions and other factors. Consider, for instance, that while the 1990 recession led to a 7 per cent reduction in Ontario employment relative to a February 1990 baseline, employment was on an upward trajectory by early 1994, although it would take until June 1997 to surpass the early 1990 peak (Figure 6.5).[46]

Different academic papers have sought to answer this question about the relative role of policy reforms versus other factors in reducing Ontario's welfare caseload and public spending on social assistance.

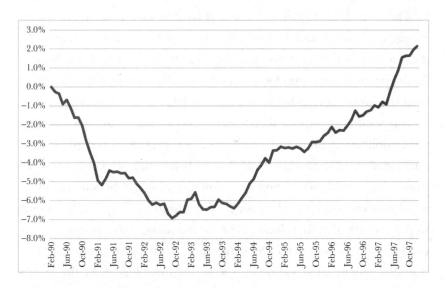

Figure 6.5 Ontario Employment Per Cent Change from Pre-Recession Peak, February 1990 to December 1997

Source: Statistics Canada (2022).

In one study, for instance, University of Calgary scholars Ronald Kneebone and his co-author Katherine White estimate that a little under half of the decline in Ontario's caseloads were due to government policy changes relative to improvements in macroeconomic conditions.[47]

In a cross-Canada analysis with a longer time horizon, Nathan Berg and Todd Gabel, scholars at the University of Otago and University of Texas at Arlington respectively, found that reforms introduced in several provinces around similar times in the mid-1990s (i.e., Ontario, British Columbia, Alberta) only explain about 10 per cent of the decline in social assistance rates between 1994 and 2009.[48] In this model, improvements in macroeconomic conditions and changes in federal employment insurance policy cumulatively explained nearly 25 per cent of the decline in social assistance rates. However, when their analysis disaggregated various types of social assistance reforms, the implementation of work requirements with strong non-compliance restrictions like those introduced in Ontario explained 27 per cent of the reduction in social assistance rates.[49]

The story is also more complicated for cost savings to the province. Provincial expenditures certainly fell, but some of this is explained by the downloading of costs to municipalities. Indeed, when Local Service Realignment entered into force in January 1998, municipalities assumed costs that were previously the sole responsibility of the province.

For example, while there were no changes to the funding responsibilities of Ontario Work (80 per cent provincial and 20 per cent municipal), ODSP funding shifted from being 100 per cent provincial responsibility to an 80/20 provincial/municipal split.[50] In addition, other social programs like social housing shifted from sole provincial funding to full municipal responsibility. The downloading of costs complicates the Harris government's costs saving legacy on social assistance. It is true that provincial spending on social programs fell under the Harris government, but some of these costs were simply shifted to municipalities and municipal tax bases like property taxes, effectively not reducing the overall tax burden on Ontarians.

While it is difficult to precisely estimate the effects of the Harris government's social assistance reforms on social assistance participation, less than half of the decline in the province's welfare caseload can likely be attributed to its policy reforms. Similarly, the cost-saving story is also more complicated. This reality serves as a check on both the Harris government's legacy and its detractors' overstated claims.

For proponents of the Harris government, claims of removing Ontarians from social assistance are more complicated than often assumed and only partially true. For its detractors, who claimed that the Harris government's policies were responsible for misery and poverty, their narrative is even more untrue. The real story is straightforward: Improved macroeconomic conditions following the deep and prolonged recession in the early 1990s did much of the heavy lifting of reducing Ontario's welfare recipients and lowering the province's social assistance costs.

Notwithstanding the nuances described in detail above, the reforms that the Harris government brought to Ontario's social assistance system were indeed transformative. Faced with an unsustainable fiscal situation and more than one-in-ten Ontarians on social assistance, the Harris government embraced ideas about the dignity of work and the deleterious effects of social assistance dependency for individuals and the society as a whole.

To this end, the government reduced social assistance benefits, created work-based social assistance and training programs, and enhanced verification to minimize fraud and overpayments. While the majority of the Ontario population supported these reforms, the backlash against the government was intense. The negative perceptions were probably not helped by the fact that Premier Harris liked to state that reducing the number of welfare recipients was one of his proudest accomplishments.

To this day, the Harris government is still framed as presiding over a dramatic increase in poverty for those on social assistance, particularly due the reduction in the generosity of welfare benefits.[51] As outlined in this chapter, the reality is somewhat more complicated: the reduction in Ontario's caseload is due to a combination of policy reforms and economic conditions. But it is both fair and important to note that poverty rates in fact fell, by any measure, in parallel with the Harris government's welfare reforms.

Although the Harris government did indeed reduce benefit rates by more than 20 per cent, it also removed caps on working while receiving social assistance, allowing recipients to make up at least part of the difference. It also did not go as far as some conservatives advocated for including time limits on eligibility and additional competition for program delivery.[52]

The structural changes enacted by the government through the creation of Ontario Works and the Ontario Disability Support Program remain in place today. Although the subsequent McGuinty and Wynne governments conducted reviews of the social assistance system, including a major one in 2012 that produced the report Brighter Prospects, relatively few changes were ultimately enacted.[53] In 2005, for example, the McGuinty government reduced the tax-back rate on employment income to 50 per cent (from 75 to 100 per cent) and extended drug and dental benefits to those who transitioned off social assistance.[54] In the 2013 budget, the Liberal government similarly announced increases in benefit rates and asset limits but otherwise left the system mostly intact.[55]

With few substantive changes to Ontario social assistance over the past quarter century or so, a new round of reforms is increasingly needed. As of March 2022, there were over 900,000 social assistance beneficiaries in Ontario, and in 2021/22, the province spent more than $9 billion on financial and employment supports.[56] The high number of recipients and significant fiscal costs are leading to renewed concerns that the current social assistance system is producing poor outcomes at a high cost for taxpayers.[57]

A major concern is that social assistance recidivism and dependency appear to once again be on the rise. In 2018, for instance, despite an improved economy and strong macroeconomic performance, only 10 per cent of Ontario Works cases exited the program for employment, compared to 13 per cent in 2014. Likewise, the average duration on Ontario Works had nearly doubled from 19 months in 2009 to 35 months by 2018. The Ford government was elected in 2018 on a commitment to address these growing issues and announced several changes early in its first four-year mandate, but then abandoned them due to political pushback.

Emerging from the COVID-19 pandemic, the time may indeed be ripe for another round of reform inspired by some of the same normative and empirical factors that influenced the Harris government. Several studies have recommended the province pursue a strategy of reducing the cost of working by adjusting claw-back rates, increasing employment income exemptions, expanding benefits to those exiting welfare, boosting rates to better match the rising cost of living, and reducing administrative burdens, among others.[58]

What is notable about many of the recommendations for contemporary reform is that they are modifications within the broader social assistance system established by the Harris government. The debate over tying social assistance eligibility to work through workfare-style programs, which were highly controversial in 1995, has become broadly accepted. Now even many progressive voices are at least rhetorically committed to this principle, although recent calls for a guaranteed income would represent a significant departure from the status quo.

The key insight here is that while *CSR* reforms to Ontario's social assistance system may have come with negative and lasting perceptions for the premier and his government, they represent a significant and substantive policy legacy.

Promises for reform were made, and these promises were ultimately kept. The government cut welfare benefits by more than 20 per cent and, with help from a stronger labour market, brought down the number of welfare recipients in the province and in turn reduced social assistance spending. Welfare reform may have been one of the government's most controversial policy changes, but what Mike Harris often described as "one of my proudest accomplishments as Premier of this province"[59] was also one of its most profound and long-lasting initiatives.

References

"Harris take Workfare to the Mayors." *CBC News* (1999, August 25). https://www.cbc.ca/news/canada/harris-takes-workfare-to-the-mayors-1.172582.

Berg, Nathan, and Tod Gabel. "Did Canadian welfare reform work? The effects of new reform strategies on social assistance participation." *The Canadian Journal of Economics* 48, no.2 (2015), 494–528.

Blank, Rebecca M. "Evaluating Welfare Reform in the United States." *Journal of Economic Literature* 40, no.2 (2002), 1105–1166.

Boychuk, Gerard W. "Federal Policies, National Trends, and Provincial Systems: A Comparative Analysis of Recent Developments in Social Assistance in Canada, 1990–2013." In *Welfare Reform in Canada: Provincial Social Assistance in Comparative Perspective*, edited by Daniel Béland and Pierre-Marc Daigneault, 35–52. Toronto: Toronto University Press, 2015.

Canadian Press. "Ontario Court lets welfare cuts stand." *The Globe and Mail* (1996, May 1).

Côté, André, and Michael Fenn. "Provincial-Municipal Relations in Ontario: Approaching an Inflection Point." *IMFC Papers on Municipal Finance and Governance* no.17 (2014).

Gabel, Todd, Jason Clemens and Sylvia LeRoy. *Welfare Reform in Ontario: A Report Card*. Vancouver: The Fraser Institute, 2004. https://www.fraserinstitute.org/sites/default/files/WelfareReformInOntario.pdf.

Government of Canada. *The Budget in Brief, 1990*. https://www.budget.gc.ca/pdfarch/1990-brf-eng.pdf.

Government of Canada. *The Budget in Brief, 1995.* https://www.budget. gc.ca/pdfarch/budget95/binb/brief.pdf.

Government of Canada. *The Budget in Brief, 1996.* https://www.budget. gc.ca/pdfarch/budget96/binb/brief.pdf.

Government of Ontario. *Ontario Fiscal Overview and Spending Cuts, 1995.* https://collections.ola.org/ser/193259/1995.pdf.

Government of Ontario. *Social Assistance Caseloads.* Last modified April 26, 2022. https://data.ontario.ca/en/dataset/social-assistance-caseloads.

Graefe, Peter. "Social Assistance in Ontario." In *Welfare Reform in Canada: Provincial Social Assistance in Comparative Perspective*, edited by Daniel Béland and Pierre-Marc Daigneault, 111–126. Toronto: Toronto University Press, 2015.

Herd, Dean, Andrew Mitchell, and Ernie Lightman. "Rituals of Degradation: Administration as Policy in the Ontario Works Programme." *Social Policy & Administration* 39, no.1 (2005), 65–79.

Ibbitson, John. *Promised Land: Inside the Mike Harris Revolution.* Scarborough: Prentice Hall, 1997.

Kapoor, Garima Talwar. *Doing More for Those with Less: How to Strengthen Benefits and Programs for Low-Income Individuals and Families in Ontario.* Toronto: Ontario 360, 2022. https://on360.ca/policy-papers/on360-transition-briefings-2022-doing-more-for-those-with-less/.

Kneebone, Ronald D., and Katherine G. White. "Fiscal Retrenchment and Social Assistance in Canada." *Canadian Public Policy* 35, no.1 (2009), 21–40.

Kneebone, Ronald, and Katherine White "An Overview of Social Assistance Trends in Canada." In *Welfare Reform in Canada: Provincial Social Assistance in Comparative Perspective*, edited by Daniel Béland and Pierre-Marc Daigneault, 53–92. Toronto: Toronto University Press, 2015.

Lalonde, Linda. "Tory Welfare Policies: A View from the Inside." In *Open for Business: Closed to People*, ed. Diana Ralph, André Régimbald and Néréé St-Amand, 92–102. Nova Scotia: Fernwood, 1997.

Lankin, Frances, and Munir A. Sheikh. *Brighter Prospects: Transforming Social Assistance in Ontario*. Toronto: Government of Ontario, 2012.

Mahboubi, Parisa, and Mariam Ragab. *Lifting Lives: The Problems with Ontario's Social Assistance Programs and How to Reform Them*. Toronto: CD Howe Institute, 2020. https://www.cdhowe.org/sites/default/files/attachments/research_papers/mixed/Commentary%20572_0.pdf.

Mallan, Caroline. "Harris promises workfare will grow if Tories reelected; Calls welfare reform one of his 'proudest accomplishments'." *Toronto Star* (1999, April 27).

Ministry of Finance. *Public Accounts of Ontario: Financial Statements, 1988–1989*. Toronto: Queen's Printer, 1989.

Ministry of Finance. *Public Accounts of Ontario: Financial Statements, 1989–1990*. Toronto: Queen's Printer, 1990.

Ministry of Finance. *Public Accounts of Ontario: Financial Statements, 1990–1991*. Toronto: Queen's Printer, 1991.

Ministry of Finance. *Public Accounts of Ontario: Financial Statements, 1991–1992*. Toronto: Queen's Printer, 1992.

Ministry of Finance. *Public Accounts of Ontario: Financial Statements, 1992–1993*. Toronto: Queen's Printer, 1993.

Ministry of Finance. *Public Accounts of Ontario: Financial Statements, 1993–1994*. Toronto: Queen's Printer, 1994.

Ministry of Finance. *Public Accounts of Ontario: Financial Statements, 1994–1995*. Toronto: Queen's Printer, 1995. https://collections.ola.org/ser/15767/1994-1995/Financials.pdf.

Ministry of Finance. *Public Accounts of Ontario: Financial Statements, 1995–1996*. Toronto: Queen's Printer, 1996. https://collections.ola.org/ser/15767/1995-1996/Financials.pdf.

Ministry of Finance. *Public Accounts of Ontario: Financial Statements, 1996–1997*. Toronto: Queen's Printer, 1997. https://collections.ola.org/ser/15767/1996-1997/.

Ministry of Finance. *Public Accounts of Ontario: Financial Statements, 1997–1998*. Toronto: Queen's Printer, 1998. https://collections.ola.org/

ser/15767/1997-1998/Financials.pdf.Ministry of Finance. *Public Accounts of Ontario: Schedules and Ministry Statements, 1998–1999.* Toronto: Queen's Printer, 1999. https://collections.ola.org/ser/15767/1998-1999/V1.pdf.

Ministry of Finance. *Public Accounts of Ontario: Schedules and Ministry Statements, 1999–2000.* Toronto: Queen's Printer, 2000. https://collections.ola.org/ser/15767/1999-2000/V1.pdf.

Ministry of Finance. *Public Accounts of Ontario: Schedules and Ministry Statements, 2000–2001.* Toronto: Queen's Printer, 2001. https://collections.ola.org/ser/15767/2000-2001/V1.pdf.

Ministry of Finance. *Public Accounts of Ontario: Schedules and Ministry Statements, 2001–2002.* Toronto: Queen's Printer, 2002. https://collections.ola.org/ser/15767/2001-2002/V1.pdf.

Ministry of Finance. *Public Accounts of Ontario: Schedules and Ministry Statements, 2002–2003.* Toronto: Queen's Printer, 2003. https://collections.ola.org/ser/15767/2002-2003/V1.pdf.

Ministry of Finance. *Public Accounts of Ontario: Consolidated Revenue Fund Schedules and Ministry Statements, 2003–2004.* Toronto: Queen's Printer, 2004 https://collections.ola.org/ser/15767/2003-2004/V1.pdf.

Mittelstaedt, Martin. "Ontario Tory Leader's attack on welfare backfires Harris cites case of civil servant who quit job under mistaken impression she would do better on social assistance." *The Globe and Mail* (1993, August 25).

Moscovitch, Allan. "Social Assistance in the New Ontario." In *Open for Business: Closed to People*, ed. Diana Ralph, André Régimbald and Néréé St-Amand, 80–91. Nova Scotia: Fernwood, 1997.

Ontario Hansard. *Opposition Day: Social Assistance Reform*, 6 November 1994 (Mr. Michael D. Harris, PCPO). http://hansardindex.ontla.on.ca/hansardECAT/35-3/l156-8.htm.

Philp, Margaret. "Social-services workers doubt lavishness of benefits Tory Leader Michael Harris says are enticing the able-bodied to social assistance." *The Globe and Mail* (1995, May 16).

Progressive Conservative Party of Ontario. *The Common Sense Revolution.* https://www.poltext.org/sites/poltext.org/files/plateformesV2/Ontario/ON_PL_1995_PC_en.pdf.

Progressive Conservative Party of Ontario. *Blueprint: Mike Harris' Plan to Keep Ontario on the Right Track.* https://www.poltext.org/sites/poltext.org/files/plateformesV2/Ontario/ON_PL_1999_PC_en.pdf.

Sabatini, E., and Sandra Nightingale. *Welfare—No Fair: A Critical Analysis of Ontario's Welfare System (1985–1994).* Vancouver: The Fraser Institute, 1996.

Sheppard, Robert. "Welfare isn't an easy way out." *The Globe and Mail* (1993, August 26).

Social Assistance Review Committee. *Transitions: Report of the Social Assistance Review Committee.* Toronto: Queen's Printer, 1988.

Statistics Canada. "Labour force characteristics, monthly, seasonally adjusted and trend-cycle, last 5 months." Last modified August 5, 2022. https://www150.statcan.gc.ca/t1/tbl1/en/tv.action?pid=1410028701.

Statistics Canada. "Population estimates on July 1st, by age and sex." Last modified September 29, 2021. https://www150.statcan.gc.ca/t1/tbl1/en/tv.action?pid=1710000501.

Tiessen, Kaylie. *Ontario's Social Assistance Poverty Gap.* Toronto: The Canadian Centre for Policy Alternatives, 2016. https://policyalternatives.ca/publications/reports/ontarios-social-assistance-poverty-gap.

Treasury Board Secretariat. *Public Accounts of Ontario: Ministry Statements and Schedules, 2020–2021.* Toronto: Queen's Printer, 2021. https://files.ontario.ca/tbs-public-accounts-2020-21-ministry-statements-schedules-en-2021-09-23-v3a.pdf.

Walkom, Thomas. *Rae Days.* Toronto: Key Porter Books, 1994.

Woolf, Avi. "We Must Restore the Dignity of Work. All Work." *The Bulwark* (2019, May 14). https://www.thebulwark.com/we-must-restore-the-dignity-of-work-all-work/.

Zon, Noah, and Thomas Granofsky. *Resetting Social Assistance Reform.* Toronto: Ontario 360, 2019. https://on360.ca/policy-papers/resetting-social-assistance-reform/.

Notes

1   "Harris take Workfare to the Mayors," *CBC News* (1999, August 25). https://www.cbc.ca/news/canada/harris-takes-workfare-to-the-mayors-1.172582.

2   This chapter uses welfare and social assistance synonymously.

3   See, for instance, https://maytree.com/welfare-in-canada/ontario/. Although this calculation is somewhat difficult given limited data availability, the need to account for inflation and the mixed effects of provincial benefits and federal income support programs (which are difficult to disaggregate), third-party analysis suggests that welfare recipients are receiving about the same in provincial benefits as they were in the aftermath of the reforms.

4   Ontario Hansard, *Opposition Day: Social Assistance Reform*, November 6, 1994 (Mr. Michael D. Harris, PCPO), http://hansardindex.ontla.on.ca/hansardECAT/35-3/l156-8.htm.

5   Ronald D. Kneebone and Katherine G. White, "Fiscal Retrenchment and Social Assistance in Canada," *Canadian Public Policy* 35, no.1 (2009), 26.

6   Peter Graefe, "Social Assistance in Ontario," in *Welfare Reform in Canada: Provincial Social Assistance in Comparative Perspective*, ed. Daniel Béland and Pierre-Marc Daigneault (Toronto: Toronto University Press, 2015), 111–113.

7   Social Assistance Review Committee, *Transitions: Report of the Social Assistance Review Committee* (Toronto: Queen's Printer, 1988).

8   Graefe, "Social Assistance in Ontario," 113.

9   Social Assistance Review Committee, *Transitions*, 259.

10   Graefe, "Social Assistance in Ontario," 114.

11   Ibid., 113.

12   Graefe, "Social Assistance in Ontario," 113. See also, Thomas Walkom, *Rae Days* (Toronto: Key Porter Books, 1994), 195–203.

13   Ontario Hansard, *Opposition Day: Social Assistance Reform*, November 6, 1994 (Mr. Michael D. Harris, PCPO), http://hansardindex.ontla.on.ca/hansardECAT/35-3/l156-8.htm.

14   Ronald Kneebone and Katherine White, "An Overview of Social Assistance Trends in Canada," in *Welfare Reform in Canada: Provincial Social Assistance in Comparative Perspective*, ed. Daniel Béland and Pierre-Marc Daigneault (Toronto: Toronto University Press, 2015), 53–60.

15   There are two ways to assess social assistance participation—cases and beneficiaries. A case refers to a single individual or a family unit on social assistance (e.g., a family on social assistance is counted as one case); whereas the number of beneficiaries refers to the total number of single individuals and heads of family units on social assistance plus all their dependents (i.e., spouses, dependent children, and dependent adults). This chapter refers to beneficiaries throughout to account for the full scope of social assistance participation. However, by way of comparison, in 1994, the average number of cases was approximately 673,000.

16   Data on beneficiaries refer to the average number of monthly beneficiaries.

17 Yearly social assistance beneficiary estimates reflect the average of monthly beneficiaries for the given year.

18 Gerard W. Boychuk, "Federal Policies, National Trends, and Provincial Systems: A Comparative Analysis of Recent Developments in Social Assistance in Canada, 1990–2013," in *Welfare Reform in Canada: Provincial Social Assistance in Comparative Perspective*, ed. Daniel Béland and Pierre-Marc Daigneault (Toronto: Toronto University Press, 2015), 35–38.

19 Ibid., 37.

20 Government of Canada, *The Budget in Brief, 1990*, https://www.budget.gc.ca/pdfarch/1990-brf-eng.pdf.

21 Government of Canada, *The Budget in Brief, 1995*, https://www.budget.gc.ca/pdfarch/budget95/binb/brief.pdf.

22 It is beyond the scope of this chapter, but it is worth noting that the welfare reforms also interacted with federal programs such as Employment Insurance that, then and now, can produce its own anomalies with respect to the regional treatment of unemployed workers. Research by the Mowat Centre for instance highlights how regional eligibility criteria often disadvantage unemployed Ontarians relative to their counterparts in other parts of the country. See: https://mowatcentre.munkschool.utoronto.ca/release-of-mowat-centre-employment-insurance-ei-task-force-report-and-recommendations/.

23 Boychuk, "Federal Policies, National Trends, and Provincial Systems," 38.

24 E. Sabatini and Sandra Nightingale, *Welfare—No Fair: A Critical Analysis of Ontario's Welfare System (1985–1994)*, (Vancouver: The Fraser Institute, 1996), 223.

25 Avi Woolf, "We Must Restore the Dignity of Work. All Work," *The Bulwark* (2019, May 14), https://www.thebulwark.com/we-must-restore-the-dignity-of-work-all-work/.

26 Rebecca M. Blank, "Evaluating Welfare Reform in the United States," *Journal of Economic Literature*, 40, no.2 (2002), 1105–1106.

27 Ontario Hansard, *Opposition Day: Social Assistance Reform*, November 6, 1994 (Mr. Michael D. Harris, PCPO), http://hansardindex.ontla.on.ca/hansardECAT/35-3/l156-8.htm.

28 Martin Mittelstaedt, "Ontario Tory Leader's attack on welfare backfires Harris cites case of civil servant who quit job under mistaken impression she would do better on social assistance," *The Globe and Mail* (1993, August 25).

29 Ibid.

30 Robert Sheppard, "Welfare isn't an easy way out," *The Globe and Mail* (1993, August 26).

31 John Ibbitson, *Promised Land: Inside the Mike Harris Revolution* (Scarborough: Prentice Hall, 1997), 146.

32 Progressive Conservative Party of Ontario, *The Common Sense Revolution*, 9, https://www.poltext.org/sites/poltext.org/files/plateformesV2/Ontario/ON_PL_1995_PC_en.pdf.

33 Ibid.

34 Government of Ontario, *Ontario Fiscal Overview and Spending Cuts, 1995*, https://collections.ola.org/ser/193259/1995.pdf.

35 The government did not reduce social assistance benefits for seniors or persons with disabilities and their families.

36 Canadian Press, "Ontario Court Lets Welfare Cuts Stand," *The Globe and Mail* (1996, May 1).

37 Ibbitson, *Promised Land*, 120.

38 Margaret Philp, "Social-Services Workers Doubt Lavishness of Benefits Tory Leader Michael Harris Says Are Enticing the Able-Bodied to Social Assistance," *The Globe and Mail* (1995, May 16).

39 Linda Lalonde, "Tory Welfare Policies: A View from the Inside," in *Open for Business: Closed to People*, ed. Diana Ralph, André Régimbald and Néréé St-Amand, (Nova Scotia: Fernwood, 1997), 99.

40 Ibbitson, *Promised Land*, 234.

41 The government also consolidated several existing social assistance programs into the two new streams.

42 Allan Moscovitch, "Social Assistance in the New Ontario," in *Open for Business: Closed to People*, ed. Diana Ralph, André Régimbald and Néréé St-Amand, (Nova Scotia: Fernwood, 1997), 89.

43 Dean Herd, Andrew Mitchell, and Ernie Lightman, "Rituals of Degradation: Administration as Policy in the Ontario Works Programme," *Social Policy & Administration* 39, No.1 (2005), 66.

44 Caroline Mallan, "Harris Promises Workfare Will Grow If Tories Re-elected; Calls Welfare Reform One of His 'Proudest Accomplishments'," *Toronto Star* (1999, April 27).

45 Progressive Conservative Party of Ontario, *Blueprint: Mike Harris' Plan to Keep Ontario on the Right Track*, 16–17, https://www.poltext.org/sites/poltext.org/files/plateformesV2/Ontario/ON_PL_1999_PC_en.pdf.

46 While this is before the structural changes to the social assistance system enacted by the Harris government, the October 1995 social assistance rate cut could explain some of the change in employment if the reduction in benefits caused individuals to look for work instead of relying on social assistance.

47 Kneebone and White, "Fiscal Retrenchment and Social Assistance in Canada," 34.

48 Nathan Berg and Tod Gabel, "Did Canadian Welfare Reform Work? The Effects of New Reform Strategies on Social Assistance Participation," *The Canadian Journal of Economics* 48, No.2 (2015), 522–523.

49 Ibid., 525.

50 André Côté and Michael Fenn, "Provincial-Municipal Relations in Ontario: Approaching an Inflection Point," *IMFC Papers on Municipal Finance and Governance* no.17 (2014), 10.

51 Kaylie Tiessen, *Ontario's Social Assistance Poverty Gap* (Toronto: The Canadian Centre for Policy Alternatives, 2016), 5; 9, https://policyalternatives.ca/publications/reports/ontarios-social-assistance-poverty-gap.

52   Todd Gabel, Jason Clemens, and Sylvia LeRoy, *Welfare Reform in Ontario: A Report Card*, (Vancouver: The Fraser Institute, 2004), 2–6, https://www.fraserinstitute.org/sites/default/files/WelfareReformInOntario.pdf.

53   See, Frances Lankin and Munir A. Sheikh, *Brighter Prospects: Transforming Social Assistance in Ontario*, (Toronto: Government of Ontario, 2012).

54   Graefe, "Social Assistance in Ontario," 115.

55   Ibid.

56   Government of Ontario, *Social Assistance Caseloads*, last modified April 26, 2022, https://data.ontario.ca/en/dataset/social-assistance-caseloads; Treasury Board Secretariat, *Public Accounts of Ontario: Ministry Statements and Schedules, 2020–2021*, (Toronto: Queen's Printer, 2021), https://files.ontario.ca/tbs-public-accounts-2020-21-ministry-statements-schedules-en-2021-09-23-v3a.pdf.

57   Parisa Mahboubi and Mariam Ragab, *Lifting Lives: The Problems with Ontario's Social Assistance Programs and How to Reform Them*, (Toronto: CD Howe Institute, 2020), 1. https://www.cdhowe.org/sites/default/files/attachments/research_papers/mixed/Commentary%20572_0.pdf.

58   Ibid.; Noah Zon and Thomas Granofsky, *Resetting Social Assistance Reform*, (Toronto: Ontario 360, 2019), https://on360.ca/policy-papers/resetting-social-assistance-reform/; Garima Talwar Kapoor, *Doing More for Those with Less: How to Strengthen Benefits and Programs for Low-Income Individuals and Families in Ontario*, (Toronto: Ontario 360, 2022), https://on360.ca/policy-papers/on360-transition-briefings-2022-doing-more-for-those-with-less/.

59   "Harris take Workfare to the Mayors," *CBC News* (1999, August 25), https://www.cbc.ca/news/canada/harris-takes-workfare-to-the-mayors-1.172582.

CHAPTER 7

Ipperwash—Editor's Note

Alister Campbell

NO RETROSPECTIVE OF THE HARRIS era is complete without a discussion of the awful events surrounding the occupation of Ipperwash Provincial Park and the shooting death of a First Nations protester, Dudley George, during a confrontation with the Ontario Provincial Police (OPP). The public outcry after this tragedy eventually led to a full-scale judicial inquiry under Justice Sidney Linden. Hearings were held, and the findings were published in a 1,400-page report in 2007. Excerpts from that final report, with a summary of the key findings, are found below.

Revelations of the last several years, particularly around the treatment of Indigenous children in the residential school system, have helped many proud Canadians of my generation come to appreciate that the history we learned in school about the building of our nation was not the whole story and that we have rather less to be proud of than we might have thought. Events of recent years, here and in the United States, have forced many of us to also understand the degree to which "systemic" biases can affect behaviour and can have consequences for the way police forces, accountable for maintaining law and order, interact with what we are learning to call racialized communities.

Given how all of us have had the opportunity to better inform our thinking about the history of settler interactions with Canada's First Nations, it is not surprising when reading the findings of the Ipperwash Inquiry now to see how comprehensively the federal government's chronic and decades-long failure to respond to the entirely legitimate grievances of the citizens of the Stoney Point reserve laid the foundations for the tragedy that followed. It is also unsurprising to learn that members of the OPP, from the leadership down, exhibited societal biases in their words and thinking, which enabled a series of unwise and ultimately fatal actions that were informed, at least in part, by those biases. Finally, as the inquiry noted, there were illegal actions taken by a single member of the OPP who was subsequently convicted and sentenced to jail time for criminal negligence causing death. Those actions directly led to the fatal shooting of Dudley George.

The Harris government was only weeks into its first term when these events took place. And, as is well documented in the Linden Inquiry, Premier Harris, members of cabinet, and members of senior staff were all informed of the unfolding events. It is also very clear that Premier Harris had a desired outcome: he wanted the occupation ended. Justice Linden found that the premier used a particularly inappropriate expletive to add emphasis to his firmly expressed view. And that vulgar expression will be part of Premier Harris' legacy. As is clear in the excerpts below, Justice Linden also found conclusively that the Premier's expression of that view was not connected in any way to the tragic outcome at Ipperwash. But the inquiries' finding will never fully absolve Mike Harris of his role in this tragedy.

A new premier and a new government aggressively driving an agenda of change were anxious in the moment not to be diverted or distracted from an electoral mission and mandate. But, in a crisis, leaders can choose between alternative paths, which may intentionally or otherwise contribute to escalation or resolution.

History will show that newly elected Premier Harris did not choose correctly in this tragic case.

Excerpts from the findings of the Linden Inquiry:[1]

1. The Premier's determination to seek a quick resolution closed off many options endorsed by civil servants in the Ontario government, including process negotiations, the appointment of mediators, and opening up communication with the First Nations people. His narrow approach to the occupation did not enable the situation to stabilize at the park. (Page 392)

2. It is evident that the Premier made it clear . . . that it was his view that First Nations people were illegally occupying Ipperwash Park, and he wanted them off provincial property as quickly as possible. I believe too much emphasis has been attached to whether the Premier directed an ex parte injunction, rather than an injunction with notice to the occupiers. Provided there is transparency in government decision making, which includes a written record of decisions made, and provided the government does not step into the law enforcement domain of the police, in my view, it was not inappropriate for the Premier to direct the Ontario government to seek an injunction as soon as possible. (Page 379)

3. Although it was legitimate for the Premier or other politicians to take the position that it considered the occupiers trespassers, that it wanted the occupiers out of the park as quickly as possible, and that it would seek an ex parte injunction without notice to the Aboriginal people, it was inappropriate to place a twenty-four-hour time limit on the removal of the occupiers from the park. (Page 357–8)

4. It is not appropriate for the government to enter the law enforcement domain of the police. Law enforcement properly falls within the responsibility of the police. To maintain police

independence, the government cannot direct when and how to enforce the law. Neither the Premier, the responsible minister, nor anyone in government should attempt to specify a time period, such as twenty-four hours, for the occupiers to be removed from the park. It is for the police to decide whether and when arrests will be made, and the manner in which they will be executed. (Page 358)

5. In the Premier's view, the police did not seem to be "as prepared as MNR would have liked them to have been." Premier Harris "wanted to be able to answer" the question as to "why a park that belonged to the Ministry of Natural Resources was now in the hands of what we deemed to be an illegal occupation." He wanted to know "how this event took place"; "were the police prepared, should they have been prepared?" (Page 370)

6. Although Premier Harris was critical of the police, I do not find that he interfered with or gave inappropriate directions to the police at Ipperwash. The Premier conveyed his displeasure that the police had relinquished control of the park to the Aboriginal people on September 4, 1995. He also said he did not think the OPP had adequately prepared for the occupation. Moreover, the Premier expressed his displeasure that the occupiers were still in the park two days later on September 6. However, the Premier did not inappropriately direct the OPP on its operations at Ipperwash or enter the law enforcement domain of the police. Although one may disagree with his view, it was legitimate for the Premier to take the position that the First Nations people were illegally occupying the park, and that he wanted them out of Ipperwash Park as soon as possible. He did not give directions on the manner in which the OPP

should enforce the law; how, when, and what arrests should be made; tactical decisions; or other actions the police should take to end the occupation. In my view, the Premier did not give instructions to or interfere with the OPP's operations at Ipperwash in September 1995. (Page 371)

Note

1 https://wayback.archive-it.org/16312/20221028230229/http://www.archives. gov.on.ca/en/e_records/ipperwash/index.html

CHAPTER 8

Municipal Reform

Ginny Roth

I GREW UP IN DON Mills, Toronto's first planned community and the kind of suburban environment one of Premier Mike Harris' greatest foes John Sewell and his fellow old-school urbanists loathe. I was born in 1989 and observed the public policy developments described in this chapter as a precocious eight-, nine-, and ten-year-old, oddly more aware of what was going on than you might think. Then again, the amalgamation of the City of Toronto, like many other major political battles of the Harris era, was hard to ignore. At the time, I remember asking my mother what "the megacity," the big word on the yellow posters, was, and she explained that it was at the centre of a big political battle. I remember vividly the way she tried to help me understand what people were fighting over: "If you lived on a street that got its sidewalks plowed in the winter," she asked, "would you want to give that up"? Well, of course not.

In certain ways, this question of forcing people to make tough choices and maybe give some things up in the process gets to the heart of almost every municipal reform the Harris government made in its years in office.

It is a simple truth that, as time moves forward and global forces bigger than any one government—growth, modernization, interconnectedness, climate change—take hold, the merits and value of existing legislation, regulation, and public policy slowly erode. Public policy status quos become untenable. Not always because the policies were ill-conceived, but sometimes just because... things change. As circumstances change, unforeseen bad outcomes emerge—disparities, unfairness, inefficiencies, and overlap. Worse still, these problems tend to creep up slowly, so for most governments, it's not politically expedient to address them.

Indeed, for the governments (of all political stripes) that preceded the Ontario Progressive Conservatives (PCs) taking power in 1995, municipal public policy challenges had almost always ended up getting "kicked down the road." So, while acute issues like overspending, deficits, inflation, and big government grew to crisis levels, and set the stage for the new Harris government's change mandate, subtler problems developed more quietly. In Ontario, after decades of inaction, property taxes were insanely out of whack, different levels of government were deeply entangled, and no one knew what to do about the pesky problem of governance for the rapidly growing greater Toronto region.

As an elementary school student, I asked my teacher why they were wearing anti-Tory pins. What even was a Tory? (I had a lot of questions.) Sensing my teacher's explanation wasn't exactly balanced, I went to my mother. "Well," she said, "they want to be paid more." Reasonable so far. "But part of the reason the new government got elected is that all kinds of people want to be paid more, not just the people who get paid by government. So, the government doesn't think it's fair to only pay teachers more." Ah. So, it was rather more complicated than my hard-done-by public school teacher was letting on. Even at seven years old, I had suspected as much. When it comes to politics, "it's complicated" never feels like a satisfying explanation. But when it comes to complete, thoughtful analysis of public policy issues, particularly those regarding local service delivery, it's often the best, most complete answer.

It is important to state, at the outset, that most of the major municipal reforms undertaken by the Harris government were not contemplated on the *CSR* platform. The *CSR* promised that property taxes would not go up and regional and municipal governments would be rationalized to avoid "the overlap and duplication that now exists." The *CSR* committed the Harris government to "sit down with municipalities to discuss ways of reducing government entanglement and bureaucracy with an eye to eliminating waste and duplication as well as unfair downloading by the province."[1]

The reality is that the vague commitments outlined in this very brief section of a rather more detailed platform barely scrape the surface of the radical and politically sensitive reforms the Harris government subsequently undertook. Despite meagre references in the *CSR* and express reservations around municipal amalgamation pre-1995, bold municipal reform made up a much greater share of the fundamental policy change brought about by the Harris government (not to mention spilled ink) than even the most well-connected insiders would have predicted prior to the 1995 election. Though it may not have been part of the plan, a series of decisions, sometimes rushed, often reasonable, led to a cascading series of outcomes that dominate our memories of this often-dramatic political period. "Downloading," "uploading," "who does what," amalgamation, and "the megacity" (measures all carried out in little more than two years) were major themes of the period, even if barely mentioned in the campaign prior. This chapter endeavours to ask and answer the following questions: Why were these reforms undertaken, and should they have been?

The easiest and most common explanations for the reforms are either that the government had a hidden philosophical agenda to pursue a preference for "subsidiarity" or that it had a hidden political agenda to pursue a mean-spirited vendetta against municipal politicians. Both confer too much credit for planning and too much blame for vindictiveness. I find that the Harris-era municipal reforms are better explained as a series of unforeseen but interconnected choices and consequences, some bad and some good, precipitated by several reasonable assumptions and actions.

The government's decisions around municipal reform cannot be properly understood outside of the following context:

- In the early 1990s, most Canadians were demanding that governments restrain themselves. The premier of Saskatchewan, Roy Romanow, closed sixty hospitals, and the premier of New Brunswick, Frank McKenna, eliminated school boards. Provincial governments across Canada were making reductions, downsizing, and consolidating.

- In the *CSR*, the Ontario PCs committed to reducing taxes, eliminating the deficit, and reforming education, factoring the first two commitments into a costing plan but not fully contemplating the ramifications of the third.

- Successive previous governments had punted necessary decisions about regional governments, property taxes, and growth planning, allowing disparities between households and among communities to fester.

- Everyone agreed, from the previous NDP government to the major national newspapers, that something needed to be done about the structure of the Greater Toronto Area, but no one could decide what that something was.

The *CSR* did not prescribe municipal reform, but its fiscal targets required tough decisions, and when the new government took office, it confronted what one former senior advisor I spoke with in research for this chapter described as a "Gordian knot" of jurisdictional entanglement, made worse by a series of long-put-off decisions. Harris and the team around him, not known for punting tough decisions themselves, set about making a series of big calls with serious long-tail consequences.

And the results were mixed. The core tensions that had scared previous governments away from acting bedeviled the Harris government as they continue to plague governments today, because they're tough. But tough challenges cry out for bold leadership. Harris and his team made difficult, imperfect decisions, and many of them still stand today, making the implicit case that imperfect change was actually preferable to indefinite delay.

In 2023, after more than twenty years of weaker leadership and public policy, the problems the Harris government tried to beat back are reasserting themselves. Crisis-level housing shortages, delayed property tax assessments, and inter-jurisdictional squabbles are all being exacerbated by booming immigration, labour and housing shortages, and technological advances. Just as was the case in the mid-1990s, no easy solutions present themselves, and avoiding the problems or tinkering around the margins will be tempting. But, if we have learned anything from Harris' municipal reforms, it's that on balance, if they want to make real change, today's leaders would be wise to channel some of his government's "revolutionary" fervour.

* * *

Ontario's 1995 government transition, policy development, and roll-out processes were meticulously planned and executed in almost every respect. Municipal reform stands apart. The Harris recipe for roll-out success was simple: clear commitment, careful planning, and competent execution. Harris and his cabinet got so much of the cut-and-dried *CSR* policy done in their first year that they were able to quickly channel their unbridled energy into tackling different, more complicated issues. In their book on the evolution of Ontario, Thomas J. Courchene and Colin R. Telmer describe "Megaweek" (January 1997, the week the government rolled out its disentanglement policy) as the result of "nature abhorring a vacuum." As they describe it, Ontario had "a pro-active government with more than four years to go before full mandate but with no apparent agenda."[2] In Megaweek alone, the government announced five major municipal reforms (in addition to reforms that would impact health care, education, and other social services):

- An updated municipal act
- The amalgamation of the City of Toronto
- Downloading property and infrastructure services to the municipalities and uploading education, health, and welfare services to the province
- Property tax reform
- School board amalgamation.

Alongside these bold provincial interventions into local communities, the government tried to unleash the power of the free market by selling off low-income housing, lifting rent control, and encouraging greater development with a more streamlined planning act. And, during its second mandate, the government pivoted back to intervening, encouraging even more amalgamations, moving to protect the Oak Ridges Moraine, and even setting the stage for "smart growth" as the public mood turned against unlimited sprawl. Understanding each reform (and assessing its merits) requires understanding its context. Tackling them one by one is all but impossible, given how interconnected they are as policies and how their development overlaps over time, particularly in the first two years of the first Harris mandate. Regardless, this chapter endeavours to explain each one and how they connect, starting with the most defining, though arguably not the most impactful: amalgamation.

Speaking of context, it's hard now to remember that when the Harris PCs took office in 1995, amalgamation was hot—memories of a narrow, right-wing, partisan movement hell-bent on fighting left-wing municipal leaders, forget the broader zeitgeist in which the PCs took over. Things felt duplicative and wasteful, and voters wanted processes to be streamlined and savings to be found. It wasn't just governments; although the federal government started to try to find similar savings and efficiencies even before the Ontario PCs did, it was the private sector, too. The number of corporate mergers skyrocketed in the 1990s, based on business strategies founded on the same core premises as amalgamation: pool resources, eliminate duplication, and achieve economies of scale. In contrast to the current day (a time when Ottawa is rethinking the competition act and bringing more scrutiny to corporate deal-making), there was then a sense that corporate consolidation, leading to bigger, more powerful companies, would allow Canada to compete globally. And, just as Canadians have recently grown weary of corporate M&A and are agitating for more competition, subsidiarity and localism have grown more popular in current public policy thinking (including among the right-of-centre), so it's difficult not to bring that contemporary bias to an assessment of the Harris government's ardent embrace of amalgamation.

While it's entirely fair to assess the merits of amalgamation on its own proponents' terms (does it create efficiencies?), less fair is the assumption that many critiques of Ontario's amalgamation period bake into their analyses: that the move to amalgamate the city of Toronto and municipalities across Ontario was a purely political decision to pursue a vendetta against left-wing municipal leaders. The sheer number of amalgamations that occurred across Ontario, often in non-urban, not left-wing-led municipalities, points to a deeper, more complicated explanation. But there is no question that Ontario's amalgamation trend in the late 1990s deserves some rigorous scrutiny.

Indeed, when the dust settled around the new City of Toronto and the municipal restructurings carried on across Ontario in this period, experts and academics, many from the centre and centre-right of the political spectrum, looked upon the fervour for amalgamation with concern and skepticism. Since then, a great deal of analysis has been conducted, and as Lydia Miljan and Zachary Spicer put it in their 2015 paper on de-amalgamation: "A vast amount of research has found that consolidation fails to produce promised cost savings, rarely leads to more efficient service delivery, and reduces the ability of citizens to be involved in the life of their local governments."[3] While the analytical case against amalgamation may seem compelling today, an assessment of the context in which the government pursued first—Toronto's amalgamation, then amalgamation across the rest of the province—is crucial to understanding why the direction was taken. And an analysis of the counterfactual—would we be better off today if none of the amalgamations occurred?—is crucial to a fair assessment of the approach.

Prior to 1995, previous Ontario governments had undertaken amalgamations here and there, using regional governments as a tool to restructure municipal regions. But when the Tories formed government, there was no reason to think they had a hidden agenda to aggressively amalgamate municipalities across the province throughout their mandate. By all accounts, they did not. The premier himself seemed to have been skeptical about amalgamation,[4] and cabinet minister Jim Wilson was on record rejecting claims of efficiency by the proponents of amalgamating towns in his community.[5] But just two months after the 1995 election, Premier Harris and his minister of municipal affairs, Al Leach, attended the annual conference of the Association of Municipalities of Ontario (AMO). Leach's ministry had undertaken a recent study into the efficiencies to be gained by amalgamation, and senior officials were thought to be eager to promote more of it. At AMO that year, Leach made it clear he was also onboard.

The best explanation for the sudden pivot toward a pro-amalgamation strategy comes from an amalgamation critic, the University of Western Ontario's Andrew Sancton, who attributes it to a shrewd effort on the part of senior public servants at the Ministry of Municipal Affairs to tie their strongly held public policy preference for amalgamation to the Ontario PCs political goals of finding efficiencies, reducing costs, and, most importantly, reducing the number of politicians in Ontario.

But whatever ignited the government's interest in pursuing amalgamation, its force was only subtle at first. A couple of months after that first AMO meeting in November of 1995, the government tabled Bill 26, the *Savings and Restructuring Act*, which contained the mechanics to implement municipal restructuring across the province. It empowered municipalities to come together and opt to amalgamate, and it gave the province tools to swoop in and impose a new structure should it so choose, though it explicitly excluded Metropolitan Toronto (it being a two-tier government) and other existing regional governments.

Despite the consensus that Harris' transition team did an impeccable job of taking over the government and imposing its political mandate on the public service, it seems clear that many of the measures included in Bill 26 came directly from the ministry and that, at the time of its tabling, its measures were only theoretical tools and not backed up by any political roll-out plan to actually use them. Just a short while later, however, the problem of what to do with Metropolitan Toronto would link the ministry's agenda to the government's unexpected political direction in a manner not anticipated by Bill 26.

Separate and apart from the question of amalgamation more generally, Ontario political parties and public policymakers saw the question of the growing Greater Toronto Area and how it should be organized as an important one. Indeed, Premier Bob Rae had commissioned a task force, led by Anne Golden, to study the issue shortly before leaving office. The fact that Mike Harris met with Golden not long after entering the premier's office and set his government to work interpreting her findings and sorting out not *if* they should do something about the GTA, but *what* they should do about the GTA, speaks to the cross-partisan consensus that something had to be done.

Thirty years later, it's now Premier Doug Ford who talks about making sure Ontario is "open for business," but he wasn't the first PC premier to fixate on competitiveness and attracting investment. When Harris took office, a big part of his new mandate was focused on attracting the kind of investment that he persuasively argued Bob Rae and his predecessors had chased off. Of course, much of the public policy manifestation of the "open for business" ethos had to do with reducing the tax and regulatory burden on business, but, according to his principal secretary, David Lindsay, ever practical Mike Harris understood that part of the problem with attracting investment was about "branding." As Lindsay told John Ibbitson in his book about the early Harris years, when Harris traveled, he discovered that "nobody knows about Ontario . . . but everyone knows about Toronto."[6] The premier understood what so many Ontarians learn when they travel the world: Toronto is what matters.

From a jurisdictional standpoint, however, Toronto wasn't Toronto. It was then six municipalities (five small cities and a borough) under the banner and uncertain governance of Metropolitan Toronto. And while everyone agreed the status quo was unsustainable, no one agreed on how to change it. Throughout the 1995 campaign, all the leaders deferred to the Rae-appointed Golden Task Force to avoid committing to a plan for what to do. Post-election, her report dropped in January of 1996, just as the PC government was rolling out its first "omnibus" legislation. Her recommendations proposed eliminating the regional governments, including Metropolitan Toronto, strengthening the cities, and establishing a region-wide Greater Toronto Council to "co-ordinate infrastructure, transportation, and economic planning."[7]

In fact, while the Ontario PCs were in opposition, the party's official policy position had also been to split up the regional government of Metropolitan Toronto and further devolve the services and responsibilities that sat at the regional government level. As the new government began to tackle the issue, however, it became clear this position made very little public policy sense. Most of the spending on metro-wide services like the police, the TTC, and community housing sat at the Metropolitan Toronto level, and it would be inconceivable to split it up, given the cross-municipality nature of the service delivery. So, as Premier Harris contemplated the problem of branding Ontario and its biggest city on the world state, he and his advisors quickly realized that reducing the number from seven to six different governments wouldn't resolve those challenges, but reducing them to *one* government might, and, in the process, the government might be able to tie fixing the Toronto problem to its political commitment to reducing the number of politicians in Ontario.

Indeed, Harris's advisors had conducted research on the notion of "fewer politicians" when they contemplated the initial *CSR* commitment to reduce the number of seats in the Legislature. The idea polled so well that the narrative around it drove the "message event" on the opening day of the 1995 campaign. Reducing the number of politicians became a core internal argument for amalgamating Toronto (an important context given the premise was ultimately abandoned when the government negotiated to a different outcome). But, while Harris' campaign advisors were gung-ho about reducing the size of the Legislature and embraced the ethos of fewer politicians and less government, they were not onboard with the new plan on the table within government for an amalgamated Toronto. The campaign advisors confronted the premier with new research showing that while the public might want fewer politicians, they were not eager to see Metropolitan Toronto amalgamated. But, significantly, internal focus groups also revealed that interest in amalgamation was low, foreshadowing that while elite opinion would come out hard against the Megacity idea, most regular people didn't care that much.[8]

Despite his advisor's reservations, the premier was set on his plan to break up the municipal fiefdoms, cut the number of politicians, and put Toronto on par with "the Tokyos and the Parises and the Londons and the New Yorks."[9] Minister of Municipal Affairs Al Leach was also a champion of the one-city approach (no doubt informed by the pro-amalgamation public servants in his ministry). So, while Leach and Harris were said to have disagreed around the cabinet table on other issues, they were certainly aligned on what to do about Toronto. Eventually, their plan leaked.

When the six mayors of Metropolitan Toronto's municipalities got wind of the news, they met to come up with a counterproposal, asked the provincial government to pause tabling of legislation, and successfully bought time for themselves until the end of the year. By then, opponents of amalgamation had organized, and the mayors put forward a joint report proposing to eliminate the Metropolitan government but effectively reconstitute it to address the issue of regional services—in a sense, to reconstitute the status quo. Further muddying the waters, a Who Does What panel, led by David Crombie, chimed in, calling for a plan that might amalgamate some of Toronto but, more importantly, would rethink the whole region.

At first, the province dug in, tabling Bill 103 at the end of December 1996. The plan was that, over the course of the coming year, they would amalgamate Toronto into one city with forty-four city councilors and a single mayor. Community councils would preserve some of the benefits of subsidiarity, focusing on hyper-local issues, and the other Greater Toronto Area municipalities outside of Metropolitan Toronto would remain as they were. Meanwhile, the early stages of the government's disentanglement plan, which involved reorganizing which areas of public policy the province versus the municipalities controlled, had also come together. The government was acting with the fervour of a strong mandate, and both disentanglement and amalgamation were being led out of Minister Leach's shop. They understood that opponents would tie amalgamation and the downloading impacts of disentanglement into one narrative, and they knew they needed to move quickly or they wouldn't get it all done. So, they decided to combine the rollout and announced it all in January of 1997.

The next section will contemplate disentanglement on its own merits, but to understand the political fallout of the Megacity (and the subsequent critique of it), it's important to understand the context for how it was introduced to the public. During one week in January—Megaweek—the government announced it would:

- Monday: Reduce the number of major school boards from 129 to sixty-six and "upload" education by abolishing local education taxes and funding education through provincial revenues.
- Tuesday: "Download" half the funding and all the administration of welfare to the municipalities, reduce provincial funding of municipally funded day care from 80 per cent to 50 per cent, and fully download social housing and public health.
- Wednesday: "Download" local public transit, regional GO train service, and secondary highways. Cut provincial funding for community policing and libraries and reduce long-term care funding to 50 per cent.
- Thursday: Standardize property taxes via the introduction of actual value assessment.

These announcements, earth-shattering for the government's ideological opponents, were made only four weeks after the government had tabled the bill to amalgamate the City of Toronto. Political orthodoxy today would suggest the government should have spread out its reforms and undertaken them quietly, negotiating with impacted stakeholders in advance and only tabling legislation when a politically palatable approach was agreed upon. But that's not what the Harris government was elected to do. More importantly, as later negotiations demonstrated, there was not a lot of common ground between what the government thought was needed and what municipal stakeholders were willing to concede. Finally, all the reforms *were* interconnected. Amalgamating Toronto didn't make sense without reforming property taxes, and vice versa. No one part of it worked without the other, so negotiating to soften one measure would threaten the viability of the rest of the plan.

In early 1997, downtown mayors and community activists, already up in arms over early Harris government cuts, mobilized to oppose the government, not just because of Megacity on its own but because, combined with the plan to download the costs of delivering key services to their service-heavy communities, their vision for local government was under existential threat. They didn't see disentanglement as a revenue-neutral part of a long put-off process toward sustainable public policy; they simply saw it as spending cuts. The chair of Metropolitan Toronto calculated that downloading would cost the city $378 million, and funding it would require an 8 per cent property tax increase,[10] sending Toronto residents, the majority of whom didn't vote PC, deeper into anti-Harris resentment. Left-wing activists like John Sewell and his grassroots citizen's committee, Citizens for Local Democracy (C4LD), were the loudest and most predictable anti-Megaweek voices, but by the time that amalgamation and disentanglement measures were rolled out, the government had also activated historically "Harris-friendly" stakeholders against the reforms. Both the president of the Metro Toronto Board of Trade and the government's own panel appointee, David Crombie, spoke up against where the government landed on who would do what, adding to the chorus of anti-government voices at this time.

By rolling out the reforms together, the Harris government had fueled public anti-Megacity sentiment in the lead up to a non-binding March 1997 plebiscite on Toronto amalgamation, which allowed anti-Megacity activists to claim that across the Metro Toronto municipalities, an average of 76 per cent opposed the merger plan. The vote was clearly not reflective of true public opinion in the general population, but opposition to Megacity had grown in the period that its opponents campaigned against it and successfully tied it to the Megaweek announcements, worrying PC MPPs in Toronto ridings. Minister Leach consequently amended the bill in late March to add a couple more city councilors and grant more power to the community councils. At the same time, he invited the head of the Association of Municipalities of Ontario to consult on the implementation of disentanglement and downloading in an effort to shore up broader municipal support.[11] In April 1997, the Liberals and NDP filibustered the legislation over the course of two full weeks. The PCs sustained further damage in the media, but the legislation passed and survived subsequent court challenges. And, in focusing their energy on amalgamation, the government's opponents let the other Megaweek measures pass, allowing the government to disempower school boards and upload education, taking major steps toward disentanglement. And by January 1 of the following year, Ontario had its Megacity.

There's a sense among Ontario politics watchers and analysts that Megacity was a political mistake.[12] For critics from the left, it represents a symbol of the ideological ruthlessness of Harris' first few years in power, swooping in to cut costs, download services, and disempower progressives. For critics from the right, including staff and MPPs from the Harris government, Megacity also tends to be a sore spot. Many of them see it as the moment the government pushed too hard, too fast, and got distracted from the core mission of clearly outlined public policy commitments in the *CSR*. But neither of those political critiques really gets at the real question about amalgamating Toronto: Was it the right policy? On the question of achieving efficiencies through amalgamation, several academic papers persuasively use the example of Toronto to prove that amalgamation does not, in and of itself, save money or reduce duplication. In fact, it's clear now that pursuing downloading at the same time as amalgamating the city of Toronto, transitioning plus absorbing the cost of delivering new services, meant that public servants' headcounts and wages experienced net increases over time.[13]

But, while achieving efficiencies became a justification for amalgamating Toronto in the heat of the debate (and was certainly an argument for amalgamating other municipalities across Ontario), it was not the core driver behind the premier's fight for the Megacity. The government needed to tackle the unsustainability of the Metropolitan Toronto structure (as any government would have had to), and the premier wanted Toronto to compete for business as a world-class North American city. Given that context, which critics of Megacity prefer to forget, it's worth asking why Toronto hasn't been de-amalgamated?

There have certainly been periods post-1998 when the political conditions—left-wing mayor with enough votes on council and a left-of-centre provincial government—could have allowed for it. But, in fact, when forced to contemplate the alternative, many analysts concede that it's hard to imagine Toronto today—its culture, its tourism, its growth, and its wealth—without amalgamation.

Amalgamation made Toronto the fourth largest municipality in North America, and it is hard to imagine the continued evolution of the province of Ontario from "heartland" to "North America's premier economic region state"[14] without an amalgamated major city at its core. Enid Slack, the director of the Institute on Municipal Finance and Governance at the Munk School of Global Affairs and Public Policy, makes a compelling case that the City of Toronto post-amalgamation has been both too big and too small.[15] But imperfect solutions are the result of tough public policy questions running up against a government predisposed to choose action over inaction. And in many ways, you can read the same data as Dr. Slack and argue that Toronto is just the right size. Indeed, in December 2014, the *Toronto Star* editorial pages (of all places) determined amalgamation to have been a "success," citing a "more uniform provision of services" and calling Toronto a "stronger, more equitable, more efficient city."[16] To quote downtown progressive and former city councilor Joe Mihevc, "I think we are now positioned for the world to see us as a city-state, and we can speak on issues with one voice," said Mihevc. "To present ourselves to the world, not as a downtown Toronto or uptown Toronto, but as a Toronto, a city with 2.5 to 3 million people, I think amalgamation achieved that."[17]

* * *

While the *City of Toronto Act* passed in the spring of 1997, other municipalities across Ontario had been slower to take up the amalgamation mandate the minister had called for at AMO when first elected.

The number of Ontario municipalities had only been reduced by fifty, from 815.[18] But in 1998 municipalities picked up the pace and made more submissions to restructure. By July 1999, 229 municipalities had been eliminated, reducing the number of elected municipal politicians by more than 1,000, most of them rural. Finally, in December of 1999, new minister of municipal affairs, Tony Clement, introduced the *Fewer Municipal Politicians Act*, which empowered the provincial government to amalgamate the two-tiered Hamilton, Ottawa, and Sudbury.

Up to that point, amalgamation had not been popular, but, unlike the contentious city of Toronto merger, the public generally took a grin and-bear-it approach to a public policy process many felt was a kind-of-necessary administrative clean-up. The implementation of the new bill pushed things further by forcibly combining some urban and rural communities in a way that many saw as an unnatural fit, particularly when it came to the cases of Ottawa and Hamilton. "In both, the provincial government merged rural and semi-rural communities with large urban centres, a measure that was met with stiff resistance."[19] Resistance, especially to Ottawa's amalgamation, came from members of Harris' own caucus and cabinet, and by the time Chris Hodgson took over as minister of municipal affairs in 2001, the government's assertive direction on amalgamation was shifting, in part because of his interventions with the premier to wind things down.[20]

Opposition to amalgamation in the 1990s, based largely on respect and a preference for local control, evolved over time into a more sophisticated critique focused on undercutting arguments around the finding of efficiencies. The Fraser Institute foreshadowed what would become the dominant analysis in its 1997 mid-term review of the Harris government with a study that eviscerated early municipal reforms, including amalgamation. The report's authors hypothesized that there was no way the creation of Megacity would cut spending and reduce the number of municipal councilors and civil servants to the extent the government thought it would.[21] While in some cases, bigger municipalities may have been able to deliver services more efficiently via economies of scale, if those services were delivered by unions, the now much bigger unions would have stronger negotiating power, getting better deals and increasing costs.

The unique argument in favour of Toronto's amalgamation, that Ontario needed a world-class city and an economic powerhouse, did not apply to the scores of amalgamations the government pushed for across the province through the late 1990s. It seems clear that, in many cases, the outcomes were at best a wash (no meaningful efficiencies found) and at worst, detrimental (lost local control *and* more inefficient service delivery). These data should be interpreted within their relevant political context, though. For instance, in amalgamated Toronto, left-wing, big-spending Mayor David Miller complained bitterly about his inability to balance the budget post-amalgamation, all while council was giving itself a raise and planning a big, expensive Nathan Phillips Square overhaul.[22] In fact, while he complained about it at the time, Mayor Mel Lastman, who inherited Megacity and its tough financial circumstances, found $131 million in efficiencies in his 2001 budget,[23] proving, along with Doug Ford a decade later, that one left-wing politician's impossible situation is another fiscally conservative politician's opportunity to stop the "gravy train."

Even if the academic analysis is correct that savings were hard to find, it's simplistic to suggest that therefore the government should not have taken a posture that encouraged, or at least enabled, municipal amalgamation. Indeed, just as this chapter's section on property taxes will suggest, there is a limit to the quality and volume of services any government can deliver for a population of a certain size. If public servants at the Ministry of Municipal Affairs were the driving force behind the push for amalgamation, why were those officials, public policy wonks in many cases, so interested in an endeavour everyone is now so certain was misguided? Perhaps because they observed the limitations of small municipalities across the province at the time (a province that was experiencing much less organic population and economic growth than it is now) and believed the municipalities could benefit from having more access to services if they could effectively crowdfund with neighbouring municipalities.

Fundamentally, as is the case with so many tough public policy issues, amalgamation represents a trade-off. For less populous areas, amalgamation represents the opportunity for greater tax revenue and the services that tax revenue pays for, but less local political influence. And for more populous areas, it represents the opportunity to exert greater political influence in exchange for sharing services with a larger pool. It's easy today to enumerate the downsides of amalgamation, but it's harder to prove the counterfactual: that a given municipality would have been better off standing on its own. It's not unreasonable to suggest that subsequent governments would then have pursued de-amalgamation if the public policy argument against it was actually so strong. But they didn't. In fact, "for the most part, the Ontario McGuinty Liberal government under Dalton McGuinty felt that the fiscal health of many smaller municipalities would be in jeopardy if they were allowed to de-amalgamate"[24].

Finally, in the context of criticizing amalgamation, "local control" is considered a good thing, but it is also the context for so many of the new problems Ontario confronts today, where local control is better understood as NIMBYism,[25] the local inclination to say "no" to projects, whether housing developments or infrastructure, that the province desperately needs to support its population growth. It would be difficult to prove that abundant amalgamation limited the power of NIMBYism in Ontario, but it's hard to imagine that the municipal landscape pre-amalgamation would have approved the transit projects, highways, gas plants, and housing developments Ontario's growth has so urgently demanded.

* * *

Just as amalgamation was barely contemplated in the *CSR* but served an enabling function for Ontario's growth, the parallel path toward disentanglement was fraught and unplanned, and it's hard to imagine today's Ontario without it. While the *CSR* did not overtly contemplate the changes disentanglement would initiate, as Andrew Sancton succinctly puts it in his *Amalgamations, Service Realignment, and Property Taxes: Did the Harris Government Have a Plan for Ontario's Municipalities?*, it did make four key, seemingly unrelated commitments without any well-thought-out plan for how to reconcile[26] them:

- To not raise property taxes
- To lower income taxes
- To reform education completely
- To reduce entanglement with municipalities.

In addition to those planned realities, an unpredictable but highly relevant political context had emerged that would initiate cabinet discussions around who does what and the process of disentanglement:

- The wheels were in motion around most major *CSR* policy commitments, creating a policy vacuum early in the mandate of an ambitious government.
- Anne Golden and the GTA Task Force she was appointed to head by the Rae government were developing a report and presenting its early findings to the premier.
- The premier and cabinet held a general, shared belief that shrinking the size of government meant "delayering" and reducing waste caused by provincial and municipal overlap.
- And, most importantly, there was still tremendous pressure for the government to find more savings.

Not only had cabinet set most of the *CSR's* key policy initiatives in motion within the first six months of forming government, but the government was also confronting concerning, unforeseen financial realities. The *CSR* called for $5.53 billion in cuts and a balanced budget by the end of the first mandate. It also called for a 30 per cent cut in provincial income taxes (despite a view within government that the cut would be more expensive than initially predicted).[27] This ambitious fiscal plan was made even more difficult by Ottawa, as the federal Liberal government's 1995 budget included massive cuts to provincial transfers, not all of which had figured into the original calculations underpinning the *CSR*.[28] Today, we know that the strong economic headwinds that blew through the Harris era (some would argue *because* of his policies) made the tax cuts and budget balance much more achievable, but in the early days of the mandate, the task looked a lot more daunting. The government needed to find even more savings than anticipated, even more savings than the *CSR* may have claimed were achievable. Moreover, the platform was clear. There were to be no cuts to healthcare spending, full stop. The PCs also promised not to make cuts that would impact law enforcement and justice or programs supporting the elderly and the disabled. Significantly, while disentanglement and amalgamation were not *overtly* contemplated in the *CSR*, it did call for a more general de-layering of government, a bias the premier and many in cabinet brought to their deliberations.

The thorough planning put into the *CSR* and the transition meant that, in the early days of the Harris government, cabinet deliberation were incredibly streamlined: "[T]here was no need for policy committees of cabinet, no need for papers presenting options or exploring the costs and benefits of alternative courses of action, apparently no significant issue for discussion which had not been pre-figured or pre-determined by the *CSR* policy framework. Action was what was required."[29] The problem with disentanglement is that while it was contemplated in the *CSR*, there was no prescribed policy path. In the "Less Government" section, the PC platform laid the groundwork for disentanglement, suggesting that Ontarians didn't need so many layers of government and that more layers lead to more bureaucracy, redundancy, waste, entanglement, and perhaps, most importantly, more *government*.[30] It even went so far as to overtly recommend resolving these issues, with a focus on "efficient local government," but it failed to prescribe a specific solution, and the new cabinet was not yet accustomed to developing and rolling out new policy. The most generous explanation for why the process became so unruly hinges on the government's obsession with revenue neutrality combined with a subsequent political need to compromise in the face of strong resistance. The most critical explanation blames an unsupervised public service for much of the unnecessary complexity.

Some officials, namely those in the Ministry of Municipal Affairs formally tasked with leading the file, felt the mess of the jurisdictional status quo (ignored by previous governments) was unsustainable. Some political advisors were sympathetic to that perspective and came around to thinking that disentanglement was the natural progression of public policy direction outlined in the *CSR*. Combined, the officials and advisors recommending disentanglement understood municipal governance and the allocation of taxation and responsibilities between jurisdictions to be so "structurally unfair" that only a wholesale do-over would begin to remedy the situation.[31] Others, namely those tasked with explaining or defending some of the unforeseen and politically unpalatable outcomes of disentanglement, look back on the series of decisions that led to the massive reforms and remember them as far less purposeful. David Lindsay, longtime principal secretary to Premier Harris, describes the process of disentanglement and amalgamation as akin to a home renovation project gone awry. Just as a homeowner thinks he's taking on a minor project when he rips out the kitchen cabinets but ends up remodeling the whole house, turning a short, low-budget task into a years-long project, disentanglement started as a series of small proposals and grew into a complete public policy overhaul. Other critics point to a combination of bureaucratic capture (disentanglement was a public service priority, not a political priority),[32] overlapping wants and needs from individual ministries, and a public policy agenda that took on a life of its own, to explain the extraordinary momentum behind the whole disentanglement process.

With an eye to exploring options before committing to a specific policy path, in May 1996, the government formally struck the Who Does What panel chaired by David Crombie.[33] It immediately became clear the panel's policy-oriented deliberations might not line up well with the political deliberations of cabinet. For instance, the panel started with a pure, core assumption that municipalities should be responsible for "hard services" and the province for "soft services." But the combined total cost of administering education and welfare ultimately made that approach untenable for the cabinet, which is equally tasked with finding savings and balancing the budget. The finance minister in particular had a tax cut to deliver and a budget to balance, and the numbers were clear; even if all other services were downloaded, they would not make up the welfare and education funding gap. As cabinet grappled with these political challenges, it was becoming clear that idealist policy-driven recommendations would not lead to easy conclusions, and no consensus was emerging. While Minister of Education John Snobelen and Minister of Community and Social Services Janet Ecker were favourable to uploading education and welfare, Minister of Municipal Affairs Al Leach was settling on the opposite.

*

The question of what to do with education was, as John Ibbitson concludes in his *Promised Land: Inside the Mike Harris Revolution*, the first innocent project that initiated the chaotic home renovation. Not only had the *CSR* committed to serious education reform, but several ministers in the original PC cabinet, including Harris himself, were former school board trustees, bringing strongly held views about how to tax, fund, and administer Ontario's education system. They agreed, as did officials, that board consolidation was necessary and understood that funding education through property taxes was a constant irritant for municipal politicians, who were held accountable for the cost to ratepayers but not for the delivery of the service.[34] Cabinet believed that teachers' unions and school boards were making education more expensive without better outcomes and that the curriculum needed a major overhaul. The broken accountability was especially evident when the government's first attempt at finding savings in the education envelope was stymied as 78 per cent of school boards responded to cuts announced in the November 1995 economic statement by raising property taxes. In the eyes of the minister, the boards "demonstrated their unwillingness to co-operate with Queen's Park and their inability to handle cuts in funding," and in the spring of 1996, as the government was in the early stages of contemplating amalgamation and disentanglement, Snobelen got to work on a plan to deal with the boards.[35]

The initial plan was to abolish the boards completely, but arguments against the complexity of implementing it won the day (perhaps ironically, given how complex disentanglement would end up being). Cabinet considered a plan to upload taxation and curriculum development powers to the province, fund the school boards from Queen's Park on a per-student basis, and disempower the boards by reducing the number of trustees in each. But uploading the school board's powers came at a $5.4 billion cost, while the government was seeking to balance the budget and cut taxes. Meanwhile, just as to address education-related CSR commitments, Snobelen had to tackle school boards, Janet Ecker needed to tackle welfare entanglement to deliver on CSR commitments related to workfare.[36] Little progress had been made on implementing workfare when she was appointed minister in August of 1996, and "the problem was the municipalities."[37]

When the PCs took office, welfare's administration was incredibly complex. Temporary assistance, which affected about half of welfare recipients, was run by the municipalities but 80 per cent funded by the province. Longer-term assistance, which affected the other half, was managed and funded by the province. The NDP had tried to tackle the complexity by uploading welfare and downloading highways and transit, but their deal with the Association of Municipalities of Ontario (AMO) had fallen through. While this approach would have provided a clearer path to implementing workfare—no fighting with municipalities over implementation—it would have cost around $5 billion[38]. The government could not completely upload education and welfare and also balance the budget. Transportation Minister Al Palladini and Solicitor General Bob Runciman proposed to download local policing and minor highways, trading some responsibilities (and costs) for others, but the cost gap was too big.

Ultimately, as cabinet deliberated through the summer and early fall of 1996 to sort out who would do what, education won. They decided welfare would become a municipal responsibility, funded 50 per cent by the province (already betraying the purist view that disentanglement should link jurisdictional funding with jurisdictional service delivery), and the province would download transit, water and sewers, certain highways and housing, long-term care, and housing. School boards were not eliminated altogether, but there would be far fewer of them, and the cost of education would be removed from municipal property taxes and fully funded by the province, education being the only major service area in question the province would do completely on its own. Even before it was renegotiated and adjusted, the package was messy. It departed from the core premises of both the platform and the Crombie panel, leaving many areas layered and entangled.

More politically problematic, it left the municipalities claiming major funding shortfalls and tough choices between cuts or tax increases. The government wasn't initially concerned about shortfalls. In addition to the $6.4 billion in education funding the province was uploading, it set aside a $1 billion reserve fund to smooth out local shortfalls in the early stages of disentanglement. Moreover, the municipal act was amended to give municipal leaders more options, loosening spending restrictions and empowering them to charge new user fees. They would also be able to point to changes in one of their omnibus bills that would allow municipalities to sell off utilities to raise revenue.[39] Finally, they argued that over time, education costs would go up while welfare costs would go down, a better long-term deal for the municipalities.

The municipalities did not agree. Minister Leach invited Terry Mundell, the head of the Association of Ontario Municipalities (AMO), to consult with the government on the proposal, and AMO countered the government plan with a proposal of their own. AMO wanted to keep 50 per cent of education funding on the property tax (with funding flowing to and at a rate set by the province), cancel the downloading of long-term care, and continue to fund day care at 80 per cent instead of reducing it to 50 per cent. What seemed in late 1996 like a reasonable, defensible plan to disentangle and delayer governments looked by spring 1997 like complicated changes that weren't worth the fight, and the government agreed to AMO's counterproposal, compromising not only the purity of disentanglement but the integrity of the revenue neutrality cabinet had originally been so intent on achieving. In August, the government compromised even further, spreading the costs of social services and regional transit across the entire GTA. The outcomes were far from the original intention, but the PCs could move on.

Though the politics of the period were tough, the government emerged relatively unscathed because it knew when to compromise with the municipalities, and their political calculation to move on turned out to be the right one. By the summer of 1997, mere months after Megaweek, the Ontario PCs were back up in the polls. But if the political impacts weren't fatal, what of the public policy outcomes? The disentanglement deal, diluted and complex as it was, did accomplish one thing. It preserved the core objective of fully uploading education and introduced a new revenue stream to the provincial government by allowing it to collect and spend a portion of property taxes. And, as time went on, disentanglement allowed the government to reduce the size of the provincial government by eliminating provincial welfare and social services administrative staff, well in line with the ethos of *CSR*.

But the province could have amalgamated school boards and uploaded costs without much of the other downloading, measures that have been blamed for countless later public policy problems, from the tragedy of Walkerton to the simple inability to build transit quickly enough. The PCs got a lot right in their first few years of government, and reforming education was a key part of that. But, in retrospect, they could have had a nicer kitchen without gutting the whole house, and there's no analysis of the results of the disentanglement process that suggests the massive overhaul was entirely worth it.

In their account of Ontario's Social, Fiscal, and Federal Evolution, "From Heartland to North American Region State," Courchene and Telmer call the Harris government's early reform of property tax to "actual value assessment" part of the "far-reaching and controversial shake-up of the internal institutional structure of the province."[40] Just as the political reaction and public policy outcomes of amalgamation were tied up in disentanglement, both cannot be properly understood without analyzing the significant tax reform the government also undertook simultaneously. When Harris and his team took office, they saw that there was no way to tackle municipal reform and the associated revenue collection and expenditure mechanisms, disentangle jurisdictional control, or amalgamate municipalities coherently without reforming property tax. And perhaps most importantly of all, the PCs were committed to getting property taxes down. When they took office in 1995, Ontario's were the highest in the country. Successive governments ignoring tax assessment and disparity problems had only made matters worse, and by the mid-1990s, the whole system was expensive, inconsistent, and unfair.

Before the Harris reforms, Ontarians were assessed for the purposes of property tax collection, based on a market value assessment (MVA) system. In theory, taxes were charged as a percentage based on an assessment of the property's value, and properties were reassessed periodically to reflect changes to the assessed value. In practice, different municipalities took different approaches to updating assessments, and most had pushed off reassessments altogether to avoid the political penalty from voters. The result led to all kinds of bad public policy outcomes.

When the new government took office, policy advisors seized with the issue immediately realized that tax rates were very out-of-date, especially in Metropolitan Toronto, where they were often still based on home values from the 1950s,[41] disparities between what families in different communities were paying were significant, and the ratios between property tax paid on single-family homes versus property tax paid on commercial, industrial, and multi-residential properties were completely out of whack. In Metropolitan Toronto, the region Harris and his team were hoping would become the engine of Ontario's economic power, "higher taxes on businesses . . . relative to the rest of the Greater Toronto Area (GTA)" provided an incentive for businesses to leave Toronto, creating what the Board of Trade of Metropolitan Toronto (1994) called the "hole in the doughnut."[42]

Fortunately for the government, in addition to making recommendations about the structure of Toronto and the surrounding region, the Golden Report also recommended finally fixing the property tax assessment mess, creating room for them to execute. Golden's task force (along with David Crombie's Who Does What panel) recommended that regions assess taxes based on a system called Actual Value Assessment (AVA), which uses data to continually reassess property taxes and smooth disparities between neighbourhoods, guarding against assessing based on speculative value. Golden also recommended collecting the education revenues paid via business property taxes regionally. At the time, the population of Metropolitan Toronto was declining, reducing the tax base and therefore the revenues available for services. Meanwhile, new office buildings in downtown Toronto had to pay much higher property taxes relative to the rest of the GTA, but more importantly for a growth-oriented government, relative to other big North American cities. This change would reduce that disparity and even-out the availability of funding for services across the region.

The government got to work implementing changes that would move the province from MVA to AVA, and once again, the practical political challenges of the implementation betrayed the pure intentions of the original public policy design. The first iteration of the legislation dictated that assessments would be done based on a three-year rolling average to try to avoid the volatility that would be caused by spikes every four years. In practice, though, it became clear the adjustments would force a crucial catch-up period, meaning property taxes *would* spike across the province, in some places more acutely than others. For instance, initially, most small businesses in Toronto were to see their property taxes more than double. While this result might have been technically fair, it would have been a clear violation of the *CSR* commitment to keep property taxes down. This process of making one-off adjustments to account for unforeseen spikes or new disparities continued throughout the long implementation. Indeed, the policy project became so complex that legislative affairs staff began to hold time in the house schedule for "clean up bills" to address the challenges as they came up.[43] For years after, and via multiple pieces of legislation, the Harris government was still introducing small adjustments—"new classes of property, new phase-in procedures, new bands of permissible rate ratios, new municipal limitations, and new deadlines"[44]—as reforms worked their way through the system.

In 1998, the government created MPAC, the property assessment agency that exists today. The province appoints its board of directors, but municipalities pay the cost to administer it. In theory, both levels of government are granted some political distance from tough reassessment decisions that cause rates to go up. In practice, though, the agency is under almost as much pressure to delay reassessments as the province ever was. At the time of writing this book, the provincial government has instructed MPAC to delay reassessments, meaning municipalities will charge rates in 2023 based on 2016 assessments. Though the Harris-implemented system is far from perfect, a two-year delay is far preferable from a public policy perspective to the forty-five-year delay some municipalities were experiencing when Harris took over.

The strongest arguments for property tax reform in 1995 had to do with evenness and urban growth. Property taxes impact how a community can fund its services, creating either a virtuous cycle of wealthy landowners funding robust services or a socioeconomic spiral of lower-income property owners reluctantly funding poorer or failing services, making a community less desirable and eroding property values and wealth for those already lower-income property owners. And, if property tax is inconsistent between communities that are close together, as it were in 1995, it can create perverse incentives, driving residents and businesses out of cities and undermining growth. Finance Minister Ernie Eves was convinced he was giving municipalities tools to better manage their revenue base, but, in practice, none of them saw it that way. For many, their pushback against amalgamation and disentanglement was founded in resentment about reassessment. Conveniently though for the government, suburban municipal politicians and their residents, who might have been inclined to oppose amalgamation, actually stood to gain from property tax reform, making it more difficult politically for anti-amalgamation downtowners to tie the two issues together.

Ultimately, how you think about property tax design probably has a lot to do with how you think about fairness. For fiscal conservative purists, property taxes should act as pure user fees, reflecting how much residents of a home will use the services the tax funds. For others who think a community is more than just a collection of individual economic units, this approach winds up appearing regressive, creating disparities between neighbours and worsening socioeconomic outcomes. The goal of the Harris government was to reset the system and then try to fix it for fairness so that, as MPP Isabel Bassett put it, "mansions in Rosedale" would not be taxed less than "a small house in Scarborough" or, as Minister Eves put it as he introduced the first bill in the Legislature, "while properties in the Niagara Falls region are assessed at 1992 values and property owners pay taxes based on that assessment, in some areas of Toronto properties are assessed at 1940 values and taxes are paid accordingly."[45] Perhaps the most important outcomes, though, came from bringing commercial rates in line. One senior advisor from the period I talked with in my research for this chapter rightly describes the ultimately unpopular tax reforms as anti-populist but good for business.

Though not entirely separable from the other reforms and not entirely municipal in focus, the Harris government's treatment of housing and its view of whether the government should be in the business of housing at all were relatively clear and consistent, and despite involving major jurisdictional considerations, they were also separate from some of the other more complex and interconnected policies. Amalgamation, disentanglement, and tax reform were all processes that strayed far from the government's original policy intent. When it came to housing, social housing, and rent control, even if the public policy outcomes were mixed, the execution was clear. Rent controls had first been reluctantly introduced in Ontario by Progressive Conservative Premier Bill Davis amid affordability challenges and under pressure from his NDP opponents.[46] While most other reforms contemplated in this chapter represent imperfect solutions to tough problems, most conservatives (indeed, most centrists and reasonable public policy thinkers) understand that using government levers to control prices in a capitalist economy rarely works to ease affordability and, even if it does temporarily, only exacerbates underlying market conditions, further throwing supply and demand out of whack.

After Davis, successive governments tinkered with rent control policy, tacitly understanding the flawed premise of price controls but unwilling to act to reverse it. The political pain of letting rent prices rise felt worse than disincentivizing new purpose-built rental apartment construction, a clearly negative public policy outcome with less obvious political fallout.

Regardless, the suppression of rents meant that, as Ontario's population grew, nowhere near enough new apartment buildings were being built. Much like today, vacancy rates were low (2.4 per cent in 1995[47]), but unlike today, rent control meant the landlords could not raise the cost of rent to fund renovations, and so the building stock was eroding. Rental supply was so low that, in 1992, the Rae government had to exempt new rental housing buildings from rent control for five years. After the Harris PCs formed government, in June of 1996, Minister Leach published a policy paper committing to end rent control altogether.

Because successive governments put off reforming rent control for so long, the Harris government knew lifting all rent control instantly would lead to big hikes, fast. The Ministry's paper proposed a gradual lifting by allowing landlords to increase the price of rent when their units were vacated and predicted that rents would normalize over the course of five years.[48] The government tabled legislation to enact the plan in November 1996, and, although the predictable groups formally opposed the legislation, it was introduced, passed, and implemented with very little actual public resistance. And for good reason. Fewer than 1,000 purpose-built apartment units per year were added to the market in the years that Rae was premier. The number ranged between 4,000 and 5,000 in the first years following the Harris reforms.[49]

From the late 1970s to the late 1980s, Canada's activist federal government played a major role in funding and managing social housing in Ontario. This approach, at the federal level, started to dry up in 1985, and as Ottawa tapered down its funding, the province stepped in, creating 37,844 units between 1986 and 1995.[50] In short, the federal government effectively "downloaded" housing to the province. Shortly after being elected on a mandate to reduce the deficit and cut taxes, the Harris government took the buck and passed it right along, canceling 17,000 nonprofit housing units in 1995 and ultimately downloading social housing to municipalities completely in 1998. While the government's fiscal plan required that social housing be downloaded, and ultimately municipalities were able to catch up, the download meant that Ontarians went years without new, affordable housing stock in a tight supply market. It's not that Harris and his advisors didn't care about making sure there was a mix of housing in the market that included affordable housing; it's that they thought the benefits of an open market would "trickle down." They hoped that while builders might build some luxury homes to meet demand at the high-end of the market, they would also build smaller condo units for the middle class and purpose-built rentals for lower-income people. While it might be reasonable to assume that, over time, deregulating housing development, with a subsequent surge in housing construction, would have a trickle-down effect that would ultimately create more housing stock at the affordable end of the spectrum, the reality is that wait lists for social housing at the time make it clear that poorer Ontarians struggled to find affordable places to live in this period.

Indeed, by the end of the Harris tenure, it wasn't even clear whether his approach of getting the government out of the business of housing was working for a majority of the province. In 2001, the public policy outcomes of lifting rental control, deregulating housing development, and downloading social housing were not looking good. The rental vacancy rate had dropped even further than when the Harris government took power, and the cost of rent was increasing faster than the rate of inflation.[51] But, by 2012, Garry Marr was writing for the *Financial Post* that Ontarians had Mike Harris to thank for the booming condo market (which at the time and since has been red hot). Since the Harris reforms, construction and overall housing supply have massively increased, but so has demand (lower interest rates obviously helped).[52] It seems likely that without Harris' reforms, demand would have outstripped supply even faster.

Taken together and in theory, the Harris government's moves to unleash the power of the free market in the housing sector by lifting rent control and selling off public housing made sense. Indeed, it is very clear that by lifting rent control alone (and deregulating planning policy), the Harris government set the stage for Toronto's condo boom, without which countless middle-income singles and families would not be able to afford to own a home, or find a place to rent, in the City of Toronto. Despite promising to repeal Harris's changes to rent control, the Liberal McGuinty government maintained the status quo for a decade, and it was only in 2018, at the end of her mandate, that a politically desperate Premier Wynne briefly reimposed rent control, before Doug Ford reversed it, again to little public opposition and in line with clearly preferable public policy. It is also clear, though, that by privatizing a service, there will always be a cohort of low-income people who cannot afford market-rate housing, even at the lowest end of the market. In its second term, the Harris government did eventually come around to supporting people legitimately unable to afford housing through new rental supplements, reflecting an admission that, while the reforms clearly drove up housing supply in general, public policy must account for housing options for low-income people in targeted ways when the market occasionally fails.

* * *

Each of the preceding sections touches indirectly on the question this section tackles directly: How should Ontario plan for the use of its land?[53] In the early days of the Harris government, the answer, more often than not, was that it shouldn't. A natural extension of the ideological positioning of the *CSR* was that the province shouldn't be in the business of over-engineering what market demand, combined with local jurisdictional preference, can jointly decide. Where highways and other major infrastructure cross big regions, it might make sense to take a more proactive approach, but in general, regions and towns should work with business interests to sort out whether land should be conserved, farmed, or developed on. Over the course of two terms of government, though, this position proved unsustainable. Not only did the general public start to demand more thoughtfulness, in the form of more environmental protection, but Ontario's economic growth necessitated a more strategic approach to ensuring Ontario's growing population had places to live and growing businesses had marketplaces to do business.

Harris is said to have "gutted" the planning act when he formed the government in 1995. It's true that the PC government reversed some of the Rae government's planning reforms, but to imply the government reversed decades of thoughtful planning policy is misleading. Through the 1970s and 1980s, localism was in vogue, and, in 1983, the planning act empowered the province to delegate autonomy to the municipalities, protecting nine areas of the province but broadly eschewing any regional approach to planning. It wasn't until the late 1980s that public concern about urban sprawl meant that the Peterson government took a greater interest in attempting to take a long-term, regional approach to planning. By the 1990s, the Rae government was deprioritizing planning. Though changes recommended by a commission chaired by John Sewell led to new environmental protections, the NDP avoided questions of amalgamation and regional reorganization, likely for the same reason they avoided countless other issues: there were no easy solutions.

The Harris government did amend Rae's short-lived changes to the planning act significantly,[54] leaving approval of municipal official plans up to regional municipalities. It's difficult to imagine today, as Ontario faces a shortage of skilled trades, but at the time, the economic context meant that unemployment was too high and voters urgently wanted more jobs, which the PCs committed to creating the conditions for. Harris' decision to "get out of the way" when it came to planning meant that municipalities could grow (or sprawl, to use the pejorative) if they chose. And many of them did, approving new developments that (among other things) created construction jobs. The government went a step further in 1996, introducing a rebate for first-time home buyers, and by 2003, "the land development and construction industry accounted for over

8 per cent of Ontario's gross domestic product, employing over 300,000 people."[55] Through the second half of the 1990s, the government wasn't just out of the business of housing; it was out of the business of planning altogether.

But just as the ideological left grappled with striking a balance between the instinct to empower municipalities through localism and the instinct to plan and protect at a higher order of government, the Harris government would ultimately need to balance its single-minded focus on growth with a different side of its coalition. Many Progressive Conservatives, and the voters who elected them in 1995, are committed conservationists. Hunters, anglers, campers, and countryfolk played an important role in the Harris voter coalition, and, while the economy benefited from a growth mindset, they (and sprawl-cautious centrists) sought a more balanced approach to the treatment of Ontario's land. And this is where the initial thinking around "Smart Growth" saw the Harris government's policy evolve from a firmly hands-off approach to land-use planning to a much more strategic long-term view.

In 2001, the government appointed a committee to study the Oak Ridges Moraine issue, focusing on an area that southern Ontario activists, at first, and then many other mainstream voters, wanted to see protected. In May, the government announced a six-month moratorium on development in the area. In his statement to the Legislature, Minister Chris Hodgson declared:

> It is my pleasure to inform my colleagues about . . . important steps the government is taking this week to move forward on Smart Growth. . . . Why are we taking these steps now? In my preliminary consultation on Smart Growth and reviewing the letters many members of this House have received from the public on urban development issues, it is clear to me that the Oak Ridges Moraine must be part of the Ontario Smart Growth Strategy.[56]

By October, a Legislative committee had produced a report attempting to strike a balance between the desire to protect the land and the need to produce aggregate (a key input in the construction boom), allowing only 8 per cent of the 469,500-acre moraine to be developed. A month later, in November 2011, the Minister of Municipal Affairs and Housing Minister Chris Hodgson announced the *Oak Ridges Moraine Conservation Act*, and the legislation came into force in 2002. The act became the precursor to Premier Dalton McGuinty's subsequent 2005 move to protect two million acres of land in the "Greenbelt," significantly curbing sprawl (and in the current view of some, curbing room for much-needed new housing) to this day.

The balancing act, factoring in both the need for growth and the desire to protect land, characterized the planning approach of the later Harris years. In fact, when the Dalton McGuinty Liberals ran their successful 2003 campaign to defeat Ernie Eves' PCs, bringing an end to the Harris era, they ran on Smart Growth, a kind of mainstream urbanism that seeks to balance the need for growth with the desire to build smart communities, prioritizing density and public transit. Anti-growth critics call Harris' Oak Ridges Moraine protection and evolution to smart growth a "death bed conversion,"[57] but the shift really speaks to the core challenge of planning policy, well understood by the more mature Harris government in its second term. In the early 2000s, the Liberal willingness to attack sprawl, which had grown to be an increasingly unpopular descriptor, meant they were able to successfully own the issue in the 1903 election. Twenty years later though, with increasing population growth and years of low interest rates, Liberals struggle to define themselves as a pro-housing party for exactly that reason. Ultimately, Dalton McGuinty and subsequently Kathleen Wynne, along with the municipalities that resisted both sprawl and densification, pushed planning so far that development could no longer keep pace with the rate of immigration.

Parties and political movements of all stripes grapple with the core contradictions of planning for the same reasons. One side of the public policy debate has a vision (often elite) of heritage, culture, local influence, and farmland. The other has a vision of unrelenting growth, often of striver suburban communities and highways that connect them on the right, and of dense urban communities connected by abundant public transit on the left. Most people want both, the contradiction manifesting itself in the problem of NIMBYism, the desire to experience the upsides of growth without having to experience the downsides of that growth in one's own backyard.

* * *

It's telling that the 1999 Ontario PC election platform, *Blueprint*, didn't cite any of the municipal reforms explored in this chapter as major wins and reasons for the public to consider reelecting the government. But just because these reforms weren't clean wins doesn't mean they weren't worth pursuing. Today's politics punish public policy experimentation and effectively reward governments that ignore non-urgent problems, leaving them for the next guys to solve. Most fans of thoughtful public policy would agree that this politically safe approach isn't desirable. The incredible momentum behind the desire for change when the Ontario PCs were elected in 1995 meant that not only did they have room to implement the incredibly clear and compelling *CSR*, but they also had the energy and political capital to tackle unforeseen issues. By tackling problems like amalgamation and entanglement without a clear road map, they set themselves up for imperfect outcomes, but in analyzing those outcomes, we must consider the alternative of inaction in order to give the Harris government its full due.

Would Toronto be a North American economic and cultural powerhouse today, attracting business investment and immigration from around the world, if not for Megacity? No. Would Ontario's education system have standardized testing and a robust, modernized curriculum without the disentanglement process that facilitated provincial control? Likely not. Would Ontario have the urban and suburban housing that facilitates the resettlement of millions of immigrants without the Harris reforms to planning and rental control? No. In fact, our current housing crisis would likely be a lot worse.

That's not to say that by opting to tackle these tough issues, the government didn't create new problems. Municipalities like Ottawa are still chafing at the awkward outcomes of amalgamating urban and rural communities into one city. Merged municipalities continue to struggle to address ever-increasing labour costs and deliver decent services across areas they weren't previously responsible for, including subsidized housing for the poorest among us, many of whom still languish on waiting lists, unable to afford basic shelter. Despite planning reforms, we still have a housing crisis, and municipalities continue to resist densification, leading to more sprawl, more pollution, and less well-connected communities. But the alternatives are equally or more fraught. There are no easy solutions. As Premier Doug Ford is learning today, along with current British Prime Minister Rishi Sunak and many other political leaders around the world, years of enabling local control, while immigration continues to increase, has led to a shortage of housing. Stepping in to set building targets is no easy task, and governments across Canada have yet to succeed at more than announcing it. Ontario is in the midst of tinkering with the much-beloved Greenbelt to free up land for development, and PM Sunak has had to water down his legislation to appease NIMBYs in his own Conservative caucus. Around the world, land-use and development planning remain a conundrum.

When it comes to amalgamation, various papers have contemplated the option of de-amalgamation, and while some see it as viable, few municipalities have pursued it. Few Ontarians miss all the municipal politicians that amalgamation eliminated, and, in fact, the Ford government recently cut the number of Toronto city councilors by 50 per cent (part of the original Megacity plan). Property taxes remain a challenge, as MPAC's current delay on reassessment makes abundantly clear, but no provincial government would reverse the adjustments made through the Harris years to make commercial property tax rates more attractive and residential property tax rates fairer. In her most interventionist and politically desperate period, Premier Wynne briefly brought back rent control, but Harris' free market approach has largely dominated policies around the regulation of rental rates. And on the matter of disentanglement, while successive governments have complained about downloaded services for years, little has been done to "re-upload" services now sitting at the municipal level.

In summary, Harris' messy municipal reforms do not add up to one coherent ideological or political agenda. They represent the ambitions of an action-oriented government tackling complicated problems that remain just as intractable to this day. No municipal reform counterfactual exists that would result in more or better outcomes. No one, the world over, has fixed NIMBYism, found a better way to balance environmental protection with the growth imperatives of an ambitious immigration policy, or preserved local culture and control while avoiding duplication, overlap, and waste. It's no coincidence that the rollout of most of the Harris reforms was rocky and that the final resting place of each public policy change represented more compromise and negotiation than the bold starting position of an ambitious cabinet. It is also no coincidence that some of the toughest reforms stuck. Because, on balance, much of that tough medicine worked. Toronto and countless other municipalities are still amalgamated, the province still has a tight grip on education, we keep re-learning that rent control does not work, and even the most ardent environmentalists understand what Mike Harris always knew: that a growing population of Ontarians needs somewhere to live, work, and raise their families.

References

Fraser Institute: The Harris Government: A Mid-term Review, 1997, https://www.fraserinstitute.org/studies/harris-government-mid-term-review.

Marc T. Law, Howard I. Markowitz, and Fazil Mihlar.

https://www.fraserinstitute.org/sites/default/files/Harris GovernmentReview_0.pdf

Amalgamations, Service Realignment, and Property Taxes: Did the Harris Government Have a Plan for Ontario's Municipalities?, 1999.

Andrew Sancton Local Government Program Department of Political Science the University of Western Ontario.

https://idjs.ca/images/rcsr/archives/V23N1-SANCTON.pdf

De-Amalgamation in Canada: Breaking Up is Hard to Do, 2015

Lydia Miljan and Zachary Spicer

Fraser Institute

https://www.fraserinstitute.org/sites/default/files/de-amalgamation-in-canada.pdf

The Growth Plan for the Greater Golden Horseshoe in Historical Perspective, 2007

Richard White, Neptis Papers on Growth in the Toronto Metropolitan Region

https://neptis.org/sites/default/files/historical_commentary/historicalcomm_web_200711291.pdf

Managing Urban Sprawl in Ontario: Good Policy or Good Politics? Gabriel Eidelman

University of Toronto 2010

https://onlinelibrary.wiley.com/doi/abs/10.1111/j.1747-1346.2010.00275.x

The Ontario Alternative Budget, 2001 Made-in-Ontario housing crisis, Technical Paper #12

Michael Shapcott, Canadian Centre for Policy Alternatives/Ontario

http://www.urbancentre.utoronto.ca/pdfs/curp/ShapcottOntario.pdf

Reforming Ontario's Property Tax System: A Never-Ending Story? 2007

Enid Slack, Almos Tassonyi, and Richard Bird

file:///Users/ginnyroth/Downloads/Reforming_Ontarios_Property_Tax_System_A_Never-En.pdf

News Articles

https://www.theglobeandmail.com/news/national/luminaries-avoid-property-tax-ordeal/article25427711/

https://www.thestar.com/opinion/editorials/2014/12/23/amalgamation_of_the_six_cities_forming_metro_toronto_has_been_a_success_editorial.html

https://www.theglobeandmail.com/news/national/ontario-to-protect-90-of-oak-ridges-moraine/article4155852/

https://activehistory.ca/2021/01/sewell-and-the-septics-the-government-commission-that-tried-to-give-community-planning-back-to-communities/

https://marksw.blog.yorku.ca/2021/02/25/ontarios-back-to-the-future-approach-to-planning/

https://torontolife.com/city/amalgamation-mike-harriss-gift-that-keeps-on-giving-to-toronto-conservatives/

https://torontoist.com/2018/01/sizing-amalgamation-20-years/

https://www.thestar.com/opinion/commentary/2014/03/17/amalgamation_made_toronto_both_too_big_and_too_small.html

https://financialpost.com/personal-finance/mortgages-real-estate/for-mike-harris-forgotten-legacy-look-up

Notes

1   *The Common Sense Revolution*, Ontario PC Platform 1995, p. 17.
2   Thomas J. Courchene and Colin R. Telmer, "From Heartland to North American Region State—The Social, Fiscal and Federal Evolution of Ontario," 1998, p. 198.
3   Miljan and Spicer, 2015, 1.
4   In fact, on the matter of amalgamation, Harris had spoken on the record in the fall of 1994 in Fergus, Ontario, *opposing* it in an almost philosophical way. He said: "There is no cost to a municipality to maintain its name and identity. Why destroy our roots and pride? I disagree with restructuring because it believes that bigger is better. Services always cost more in larger communities. The issue is to find out how to distribute services fairly and equally without duplicating services."[7]
5   Sancton, 2000, 137.
6   John Ibbitson, "Promised Land—Inside the Mike Harris Revolution" 1997, p. 241.
7   Report of The GTA Task Force, January 1996, p. 196.
8   In fact, in one focus group a citizen referred to the plan as MeGAcity (emphasis on the wrong syllable) and asked others in the room what the word even meant, revealing just how far away the newspaper debate was from people's everyday lives.

9   Ibbitson, 1997, 242.

10   Ibid., 257.

11   Ibid., 264.

12   Liberal strategist John Duffy famously christened it "The Issue that Ate the Agenda."

13   Fraser Institute, 2015, 7.

14   Courchene and Telmer, 1998, 173.

15   Toronto Star, 2014.

16   Toronto Star, 2014.

17   Torontoist, 2018.

18   Sancton, 2000, 139.

19   Fraser Institute, 2015, 17

20   Tony Clement interview.

21   Fraser Institute, 1997, 39.

22   Toronto Star, 2007.

23   CBC, 2001.

24   Fraser Institute, 2015.

25   Not In My Backyard— NIMBY.

26   Sancton, 2000, 148.

27   Courchene and Telmer, 1998, 183.

28   Courchene and Telmer, 1998, 183. The Harris Campaign published a "post-Martin Budget Update" to the *CSR* in the run-up to the June 1995 election, which reaffirmed the tax cut and balanced budget pledges. But the additional cuts to provincial spending required to achieve these targets, given the federal transfer cuts were to be found in "waste and mis-management," always easier to say than to find.

29   Cameron and White, 1996, 21.

30   Courchene and Telmer, 199.

31   Quote and context from Sabine Matheson interview.

32   Quote and context from John Toogood interview.

33   Ibbitson, 1997, 236.

34   David Lindsay.

35   Ibbitson, 1997, 230.

36   Ibbitson, 1997, 233.

37   Ibbitson, 1997, 234.

38   Ibbitson, 1997, 235.

39   Fraser Institute, 1997, 41.

40   Courchene and Telmer, 1978, 70.

41   Ibbitson, 1997, 245.

42   Bird, Slack and Tassonyi, 2007, 14.

43   John Toogood interview.

44   Sancton, 2000, 152.

45   Hansard, 1997.

46   Ibbitson, 1997, 180.

47   CMHC.
48   Ibbitson, 1997, 181.
49   Financial Post, 2012.
50   Ontario Non-Profit Housing Association Timeline.
51   Shapcott, 2011, 3.
52   *Financial Post*, 2012.
53   I encourage interested readers to also look at Gordon Miller's excellent chapter on environment for another perspective on Harris and land-use planning in the context of the Oak Ridges Moraine and the "Lands for Life" provincial parkland expansion.
54   Ibbitson, 1995, 250.
55   Eidelman, 2010.
56   Hansard, May 17, 2001.
57   Hamilton Spectator, 2021.

CHAPTER 9

Labour Relations

Howard Levitt

I N 1995, IN THE MONTHS before Mike Harris first attained office, conspicuously located billboards could be found around the province announcing NDP Premier Bob Rae's having just been named "Businessman of the Year." The gag was that he was named "Businessman of the year" for Buffalo, New York, because of all the jobs and investment Rae and his policies had sent south of the border. The gag wasn't that funny for the hundreds of thousands of unemployed in Ontario during those very difficult years.

I will leave it to the authors of chapters on Ontario's economic and fiscal performance during the Harris period to provide the detail, but let me just summarize the sad state of affairs when Harris was first elected. The provincial annual deficit had spiraled to $11 billion, astronomical at the time. Ontario was experiencing record unemployment and rapidly climbing welfare caseloads. Government spending had doubled, and taxes had been increased sixty-five separate times over the previous decade. Despite all the tax increases, government revenues fell, and as a result, Bob Rae had increased the province's debt by 114 per cent. This meant that interest payments on the debt were almost three times what they had been just one decade earlier, crowding out spending on healthcare and education.[1] In the *CSR* plan, Harris promised to create private sector investment, which he claimed would lead to private sector job creation and to have a government employing as few civil servants as possible. He pledged to reduce spending and reduce taxes in turn, so that the private sector would be better situated to create more jobs.

Changes to labour legislation were at the very forefront of his plans. In a particularly powerful paragraph in the *CSR* platform, Harris pledged as follows (boldface in the original):

> We will repeal the NDP's labour legislation—Bill 40—in its entirety. Period. It's a proven job killer.[2]

In fact, as Harris crisscrossed the province during the early summer campaign of 1995, he promised that "scrapping Bob' Rae's job-killing Bill 40" would be the very first act of his new government. Critical to the ambition of the Harris "revolutionaries" was a plan to dam the excesses of Rae's Bill 40 misadventure. And it worked.

Although unions, the opposition parties, and much of the media argued that there were other factors more impactful than his labour legislative changes, almost a million new jobs were created under Harris, and the province moved from a huge deficit when he took office to a $3 billion surplus in 2002 when he left. And the record of success was not just on the fiscal side.

Union supporters argued that Ontario's decreasing employment during Rae's term was not caused by Bill 40 but by "economic restructuring, increased global competition, the Free Trade Agreement, currency exchange rates, interest rates and other federally driven economic policies," according to the NDP's minister of labour at the time. But Harris had to contend with all the same challenges. And his job creation record speaks for itself.

I believe, as does Harris to this day, that his labour law reforms were the primary cause of this job-creation success story.

As we will discuss in detail below, Harris had big plans for labour law reform. But Harris had other labour-related issues he wanted to tackle at the same time. Harris came in promising to cut Workers' Compensation Board premiums, eliminate Ontario's massive unfunded WCB deficit of $10.9 billion (the most severely underfunded WCB in Canada).[3] And the late-Rae-era NDP government had introduced American-style "affirmative action" to Ontario. Harris also promised to "scrap the quota law."

It is hard to appreciate now (precisely because the Harris-era reforms were so successful), but the unfunded WCB deficit was a huge problem for Ontario. I recall being personally anxious at the time as to what impact that liability alone might have on the economic future of myself and all other Ontarians for decades to come.

One of Premier Harris' first acts was firing the Ontario Labour Relations Board's chair, Judith McCormack on July 26, 1995, several months before Bill 7 (the Harris government's replacement for Rae's Bill 40) was passed, with three other vice chairs of the OLRB let go six weeks later. The PC campaign had presaged this announcement on May 25, referring to the pro-union labour board without naming her. Before her first three-year term had ended, and in advance of the election, Bob Rae had reappointed her for another three-year term and it was this appointment which Harris rescinded.

The Ontario Divisional Court later ruled these revocations invalid,[4] but the ruling was too late to stop their actual ouster. I take some personal credit for their removals since I had written a column in the *Toronto Star* during that election, exposing the union-side background of the vast majority of Rae's appointments to the board, including Chair McCormack. The Labour Board sent out a rebuttal of my column to the entire labour relations community, attacking me for purportedly "bringing the administration of justice into disrepute." However, the soon-to-be labour minister, Elizabeth Witmer, took note of my column and acted quickly to dismiss those appointees when in a position to do so, dismissals which were judicially challenged by union and certain "neutral" establishment, management-side labour lawyers acting in tandem.

* * *

Professors Harish Jain and Muthu Chidambaram from the universities of McMaster and Regina respectively published "Approved Bill 40 Amendments to OLRA: An Overview and Evaluation" in September 1993. The article clearly supporting Bob Rae's Bill 40:

> the centrality of work in human life has various dimensions. The spiritual and temporal values as the well as intrinsic and extrinsic values. Work has always been connected to moral and ethical, as well as economic values. Although our laws and moral codes do not specifically recognize a right to work, they do acknowledge strong, protectable interests in fair work opportunities and freedom from occupational injury and illness.
>
> Employee's rights to form themselves into unions, engage employers in good faith bargaining and invoke meaningful sanctions in support of that bargaining is fundamental to achieve dignity and fairness in the workplace. The Bill 40 amendments have reinforced this right. We need industrial peace but not peace at any cost. We need a competitive marketplace but not without compensation. We need structural change and progress to compete in the international marketplace, but labour should not be the sole party to bear the cost of such a change. Bill 40 is an attempt to find synthesis between these competing values.[5]

This passage sets out the core philosophy of the union movement's and NDP's arguments in favour of Bill 40. This thinking around centrality of work to human dignity, self-worth and meaning was similarly expressed by the Supreme Court of Canada[6] in which Justice Iacobucci, citing another SCC case, declared that

> work is one of the most fundamental aspects in a person's life, providing the individual with the means of financial support and, as importantly, a contributory role in society. A person's employment is an essential component of his or her sense of identity, self worth and emotional well-being. Work is fundamental to an individual's identity.[7]

In my view, these arguments distracted from the specifics of the bill itself and were irrelevant to its impact, however arguably laudatory its purported intent. Bill 40 was naively designed legislation which disregarded how unions would use it, as well as how intimidating unions often were, to employees who oppose them. It also, not coincidentally, forsook basic democratic principles.

The explanations provided for the need for Bill 40 were that the number of part-time workers had almost doubled from 1975 and 1991 to almost 17 per cent of the total labour force, and that the service sector had increased dramatically, from 63 per cent to 71 per cent, and that visible minorities had increased 50 per cent between 1981 and 1986, mostly in the service sector where they were earning 25 per cent less than others. It was also pointed out that workforces were moving from cities and towns to suburban areas and new certifications were moving from larger to smaller workforces so that, in 1990–1991, the majority of bargaining units certified had twenty or fewer employees.

Although those societal changes were real, they did not translate, as argued, into the need for Bill 40's actual provisions. It is a common rhetorical trick, which the Rae government used in this instance, to use genuine problems to justify unrelated solutions.

Before Bill 40 was pronounced, a committee was set up under former OLRB Chair Kevin Burkett. A ninety-five-page report was filed by its labour representatives with sixty proposals for reform and a thirty-nine-page report came from the management representatives, which saw no need for any change. Burkett himself abstained.[8]

The major changes in Bob Rae's Bill 40 were as follows:

- Formerly there was no purpose clause in the *Labour Relations Act*, only a preamble. A purpose clause was now inserted into the act itself, stating that the *Labour Relations Act*'s "purpose" was to encourage collective bargaining and to ensure the rights of employees to participate in collective bargaining. This was, at law, an interpretive clause for all other aspects of the legislation which would govern the interpretation required by the labour board in the event of any ambiguity and in exercising its discretion in the development of its jurisprudence. It set the legislative tone and was a cloak which the Rae-appointed OLRB could hide behind in making its decisions;

- A union could now apply for certification when only 40 per cent of the bargaining unit had signed membership cards, rather than 45 per cent in the past, with automatic certification granted when 55 per cent had signed;

- If unions applied for certification with 55 per cent under Bill 40, the union was now certified and there was no period permitted, after the union's application, for employers (or anti-union employees) to make speeches, send letters or otherwise convince employees to change their minds in the form of petitions or revocations after the application date for certification;

- Membership support was now determined on the date that the union applied for certification. Previously it had been the "terminal date," some days later, as determined by the OLRB. Previously, in the period between the application and terminal dates, opposition to the union, in the form of anti-union petitions, could be signed so as to reduce the number of employees who had signed membership cards back down to below 55 per cent, thereby requiring a vote rather than automatic certification. That now ended. If the union applied with 55 per cent signed, the union was certified, without any opportunity for the affected employees to hear management's or other employee's perspective. If the union was able to conceal its organizing drive until that point from employees supporting management, as often occurred, those employees lost any opportunity to organize against the union;

- Picketing was permitted on third-party property;
- Bill 17 extended Bill 40's orientation toward unions by permitting more classes of managerial staff to be organized and the previous professional exclusions from certification were repealed so that lawyers, architects, dentists, and land surveyors could now be organized as well as agricultural and domestic workers;
- Government employees and essential service providers were given the right to strike;
- Before Bill 40, if there were unfair labour practices committed by the employer such that the true wishes of employees were not likely to be ascertained and the union had "membership support adequate for collective bargaining" (which could be much less than 50 per cent), the union could be automatically certified even if it did not win a vote. Under Bill 40, employees no longer had to have "membership support adequate for collective bargaining" to be automatically certified. This resulted in the Royal Shirt case with only two employees signing union cards out of over forty but with the union automatically certified;[9]
- Bill 40 permitted the labour board to consolidate two or more bargaining units so as to provide unions with more bargaining power when a company had more than one bargaining unit with the same union.

- Replacement workers were prohibited if the strike vote had 60 per cent or more supporting the strike. Prohibited workers included employees in the bargaining unit, new employees and even managers from other locations;

- Previously, when there was a contract for cleaning, food or security, the union certification and any associated collective agreement ended when a new contractor took over the contract and any collective agreement was lost. Bill 40 granted successor rights in this contract service sector, which made all of those businesses immediately less valuable;

- The Ontario Labour Relations Board was provided the power to determine the terms of a new collective agreement as a remedy for an unfair labour practice when it viewed other remedies to be insufficient. Furthermore, Bill 40 gave the OLRB the power to issue interim relief prior to the completion of any proceedings;

- Benefits were to be continued during a strike or lockout as long as the union made the necessary payments for both the employee and employer's share of benefits during the strike;

- The board was provided the power to speed up its procedures, issue interim orders and consolidate bargaining units;

- Previously, part-time employees were in separate bargaining units, on the basis that they had a different "community of interest" than full-time ones. Bill 40 had them generally included in newly certified bargaining units along with full-time employees;

- Unions could now apply for an arbitrator to be appointed to impose a first collective agreement (when the union lacked the bargaining support to negotiate a collective agreement) without any grounds at all. Previously, before such compulsory arbitration could be granted, a union had to establish that the employer was not recognizing its bargaining authority, was making uncompromising demands without reasonable justification or was not making reasonable or expeditious efforts to conclude a collective agreement. This was intended to prevent an employer from using its greater bargaining power to negotiate a weak collective agreement;

- The *Trespass to Property Act* was overridden, such that unions could picket wherever the public normally had access, such as shopping mall parking lots, for the purpose of union organizing even if the mall owner did not wish them on its property;

- Previously, there had been a limit of six months during which striking workers had the right to return to work. This six-month limitation was removed, and striking employees were required to be recalled at any time, in preference to any replacement workers, whenever the strike ended;

- Section 40 imposed a new obligation to bargain a workplace transition plan in good faith where the employer provided notice of the termination of fifty employees or more because of the closure of part or all of a business.

A CD Howe study, "Legislation Governing Collective Bargaining, Certifications and Labour Disputes," [10] commented on Bill 40 and found that banning strikes increased public service wage levels significantly and that bans on temporary replacement workers both lowered wages and increased the length of strikes. It concluded that union certification through signed cards rather than a vote increased both the number of strikes and the wages of unionized employees and emergency back to work legislation had a chilling impact on negotiations in subsequent bargaining rounds.

Frank Stronach of Magna Corporation pretty much summed up employers' reaction to Bill 40: "You know a lot of people mean well, the Premier means well, but in the final analysis, we have to be careful when it comes down to wealth creation . . . wrong time and wrong formula . . . scrap it, scrap the whole thing and start over." [11]

Employers argued that the various changes in the workforce were adequately dealt with through various other initiatives, such as employment standards, pay equity, occupational health and safety, and workers' compensation. The response to Bill 4, by the Canadian Manufacturers Association was "Bill 40 works against this because it is geared to benefit a select group of senior trade unionists at the expense of individuals, employers and the greater public interest. The bill is a result of cherry-picking parts of other labour legislation in Canada to create a bill completely out of step with economic reality. The government must work at improving our competitive position, not undermining it."[12]

An Ernst and Yonge report for the Council of Ontario Construction Association entitled "The Impact of the Proposed Changes to the *Ontario Labour Relations Act*"[13] found that employers believed 295,000 jobs were lost and $8.8 billion in investments were gone in five years because of those labour law changes.

Another business coalition claimed that a half million jobs were lost along with $20 billion in investment.[14] The More Jobs Coalition chimed in that "balance and fairness were sacrificed to Trade Unions. Meaningful reform gives way to trade union empowerment. This is a recipe for a destructive labour relations climate."[15]

As Mike Harris himself stated at the time: "It will destroy as much as anything else the future for my children and for others in this province and the Liberals say it's not the right time. . . . When's the right time for wrong legislation?. . . No time is the right time for legislation that is twenty years behind the time."[16] Harris also pronounced: "Bill 40 was the brainchild of the "three Bobs" (Bob Rae, Bob Mackenzie (minister of labour) and Bob White (CAW leader).[17]

PC MLA Margaret Marland summed up the general view of employers and the Tory caucus: "Knowing the impact of Bill 40 and businesses, many investors will choose not to do business in Ontario. We are in serious trouble."[18]

The PC Party proposed ninety-four amendments in an attempt to stop it when it was tabled in the Legislature. The political environment was rancorous with billboards around the province depicting pictures of Marx alongside Rae. Rarely had labor legislation been such a central element in a provincial election campaign in Ontario or any other province.

The contention around Bill 40 and the record levels of unemployment and economic distress for business in the early 1990s set the table for the big changes Mike Harris promised to bring to labour law in the *CSR*.

* * *

Seizing their opportunity shortly after their landslide election in 1995, the Tories quickly enacted Bill 7 which virtually entirely repealed Bill 40. It was understood that Mike Harris was not going to get votes from union supporters (or the left more broadly) and thus he had no hesitation in doing exactly what he promised Bill 7 was entitled An Act to Restore Balance and Stability to Labour Relations and to Promote Economic Prosperity. We will now take a close look at the legal changes in this dramatic change of course for labour law in the province. The Key Elements of Bill 7 were:

- Allowed employers to hire replacement workers in the event of a strike;
- Required a secret ballot with majority rule for all votes on new collective agreements, certifications and de-certifications. This by itself gutted the most pernicious provisions of Rae's Bill 40. The most significant change was the requirement that a secret ballot vote be held with every certification application so that unions could not browbeat employees into signing cards, with certification previously occurring when 55 per cent or more of employees signed such cards. The union now had to achieve a majority in a secret ballot vote and there would be no automatic certification based on the percentage of cards signed;

- Votes were required for all strikes and ratifications of collective agreements except in the construction industry. There was now, also, a requirement that unions hold secret ballot votes before engaging in strike activity, thereby introducing more democracy into the workplace so that employees could no longer be browbeaten by their union into striking;
- Bill 7 eliminated many groups of employees from potential certification. Agreements covering agricultural workers and some professions were rendered nugatory and welfare recipients, who now were going to have to work in order to get welfare benefits, were also prohibited from joining unions;
- It restricted the power of the OLRB to grant lesser remedies such as a second vote if there was employer illegality during organizing and during the certification process.
- The government also reduced the number of employees in the public sector through privatization, contracting and layoffs;
- If a union lost a certification vote, it was restricted from reapplying for certification of that bargaining unit for one year following its loss;
- Successor rights were eliminated where a sale of business related to buying a business from the crown;
- It created a stricter approach to procedural time limits in the arbitration process;
- It required mandatory strike and ratification votes with the secret ballot;
- It reduced the power of the OLRB to grant first contract arbitration and reduced its power to determine outstanding terms of the collective agreement if the duty to bargain in good faith was violated;
- It removed successor rights in the contract service sector;
- It reduced the support required for a vote for certification and decertification from 45 per cent to 40 per cent;

Following Bill 7 coming into effect, there was a significant test case involving Wal-Mart in April 1996. The union obtained ninety-one signed cards out of 205 employees providing the requisite percentage for a vote. A vote was ordered held. The employees roundly rejected the union, 151 to forty-three, so even many of the initial card signers voted against the union.

The union alleged that the employer's conduct influenced the vote unlawfully and justified its automatic certification. Its arguments were that the company allowed an employee to make an anti-union speech at a company meeting, managers had walked around the store for a number of days (which the board viewed as a subtle intimidation) and, when an employee asked during an open meeting about whether the store would close if Wal-Mart was unionized, Wal-Mart management refused to answer, which the board found amounted to a job security threat.

The union was automatically certified by the board and Wal-Mart's application to have the decision quashed by Divisional Court of Ontario was unsuccessful in July 1997.

This resulted in further legislation by the Harris Government, Bill 31, requiring secret ballot votes in every case and no longer permitting any automatic certifications.[19] This bill took away the OLRB's ability to certify unions without demonstrated majority support even if the employers created a "environment in which a vote might not reveal the true wishes of the employees," an exception which Bill 7 had left in place. Bill 31 also reduced access to relief from the OLRB to address alleged employer illegal activity and prohibitions on the reinstatements of terminated employees. Finally, Bill 31 significantly reduced success in certifications, the volume of organizing activity, and unfair labour practice activity, even compared to Bill 7, according to a study by Timothy Bartkiw called "Manufacturing Decent? Labour Law and Union Organizing in the Province of Ontario."[20]

It is worth noting that Bill 31 was subsequently repealed by the Liberals after the defeat of the Ernie Eves government, so that automatic certifications are again actively fought at the OLRB with unions alleging unfair labour practices.

The impact of Bill 7 was quick and powerful. The number of private-sector strikes in Ontario was 400 per year in 1989, 300 per year in 1991, 250 per year in 1995, and it stayed at around 200 per year throughout the Harris years.

According to a paper in 2000 by Felice Martinello of Brock University, certifications increased and decertifications decreased after Bill 40 was passed. Not surprisingly, the opposite occurred after Bill 7's passage.[21] In fact, Bill 7 more than reversed the impact of Bill 40.

As Martinello found, after Bill 7 the number of certifications attempted fell 19.4 per cent below the 1987 to 1990 period and the success rate fell 11.9 per cent below that pre-NDP period, resulting in a 28.7 per cent drop in the number of new union certifications actually granted. This decline relative to the Bill 40 period was even more dramatic as certifications significantly increased under Bill 40.

Similarly, decertifications decreased from the pre-Bob Rae era to when the NDP governed and increased during Mike Harris' tenure. After the NDP was elected, the number of decertifications attempted fell by 11.9 per cent and those granted fell by 25.8 per cent. Once Bill 40 took effect, both decertification attempts and decertifications granted fell yet another 10 per cent. Decertification activity after Bill 7 increased dramatically relative to the pre-Rae era, the attempts increasing by 32.2 per cent and decertifications granted by 28.3 per cent. The number of decertifications granted during the Harris years was roughly 50 per cent higher than in the Bill 40 era. This was not surprising, as Bill 7 required unionized workplaces to post information on how to decertify.

In the same way, the number of unfair labour practices complaints increased significantly under Bill 40, by over 50 per cent, and then reduced by more than half after Bill 7 was passed.

After Ontario's "Lost Decade" under Premiers Peterson and Rae, Ontario's private sector employment numbers had taken a severe beating.

Bob Rae's Bill 40 made thing worse for working people, not better. In the Harris era, from 1995 to 2004, more than 1,000,000 private sector jobs were created in Ontario. That dramatic increase in prosperity enabled health care funding to increase by more than 10 billion dollars and access to hospital emergency departments improved substantially. Waiting times at hospitals were cut by 53 per cent and $1.2 billion were invested to provide long-term care beds, a 35 per cent increase. These non-labour-law related benefits are in my view a direct consequence of the transformational impacts of Mike Harris' firm handling of labour law reform.

* * *

On May 15, 1995, policy changes to WCB legislation were announced. Upon the new government becoming elected, Glen Wright was appointed chair of WSIB. As he explained to me in an interview for this chapter, his goal was to change the emphasis of the organization to more of a true insurance program and one focusing more attention on the injured worker. The objective of this change in emphasis was to change the way employers viewed worker's compensation premiums. In the new model, employers would stop seeing their worker's compensation premiums as constituting a form of taxation but instead understand those costs as similar to their insurance premiums for property or liability coverage where premiums resulted from actual risk experience ratings.

WCB was originally designed for employees suffering losses because of the nature of work in the early 1900s. It could not leave workers without recourse, but employers had become disgruntled by the cost of the program by 1995. To make matters worse, injured workers were not being serviced adequately either and satisfaction levels were very low for both stakeholder groups, workers and employers, with low approval ratings. Overall, there had been a sense of complexity and of a government programme punishing employers. And hanging over all of this was a nearly $11-billion unfunded liability which had accumulated over decades and represented a major financial problem for a province already struggling under an accelerating and costly debt load.

Wright's business background had been in insurance. And he understood that properly priced risk has a positive impact on behaviour. Traditionally, ratings were based on where one lived. This was changed to industry groups so that WSIB administrators became more expert in their sectors, that is, miners were not lumped in with teachers. Wright also made clear to employers that experience ratings were what would count in determination of future premiums, so that if they wanted lower rates, they would have to keep their workplaces safe. These common-sense changes had a big impact. There was a dramatic increase in approval ratings, 60 per cent by the end of the Harris era for workers and employers, ratings even higher than for private sector insurers.

The WSIB also worked on improving its relationship with injured workers, especially those with serious injuries, and began to engage much more strategically in supporting health and safety practices.

The change in approach to workplace safety included one major step: replacing the Workers' Compensation Board with a new Workplace Safety and Insurance Board. Bill 99, which enabled this transformation, went through a process of public hearings and numerous amendments and passed final reading and was given royal assent in November 1997.

David K. Wilken, in his 1998 paper "Manufacturing Crisis in Workers' Compensation" described the bill as follows:

It is no exaggeration to characterize Bill 99 as an attempt to place the worker's compensation system on new foundations. It replaces the WCA with the new *Workplace Safety and Insurance Act*, 1997 [hereinafter WSIA], which came into force on January 1, 1998. The change in name also affects the Board, which has become the Workplace Safety and Insurance Board (WSIB), as well as the Appeal Tribunal (now the WSIAT).

The WSIA also introduces a new purpose clause which moves compensation for injured workers from first to last place in order of importance and even removes the qualification that such compensation should be 'fair'. Among the more important and substantive changes, it creates time limits for claims and appeals, reduces the rate of compensation from 90 per cent to 85 per cent of net average earnings, eliminates entitlement for chronic stress, allows for limits to be placed on benefits for chronic pain by regulation, and replaces the concept of vocational rehabilitation with that of "labour market re-entry."[22]

The WCB bureaucracy and governance model were completely restructured. Key changes included:

- The act was amended so that the board of directors administering the act were required to act in a "financially responsible and accountable manner".
- The act provided that at least one program had to be evaluated each year for cost efficiency and effectiveness.
- There was legislative encouragement of early return-to-work programs so that workers would be quickly re-employed and off the WCB payroll.
- Workers were now required to disclose all information provided by health professionals as a condition of being entitled to WSIB benefits. Employers and workers were required to cooperate for the early and safe return to work.
- The Workplace Safety Insurance Board was authorized to recover overpayments made to workers and their dependents. Fines were created for providing false or misleading statements to the board. There were also sanctions for directors and officers guilty of acquiescing in the commission of an offence by the corporation.

The new organization had a lot of work to do to change the WCB's old and dysfunctional operating model. Internal and external fraud cost the WCB an estimated $150 million a year. There was criticism that false claims were being paid, so WSIB setup a fraud unit with almost fifty former OPP/RCMP officers and snitch lines to go after cheaters. According to Wright, the cheating was primarily conducted by employers, not workers, claiming someone was not injured and wanting them to come back to work so they could avoid lost time injury ratings. There were issues around misreporting and underreporting injuries to protect employers' experience rating, including among well-known companies. Some, particularly smaller companies, often lied about their payroll.

Employees off work with fraudulent claims were now pursued with vigour. The WSIB made deals to share information with the CRA to seek out employers which were not properly registered or who falsified payrolls.

The hard-nosed focus on fraud, by employers or employees, was quite helpful to the reputation of the new WSIB and, over time, issues on both sides declined.

Perhaps most significantly, The WCB's unfunded liability was two and half times greater than all of the other provinces combined, and increased from $2.025 billion in 1983 to $12 billion in 1995. This unfunded liability and high Ontario assessments impacted Ontario's cost of borrowing and had an adverse impact on job creation.

To deal with this crisis, the WSIB moved funds to private sector fund managers and put together an investment advisory group with professional expertise. The unfunded liability was reduced through better investment, the number of accidents were reduced through an emphasis on health and safety since employers' personal accidents affected their ratings, hence their own payments. Deaths came down, as did injuries.

The results were transformational. This liability decreased to 7.09 billion dollars by the end of 1998. By 2000 it was down to under 6 billion[23]

Apart from Bills 7, 31 (labour) and 99 (WSIB), Harris did even more in an effort to entirely dismantle the legislative legacy of Bob Rae's NDP government.

If it wasn't already a surprise that Bill 40 had made labour law a major campaign issue, the effort to introduce affirmative action into Canada was a real shock to many. Opposition to this became a key plank in the final waves of television advertising in the 1995 election campaign where Harris promised to "Scrap the Quota Law." In September 1994, the Rae government had passed Pay Equity Bill 79 which required Ontario employers to conduct workplace surveys and create timetables to hire and promote Aboriginals, persons with disability, racial minorities, and women. It did not permit employers to hire the best qualified candidate but required reverse discrimination as part of the Liberal/NDP accord agreed between Peterson and Rae on May 28, 1985, resulting in pay equity then being introduced. Equal pay for work of equal value and employment equity, perceived as job quota legislation, came later when the NDP had a majority.

Having promised to do so during the election campaign,[24] Harris immediately repealed Bob Rae's *Employment Equity Act*, which required positive discrimination in favour of designated minority groups over others based on race, gender and disability, and replaced it with an Equal Opportunity Plan providing funds, support, access and accommodation to Ontarians with disabilities and a variety of public education initiatives to incent employers to promote the integration of women, the handicapped and visible minorities. Bill 8, the *Job Quotas Repeal Act* repealed the *Employment Equity Act* and to ensure it was not reversed, required all information collected from employees to comply with the former *Employment Equity Act* be destroyed. The fact and impact of this is particularly notable today, when DEI initiatives are increasingly moving to overt affirmative action.

Here is a summary list of additional Harris reforms in labour law:

- Harris imposed a freeze on the minimum wage at $6.85, which was then one of the highest in North America. At that time, Ontario's minimum wage was higher than any other neighbouring province or state. It had just increased from $6.70 to $6.85 an hour on January 1, 1995 (having been $4.00 an hour 10 years earlier). The highest minimum wage in any bordering state was Pennsylvania at $4.75, with Michigan and Indiana only $3.35 an hour. Every Canadian province had a lower minimum wage. The NDP had promised to increase the minimum wage to 60 per cent of the average industrial wage over four years and eliminate a lower wage for younger workers which had been in effect;

- Bill 22 was passed, the *Preventions of Unionization Act* (Ontario Works) precluding employees involved in community participation under the *Ontario Works Act* from being unionized;

- Harris passed the *Public Sector Salary Disclosure Act* disclosing publicly the salary and benefits of public sector salary employees earning 100,000 dollars or more, including private sector employees of employers which received significant funding from government and were "not for profit";

- The *Crown Employees Collective Bargaining Act* was amended so that arbitrators could no longer guarantee job offers to employees whose jobs were eliminated other than in Crown Agencies;

- Successor rights under the act were made inapplicable to anyone buying a business from the crown;

- The maximum amount an employee could receive from the wage protection program was reduced from 5000 to 2000 dollars;

- The *Employment Centers Improvement Act* provided that money cannot be recovered if it became owing more than six months before the claim was brought forward, reduced from two years;

- Under the *Employment Standards Improvement Act*, the limitation period for recovering money was changed from two years to six months;
- An employee who filed a complaint under the *Employment Standards Act* could no longer bring a claim for wrongful dismissal or other civil proceeding.

It is important to understand the ease with which a carefully established balance in labour law can be altered by a stroke of the pen. The fall of the Ernie Eves Government gave the new governing Liberals the opportunity to make big changes to the Harris-Era balance and begin to undo the results of Bill 7. The *Labour Relations Statute Law Amendment Act* 2005 was announced by the McGuinty government as an "act to restore balance" between the strong pro-union Bill 40 and anti-union Bill 7:

- Employers were no longer required to post information on decertification in unionized workplaces;
- Union did not have to disclose the earnings of their directors, officers and employees earning 100,000 dollars per year or more;
- It restored the power of the labour board to certify if there were unfair labour practices during an organizing drive that impacted on the voluntary nature of any potential vote.
- It established card-based certification in the construction sector if more than 55 per cent of employees signed cards. The restoration of automatic certification in just the construction industry certifications was justified as appropriate because of the quick workforce startups, shutdowns, and the mobility of construction projects and workers;
- It restored the OLRB's powers to reinstate workers, on an interim basis, fired or disciplined during organizing drives because of their efforts to organize, even prior to a hearing.

And there was more from the new Liberal government. In June 2005, Bill 144 was passed with further changes:

- Remedial certification can be granted "if no other remedy was sufficient to counter the effect of the contravention," which was not as strong as the pre-Bill 40 version which provided automatic certification when "the true wishes of the employers are not likely to be ascertained";
- Granting interim reinstatement for firings during organizing drives;
- There was a partial restoration of remedial certification power;
- There was also a partial restoration of the power to grant the interim reinstatement of fired employees in organizing drives;
- There was a repeal of the requirement to post instructions on how to decertify and of union salary disclosures.[25]

And so, the pendulum continues to swing in labour law.

* * *

In 2023, the world is a very different place than in 1995. Since the days of Harris, we have seen a high percentage of unionized employers cease operations or shed their workforces relative to nonunion ones. During my own career (since 1979), I have seen more changes in workplace legislation and common law development in the labour law field than in any other area of law, and it has become a central point of interest for many. Far more non-union cases occur today than union ones, and they occupy more public attention. Today, newspapers, radio, and even TV are permeated by topics of employment law. The consequent reality is that workers have far more protection outside of a union than they ever had before and, in many respects, more protection than inside. They cannot be laid off without triggering a constructive dismissal claim, while the very concept of constructive dismissal does not even exist under arbitral jurisprudence. Whereas non-union employees can sue for any breach of their terms of employment, unionized employees are subject to the whim of their union, which has very broad legislative latitude to not take particular, even meritorious cases, subject to a narrow exemption under the OLRA which unions have little trouble finding their way through.

Unions, locked into long-term contracts, often have less bargaining power at present (when there is essentially full employment) than non-union employees, who are commanding significant wage increases. The point is that there is less reason for unions than ever before. The rigid structures, byzantine inefficiencies, and lack of motivation (because of the difficulty of dismissing them and the inability to provide merit-based increases) have put unionized employers at a distinct disadvantage. Particularly as, workers already have the protections unions promised, as a result of legislation and common law developments. Today, as a result, unions are fighting to find purpose.

The Harris legislative changes were profound in the impact they had on the economy. The rollbacks since his time have generally been counterproductive, a sop for union votes and often a cynical measure to encourage increased campaign donations to the Liberals.

Interestingly, the Ontario Liberals have, since the Harris era, become the party of labor more so even than the Ontario NDP and the largest lobbying groups around election time have been union-sponsored and funded groups, taking dead aim at Conservatives in an effort to ensure that the Harris changes are not reinstated.

Although many of the issues which triggered so much debate at the time are less salient today, a return of some of the key Harris policy measures, which have since been rescinded, would be in the clear interests of Ontario and its workforce.

Notes

1   See "Fiscal and Privatization" chapter of this book by Jack Mintz and Terence Corcoran for more on this.

2   *The Common Sense Revolution*, 1994, p. 15.

3   The Harris Government. A Mid-term Review, Marc T. Law, Howard I. Markowitz and Fazil Mihlar, Frazer Institute, October 1997, p. 24.

4   *Hewat v. Ontario (1997)970 OAC 76 aff'd (1998) 108 OAC 117 (OCA).*

5   Jain and Muthu Chidambaram "Approved Bill 40 Amendments to OLRA: An Overview and Evaluation," 1993.

6   Incidentally, the first decision before that Court in which I acted.

7   *Machtinger et al. v. HOJ Industries* 1992 1 SCR 986.

8   See quote from *The Politicization of the Ontario Labour Relations Framework in the Decade of the 1990s*. Kevin M. Burkett, Sefton Lecture, 1997, p. 11. "…on April 19, 1991 the committee filed two diametrically opposed documents; one from the union members of the committee containing over 60 reform proposals and one from the management members recommending the status quo. I dissociated myself from both documents and in the covering letter made a plea for meaningful consultation."

9   I began acting for Royal Shirt after that case was decided. Not surprisingly, the employees decertified at the first opportunity as the union never developed employee support regardless of the legislative support Bill 40 provided the union. That is an obvious difficulty with forcing automatic certification on employees who do not wish to deal with their employer through a union.

10 CD Howe Institute, Commentary 304, Benjamin Dachis and Robert Hebdon, June 2010.

11 Harish C. Jain and S. Muthu Chidambaram, "Bill 40 Amendments to Ontario Labour Relations Act: An Overview and Evaluation" (working paper #385, September 1993), 13.

12 Ontario, Legislative Assembly, Standing Committee on Resources Development, 35th Parl. (31 August 1992).

13 Toronto Star, Page D1, July 8, 1992.

14 Ontario, Legislative Assembly, Standing Committee on Resources Development, 35th Parl. (5 August 1992).

15 Facing reality, sharing responsibility: a comprehensive assessment of Ontario's labour legislation proposals and the need for meaningful, all-party discussion. Submission to the minister of labour on proposed changes to the *Labour Relations Act*, February 1992.

16 Ontario, Legislative Assembly, *Hansard*, 35th Parl, 2nd Sess, (8 July 1992) at 1620.

17 Ontario, Legislative Assembly, *Hansard*, Parl, 2nd Sess, (October 1, 1992) at 2280.

18 Ontario, Legislative Assembly, *Hansard*, Parl, 2nd Sess, (November 4, 1992) at 3160.

19 *Economic Development and Workplace Democracy Act*, 1998.

20 *Canadian Public Policy*, Volume 34, No. 1, 2008.

21 Canadian Public Policy, Volume 26, "Mr. Harris, Mr. Rae and Union Activity in Ontario."

22 *Wilken, David K. "Manufacturing Crisis in Workers' Compensation." Journal of Law and Social Policy* 13 (**1998**): 124–165.

23 WSIB Funding Review, Mackenzie Associates, Joint Submission OCEU and CUPE ...

24 Campaign event, May 5, 1995.

25 *Public Policy.* Volume 34 No. 1, 2008, by Timothy Bartkiw.

CHAPTER 10

Energy

Will Stewart

NYONE WHO HAS DRIVEN ON University Avenue, the grand boulevard in the centre of Toronto, has likely seen, but perhaps failed to fully appreciate, the imposing statue of Adam Beck, architect of Ontario's electrical system. He stands atop his podium, which itself is covered with the names of the rivers across Ontario which have had their energy harnessed to produce public power for all. Despite his perch in the middle of one of Toronto's busiest and grandest avenues, Beck holds his steady glare fixed on the Legislature at the north end of the road, where he spent considerable time and invested much energy. In the early 1900s, Adam Beck moved from being a cigar manufacturer, horse enthusiast and mayor of London, Ontario, to the Legislature, where he dove headfirst into issues of public power generation and supply. Shortly thereafter, Beck's Party leader, Sir James Whitney, became premier of Ontario, ousting the Liberal premier, George Ross in what was Ontario's first (but definitely not last) election centred, at least in part, on electricity and pricing.

Adam Beck, and the Conservative party in Ontario, took issue with the Liberal government's decision to rely on private sector power companies for the electrification of the province. In a move that might shock many current day Ontario conservatives, and certainly those of the "Mike Harris conservative" variety, Whitney and Beck ran on a platform of public power, with the slogan "Power at Cost," and going so far as to declare that the "gifts of nature are for the public." By this they meant that the rivers and falls across the province would be used to dam and create this public power. The creation of Ontario Hydro started with a political mandate to provide power to "even the poorest working man" who "will have electric light in his house."

Beck was a man of such force and vision that the structures he put in lasted almost 100 years, from the early 1900s until the mid-1990s, when a very different Progressive Conservative Premier, Mike Harris, came to power with a very different vision for the system and with a plan to rely more and more on the private sector for energy, a policy option that conservatives had explicitly rejected some ninety years earlier.

While Beck acolytes of today might still hold his biases for "power at cost," by the mid-1990s in Ontario, his party had abandoned this long-held policy position. Importantly, so had the Liberal Party, leaving very little differences in their policy approach. Of course, we all have our biases. In full disclosure, the author of this chapter certainly does. As soon as I was done with my university studies in political science, I started my career in the Ontario civil service at the Ministry of Education and Training working on apprenticeship programs and certification. It quickly became clear that I preferred the pace and stimulation of politics more than the rigour of implementing effective program delivery and so I managed to find myself in the employ of John Baird, the MPP for Nepean-Carleton at the time, who had the added responsibility of being the parliamentary assistant to the minister of finance, one Ernie Eves.

Baird and I clicked right away and I spent much of my formal political career with him. I owe him a massive debt of gratitude for his faith in me, and his (sometimes?) willingness to listen to reason, advice, and strategy. As Baird's chief of staff, the two of us were inseparable for many years. The political ups and downs and the stories are ones I will never forget. I served as his chief of staff when he served as minister of community and social Services, where we were then also assigned the additional responsibilities for children and francophone affairs. We spent some time in the Office of the Chief Government Whip, which gave me a great understanding of legislative process and committee work. Finally, we went to the Ministry of Energy together as our last post in government prior to the PC's electoral defeat in October 2003. It is there that I developed a comprehensive understanding of the complexities of Ontario's Energy/Electricity file.

In my view, it is entirely fair to say that Premier Harris brought about many needed changes in the energy space, as the province and its electrical system were in a much different place than it had been in Beck's time. Ontario began as a vast geography possessing very little generation infrastructure and no significant transmission capacity. But the transformation that Beck's Ontario Hydro enabled, primarily by damming rivers for the generation of power, saw the province become the industrial powerhouse for the nation. Subsequent decades saw many changes in the provincial, regional and North American industrial context, and when Premier Harris came to office in 1995, he inherited a system that was far over capacity, mired in public debt (almost $40B dollars) and facing the very real challenge of retrofitting the province's nuclear reactor fleet which had still not been paid for, despite generating electricity for decades.

The Harris Government's controversial moves to engage the private sector were in fact by far from being the first. In fact, the move to "private power" began a decade before Premier Harris took office, in the government of Liberal Premier David Peterson, who first issued a request for proposals for Non-Utility Generators (NUGs), in an effort to fuel new industrial investments in power generation to support the province as the economy expanded. NUGs were seen as a way to reduce the risk of construction cost overruns, which the province had repeatedly experienced in the construction of its nuclear plants. The NUG strategy was also intended as a way to move these assets off the provincial books, at a time when Ontario was already struggling to fund the debt costs associated with previous electricity generation construction projects. These private sector generators received contracts from the Ontario government, who entered into power purchase agreements with them. In short, this meant that the government would purchase a set amount of electricity, at a set price, so long as the private sector corporation built, maintained, and staffed the power plant. A keen observer would note that the public policy shift to private sector power continued via the NUGs *through the entire five years of Premier Bob Rae's NDP government in the early 1990s,* despite their oft-voiced insistence that private power had no place in the province.

* * *

By the time the NDP were defeated in 1995, the troubles with Ontario Hydro were many. So much so that Mike Harris, as the leader of an opposition party in Ontario, defined electricity in Ontario as one of the significant obstacles which was holding the province back from realizing its full potential. Just as Whitney and Beck did almost 100 years before, Harris and his "revolutionaries" saw fit to define a new paradigm for electricity in the province in their campaign platform. Occupying just one paragraph in the *CSR* platform under the heading of Reforming Ontario Hydro, the PCs promised:

> A 5-year freeze will be placed on Hydro rates to give consumers, employers and industries guaranteed stability in planning their budgets. This may mean more changes at Hydro, including some moves towards privatization of non-nuclear assets. The current

Hydro chairman has already begun to lead this huge corporation back in the right direction. We will work with him, and many others, to bring Hydro back to its proper role, providing reliable and affordable electrical power to Ontario.[1]

It was that tiny paragraph, in a traditionally unimportant campaign platform that in fact set a new course for the electricity sector in Ontario. And it is critical to appreciate that this new course is the one that Ontario continues to follow to this day. Despite all the political debates, the accusations, the price interventions, and even through multiple Liberal governments and mandates, we largely have the electricity sector today, in Ontario, that grew out of that four-sentence promise made in 1994.

Of course, as is often the case, election promises in campaign platforms are not fully articulated and frequently lack specifics on how the government will actually do what they intend to do. But it is particularly interesting to note something that the Harris Revolutionaries explicitly said they would not do. The nuclear industry was specifically carved out as not being subject to "privatization." Such is the delicate nature of politics when it comes to nuclear power. In many ways, the costly nuclear plants in Pickering, Darlington, and on the Bruce Peninsula, were responsible for the massive debt that Ontario voters had been shackled with. On the other hand, the Mike Harris "revolutionaries" knew full well that playing around with nuclear power and its ownership could be a "bridge too far" for voters. This is worth special note at the outset because, in fact, the Harris Government did engage with the private sector in the nuclear space and the Bruce Power public/private partnership represents one of the most revolutionary elements in the Harris Legacy.[2]

Once the votes were counted in 1995, Mike Harris and the common-sense revolutionaries found themselves moving from third place party to government, and with that move came the challenge of implementing the promised reforms—actually "doing what they said they would do," a phrase that would become a mantra for the Harris government and a frequent touch point for those working inside of it.

To help provide practical answers to the question "What now?" the new government looked to former federal Liberal Energy (and Finance) Minister Donald MacDonald, who was asked to convene a group to provide that roadmap. MacDonald and his committee were tasked with considering how the industry could be improved, in recognition that there were significant structural and financial challenges with the status quo, a sector largely unchanged from that Beck conceived some ninety years before. The terms of reference were fairly clear: "The Government of Ontario is committed to upholding the objectives of sustainable affordable electricity rates, enhancing provincial competitiveness, preserving financial soundness and safeguarding Ontario's quality of life."[3]

In May 1996, "A Framework for Competition" was presented to the government by MacDonald and his team. The framework laid out the challenges with the current sector structure, discussed why that structure did not work in the later part of the twentieth century as it had at its inception, and set out a vision for how to increase competition across generation, transmission, and even local distribution of electricity. The headlines, of course, largely focused on the "break-up" of Ontario Hydro, the Crown corporation which had long been at the centre of the electricity, and in some ways industrial, and even natural resources policy in Ontario.

Bound by the promises in the *CSR*, and with the price of electricity "frozen," the new Government set about reorganizing the sector to align it with this new vision, a realignment and a vision that remain largely unchanged to this day.

The framework called for the creation of a series of new corporate entities as a first step in the move to promote competition. The generation assets were to be moved to what we now know as Ontario Power Generation (OPG). The mandate for safety and inspections moved to a newly created organization called the Electricity Safety Authority. Long distance transmission, and a considerable number of smaller distribution systems were housed in Hydro One. Rates and regulations, policies, and rules for electricity were to be assigned to the Ontario Energy Board (OEB).

As a way to further encourage and accelerate competition in the commodity of electricity, the Macdonald framework also called on the government to sell off non-nuclear assets, or at least use traditional equity markets to find investment or debt to fund the newly created companies and even assets such as individual power plants. Further, while municipalities would still be the focus for distribution assets through Local Distribution Companies (LDC), they too were encouraged to amalgamate, consolidate, or otherwise reduce their own numbers in the interests of efficiency and better service.

The framework was built on the belief that the new approach would not only modernize the system but would also lower prices for consumers:

> Under conservative assumptions, the Advisory Committee's analysis shows that its recommendations for a competitive generation market are likely to result in future wholesale electricity rates that are lower than those which can be expected by maintaining the current system. Moreover, these electricity price benefits can be achieved without imposing a burden on Ontario's taxpayers.[4]

While the work of MacDonald was welcomed with open arms by the Harris government, and largely implemented as written and advised, the advisory committee had clearly not foreseen the challenges that would lay ahead with regard to the volatility and elasticity of the price of electricity when it made its "conservative assumption" on that price. It was this "miss" which ultimately proved to be at the centre of every political crisis in electricity policy in Ontario for the next ten to fifteen years.

Harris and his cabinet moved forward at a considerable pace (as you may note is a theme across most chapters in this collection), taking the recommendations of the committee, and replying in 1997 with their own interpretation in the Direction for Change: Charting a Course for Competitive Electricity and Jobs in Ontario,[5] which set Ontario in motion to fundamentally change course from the one that Beck originally envisioned. Of course, that meant the considerable overhaul of Ontario Hydro and its "break-up" into the separate entities proposed in the report. It was thought that this fundamental reform would set the stage for competition, and in turn bring to bear the needed market forces, which would spur private development of generation assets, while leaving the taxpayer of the hook for these costs.

It is easy to gloss over the significance, the importance, and the sheer effort it takes to break up any government monopoly, never mind one that has been in existence for 100 years and provides the lifeblood of Ontario's economy to every home, business, and community building. As an author, it is easy to simply report that the Harris government passed the *Electricity Competition Act* in 1998 and brought a close to Sir Adam Beck's vision at the outset of the new century . . . but that simple sentence does not do justice to the massive undertaking that it was.

This reform was not simply a reassignment of responsibilities. Ontario Hydro had grown to be one of the largest integrated electrical utilities in North America. Untangling ninety-plus years of Ontario was no easy task. Simply breaking up a utility of this size, powering the country's largest provincial economy, with shared "interties" with both of Ontario's provincial neighbours as well as many American states, was a massive task. Ontario Hydro not only had nuclear, gas, coal, and water generating stations, but it also was one of the world's leading transmitters of electricity across massive distances. Simply separating the crown corporation into two commercial driven entities (Hydro One and Ontario Power Generation) would have been enough for most governments. But half measures and incomplete initiatives were certainly not the modus operandi of the Harris PCs as they pushed to reach a desired end state in just a few short years. Harris was elected in 1995, and by 1998, the government had already passed their *Electricity Competition Act* and a fundamental reorientation of the way our province actually works was underway.

The significance of this bill was not lost on the Liberal member from Renfrew North (at the time), Mr. Sean Conway.[6] Now, there is a lot to say about Mr. Conway and his impact on Ontario's electricity sector. He spent much of his time in politics, and afterwards, debating, discussing, and certainly speaking on electricity policy in Ontario. Mr. Conway foretold of the ongoing, and perhaps never-ending, debates on electricity policy, when he rose to discuss the Bill and said:

> Because it is so complicated, because it is so technical, it misses a great deal of public attention. In one way, I deeply regret the process I've seen since the introduction of this bill on June 9. We have paid very little attention, and not just the Legislature. I would chastise my friends in the press. I think this bill deserves a lot more attention than it has received, particularly from the print media. I understand that other things are going on, particularly in the print media. It's certainly not a television story. But there was a time when a newspaper like the *Globe and Mail*, perhaps even the *Toronto Star*, would assign two or three reporters with a strong business background to go at this story and develop it over the course of several days. That has not happened. But, trust me, the day will come when it will capture a lot of attention."[7]

Close readers will have learned to appreciate by now that the dissolution of Beck's Ontario Hydro was a big change. But perhaps the biggest change was the creation of the Independent Market Operator or IMO (now the Independent Electricity System Operator (IESO). The creation of this new entity was necessary as the province moved to a market price for electricity. The thinking was sound. The new framework was based on a firm belief that market prices would drive the creation of new, private sector power generation, which would mean that the fiscal risks around construction costs that Ontario Hydro had historically struggled with would become a thing of the past. New, private producers would rely on market signals to determine if they were to build capacity or provide power to the grid. The guiding theory was simple. When prices went up due to a lack of supply, producers would build new capacity, just as oil companies look to the global price of a barrel of oil to determine if, when and where investments in production can and should be made. Despite the many subsequent changes in the energy sector, by Liberal and Conservative governments, over the several decades since the end of the Harris era, this theory of rational market behaviour by suppliers underpins the structure we still have today.

With the stage set, the wholesale and retail markets were opened to competition at midnight on May 1, 2002, after considerable delays. According to the IMO (now IESO), the new market in Ontario had a total of 239 market participants, which was made up of ninety-three local distribution companies which primarily were (and continue to be) owned by municipalities; eighty-nine industrial customers who had such high electricity demand that they tie directly into the high-voltage lines under direct current, nineteen generators owned by both private entities, and the newly minted Ontario Power Generation which continued to hold more than 70 per cent of the generating capacity of the province and the fleet of nuclear reactors (retained in public hands as promised in the *CSR*).

* * *

As already noted, one of Premier Mike Harris' first acts was to cap the price on electricity at 4.3 cents/kWh, after rates had been raised consistently under the NDP government of Bob Rae from 1990 to 1995.

While this populist move was welcomed by Ontarians as a measure of relief, setting the price at that rate, which many considered too low, would ultimately end up costing the Harris government dearly before the end of the second mandate. If that "frozen" price from 1995 had not stayed fixed in the years until market opening, and had better reflected the true costs in those seven years, perhaps the change in prices after opening up to competition might not have caused such significant backlash when the market actually opened.

The market structure that Harris implemented consisted of two distinct parts: the wholesale and the retail market. The wholesale market was administered by the IMO. In its most basic form, the idea was that every five minutes there would be a fresh market price set. This spot market price would fluctuate based on which generators bid their power supply into the market and at what price. The system operator would then select the generators that had what was needed to provide power in particular parts of the province for servicing customers and at what price. Generators would have their bids accepted or rejected and the accepted power would be placed on the grid at the agreed price.

At first, the move to a market price was either welcomed or simply unnoticed by rate payers. The date of market opening had been deliberately set in the Spring, when the demand for electricity drops as furnaces are turned off in homes, the days become brighter and longer reducing the need for lights, but at a time when air conditioners and pool pumps have not yet been activated for the season. With lower demand, the market should respond with lower spot market prices. And it did, at first.

In the first month of this new approach to market-based power pricing in Ontario, the price did in fact fall. By averaging out the spot market price of power, based on the five-minute interval spot price, we can get an indication of what that monthly cost would be per kilowatt hour. The average spot market price of wholesale power in May of 2002 was 3.01 cents per kWh, considerably lower than Harris' frozen price of

4.3 cents per kWh, which many critics saw as too low to recover costs.[8] In short, the wholesale market was working. But, at the same time as Harris opened the wholesale market, he also allowed the retail market to open. Ultimately, this would be seen as perhaps the gravest misstep made. among all the changes to the electricity market. It certainly led to the political challenges that plagued the province in the years that followed.

The second component of the structure was the retail market, which is made up of "end use" customers, both residential as well as small and medium-sized businesses. In other words, the vast majority of the province. In most cases, the municipally owned electricity companies, or LDCs, took the position that they would pass the spot market price of electricity on to the customers, meaning that each month, homeowners would see a different average spot market price on their bills, which would then be used to calculate the price charged for what they consumed. After all, the LDCs were, and are, municipally owned, regulated monopolies with capped rates of return and they had no ability, or desire, to take on commodity price risk.

While the market opening was a success from a market function point of view, and initially resulted in lower prices, celebrations of the successful work and policy changes were short-lived. By the second month, prices had begun to rise, but even then, there was no immediate public outcry, as it was commonplace in the LDC billing cycles at the time to only have a bill every two months. So, consumption, at whatever the floating commodity price, did not come through to the customer as a bill to be paid for up to two months. But as Spring slowly turned into summer, the problem of a lack of supply for electricity began to surface.

It had long been assumed by planners of the system reforms (incorrectly as it turned out), that the shutdown and retrofit of the Pickering A nuclear plant would be completed well before market opening. In fact, many saw this as a necessary precursor to a successful market opening, as it would provide a large amount of power, and at a relatively low price.

Due to the nature of the technology, nuclear power cannot be easily stopped and once started must run 24/7. With low demand overnight, it was assumed that they would be "bidding in" very low-price power, in order to ensure their bid was accepted by the IMO. The conviction at time of launch, was that Pickering A could provide downward pressure on the spot market price, and the price that consumers would ultimately pay. In retrospect, opening the market prior to Pickering A actually refiring was a critical flaw in the planning. But it was not necessarily fatal on its own. If only the wholesale market had been opened, and customers were still on fixed price or averaged contracts (as many are for natural gas), the retail market could have still survived.

But there was an added challenge that could not have been predicted: 2002 ended up being the hottest summer in Ontario for fifty years. Ultimately, this meant that in addition to the price of power going up considerably in the early months after market opening, the added air conditioning load in the record hot summer temperatures meant that bills skyrocketed over the months that followed.

Opposition parties saw blood in the water and took to the airwaves to complain that "private power" was responsible for skyrocketing bills. Obviously, a less partisan look at the issue would have yielded a different result. Increased demand in a particularly hot summer, decreased supply due to Pickering A mismanagement, and a first-in-a-lifetime spot market price of power being passed through to customers were the true culprits.

For their part, the "market design committees" continued to espouse the wonders of the open market, telling anyone who would listen that the market was doing what it was supposed to do.[9] That is to say, that prices go up when demand it high and supply is low. Economics 101 they would tell the government. But numbers and market theories do not vote. By the time the summer bills ended up in the mailboxes of residential customers in the fall of 2002, the Ontario electorate had had enough of the experiment. On some days in the Legislature, Minister of

Energy John Baird was facing every single question in question period. Electricity prices were front page news daily. The Harris government was under siege and had to act.

The political opposition at Queens Park was successful in making the pricing of electricity entirely a political decision (and one they would come to regret when the Liberal party of Ontario assumed power in October 2003). For the Liberals, the strains in the electricity market gave them a proof point that the PCs were past their best, that they were not competent to govern and in the parlance of the Liberal party, the changes to the electricity market were to help the PC's ever-mysterious "rich friends" as part of the "hidden agenda."

While this rhetoric is to be expected from opposition political parties, it was a disappointment to the Harris Conservatives that those who had fought long and hard for a new market system for electricity for decades were suddenly silent. When the government was taking massive body shots each and every day on electricity, the executives of private energy companies, those who helped design the market, as well as those at law firms and financial corporations who would be paid to help bring new private power to Ontario proved unwilling to put their hands up, or necks on the line, to speak positively about the changes. Without supporting voices, the government had no choice but to act, as it was the only entity publicly defending the move.

It is important here to note that while there were certainly errors in the implementation process (opening retail and wholesale at the same time; not protecting the end residential customer from the fluctuating spot price) and in the timing of market opening (lack of supply due to Pickering A; hottest summer in decades), not everyone was adversely impacted. As an example, the residents of Toronto, and by extension the customers of Toronto Hydro, were protected from fluctuating spot market prices, as the utility decided to keep the commodity price at the frozen rate of 4.3 cents/KwH and create a variance account to true up the differences (much like the standard billing approach that customers were familiar with on natural gas). Despite this, opposition MPPs, media, and residents of Toronto were included among the loudest voices on the "massive increases in power costs." Of course, with the commodity price the exact same on their bills, the increase in bill amounts would have been 100 per cent attributable to their own usage in the hot summer. Despite pointing this out repeatedly in public communications, the narrative of Tory mismanagement proved far more appealing at the time than the realities of power usage. As is human nature, nothing was seen as an individual responsibility regarding usage . . . it simply must be someone else's fault.

In November 2002, the Ontario government moved to close the retail market. The pressure had become too much, especially for Harris' successor, Premier Ernie Eves, as he drew ever closer to an election window in what was assumed to be 2003 or early 2004. The government rolled out three successive announcements over three days which were intended to change the public narrative on electricity. The first was the big one—an announcement that the price of power would be once again capped at 4.3 cents/kWh for all customers. The second was a renewed commitment to conservation programs and demand-side management. The third was a plan to change the structure of the Ontario Energy Board in order to "put customers first."

If the government needed any validation that they were in this alone and could not rely on energy companies to defend the reform of the system, they did not have to wait long. Standing at a podium the morning after the first announcement, one Toronto energy executive began his remarks with "Welcome to California Hydro"[10] which was welcomed with chuckles and guffaws from the collection of energy executives and advisors in the room. His reference was to the challenges of prices and blackouts in California at the time.

At the time, the idea to close and cap the retail market was seen as one that could ensure the survivability of the wholesale side of the market. And in this it proved successful as it remains the basis for the electricity system Ontario has today. The thinking was that the price of power would continue to fluctuate but would be lower in the "shoulder seasons," higher in the summer and winter peaks and with Pickering A about to come back online, the province would soon have more supply, cooler weather, and the price would drop. This combination of factors would allow the province (accountable for financially backstopping the variance accounts) to remain close to balance. The common refrain in the key messages at the time was "The plan will pay for itself over the course of the plan."

We had just seen this movie, however. The government plan was essentially replicating the experience of Toronto Hydro on a province-wide basis and, as already discussed, we know that Toronto residents were just as angry as the rest of the province with the exact same set-up. The announcements in November 2002 did help stop the bleeding for the Ontario PCs, but it did spell the end of the retail market, much to the frustration of energy retailers who had gone door-to-door, selling stability in pricing at a time when the narrative of the day was focused on skyrocketing prices. These retailers, many with questionable sales tactics that remain memorable, certainly contributed to the confusion, but it is hard to assign too much blame to them, as the government allowed these tactics to happen within their system design.

The wholesale market, and the other market players that were created by the Harris break-up of Ontario Hydro continue to operate much as it was envisioned they would by the new system's designers. The goal was always "to get politics out of the sector." Ontario Hydro had always been a power producer but given that it was under the control of the government, it had also been used for economic development, and, in some cases, social policy. When the Liberals took power in October of 2003, they returned to using hydro policy as social policy, a move they almost had to make after all the criticism they heaped on Harris' design of the new system.[11]

Simply because the Eves government had succeeded in managing down the temperature on electricity prices did not mean they were "off the hook" on Energy. Given the size and scale of the electricity issue in the 1.5 years prior to the next election, the PC team knew this was something they had to defend against and where the Liberals were expected to attack. But their choice to attack on the subject of coal-generated power was a surprising one, and the Liberal leaned in heavily on this issue.

* * *

Throughout Premier Mike Harris' time in office, there was ongoing discussion on the health impacts of coal-fired generation facilities. Included in this public policy debate was the OPG-owned facility at Nanticoke, which had the distinction at the time of being the single largest smog-emitter in North America. By the early 2000s, Ontario saw health advocates and the Ontario Medical Association all releasing reports on the issue, which served to refocus the debate from one of economics and industrial development, to one regarding health outcomes, a much different fight.[12]

With the recognition of a need for a new approach to air quality, the Harris PCs looked for a new solution to a political challenge that had begun to plague the government. In August 2001, the Select Committee on Alternative Fuel Sources began new work, tabling a final report in June 2002 in the Legislature. It is important to note that this committee had representation from all three parties, but with a majority of the members being from Mike Harris' caucus. The various MPPs had robust and meaningful debate on what steps the government, and by extension the province, could take to encourage lower or non-emitting sources of fuel adequate to generate what appeared to be the unquenchable thirst for more power, but newly coupled with environmental considerations previously ignored in the industrial heartland of confederation.

Another chapter in this book will discuss Premier Harris' record on the environmental front, but the importance of this select committee cannot be overlooked. In fact, the role that it played in the "greening" of our electricity sector in Ontario is paramount. It was this committee, made up of entirely of partisan MLAs, who came together to draft a report which called for, among other things, a ban on coal as a fuel for generating electricity in the province. Their report came as the electricity market opened, with skyrocketing prices (in the eyes of the voters and critics) with all-party, and indeed unanimous support.

The PCs could have easily used their majority on the committee to change the terms of reference, stall, and/or craft a report as they saw fit. Such is the power of a majority government of any partisan stripe in our parliamentary system. Instead, what the people of Ontario received was a bold report which, in many ways, set the stage for how the electricity sector would continue to be transformed and modernized. It is extremely rare for any report, from any legislative or parliamentary committee for all parties to unanimously agree. This is doubly true when the committee has a topic where one or more parties believe they have an advantage politically in causing embarrassment to the other party or parties. The Liberals and the NDP could have withheld their support, just as the PCs could have used their majority to craft any report. Instead, Ontario received a genuine, multi-party report on green energy, sustainability, and environmentally focused power generation.[13]

The marquee recommendation in the select report was to phase coal out of the energy mix in Ontario by 2015. This recommendation had Premier Harris' strong personal support as evidenced by his own comments at the time.[14] This phasing-out of coal would be no small feat for a province with five coal-fired generation plants in full production. Coal is also very low priced as a fuel source compared to many other alternatives, especially natural gas. It took some fortitude for the committee members to knowingly recommend that the province move to more expensive fuel sources, at a time when electricity prices were also rising as a result of the changes to the electricity market's structure.

Nevertheless, the recommendation was made, accepted, and the planning began with a write-down of OPG's coal fired assets, which now would be terminated prior to the end of their planned production life. But what appeared, in 2002, to be a multi-party agreement on a process and a goal, quickly changed only a year later. Of course, all parties still supported the phase out of coal, but the Liberal Party of Ontario must have realized that they had made a strategic political error. By agreeing to the orderly phaseout of coal, the Liberals under opposition leader Dalton McGuinty had lost a weapon which they could otherwise use to attack the PCs in the 2003 general election. Additionally, they lost the opportunity to attack the Tories on an issue where the population was eager for battle. Ontarians were still angry at the electricity policy changes, and many were also inclined to see a weakness in the Harris Government's records on the environmental front.

Once the political operatives on the Liberal side of the aisle realized their error, policy changes driven from a political and campaign point of view trumped the sound energy policy previously agreed to by all parties through the deliberative committee process. When it came time to fight the 2003 general election, McGuinty's Liberals decided that 2007, just four years after the 2003 election, would be a better date for the complete removal of coal from the Ontario electricity sector. Their argument was that air quality issues could not wait, that better health outcomes could not wait and the removal of coal-based power generation from the Ontario system must be done faster. The attack was powerful and successful, wrong-footing the Tories and certainly helping the Liberals gain valuable political points in their victorious 2003 campaign.

Ironically, this politically fueled decision would ultimately lead to worse air quality in Ontario in the short term and all the way to 2015. Despite the 2015 goal of closing coal plants, OPG had developed government-approved plans to clean the emissions from the plants to mitigate adverse health impacts between the early 2000s and their planned closure in 2015. OPG had moved to install "scrubbers" to remove nitrous oxide and sulfur dioxide particulates. This investment in plants soon to be closed was still warranted given the positive environmental impacts and the length of time between the installation date and the eventual plant closures twelve years later.

When the Liberals chose to radically alter that timeline (from twelve years to only four), the business case for the scrubbers disappeared as, in industrial planning, four years is almost next month. So, the investment in scrubbers was canceled. It was clear to anyone who looked at the system, understood the province's industrial load, or even knew the first thing about system planning and the need for a grid that has major and minor generation facilities placed in a province in the right places to support a properly functioning grid, that the Liberals promise was simply impossible to achieve. The PCs jumped, suggested that this was a proof point that McGuinty was "not up to the job" as the PCs campaigned on for the second straight election. But as is so often the case, emotions and aspiration in an election campaign can often beat out facts and reason.

The PCs were eventually proven right. The coal plants could not be closed in four years as the Liberals promised. In fact, the last of the coal plants closed on the last day of 2014, meaning the Select Committee on Alternative Fuels had seen the achievement of its original objective of having them all gone by 2015. In reality, the Liberals beat the original all-party, multi-year target by only twenty-four hours. This was a fact the PCs were happy to point out as proof that their policy position had been correct. Of course, they pointed that out from the opposition benches to a populace which had long since forgotten the nuances of this issue.

What was lost at the time and is sadly still under-appreciated is that the Liberal's completely political decision in 2003 and the resulting cancelation of the scrubbers' installation meant that Ontarians had to breathe dirtier air for twelve years more than they would have had to if the original recommendation of the all-party committee recommendation had been adhered to.[15]

* * *

In many ways, electricity policy discussions during the campaign in 2003 were centred on the Mike Harris policies regarding electricity reform, even though it was Premier Ernie Eves who led the PCs into battle in that general election. The price challenges, rapid policy changes, and of course, the blackout in Ontario and many US states, were all fresh in the minds of the electorate and the Liberals clearly capitalized on this political opportunity. Frequently, the Liberals pointed to the challenges in the electricity sector as part of an overall campaign narrative that the PCs were simply not capable of managing the province, and specifically, that the policies of the Harris/Eves PCs were making life worse for Ontarians.

Other than rising prices and the timing of exit from coal-fired generation, there were two other fronts in the Liberal attacks, both focused on what the Liberals and the NDP said were adverse consequences of "private hydro" and which successfully capitalized on the fears of the electorate.

First, the Liberals took aim at a public/private partnership ("P3") which the Harris Government had created for Bruce Power, the nuclear plant on Lake Huron. Given that OPG had massive generation assets and that their dominant position would likely constrain the hoped-for benefits of a free and open market, the Harris government opted to outsource the operations of one of OPG's largest nuclear assets. By having it run by a new, private sector corporation, there was a belief that Bruce would act as a counterbalance to the market dominance of OPG. The P3 arrangement removed both the actual power generation, as well as the pricing of the output of the Bruce plant, from OPG's management oversight. The belief was that a privately managed Bruce plant would also provide a direct and real time benchmark for the efficiency of the OPG plants and operations, given that Bruce would have the same type of reactors as OPG—AECL, heavy water CANDU reactors.

The innovative approach in this P3 deal was that OPG would still remain the owners of the facility, just not act as the operators. Given the long-term liability of spent nuclear fuel, this approach of outsourcing operations instead of transferring the asset was key to making the P3 politically workable for all. At the time, critics characterized this arrangement as a move to "more private hydro" (in a similar way as the Liberals and NDP continue to communicate to this day on other policy areas such as healthcare).

Once again, the lasting impact of the Harris-Era policy reforms can clearly be seen. Once in power, the Liberals saw the benefits and workability of the arrangement and, instead of canceling the deal, in fact continued to renew and promote it. They fully embraced what has become known as one of the most successful public–private partnerships in the country, if not beyond. The Bruce Power P3 deal has now celebrated 30 years, and the nuclear plant has gone through countless renovations and retrofits, fully funded by the private sector, which have served to extend the plant's working life and increase output. It has even become a supplier of medical isotopes for cancer treatments.

The second focus of additional attacks from the Ontario Liberals and the Ontario NDP focused on private hydro as it pertained to Hydro One, which Harris had created as the province's transmitter (and sometimes distributor) of electricity. Hydro One, at the time, controlled well over 90 per cent of the province's long-distance, high voltage electricity lines—the lines that move massive amounts of power from power plants to markets. This transmission essentially functioned as a "pass-through" monopoly, with rates and returns set by a government body. And there is no doubt that the Harris PCs certainly did have Hydro One in its sights for eventual privatization.

With all the other challenges the Harris government faced on the electricity file however, a decision was made not to pursue this policy in the immediate term, especially after the blackouts experienced in the United States and Canada. The opposition continued to belabour the government, in this case communicating to an electorate that was evidently willing to listen, about how the recently experienced blackout was another example of PC mismanagement and the direct result of "private power" in Ontario (despite the fact that there was little to no private power in the province at this time). In fact, Hydro One was still owned by the government, and the blackout was actually caused by mismanaged tree maintenance in Ohio, and had nothing at all to do with Ontario, Mike Harris, or any policy changes from the PC government in Ontario. But the Liberal narrative was far more concise, direct, and played on pre-existing concerns about the open market in Ontario.

And here again, we find a big proof point regarding the long-term merits of the Harris-era policy reforms in the electricity sector. Despite arguing against private sector involvement in the electricity sector and whipping up price and reliability fears attributed to the actions of non-government actors, it was the Liberals themselves who would ultimately sell off a controlling interest in Hydro One and see the organization move from a crown corporation to one that is public traded on the Toronto stock exchange. The Liberals not only did not reverse the decisions they campaigned against, but in fact "doubled down" on the Harris vision and pushed privatization further than even Premier Ernie Eves was willing to do!

* * *

It is now commonplace in Ontario to think about electricity policy in Ontario as private sector led. This is a massive change from when Premier Harris first sat in his premier's office chair in Whitney Block at Queen's Park. While Beck's steely glare continues to be immovably fixed on the "Pink Palace" up the road on University Avenue, one can't help but wonder what he may have thought of the big changes Mike Harris made happen. On the one hand, Harris' policies were very different from those Beck envisioned. But to simply conclude that Adam Beck would have never supported such changes may be premature. There is no debate that Beck's policies ensured that Ontario had the integrated, affordable, and expertly moved electricity needed to turn our province into the economic engine of confederation. But, by the 1990s, Beck's vision had moved to the end-state of most government monopolies, bloated, in debt, lacking needed investments for modernization, and yet still, somehow, facing electricity shortages in the immediate term.

Before Beck was a master central planner, he was a businessman. Beck understood as a cabinet minister that he had a product that businesses needed: the lifeblood of manufacturing is electricity. But it is fair to wonder if Beck would have seen that, by 1995, the time for Ontario Hydro was past, and that it was time for the business sector, with global experience and insight, to help Ontario built the electricity sector it would need for the next 100 years.

As we look back on the Mike Harris era, almost thirty years after he first rode the *CSR* to power in 1995, we certainly see his lasting legacy in the market-driven system we have in Ontario today. We are blessed with multiple, new, generating plants built without taxpayer dollars, including significant, private sector, non-emitting sources. To this day, we have one of the most successful public–private partnerships ever, operating a major nuclear plant, and we have successful conservation programs that see private sector companies rewarded for encouraging less consumption. We have a series of integrated government entities to ensure the effective management of the electricity system. We have rid our province of coal-generated electricity, making our grid one of the cleanest in the world with over 95 per cent of our power coming from non-emitting sources. And, in perhaps the biggest success of all, we saw the Liberal government that replaced Harris' revolutionaries continue down the same path he had marked out for them and even go one step further, pushing Hydro One into a privately held, for-profit, publicly traded organization.

It may be ironic, but the role of ensuring Mike Harris' vision for energy policy was permanently entrenched fell to the Ontario Liberals. But enshrine it they did, perhaps the most compelling proof you can find of the enduring nature of the Harris electricity legacy.

Notes

1   *The Common Sense Revolution*, 1994, p. 14.

2   I will come back to Bruce Power later in this chapter, but interested readers can also find another perspective on this important policy file in Jack Mintz and Terry Corcoran's chapter on Fiscal Policy and Privatization.

3   Terms of Reference, included as Appendix A in the final report of the Mcdonald Commission Report - https://archive.org/details/frameworkforcomp00adviuoft/page/134/mode/2up?view=theater

4   Page VIII—Introduction - A framework for competition: the report of the Advisory Committee on Competition in Ontario's Electricity System to the Ontario Minister of Environment and Energy (https://archive.org/details/frameworkforcomp00adviuoft/page/n15/mode/2up?q=conservative+assumptions)

5   https://archive.org/details/directionforchan00ontauoft/page/n7/mode/2up

6   Sean Conway was certainly a great legislator, and a great orator. He was certainly a thorn in the side of the government generally, and the minister of energy in particular. But he was also dedicated to our province and the betterment of public institutions. When Sean retired from public life, we lost a truly great legislator who was always ready for a political story on the history of our province. He was recognized for his efforts by being awarded the Order of Ontario. Despite our policy fights both public and private, I consider Sean to be friend to this day. We continue to disagree, but his contributions to this province are clearly with us for a long time.

7   Parliament-36, session-2, 1998-10-28. https://www.ola.org/en/legislative-business/house-documents/parliament-36/session-2/1998-10-28/hansard-1. It is quite telling that even in 1998, politicians were already noting the depleting resources, interest, and ability of the press to adequately cover the significant debates of the day, even before the widespread rise of social media and the collapse of the "mainstream media" funding model of advertising and subscriptions.

8   IESO Historical Price of Power Reports - http://reports.ieso.ca/public/PriceHOEPAverage/PUB_PriceHOEPAverage_2002.xml

9   Comments from MacDonald, Carr, Budd saying the market was working as it should. https://www.theglobeandmail.com/report-on-business/power-failure-ontarios-aborted-plan/article25426056/

10 This is a personal recollection. It was Courtney Pratt speaking at a podium 3 feet from me at a head table at an energy breakfast. Hard to forget.

11 As an editorial comment beyond the defined time-scope of this article. . . . Not only did the Liberals ensure politics stayed in energy, but they in fact made the process worse by returning to the old mindset, if not the old structure, by creating an additional fee for customers for renewable power. While the goals were environmentally laudable, the government paid very large premiums on that power, in some cases as high as 80 cents/kWH. With the price to the customer closer to

5 cents, the Liberal government needed a way to pay for the loss of purchasing something at 80 cents and selling it for 4.3 cents and thus returned Ontario to taxpayer-funded social policy via electricity rates.

12 OMA report, May 1998. Interested readers will also want to read former Ontario Gord Miller's section on Smog Abatement in the Environment Chapter of this book

13 https://www.ola.org/en/legislative-business/committees/alternative-fuel-sources/parliament-37/transcripts/committee-transcript-2002-may-15

14 https://www.theglobeandmail.com/news/national/ontarios-electricity-deregulation-to-have-green-benefits-harris-says/article4145002/.

– Mr. Harris's speech yesterday stated the government's commitment unequivocally. "I believe in open, competitive markets, because they help keep costs low and encourage innovation. And I believe we need to apply the same thinking to the electricity sector." One of the benefits of an open market, he said, would be a shift to renewable energy sources as the price of fossil fuels rises. "Fuel cells, wind power, other alternative sources of power will become increasingly important and will become more and more competitive," he said.

15 It is worth noting that the PCs have only won two elections since the second Mike Harris majority in 1999. Their focus on thoughtful, long-term policy positions in the energy space had long-term and adverse impacts on their political prospects. Interestingly, the PCs eventual return to power under Premier Ford was also driven in large part by politically successful but perhaps short-term policy regarding Ontario's energy system.

CHAPTER 11

Environment

Gordon Miller

THE ENVIRONMENTAL POLICY CONSEQUENCES OF the Mike Harris era including his famous the *CSR* are not as simplistic and negative as many opponents and commentators would report. They are, in fact, a complex mix of outcomes that include both mundane attempts at efficiency, and at least one serious failure with disastrous consequences. They also include several bold and far-reaching initiatives for which due credit has not yet been paid.

In any case they are all best understood if one considers them in light of three major influences that were molding the government initiatives in environmental, conservation and natural resources policy during the tenure of Premier Harris.

The first and most obvious influences were the priorities and focus of the people advising and staffing the offices of the new government at Queen's Park. One of the main reasons the *CSR* political platform was such a success was that it was communicated with intensity and deeply understood by all those involved in the election process.[1] That process discipline permeated the political campaign and very much carried through into government as it produced a cohort of "troops of the *CSR*" that went on to serve as the political staff of the premier's and cabinet ministers' offices.

Many of these (mostly very young) staffers were deeply immersed in the teachings of Milton Friedman, someone who didn't really understand the natural environment and largely viewed it as an irrelevant externality. In that context the Ministry of the Environment (MOE) and Ministry of Natural Resources (MNR) were seen to be of little political importance other than as a source of budget cuts (the first priority of the *CSR*) to help address the financial crisis that the province was clearly in. Their initial naivety (which some would excuse as inexperience) in this regard would come to play an important role in future environmental management events.

Other prime concerns of the Harris government were the overall size of government as well as its intrusive regulatory environment. Another big concern crystallized in the course of the first few years, the search for cost savings dictated the need for the disentanglement of the provincial government from the municipal level of governance. As a bureaucrat who was working on the inside of government at that time, I could see the seriousness of the problems they were trying to address. But I could also again see the naivety of their, often simplistic, policy approaches, as they tried to tackle a sophisticated and complex governmental system that had been emerging as a response to the evolving Ontario economy.

The second significant influence involved in forming the environmental performance of the government during the *CSR* was the powerful, well-structured bureaucracy of the provincial civil service. At that time, the civil service was still largely functioning with the organization and efficiency which was a legacy of the Bill Davis government, but it had been subjected to some restructuring as well as an infusion of more radical leftist elements through five years of NDP rule. Consequently, there were forces within the civil service that would ideologically oppose the initiatives spawned by the *CSR* and try to thwart them. But, by and large, the greatest resistance to budget cuts and restructuring would come from a proud public service that truly understood the role and function of government in Ontario and although not philosophically opposed to constraints, were very concerned that change be done "correctly" and in a proper policy context.

The third and perhaps most profound influence that would shape the evolution and outcomes of the environmental policy agenda of the Harris years, was the character, personality and cultural heritage of the premier himself. Mike Harris was not a product of the elite culture that permeates the GTA and the university cities of southern Ontario. He was, and is, a northerner, and even now that concept is alien to the understanding of much of the southern Ontario populous, I know what that means because I am one too.

Growing up in northern Ontario gives a person a different perspective of the land, the natural environment and the people who live and build their lives there. In the south, the land is privately owned and usually modified to a purpose such as agriculture or rural estates. Southerners are restricted to life in an urban landscape and the narrow worldview that implies. To reach nature, one must travel significant distances, and so it is difficult to cultivate a comprehensive understanding of the natural landscape.

In the north, you may live in an urban municipality, but the land around a short distance away is public, termed crown land. You can fish, hunt, camp, ski, snowshoe or canoe the wilderness and, outside of the provincial parks, it is all free and open and minutes away. With an inexpensive permit, you even can cut enough firewood to heat your home. For northerners, much of life revolves around camps (cottages), boats, snowmobiles, all-terrain vehicles and pickup trucks. The lifestyle shapes your perceptions, and it certainly did so for the twenty-second premier raised in North Bay, where the family business was a tourist fishing camp.

It did not take long for the wide-eyed innocence of the "troops" with respect to the environment and natural resources file to display itself.

As an unsuccessful candidate, on the day the new cabinet was sworn in, I was an invited guest to the event in the Legislature and the following reception at the lieutenant governor's suite. But I was also a current district manager for the Ministry of the Environment in North Bay (still on unpaid leave). So, I was known as someone who had a perspective on matters of the environment. I was buttonholed at the reception by some of the new zealous young staffers who were anxious to hear my comments on the just-sworn-in minister of the environment, Brenda Elliott. They were somewhat downcast at my response that I was unfamiliar with her and totally unaware of Ms. Elliott's credentials for the job. They quickly and enthusiastically piped in, "but she runs a green store in Guelph." They became more deflated and despondent when I explained that, while I was sure Minister Elliott's business experience would serve her well in cabinet, the MOE mandate was about challenging problems like sewage treatment, air pollution and waste management, not experience generally acquired in the retail "green" trade. It was then I realized that navigating through future environmental policy reforms was going to be an educational challenge for the new government *and* the experienced bureaucracy.

One of the early Harris Government attempts to disentangle the provincial and municipal roles happened to be the reform of the structure and function of Conservation Authorities, an important player in environment and natural resources policy in Ontario. Despite the substantial disruption of the status quo involved, I would have to say that from my perspective, in the end, it worked out reasonably well for governance of these institutions. But it must be recognized that at the start of this initiative, the Harris team were driven to reduce duplication and save money and they may not have had a complete understanding of the roles and responsibilities of the agencies involved and the implications of completely devolving governance to the municipalities.

Conservation Authorities (CAs) oversee flooding and land use activities in areas of land defined by one or more watersheds, the boundaries of which reflect the natural landscape. At that time, Conservation Authorities were primarily creatures of municipal governments who occupied the lands in the watersheds the CAs oversaw. The local governments appointed most members to the CA's board of directors and were levied, or voluntarily granted, most of the operating funds. But the province, through the Ministry of Natural Resources (MNR) also provided grants, in support of various activities, and in exchange retained the right to appoint a specified number of board members as well. As an informed third-party observer at the time, I would say that the model did not work well.

Years of constraints of the MNR budget before 1995 had been reflected in the CA budget transfers and caused tensions in the CA board structure. The MNR bureaucrats were content to pass on constraints, but they were reluctant to release the degree of control they had over CA activity. The situation was ripe for *CSR* reform, and it came in tandem with the cuts. Early in the Harris era, the MNR funding for CAs was dropped completely and the province withdrew its appointees to the boards. Going forward, the CAs' funding would all have to come from its member municipalities (and any grants or programs they could acquire from other ministries or the federal government).

The impact of this initiative is best illustrated by the example of the North Bay-Mattawa Conservation Authority (NBMCA) in the premier's home riding. At the time, the NBMCA occupied an industrial building in the industrial park of North Bay. It was not huge, but it had yard space and was large enough to accommodate the vehicles, equipment and staff of a busy CA. When the provincial austerity measures hit, that lease was terminated, the staff was trimmed and the whole operation had to be shoehorned into a tiny (I would say substandard) office space in an old municipal building. I cite this example as an illustration of the commitment of the Harris government to its ideals. Not only was this disruptive to the local programming of the CA and annoying to the municipalities of the premier's riding, but the vacant industrial building (now without a tenant) was owned by a couple, the husband who was the premier's best friend and the wife who was his campaign manager. There were no favourites to be spared in this revolution.

* * *

All things considered, and despite the painful transition, the governance change turned out, in the end, to be a prudent and wise move. The provincial ministry was removed from meddling in local government activities and municipalities had to reconceptualize and rationalize their relationships with their CAs. New programs were developed, and new funding sources were created. The NBMCA and all of its companion CAs in the province survived, and (after some hardship) eventually prospered again.

But one austerity and outsourcing initiative, implemented by the well-intentioned but naive and inexperienced government, played an unfortunate role in what turned out to be the most serious environmental tragedy in Ontario in living memory. To begin to comprehend what happened at Walkerton and how the fiscally driven decisions of 1995–1997 had such an unintended, but undeniably tragic impact, in 2000, one has to go back and consider the history of the regulation of drinking water supplies in Ontario. In 1970, various public health and pollution control functions of the province and municipalities were consolidated as the responsibility of the newly formed Ontario Ministry of the Environment by the Bill Davis government. Included in that package was the responsibility for the approval, regulation and inspection of communal drinking water supplies (including but not limited to municipal-run drinking water systems). This seemed logical to most because, at that time, the Ontario Clean Water Agency (OCWA), an agency of the province, still played a major role in operating both municipal sewage and drinking water treatment utilities for the municipalities on a contract basis. This was necessary because in those days many municipalities did not have the sophistication or capacity to run utility operations on their own. But, not all in the bureaucracy accepted this structure as desirable. Some believed that the MOE was an organization that should be focused on a clean healthy environment and stopping the pollution of same. In their eyes, safe drinking water was clearly a job for public health units, just like food systems and restaurant hygiene.

Nonetheless, municipal water systems stayed under the regulatory authority of MOE through the 1970s and 1980s. In the early 1990s, however, the debate over appropriate responsibility resurged again within the MOE. The NDP government of Bob Rae had begun applying severe constraints to ministry budgets and there was much internal discussion as to what responsibilities the MOE could get out of. The question was raised internally, "Why do we regulate municipal drinking water plants?" The debate didn't result in changes to the regulatory system, but it did cause bureaucrats to deprioritize drinking water plant regulation.

This was the state of things when the Harris team took the reins and started looking for efficiencies in the MOE file. The idea of passing regulatory authority for drinking water to public health was given a pass, but another opportunity presented itself. As a relic of its historically dominant role in utility-operations, the MOE still used its significant laboratory capacity to give a highly discounted analytical service to water and wastewater utilities of municipal utilities (this involved hundreds of thousands of samples per year). This service was seized upon as an unnecessary intrusion of government into the private analytical laboratory business and, quite frankly, it was. The situation had developed innocently enough. MOE laboratories were initially world-class and originally filled an un-serviced need for high quality analytical services. They were, at first, the only place available to provide the service at the required quality and quantity. But by 1996, the private sector had developed and expanded considerably, so it made sense to tell the municipalities to seek private labs for their analytical needs. The political staff saw this as both a route to cost-savings and a legitimate example of how "reinventing government" through outsourcing could be put into practice. The MOE staff saw benefit in "disentangling" themselves from drinking water regulation. And so, that is what the province did. Unfortunately, in that move, a serious procedural error was tragically embedded in the drinking water protection system.

In the summer of 2000, the Walkerton tragedy occurred, with seven fatalities (confirmed in course of the subsequent public inquiry) and widespread serious illness. The details and consequences of that event were thoroughly dissected and comprehensively documented by the O'Connor Commission Report. O'Connor found that there were multiple causal factors, including:

- the well system was unsound and unsafe;
- an unusual rainfall event had massively contaminated the source;
- most importantly, the operators responsible, Stan and Frank Koebel, deceived the regulators in various ways and had submitted fraudulent samples for "chlorine residuals."[2]

Subsequent to the investigation, the fraudsters, whose dereliction was directly accountable for the tragedy, plead guilty to common nuisance and were convicted for their crime. Although the MOE's lack of enthusiasm for being responsible for drinking water regulation was revealed through various testimony, no fault was found with the MOE inspector. Simply put, the inspections had been properly done but the inspector had been deceived. In essence, as with many regulatory regimes in place today, when one level of government regulates another, it does not usually contemplate outright fraud by the regulated entity.

But this is not the whole story. Because there was also a fatal flaw in the system that had been introduced by the privatization of drinking water testing and which inadvertently removed a safety mechanism that may have made all the difference at Walkerton in 2000. Prior to the privatization, the analysts at the MOE labs would flag any drinking water sample from a communal supply that appeared to violate drinking water standards. In addition to immediately advising the utility, procedure required them to directly alert the district manager (DM) of the relevant MOE District Office. As a district manager myself, who worked under these procedures. I had, over the years, received such calls and would immediately dispatch an environmental officer to the utility to inspect, re-sample, investigate and take such action necessary to confirm and correct the problem. The officer sent was normally skilled in the science and technology necessary to understand the situation and, typically, they had inspected the facility previously and knew the staff personally. This was a failsafe in the regulatory system that had served the public of Ontario well over the years by heading off drinking water quality problems as quickly as possible. And this was the failsafe that had been unintentionally disabled in the rush to outsource the lab analysis system.

The requirement to notify both the utility and the MOE DM had not been set down in regulation. Why would it be? It was required by MOE procedure and the MOE was the ones analyzing the water samples. The procedure had worked well for years. But, when municipal utilities moved to contract private labs to do their analyses, no such requirement to notify the MOE was built into the contracts because no regulation required it. It is in fact entirely likely that neither party were even aware that MOE had been operating such an internal procedure as a safeguard.

This is the risk of implementing any change in complex environmental policy structures. The subtle nuances of existing policy can be skimmed over in the zeal to achieve other goals such as austerity and efficiency. Clearly it is always best to ensure that changes to such policies involve third parties, public consultation and considered review. Ultimately, as the government in power, Premier Harris accepted the appropriate responsibility for the Walkerton tragedy and all the recommendations of the O'Connor commission were enacted.

* * *

Sometimes environmental legacy outcomes are the result of a thoughtful step-by-step progression of a plan and sometimes they emerge somewhat unexpectedly from the fog of war. This I believe was the case in the ultimate definition and protection of the landform called the Oak Ridges Moraine (ORM).

The Oak Ridges Moraine is a ridge of, primarily, sand and gravel, left by the termination of the glaciers and which runs parallel to and about sixty kilometers north of Lake Ontario. It extends from the Niagara Escapement in the west to the Trent River in the east. The landform is particularly important because its permeable surface allows rain to penetrate and recharge the groundwater aquifers servicing local populations and gives rise to all the streams and rivers that flow south through the Greater Toronto Area into Lake Ontario.

Being hilly and with coarse soils, the ORM was never fully cleared for prime agricultural land so, in 1995, it remained a rolling landscape of fields and woodlots with interspersed small community development. But that was about to change.

The great sprawl of urban development was rapidly spreading north, as water and sewage infrastructure was extending north from Toronto and Durham Region. Speculators had secured vast areas of this land and the expectation was that they would facilitate burgeoning suburban development for years to come. It looked like a great engine for Ontario's economic growth and the ambitions of the *CSR*. But there was one environmental policy weakness that would come to plague the hopes of the new government.

Land development in Ontario was and still is governed by *The Planning Act*, which mandated individual municipalities to undertake studies and consultations and produce official plans (OPs) that would govern how lands could be subdivided, what kinds of land use were permitted and how appropriate infrastructure would be secured. Changes or variance from the OPs were challenged at and adjudicated by the Ontario Municipal Board (OMB) an independent tribunal appointed by the province. The system had, over the years, been reasonably efficient in organizing development within municipalities (although not without some colourful conflicts). But this planning system simply was not designed to deal with landscape-level natural heritage or integrate thinking about cultural values that transcended municipal boundaries. And, with suburban sprawl climbing up the south-facing slope of the ORM, unrest and concern was developing among the communities on the Moraine, as well as the urban centres along the plains adjacent to Lake Ontario. It could not be ignored that excluding Toronto itself, these were electoral districts which had voted strongly for Harris and the *CSR*.

The first response of the government was a wise one. In 1996, they announced the first provincial policy statement (PPS). This was a document that required municipal planners to "have regard to" a variety of provincial government priorities in their OPs. Significant among these priorities were various environmental objectives, like protecting significant woodlands and wetlands on the landscape. The PPS was an important development in land-use policy and lead to changes in the conceptualization of planning. But, alas, when it came to facing the political challenges of the ORM, it was not enough.

As development continued apace north up the moraine, a coalition of interests opposing this rampant land development emerged. On the moraine, residents feared that the rural landscape, with its interconnected matrix of forests, wetlands and heritage agricultural features, would be obliterated. Further south, people worried about the quality and flow of their well water and the health of their streams and rivers. A focal point emerged when it was realized that current planning approvals pending in Richmond Hill would result in the severing of the last east/west corridor of natural heritage lands. The ORM would lose ecological connectivity and be cleaved into two isolated zones. A challenge was raised at the Ontario Municipal Board (OMB) and the City of Toronto stepped in and approved funds to support those groups fighting the development approvals at the OMB. The media leapt upon the emotive issue and the game was on.

Another major public challenge came in March 2000, when two requests for review were filed pursuant to The Environmental Bill of Rights, citing the need for a new policy, act, or regulation to produce a long-term strategy to protect the ORM. One was filed by environmental groups and the other by two Toronto city councilors.

The government response was quick. In May 2000, the requests were denied in a letter signed by the three cabinet ministers having jurisdiction (the ministers of municipal affairs and housing, natural resources and environment). They stated, "the provincial government is committed to the environmental integrity of the Oak Ridges Moraine. We believe the guidelines, policy and legislation comprising the current land-use planning system in Ontario provides that protection. Since this sound provincial and municipal framework of policy, guidelines and legislation exists, each of us does not believe that a further review is warranted."[3]

I suspect this position was taken on the advice and assurance of the public servants of those ministries who truly believed in the system they had created. But those with experience and insight into the process knew that the premise of that argument was deeply flawed. The planning challenges of the rapid buildout of GTA suburban construction had far outstripped the capacity of the historic planning process to cope. Failure of the case before the OMB was imminent and a crisis in municipal land use was at hand.

What was needed was a planning policy system that would not be subject to the narrow priorities of individual municipalities and local developers. Planning was required at the level of the Oak Ridges Moraine as a landform. Fortunately, there was prior success to draw on.

Recognizing and protecting a landform was not new to a Progressive Conservative government in Ontario. In 1973, the Bill Davis government had passed the *Niagara Escarpment Planning and Development Act*.

The legislation was controversial at the time, and it required the adoption and acceptance of a new way of thinking about land use and land-use planning that was not easily reconciled with the way business had been done up until that day. But it worked, and by 2001, it was internationally recognized as a successful model. Moreover, the "father" of the Niagara Escarpment Plan, Norm Stirling, was still sitting at the Harris cabinet table.

So, out of the tension and confusion of the political battle on the moraine the debate suddenly turned. The need for a dramatic new approach was recognized. Without prior notice, the minister of municipal affairs and housing, Chris Hodgson, rose in the Legislature and tabled the *Oak Ridges Moraine Protection Act*, which placed a six-month moratorium on development on the ORM to afford the opportunity for a rapid but comprehensive program of public consultation. The opposition's surprised reaction was to call for the government to "do it now." With a glance to the government house leader, Janet Ecker, and her affirmative nod, Minister Hodgson called the opposition challenge and the bill was immediately and unanimously given first, second and third Reading and became law. Subsequently, the necessary consultation was completed and culminated in the *Oak Ridges Conservation Act* in December 2001. That legislation, in turn, lead to The Oak Ridges Conservation Plan the following year.

The new plan focused on protecting and improving the ecological and hydrological integrity of the ORM and ensuring that the moraine is maintained as a continuous natural landform, while providing opportunities for continued development in existing urban and rural settlements. It was a complete "rethink" of land-use planning in Ontario and it brought new and innovative approaches into play. The crisis was averted. The solution was well received and a legacy for the Harris government was created. Even the often-critical Environmental Commissioner opined, "The ECO commends the government for enacting the ORMCA and the plan and recognizes the work of the staff of the various ministries involved, the members of the external advisory panel, municipalities and environmental groups, and the thousands of Ontarians who made submissions. The ECO acknowledges the difficulty of doing this work so quickly. Developing and finalizing the plan within a year was a remarkable achievement. Overall, MAH (Municipal and Housing) did an excellent job of balancing the competing interests and submissions."[4]

* * *

One environmental issue that clearly captured the attention of the Harris government was that of air quality, especially in the GTA airshed. Smog, although it involves complex science in origin, is easily understood by the public and their elected representatives. Smog alerts were far too common in the late 1990s and the adverse health effects were well documented.[5] Doctors and other health professionals were vocal in their concern and exhorted the government to take action.

One contributing factor to smog days was the automotive emissions from the increasing traffic congestion in the urban areas. Cars in the 1990s were still significant emitters of hydrocarbons and particulates compared to their successors in subsequent decades. The volatile organic compounds that result from poorly tuned engines were key components in catalyzing the atmospheric formation of smog. The question was, how could the province address and mitigate this situation?

Direct emission controls installed on each car was the best solution, but there were a number of practical constraints. Emissions control technology was developing rapidly, but standards that would require new cars to meet more stringent pollution reductions could not feasibly be set by Ontario alone. Auto standards were generally negotiated and set on a North American level for all manufacturers (with input from the major overseas companies). Ontario was a participant in those negotiations, but the Harris government had to accept that, for the time being, the auto emission standards applied to the model year 1989 were what they had to work with.

Another problem was the large existing inventory of cars on the road. In 1995, the protracted recession had been taking a severe toll on the economy. The average age of cars on the road was thus quite high, as Ontarians with limits to disposable income (including those unemployed or on welfare) were trying to keep old "clunkers" on the road as long as possible. Even the cars in the fleet equipped with the current technology were six model-years old and there were many vehicles that predated the cleaner 1989 standard. But one possible solution that was within Ontario's reach, was to get those cars tested for emissions and running well or get them off the road. That's how and why Drive Clean was conceived.

But a Progressive Conservative government introducing a program requiring people to get their vehicle tailpipe emissions tested surely would be controversial among more libertarian elements of their electoral base. Due to this concern, the environment minister of the day, Norm Sterling, appealed to cabinet and was granted an unprecedented multi-million dollar budget to engage Ontarians with a multi-channel advertising campaign, beginning months before the policy was announced and starting with a focus on one core message, the public health and environmental toll of improperly tuned cars with an underlying theme that appealed directly to a fundamental conservative value: personal duty and responsibility.

Even so, it was unexpected that when the first proposal for the Drive Clean program was posted on the Environmental Bill of Rights (EBR) Registry[6] in October 1997 for a thirty-day comment period, no comments were received at all! This signaled that even the most libertarian elements of the PCs right-wing had accepted that this highly intrusive policy had a reasonable foundation. Thus, with further details and refinements worked out over a pre-implementation process, the full Drive Clean program came into effect in April 1999.

The initial program only applied to highly populated and vehicle-intense portions of southern Ontario. It was delivered by private (many quite small) automobile servicing facilities that had to invest in the necessary testing equipment and certification to be approved by the MOE. Cars and light trucks that were over three-years old had to have an emissions test taken at the tail pipe every two years as a precondition to their license plate renewal. Various standards and procedures of the program were revised and updated over the ensuing years to keep the program current. As better, newer car technology was phased in and there were additional tail-pipe regulations, clean fuel standards and better onboard diagnostic systems, the need for the initiative waned. But it did its job to bridge the critical gap. Emissions from the auto sector were reduced and grossly polluting "clunkers" were decommissioned and taken off the road. The air was cleaner in southern Ontario partly because of this initiative.

Auto emissions were an important component of smog, but they were not the biggest problem. The largest source of smog generating pollution was the nitric oxide and particulates produced in huge quantities from the combustion of coal to produce electricity. Undoubtedly, a substantial portion of this was of trans-boundary in origin but, some of the problem was made-in-Ontario. In 1995, we had major coal plants emitting pollutants right in the key transportation corridor most plagued by "smog days." The ageing Lakeview Generating Station was on Lake Ontario in Mississauga and the largest coal-fired generating station in North America, Nanticoke was not far away, on the shores of eastern Lake Erie.

There was, in fact, a will to tackle the dicey problem of coal plants at the Harris cabinet table and this was largely driven by the premier himself. But due to the sudden and unexpected closure of seven units of Ontario's nuclear generating plants in October 1997, the surplus electrical capacity that might have allowed for the closure of these coal plants was eliminated. However, the useful life of the boilers at

Lakeview was expiring, and that gave the government the opportunity to announce the intent to get out of coal-fired generation starting with an announcement in 2003 of the closure of Lakeview in 2005.

* * *

Not every government leaves an imprint on the province that positively and permanently impacts the way of life for its people and the structure and progress of its industrial economy. Yet, that was in fact the most significant legacy of the environmental policies of the Harris era.

In 1995, far from the Toronto, there was significant, long-standing unrest and conflict regarding the vast landscape of forested public lands that extended from Algonquin Park and the Haliburton County, all the way north and west to the shores of James and Hudson Bays. These were Ontario's Crown lands, which compose approximately 87 per cent of the province.[7]

Of course, these lands were, and still are, the subject of disputes with the First Nations and Metis over ownership, stewardship, and control. But that was not the source of the conflicts that were brewing within provincial jurisdiction at this time. Of course, the province has dealings and responsibilities relating to indigenous communities, but such matters are constitutionally dealt with nation-to-nation, by the federal government. The conflict developing in the woods of the crown forest involved a wide range of non-indigenous parties.

The crown lands were seen through separate lenses by the many and various residents, visitors, commercial and industrial businesses that frequented its expanses. The forest industry was the dominant presence on the landscape and the source of significant wealth creation and employment. Mining was a close second in economic activity. Both industries saw the crown forest as a source of resources that should be open and unencumbered, to allow them to create wealth from public natural resources. But there were other commercial players. Fishing and hunting lodges and other outfitters had developed a prominent tourism industry that serviced an international clientele. The annual Fur Harvesters Auction in North Bay, Ontario was internationally recognized as offering the finest in wild fur by the fashion houses of the world. And expanding forestry roads and snowmobile proliferation had widely expanded the recreational opportunities for Ontario anglers and hunters. To add to this, an expanding group of canoeists, hikers, nature photographers and other outdoor adventures were increasingly present on the landscape.

In previous years, all these uses occurred concurrently and there were, of course, various localized conflicts, but the vastness of the landscape buffered and diluted the discord. But by the 1990s, the scale and magnitude of the forestry and mining industries had increased substantially and the strife between the various interests became much more prominent.

Added to these tensions was the growing international recognition of the importance of biodiversity conservation. In late 1992, Canada became the first industrialized country to sign the United Nations Convention of Biological Diversity. In 1996, the Ontario government affirmed its commitment, along with all other provinces and territories to fulfil those obligations.[8]

Specifically, Article 8 of that convention was a requirement to set aside parks and protected lands as representative of that biodiversity, and as a refuge against more consumptive or disruptive land uses. There was no formal specification of the area of an ecological landscape to be protected, but the figure of 12 per cent was widely discussed, and that figure would play a significant role in the catharsis that emerged from the new initiative that the Harris government launched in February 1997.

At first blush, it seemed straightforward enough. The existing land use plans that governed Ontario's crown Land were fifteen- to twenty-years-old and clearly were not adequate to resolve the emerging conflicts that were arising. A new comprehensive planning system would be developed called "Lands for Life."[9] It wouldn't cover all the crown land in the province, but it would involve most of the area where industrial, commercial and recreational activities were active. The 39 million hectares involved had been previously delineated by the Class Environmental Assessment for Timber Management on crown lands in Ontario as "the area of the undertaking" (AOU).[10] In a wise move that recognized that a regional diversity of priorities and opinions would exist across such a wide geographic expanse, the process was divided into three planning areas, Boreal West, Boreal East and the Great Lakes-St. Lawrence. Each was headed by a round-table board of local citizens drawn from diverse backgrounds. The round tables embarked on an ambitious public consultation. And then all hell broke loose.

Never before (or since) had the provincial government undertaken such an extensive public involvement initiative. There were public meetings throughout the affected regions. There were community workshops, open houses, questionnaires and written submissions. The Ontario public (especially in the North) was taken aback by the open process. The energy brewing up from the conflicts erupted in surprising levels of participation. "What was going on?" Some public meetings in small northern communities had 1,500 people show up. There was anger and suspicion at first, but that quickly dissipated when people saw that the round table members were "their own people" and that the process was sincere. What emerged was mass participation. The three tables heard directly from 15,000 people by various means.

After just thirteen months, the round tables submitted draft recommendations to the minister of natural resources. These were consolidated into a report by MNR and that report again went out for public consultation. Over 14,000 more submissions were received. By this stage, the results of the process were seen positively by various formerly antagonistic groups. The forest industry sat down with a coalition of environmental groups called The Partnership for Public Lands and that eventually lead to an agreement called the "1999 Ontario Forest

Accord—A Foundation for Progress." There was trepidation among hunters over the creation of more provincial parks, but that was calmed by the decision to create conservation reserves that were protected from logging or mining but open to hunting and unrestricted camping. And, although it was recognized that the forestry and mining industries would lose access to the lands put under protection, this would be more than compensated for by the clarity of access to the undesignated landscape and the freedom from risk of disputes with environmental and recreational groups.

It must be noted that consultation with the indigenous people on this landscape was part of the process, but this was done in recognition of the existing aboriginal and treaty rights protected under the Canadian constitution. Nothing in the results of this initiative was meant to limit, compromise, or abrogate those rights. However, there was a good faith and genuine effort to hear the inputs, ideas and include concerns of the indigenous peoples.

There were many other outcomes of the Lands for Life initiative that are beyond the scope of this discussion. However, as the process progressed to this late stage, it was evident that there was goodwill among the parties and considerable consensus. But one major step remained. How much of the affected areas would be open to industrial and commercial activity and how much would be lands to be protected in order preserve ecological integrity and cultural values? What would the split be?

The parties sat down for a final negotiation and came up with a deal that all could live with. But it had to be brought to Premier Harris for the final nod before bringing it forward to the public. It was at this point that Mike Harris the "northerner" emerged. His intimate understanding of the land and the importance of our natural heritage came into play. The plan presented was for an unprecedented expansion of Ontario's system of parks with protected areas to cover 9 per cent of the AOU. He is reported to have looked at the package and then up at the presenters and said, "What part of 12 per cent did you not understand?" (or words to that effect). Go back and bring me a deal that is agreed to at 12 per cent." They did, and he signed off and the final plan was announced as "Ontario's Living Legacy."

Ontario's Living Legacy was true to its name. Sixty-one new provincial parks were created and forty-five were expanded. Two hundred and seventy-one new conservation reserves were designated and one existing one was expanded. In total, there were 378 new protected areas in the AOU covering almost 2.4 million hectares. No jurisdiction in North America (perhaps in the world) had ever accomplished this magnitude of expanded biodiversity protection in such a short time. It truly was a remarkable achievement of problem identification, public consultation, stakeholder participation and consensus development. The plan was implemented with little controversy and broad approval. It was the definitive example of good government in a parliamentary democracy.

* * *

The *CSR* brought to power a government filled with newcomers that were ideologically challenged by the concepts of ecology, environmental policy and planning. But, fortunately, the "common sense" part of the mantra, and the presence of a few old hands who were in government in the 1970s and early 1980s, allowed Premier Harris to navigate the challenges presented by the environment file with reasonable success. The conservation authorities were disentangled from the province, but they all survived with new governance. The Walkerton tragedy profoundly shocked everyone and shook the people's confidence in environmental protection institutions. But major lessons were learned and new policies and structures put in place. The Oak Ridges Moraine was protected as a landform and in ways that changed land-use planning permanently in the province. Drive Clean and the coal closures initiative set an agenda that was picked up and advanced by the subsequent government and ultimately gave the province air quality now essentially free of "smog days."

But Ontario's Living Legacy will be true to its name and form the most significant chapter in the environmental history of the Harris government, one that will bring lasting benefit to future generations. It will be remembered not just for the peace it brought to a landscape challenged by the multiple use demands of a growing human population and expanding industrialization. It will also be seen as an endowment of ecological and cultural riches that were given to us from the past and now are secured for future generations. It was, and is, a true legacy for Premier Harris and the *CSR*.

Notes

1   I was a nominated candidate for the PCs in that election and I actually had to take, and pass, a test on the details of the CSR. I was told that if you failed, you would be dropped as a candidate (I don't know if that actually happened).
2   Which is the major tool to confirm that drinking water is protected from organic infections such as the e-coli bacterium.
3   Province stands pat on its rules, *The Globe and Mail*, May 30, 2000, p. A21.
4   *Developing Sustainability*, Environmental Commission Annual Report, 2001/2002.
5   Air Quality Report 2002 Report, Environmental Monitoring and Reporting Branch of the Ontario Ministry of the Environment, Queen's Printer for Ontario, 2003.
6   Open Doors, Ontario's Environmental Bill of Rights, Environmental Commissioner of Ontario Report 1998, p. 45, Queen's Printer for Ontario, 1998.
7   Currently, 87 per cent according to the Ministry of Natural Resources and Forestry, 2022.
8   Canadian Biodiversity Strategy: Canada's Response to the Convention on Biological Diversity (https://www.cbd.int/doc/world/ca/ca-nbsap-01-en.pdf).
9   https://www.fao.org/3/XII/0556-C1.htm
10 https://www.ontario.ca/document/forest-resources-ontario-2016/management-zones

CHAPTER 12

Democratic Reform

Guy Giorno

VERSHADOWED BY THE GLAMOUR OF tax cuts and the controversy over spending restraint, Mike Harris's democratic reform agenda has been infrequently explored and poorly understood. Those who consider the topic at all often assume that referendums and democratic renewal were peripheral to the *CSR*, unimportant and almost an afterthought. This myopic assessment disserves both the concept of democratic reform and the *CSR* itself. [1]

Viewed from a narrow perspective, Harris's 1995 campaign platform was entirely a fiscal and economy project: reduce (non-priority) spending, cut taxes, balance the budget and, in the process, unleash the private sector to create 725,000 jobs. In this context, democratic reforms were outliers, their existence in the platform explicable only to the extent they made the budget projections work. Thus, public disclosure of government salaries was billed as making government do better with less,[2] while slashing the number of legislators was classified as a cut to non-priority spending.[3] Even conflict of interest rules were considered a fiscal measure, included in the platform section on privatization (euphemistically described as "asset sales").[4] Similarly, Harris's 1999 *Blueprint*[5] reelection platform stuffed proposed democratic reforms into buckets of fiscal and economic policies.[6]

An alternate viewpoint, based on a nuanced and deeper understanding, is that democratic reform was at one with the spirit of the *CSR*. While fiscal and economic policy was the platform's bone and muscle, the breath of populism animated the body and gave it life. A desire to shake up the political system was not a sub-text in the *CSR*. This populist theme was in fact the leitmotif of the text, screamed by the critical last word of the title ("Revolution"), and displayed in its strongly worded introduction: "[G]overnment isn't working anymore. The system is broken. . . . Our political system has become a captive to big special interests. . . . It is full of people doing all too well as a result of the status quo."[7]

In this context, policies of direct democracy, accountability, transparency and populism (collectively, democratic reforms) are properly understood as sharing the same philosophical lineage as the more high-profile (fiscal, economic and other) measures to which the rest of this book is devoted. Harris's commitment to democratic reforms was established and genuine, though it would prove to be challenged by the realities of governing. While some reforms were eventually abandoned, and others short-lived, several, notably substantial and lasting reforms to enhance transparency, have endured, in many cases, spread nation-wide and are unquestionably part of his legacy.

The theme of democratic accountability runs through Harris's provincial political career. As a backbench member of the 32nd Ontario Legislature, Harris dutifully supported the PC government's initiatives, but privately chafed at the influence of unelected advisors to Premier Bill Davis, including the so-called "kitchen cabinet" of "Big Blue Machine"[8] insiders that met weekly at the Park Plaza hotel on the northwest corner of Bloor Street and Avenue Road.[9] When Bill Davis announced his retirement from politics in 1984, Harris supported the leadership campaign of Frank Miller, and subsequently served as minister of natural resources in both short-lived Miller cabinets.[10] The Miller leadership campaign was partly based on a pledge to break backroom power brokers' control over both MPPs and ordinary party members, a goal that Harris shared.

At a 1989 special meeting, the Progressive Conservative Association of Ontario adopted a new constitution that included the then relatively novel method of leadership election by university member suffrage, more commonly called "one member, one vote." The stated and actual goal was to break the ability of party elites to influence selection of the leader,[11] by transferring power to rank-and-file members.[12] When Harris himself ran for party leader in 1990, he pitched his appeal to the grassroots members who would be directly electing the leader. He promised to reduce the influence of backroom advisors, to base policy on principle not polling,[13] to empower the legislative caucus, and to listen more closely to party members. The loss of power, the reality of a long stay in opposition,[14] and the siren call of consecutive national majorities[15] had taken their toll on the provincial party. Those seeking influence, employment, and lobbying opportunities were now focused on federal politics. Among the diminished numbers who remained active in the Ontario PCs, populist, anti-insider sentiment was, consequently, less diluted. Harris's message appealed to the residual membership,[16] especially the PC youth.[17] Even then, he won the leadership with just 54.6 per cent support.[18] Once elected as leader, Harris continued to echo the populist themes on which he had based his campaign.

The constitutional reform initiatives of the late twentieth century, in particular, debate over the Meech Lake Accord[19] and Charlottetown Accord, offer some of the clearest, early examples of the future premier's populist thinking. One of his first major legislative speeches as party leader outlined Harris's vision:

> . . .in a participatory democracy, which this country supposedly embraces, people have a right to participate, not just in a token way after the fact but directly and in a meaningful way before public policy and especially constitutional decisions are made.[20]

While Harris supported, more or less, the substance of the proposed constitutional reforms,[21] he criticized the process, and decried the subordination of ordinary people's priorities to an agenda of political interests and special interests.

From the outset, Harris had misgivings about the Meech Lake process. He and Ernie Eves were members of a select legislative committee that unanimously panned the closed-door dealing that produced a *fait accompli*.[22] Harris and Eves then issued their own minority report that decried the rush to ratify without impacts being properly understood.[23]

Ratification of the Meech Lake Accord failed just five weeks before the start of Mike Harris's first general election campaign as PC Party leader. Repeatedly during that campaign, Harris excoriated the elitist and secretive genesis of the Accord, and insisted that future constitutional amendments be subject to voter approval in a referendum.

When Liberal Leader David Peterson interrupted his own election campaign to participate in the annual conference of premiers,[24] Mike Harris declared that the secretive Meech Lake process ("horse-trad[ing] with the constitutional future of Canada . . . behind closed doors, in the dead of night . . . [then] presented the Canadian public with a fait accompli") had scarred Canada, perhaps permanently.[25] Harris announced principles of a "new style of constitutional discourse," including the following:

> No constitutional reform should be imposed on the people of Ontario unless they have first had the opportunity to pass judgment on it through a binding province-wide referendum. Only if approved by such a referendum should any amendment resolution be presented to the Legislature.[26]

Nine days later, before an uncomfortable and unimpressed lunchtime audience of Mulroney government officials in Ottawa, Harris combined another withering attack on the accord with the renewed pledge of citizen involvement by referendum. Blaming failure of the Meech Lake Accord on "a closed-door process of exclusion and secrecy" that shut out women's groups, Indigenous peoples, new Canadians, the Territories, and ordinary Canadians,[27] Harris twice promised, as Ontario PC Party policy, that future proposed constitutional amendments would be placed before the people in "a full, broad and binding referendum."[28]

He pledged to, "serve notice on first ministers across the nation that no new arrangement will be put to the Ontario Legislature unless it has been ratified in a public referendum."[29]

Today insistence on a referendum for such matters may seem unremarkable, even obvious, but back then Harris was an outlier among party leaders, especially conservative leaders, in demanding a popular vote on constitutional amendments.

Two years after the death of Meech, the next proposed package of constitutional amendments, the Charlottetown Accord, was put to Canadians in a referendum, and rejected. Harris had been prepared to endorse the substance of the Charlottetown compromise, but was an early demander of a public referendum on the proposals.[30] In the wake of its defeat, the Ontario PC leader denounced its brokered process as elitist and out of touch.

"The paternalism and the elitism of the past will not sell today," Harris told MPPs the day after the 1992 referendum. "We need more genuine reflection of the will of the people in our deliberations. We need more free votes in the Legislature. We need more recognition of the sophistication of the electorate."[31] Harris felt that the obsession with constitutional reform, a preoccupation of politicians and special interests, was out of touch with the priorities of ordinary people. The problem, as he saw it, was that politicians were advancing their own priorities and elite interests' priorities, instead of addressing what was genuinely important to the public, indeed, addressing what angered the public.[32] The same sentiment would find expression in the *CSR* that Harris released some eighteen months later.

Harris's insistence on putting constitutional amendments to a referendum would subsequently force Prime Minister Jean Chrétien to abandon an attempt to secure quick approval for constitutional reform based on Chrétien's Verdun Declaration.[33] In a private meeting at the top of the Harbour Castle hotel in Toronto, Harris told a surprised Chrétien that the Legislature would only vote on constitutional amendments after they were approved by Ontarians in a referendum. His blunt assessment was that the proposals would not pass a province-wide vote.[34]

* * *

Harris's commitment to direct public participation in decision-making was not limited to constitutional reform. As party leader, he supported decision by referendum on provincial budgetary policy,[35] on Sunday shopping,[36] on the introduction of casino gambling,[37] as a precondition to tax increases,[38] and on any matter within provincial legislative jurisdiction that 15 per cent of the electorate petitioned to place on a ballot.[39] Prior to becoming PC leader, Harris had voted for referendum legislation with an 8 per cent trigger.[40] (During Harris's leadership, in 1993 and 1994, PC MPPs twice supported "voter recall" measures, but Harris himself was not present for either vote.[41])

The *CSR* platform did not mention referendums, but a more detailed policy document,[42] drafted by party researchers on the basis of Harris's and caucus policy statements, then vetted, approved, and printed in multiple copies, listed numerous ways in which a Harris government would be "giving power to the people." An eleventh-hour campaign decision nixed public distribution of the longer document, not because its content was inconsistent with party policy, but out of fear that a large policy dump might distract from the precisely calibrated pledges of the *CSR*. According to the party's unreleased policy plan:

> We will initiate the first use of referenda on a regular basis to give the public a direct say in determining deficit, tax and spending policies.

These votes can be held on a local or province wide basis, depending on the scope of the issue involved. To begin with, we will have a process for referenda whenever there are province-wide federal, provincial or municipal votes.[43]

During the 1995 election campaign, Mike Harris and the PC Party did commit to referendums on one particular issue: the expansion of casino gambling. Instead of taking a firm stand on casinos, Harris promised to let the public decide. The complex evolution of that promise, and its eventual abandonment, foreshadowed the implementation difficulties that would later affect other direct democracy initiatives.

As early as 1993, the PC Party had tried unsuccessfully to include in the new *Ontario Casino Corporation Act* a prohibition of the operation of any casinos in Ontario unless and until voters approved through a province-wide referendum.[44] Eventually party policy solidified into a promise that casino gambling would require double-referendum approval: a province-wide referendum on whether to allow casinos at all, and then a local referendum in each host community.[45] In March 1995, Harris clarified that the NDP government's interim Windsor casino, operating on a temporary site since May 17, 1994, and the pending Rama casino, announced in December 1994, would be grand-parented, but further expansion of casino gambling, whether at a permanent Windsor site or elsewhere in Ontario, would be decided by the public.[46] Soon after winning the election, the Harris government began to backtrack from the commitment. In November 1995, the government announced that it was still committed to a province-wide referendum, no earlier than November 1997,[47] but meanwhile would authorize the establishment of a casino in Niagara Falls. The finance minister claimed that, "Ontarians will have the information on the impact of casinos in three different communities by the time a referendum is held."[48] Within months, the minister announced the establishment of charity casinos[49] (though the government declined for several years to call them "casinos"[50]), making no mention of a province-wide referendum. Then, in 1998, the government introduced a "Slots at Racetracks Program" that effectively placed casinos at multiple racetracks.[51]

Feeling pressure from public opposition to the pace of gaming expansion, the Conservatives announced in July 2000 a three-year pause in the establishment of new casinos and charity casinos. By then, however, the government was operating or had announced four commercial casinos and six charity casinos, and had allowed or approved 8,700 slot machines at sixteen raceways,[52] all without the blessing of a province-wide referendum. The responsible minister noted that casinos and charity casinos had only been placed in communities that confirmed by referendum their willingness to be hosts, and a new law provided that any new casinos and charity casinos (once the moratorium ended) would only be located in communities that showed referendum approval.[53] Nonetheless, Harris's original policy clearly stated that referendums would be both local and province-wide. The promised provincial referendum on casino gaming was never held.

While multiple factors contributed to the quiet death of the casino-gaming referendum pledge, the dominant cause was fiscal. Payments into the consolidated revenue fund resulting from commercial casinos more than quintupled during Harris's first term.[54] During his second term, charity casinos and racetrack slots would prove to be even more lucrative than commercial casinos.[55] With gaming taps spilling such revenue into provincial coffers, no serious consideration was given to a referendum that might interrupt the flow.

The casino referendum pledge was still nominally alive when, in August 1996, Harris's office launched what would become a four-year referendum project. Beginning with the soft launch of a consultation paper, followed by legislative committee review, and then further consultation, the initiative would ultimately produce a draft provincial referendum law and an actual bill governing municipal referendums.

The latter was gutted before being passed, while the former was unceremoniously abandoned.

Prepared by the cabinet office and premier's office, the discussion paper, Your Ontario, Your Choice: A Preliminary Look at the Referendum Alternative, invited Ontarians to write directly to Harris with thoughts on how, not whether "to implement a referendum strategy in Ontario." The document was notable for at least two reasons. First, though written in clear and accessible language, it delved deeply into the details of direct democracy alternatives, distinguishing among plebiscites, referendums, initiatives and voter recall, asking for input on thirty-five specific questions in twenty-one categories, and candidly addressing the constitutional impediments to reform, most significantly that any derogation from the Legislature's law-making function would require a constitutional amendment.[56] This precision was intentional. Anticipating a rocky road ahead, the premier's office wanted to avoid off-hand rejection based on any sentiment that the paper was not well thought-through.

Second, the discussion paper was heavy with references to Harris's personal commitment to referendums, including five direct quotations. The audience for these was not the general public, but Progressive Conservative MPPs and party members who might be skeptical of the initiative. Particularly because the CSR had been silent on direct democracy, the paper's authors wanted to blunt internal arguments that referendums were extraneous to the plan.

Brampton South MPP Tony Clement was tapped to head the referendum project, and maintained this responsibility after he entered the cabinet the following year. Clement's first task was to guide the discussion paper through public study by the Standing Committee on the Legislative Assembly. After hearing from fifty-six witnesses, the committee voted on party lines (with Liberals dissenting completely and New Democrats dissenting in part) to recommend the introduction of legislation that would allow either citizens or the government to trigger a provincial referendum. The recommended threshold for a citizen-initiated referendum was signatures of at least 10 per cent of eligible voters, collected within 180 days. The government would be required to introduce a bill to implement the will of more than 50 per cent of voters. The committee majority also recommended that referendum approval be obtained before the Legislature voted on a constitutional amendment and the government introduced a bill that would impose a new tax.[57]

The Progressive Conservative majority was careful to stress that it saw referendums not as an alternative to representative democracy, but as a "supplement" to the current system.[58]

The committee held public hearings in September and November 1996. It issued its final report in June 1997. During the intervening months, the government's critics, inside and outside the Legislature, were roiled by the controversial Toronto amalgamation bill.[59] The legislated merger of East York, Etobicoke, North York, Scarborough, Toronto, and York into a single City of Toronto, occurred despite widespread opposition, including simultaneous March 3, 1997, mail-in referendums in which local voters overwhelmingly rejected amalgamation.[60]

Ironically, one week before introducing the Toronto amalgamation bill, the Harris PCs had passed legislation making it easier for municipalities to place referendum questions on local ballots.[61] Now they were ignoring the clear results of six local ballots.

On one level, there was no comparison between the so-called "Megacity" referendums and what the Harris government proposed in Your Ontario, Your Choice. Both constitutionally and as a matter of public policy, the parameters of municipal structure and organization have always been provincial, not local decisions. (It is obvious that the size and structure of a provincial capital are important to the entire province, not just the city's inhabitants.) Further, the wording of the Megacity questions lacked the objectivity required of a proper referendum ballot.

Yet on another, more basic, level, the government's disregard of the Toronto amalgamation referendums called into question the sincerity of its commitment to direct democracy. An obvious and not unreasonable take-away was that the Harris government supported referendums except when it disagreed with the results. More problematic (to those who listened closely) was that several of the government's arguments about municipal referendums were fundamentally antithetical to its own direct democracy agenda.[62]

After the standing committee issued its pro-referendum report and recommendations in June 1997, the Harris government then established a Referendum Ontario secretariat within cabinet office, complete with its own web page and logo. In March 1998, Clement, by now also serving as the minister of transportation, released two more consultation documents: a draft *Referendum Act*, providing for votes on provincial questions, and the Municipal Referendum Framework: A Consultation Paper. Clement personally traveled to nineteen Ontario communities to conduct town hall meetings and solicit public input.

Under the draft provincial legislation, the threshold for citizen-initiated referendums was more onerous that the standing committee had recommended: a petition signed by 10 per cent of eligible voters in each of the seven regions of the province. The organizers would have just 180 days to amass signatures. The draft bill would also have required that referendum approval be a precondition to (1) a vote by the Legislature on a proposed amendment to the Constitution of Canada and (2) introduction in the Legislature of a bill that would impose a new tax or increase an existing tax. The former reflected Harris's 1990 position on constitutional amendments; it was never enacted. The latter would be introduced as the *Taxpayer Protection Act*, and pass. The draft legislation did not specifically mention referendums on casino gaming: further evidence that by March 1998 the pledge had been abandoned.

Comprising forty sections that ran for twenty pages, the draft provincial referendum legislation reflected careful consideration of implementation issues, including campaign spending limits, rules for advertising, a new

Referendum Commission, and enforcement. Though Clement was the responsible minister, the legislation was an official government initiative that had been sanctioned by cabinet. In fact, the policy-and-priorities-board's[63] and cabinet's consideration of the bill's content had begun in summer 1997 (shortly after the standing committee reported) and Harris was personally engaged. Despite the effort the government, and the premier himself, had invested in the referendum legislation, the bill never proceeded beyond a consultation draft.

Some of Harris's advisors (trusted friends whom he used as a regular sounding board and who did not belong to his caucus, his staff, or his campaign team) were leery that citizen initiatives might place controversial issues on the political agenda, but their hesitance was not why the referendum bill was sidelined. Indeed, Harris was willing to see a citizen-initiated referendum on any issue, even a constitutional amendment, as long as the 10 per cent signature threshold was met in each of seven regions.

The proposal stalled because, on the eve of a general election, it was felt to be too unfocused and potentially distracting from the PC campaign's precise, planned message on taxes. The PC Party was already planning to brand Dalton McGuinty, the new Liberal leader, as a weak tax-and-spend politician who would jeopardize Ontario's economic gains. The campaign team saw tax-increase referendums (dubbed "taxpayer protection") as an opportunity to draw attention to the tax policy difference between the Harris and his rivals, McGuinty and NDP leader Howard Hampton. Both opposition parties had vehemently dissented from the tax-referendum recommendation in the standing committee report, and the PCs would claim both were planning to hike taxes: The NDP was promising to reverse Harris's tax cuts, and the Liberal leader had pledged to restore the power of school boards to increase education property taxes.

* * *

Referendums were not mentioned in the *CSR*, but in the middle of the 1995 election campaign, Harris announced that net tax increases should be permitted only upon approval in a referendum or following a general election. In the same announcement, he promised a legislated requirement to achieve deficit reduction targets and then to maintain a balanced budget.[64] He also publicly signed a Canadian Taxpayers' Federation pledge containing similar language.[65] Despite the promise of "immediate passage," it was not until four years later, just months before the anticipated date of the 1999 general election, were the proposed tax-increase referendum provisions redrafted as stand-alone legislation, then paired with another new law, requiring balanced budgets, to form the *Balanced Budget and Taxpayer Protection Act*.[66]

To the surprise and disappointment of Harris and his campaign team, McGuinty supported the taxpayer protection law from the moment it was placed before the Legislature.[67] In fact, during the 1999 election campaign, McGuinty criticized Harris for not being fast enough to pass a *Taxpayer Protection Act* and pledged that Liberals would enact such a law within 100 days.[68] (The Canadian Taxpayers' Federation, too, condemned the PCs for rolling into their 1999 platform the unfulfilled pledge from 1995.[69])

Reintroduced again following the 1999 general election, the *Taxpayer Protection Act* became law with Progressive Conservative and Liberal support.[70] As enacted, Harris's taxpayer protection legislation was the most comprehensive in Canada,[71] but the act's impact was short-lived. Two months after Harris resigned as Premier, his own party neutered the tax-referendum requirement and left the hollowed-out law on the statute books.

In its 2002 provincial budget, the Ernie Eves government proposed a one-year delay in four previously legislated tax cuts.[72] Under Harris's *Taxpayer Protection Act*, postponement of an already-legislated tax reduction, considered tantamount to a tax hike, was subject to referendum approval. The Eves PCs bypassed the requirement by amending the act to provide that the referendum rule would not apply to the tax measures in the 2002 Budget.[73] Thus a pattern was set: to circumvent the *Taxpayer Protection Act*, a finance minister merely includes in the first budget bill of the year an exemption for that year's tax measures. The Superior Court of Justice would later confirm that this work-around is lawful.[74] In such manner, the act has been bypassed nine times.[75]

Ironically, during the 2003 election campaign, the PC Party and the Liberals went through the motions of formally registering, with the Chief Election Officer,[76] certain tax changes that they would make if elected. (The *Taxpayer Protection Act* provides that referendum approval is not required if a tax increase or new tax is clearly and transparently disclosed as part of a platform.[77]) In no subsequent election has anybody registered a proposed tax increase. There is no need, as it has proved far easier to carve out exemptions from the act than to comply with it.

Outright repeal and a decent burial of the Harris *Taxpayer Protection Act* would have been more dignified than the present spectacle: a statutory corpse, riddled with nine legislated holes, that notionally remains in force but has not once accomplished the purpose for which it was enacted, and presumably never will.

* * *

The Harris government did introduce and secure passage of municipal referendum legislation, but only after gutting its consultation proposal. The Municipal Referendum Framework: A Consultation Paper included draft legislative text that had been approved by Cabinet. Notably, the consultation paper suggested that citizens be permitted to initiate referendums by obtaining the signatures of at least 10 per cent of voters within a 180-day period. This was more than a trial balloon. According to the government:

> We believe that the right to initiate a referendum is as much a right to participate in the democratic process as is the right to

vote in an election. Any individual who is qualified to vote in a municipality should be able to initiate a referendum in that same municipality as long as the proposed question meets the criteria.[78]

When Tony Clement, by this time the minister of municipal affairs and housing, placed before the Legislature Bill 62, the *Direct Democracy Through Municipal Referendums Act*, 2000, any provision for voter-initiated questions had been stripped out.[79] The act essentially provided that municipalities choosing to hold referendums must live with the results, but whether to conduct a referendum is up to each municipal council. All mention of citizen-initiation having been excised prior to first reading, the legislation was subsequently enacted[80] and remains in the municipal elections act to this day.[81]

In contrast, not even a framework for provincial referendums exists: no statutory and administrative infrastructure waits in place should the government or the assembly ever decide to conduct a province-wide ballot. Inexplicably, Harris's bold leadership on public participation in constitutional reform, the precondition of referendum approval before the Legislature votes on an amendment, was never enshrined in law. That a banal framework for municipal referendums is the only enduring legacy underscores the lost promise of Harris's early embrace of direct democracy.

Ultimately, the failure of Harris's direct democracy agenda can be traced to the limitations imposed by our constitutional order. Within its jurisdiction, parliament and each Legislature are supreme, and its law-making powers are constrained only by the constitution as interpreted by the courts. Direct democracy succeeds only with the Legislature's consent; the assembly cannot be forced to yield legislative authority. Whether on taxes or casino gambling, provincial politicians proved simply unwilling to share power with the people.

* * *

Unlike direct democracy, which focused on decision-making, other populist measures implemented by the Harris Government targeted the prestige, perquisites, and pay of politicians. These reforms met with greater success, partly because they did not directly challenge constitutional legislative authority, but primarily because politicians were hesitant to champion their own status and self-interest. Three of Harris's populist initiatives, fewer politicians, compensation reform, and a balanced budget law, ranked among his signature policies and only the latter has been repealed.

The *CSR* was built on the premise that government was working too well to promote the interests of politicians and elites and not working well enough for ordinary citizens. As Harris understood, it was not enough to introduce reforms that benefited hard-working Ontarians. To demonstrate that the paradigm was being inverted, Harris needed to show proof that the political and elite classes were losing—losing clout, losing status, and losing financially.

Symbols are communications that convey information simply and directly. The use of policy as a symbol is beyond the scope of this chapter. Suffice it to say that sometimes a policy can be emblematic of a politician's values and priorities: conveying a message about what is cherished and what is disregarded.

Despite the notional saving estimated by *The Common Sense Resolution*, Harris's proposed reduction in the size of the Legislature was not primarily a cost-saving measure. It was a symbol conveying a message that elected officials were expendable, part of the problem, and being put in their place.

The policy itself was symbolic, as was the means of announcing it. During the 1995 election campaign, and again when the *Fewer Politicians Act* was introduced in October 1996, Harris announced his policy beside a flat-bed trailer carrying one chair for each legislative seat that would be eliminated. After Harris had finished speaking, the chairs were hauled away. The event evoked Premier Mitch Hepburn's 1934 public auction at Varsity Stadium of government-owned cars: it too, had been an emblematic policy, presented to the public in dramatic fashion.

Reducing the size of a legislature by roughly 20 per cent, to align with the number and the borders of federal ridings, does not harm democracy, provided the boundaries are fair. In Canada, the constitutionally protected principle is "effective representation" that primarily means parity of voting power, subject to other considerations, such as geography and community, that may be relevant.[82] Effective representation is not undermined by an impact that is more or less the same on all electoral districts.

One small democratic enhancement was to make district boundaries and names more understandable to ordinary Ontarians. Prior to 1999 (the election when the change took effect) confusion about the names and boundaries of overlapping federal and provincial constituencies was rampant. Making this aspect of the electoral process more accessible to the public was a positive change. For similar reasons, effective 2000, the Harris government made the federal-provincial electoral districts the basis of City of Toronto municipal wards, with each riding divided in half to form two wards.[83] Since 2018, each federal-provincial electoral district now corresponds to one city ward.[84]

The adoption of federal boundaries, which contemplated natural growth as Ontario's representation in the House of Commons increases, has been maintained to this day, with one exception. In 2005, a Liberal majority in the Legislature separated Northern Ontario from the mirroring of federal boundaries.[85] While electoral districts in Southern Ontario continue to evolve according to the boundary changes and name changes of federal ridings, the number of seats in Northern Ontario is insulated from erosion as relative population declines. Indeed, in 2017, two additional constituencies were created in Ontario's far north.[86]

Harris's government also used the "fewer politicians" brand to describe its amalgamations of municipalities and school boards. Al Leach frequently touted "fewer politicians" as a benefit of municipal mergers and restructuring in Toronto and elsewhere.[87] The *Fewer Municipal Politicians Act*, 1999 combined small rural communities and big cities in Hamilton (formerly Hamilton-Wentworth), Ottawa (formerly Ottawa-Carleton) and Greater Sudbury.[88] The government's *Fewer School Boards Act*, 1997,[89] reduced the number of major school boards from 129 to seventy-two and reduced the number of school trustees (whom the government called "school board politicians") by two-thirds.[90]

The simplistic "fewer politicians" branding diverted attention from the more deleterious effects of municipal and school board amalgamations, including leveling-up of costs, entrenchment of unionized contractor preferences, loss of voice for rural communities, erosion of community identity, rural–urban service disparities, and weakened council (and school board) oversight of administration. Toward the end of Harris's time in office, the government began to acknowledge the other side of the argument. The 2001 Speech from the Throne conceded, at least in relation to school boards, that "while economies of scale and common accountability standards promote excellence and efficiency, so do innovation, competition, flexibility and choice."[91]

The *CSR* called the downsizing of politicians and their compensation "leadership by example," but the slogan was only partly true. Politicians were subjected to shrinking numbers and shrinking pay, whether they liked it or not. Being pushed first on the gangplank is not necessarily "leadership," and to be *made* an example is different than *setting* one.

Symbolism aside, fundamental compensation problems did exist. A top-up of one-third of MPPs' salaries, tax-free, as a so-called expense allowance, obscured the true value of MPP compensation, and falsely implied that it reimbursed expenses (which were already paid separately).[92] A generous retirement scheme that was not self-funding was deceptive and unfair to everyone but the MPPs who enjoyed it. The emergence of the urban school board trustee as a full-time job (with full-time pay), with no indication (and no way of measuring) that it resulted in better representation or oversight, suggested that sight of the original function had been lost.

Under Harris, effective April 1, 1996, Ontario became the first province whose legislators scrapped their own tax-free allowances.[93] Starting next with British Columbia,[94] almost every other jurisdiction did likewise, including the House of Commons, which eliminated MPs' non-accountable, tax-free, incidental expense allowances in 2001. Effective 2019, the federal income tax act was amended to ensure that any remaining public office holders' non-accountable allowances were fully taxable; by then, Quebec was the only province still paying a tax-free allowance to its lawmakers.[95]

By any objective measure, the MPP pension scheme, or *Legislative Assembly Retirement Allowances Act* (LARAA),[96] was even more egregious.[97] Members contributed 10 per cent of their pay (excluding the tax-free allowance) and became entitled to an annual pension when age plus service (of at least five years) totaled fifty-five years. The maximum possible pension (reached after a mere 15 years' service) was equivalent to 75 per cent of annual pay based on the best thirty-six months. By comparison, in 1996, Ontario teachers (whose pension benefits were superior to those of most other Ontarians) needed a ninety-factor (age plus service equals ninety years) to qualify for an unreduced pension of 70 per cent based on their best five years;[98] for this, they made contributions of between 7.3 per cent and 8.9 per cent.[99]

The *CSR* decried "the sweet deals politicians have created for themselves" and pledged to abolish MPP pensions. Not until the general election campaign did Harris describe them as "gold-plated";[100] from that point, the term was used repeatedly. Two months before the 1995 election, Ernie Eves was claiming that MPP pensions were "miniscule,"[101] but eventually he rallied behind the "gold-plated" label.[102] In April 1996, Eves introduced legislation that eliminated the LARAA, replacing it with what the government called "an RRSP-type plan," actually a money-purchase pension funded by employer (government) contributions of 5 per cent of salary, accessible to members upon leaving the Legislature or reaching age fifty-five, whichever came last. The bill preserved, and indexed to inflation, benefits for MPPs who had already retired, as well as their spouses and qualifying dependent children.[103]

The legislation, which passed with all-party support, dealt differently with the sixty-one MPPs who had been reelected on June 8, 1995. From that day forward, they would belong to the same money-purchase pension plan as other MPPs. Their past participation in the LARAA would, however, be recognized. Each MPP had the option of leaving, in the new plan, credit for service prior to June 8, 1995. Alternatively, each MPP could transfer to a locked-in retirement account the commuted value (essentially, a cash-out) of the LARAA pension to which the prior service entitled the member.[104] The new legislation provided that the LARAA would be subject to indexing before the commuted values were calculated; significantly, until that point, LARAA pensions were unindexed, though subject to irregular, ad hoc adjustments.[105] Eventually, all sixty-one members chose to transfer their cash-outs into locked-in retirement accounts.[106]

The cash-outs contradicted the premise that the LARAA scheme was undeserved, inflated and larded with fat. If those indictments of the old system were accurate, and they were, there was no justification for paying incumbents the present value of the LARAA pork. More to the point, there was no evidence that anyone in the Legislature had actually foregone outside opportunities more remunerative than the old MPP pay scheme (including the LARAA). Indeed, then, as now, most MPPs were collecting bigger paycheques than in their previous occupations.

The old system of retiring allowances was excessively generous, actuarially unsound, and unfair to taxpayers, so the assumption that the LARAA created vested rights that needed to be preserved was dubious. Moreover, it is a basic constitutional principle that a legislature can repeal statutory entitlements at any time, subject to the Charter of Rights. Even if vested entitlements *were* the basis of the cash-outs, there was no reason to enrich the LARAA (by indexing it) prior to commutation. It didn't help that Harris and Eves, who were guiding the policy, were among the MPPs most directly affected. (Integrity Commissioner Coulter Osborne subsequently examined Eves's involvement and found that, because the compensation reform affected all members of the Assembly, including sixty-one returning members, there was "no merit" in the suggestion that Eves needed to recuse himself from decision-making.[107])

Years later, it emerged that the payments to long-time MPPs exceeded federal *Income Tax Act* limits on transfers to registered retirement savings plans. The news media reported that the Ministry of Finance had been warned the cash payouts were non-compliant,[108] but Integrity Commissioner Osbourne found that it appeared to the provincial government that its plans were acceptable to the Department of National Revenue (now Canada Revenue Agency).[109] The Ontario government covered the personal tax liabilities of the affected individuals; the total cost of making them whole was reportedly $10 million.[110]

While the commutations and their handling can be criticized, the fundamental policy of replacing an unsound, excessive, defined-benefit plan with a modest, defined-contribution plan has been widely accepted in Ontario. The last two decades have seen no calls to return to any sort of defined-benefit pension for provincial politicians. Just before Christmas 2006, however, Liberal and PC members quickly voted to double, to 10 per cent, the government's contributions to the defined-contribution plan.[111]

While it was laudable to simplify MPP compensation and make it transparent, Ontario politicians simultaneously used the 1996 pay reforms to enhance their earnings. Hidden in plain sight was a significant salary increase,[112] which few journalists noticed or reported. Proper discussion of that topic is beyond the scope of this chapter.

Mid-way through its second term, the Harris government attempted to take decisions about future compensation increases out of the hands of politicians and to give the Integrity Commissioner the power not to recommend, but actually to determine, changes in the base salary. Bill 82, the MPP compensation reform act (arm's length process), 2001,[113] passed with Progressive Conservative and Liberal support.[114] The independent salary-setting process was short-lived. In August 2001, Integrity Commissioner Gregory Evans decided that MPPs would receive a 25-per cent pay increase immediately after the next general election.[115] Two years later, during the general election campaign, Evans's successor, Osborne, rescinded the pending increase at the request of all three party leaders.[116] The Commissioner had also decided on a small inflation adjustment, but the Legislature froze MPP salaries for eighteen months until April 1, 2005, and terminated the increase.[117] It was clear that MPPs did not support independent compensation setting in practice, despite professing to support the theory. In 2006, the Integrity Commissioner recommended that MPP pay be set at an unspecified percentage of MP pay, but declined to exercise his statutory power to make a binding determination.[118] Within two weeks, MPPs eliminated the Commissioner's role in determining increases and tied their salaries to the compensation of federal MPs, paying themselves 75 per cent of an MP's annual sessional allowance.[119] In 2009, the MPP base salary was frozen (that is, detached from future increases in MPs' pay).[120] Pursuant to various subsequent amendments, MPP salaries remain frozen.[121]

* * *

Another compensation-based reform was Harris's *Balanced Budget Act*.[122] The legislation would have reduced cabinet ministers' salaries if the provincial government ran a deficit. Salaries would have been reduced by 25 per cent following the first deficit year and by 50 per cent following each subsequent deficit year. The reductions would not have applied to ministers' base MPP salaries, only to the additional amounts to which they were entitled by virtue of their cabinet posts. The act provided exceptions in the event of disaster, war, and a 5 per cent revenue decline not attributable to a tax cut. The act would also have permitted a deficit of up to 1 per cent of annual revenue, provided it was offset by a surplus in the following year.[123]

In 2004, the Liberal legislative majority repealed the *Balanced Budget Act*[124] and replaced it with new legislation that basically required planning for balanced budgets (but not a requirement to avoid deficits) and greater transparency around fiscal planning.[125] The new law did not include salary-reduction provisions. In 2018, the Progressive Conservatives voted to repeal the 2004 law[126] and enact their own, similar replacement.[127]

While Harris's balanced budget law was not long in force prior to repeal, the underlying notion that politicians' pay should be linked to fiscal performance was a theme of other Harris-era legislation and was later adopted by Kathleen Wynne's Liberals. The original 1996 MPP salary reform provided for an arm's length commission to recommend increases, but only when the budget was balanced.[128] In 2014, the Liberals introduced and adopted an analogous legislative amendment, under which MPP salaries would remain frozen until after the provincial budget was balanced.[129]

The Harris government agenda also included significant reduction of school board trustees' remuneration. Until 1982, school board members' allowances had been capped at $600 per month for large boards, and lesser amounts for smaller boards.[130] In 1982, the caps were removed[131] and, in some places, compensation soared. By 1995, urban school boards were paying trustees as much as $40,000 per annum[132] ($70,000 in 2022 dollars); in Toronto, trustees received $49,683[133] (equivalent to $86,400 in 2022). The education act was amended in 1997 to cap school trustees' honoraria[134] (the old term, "allowance," was repealed) at $5000.[135] At the same time, implicitly rejecting the need for full-time education system politicians, the Education Improvement Commission recommended that responsibilities of school boards and board members should not be operational or managerial but, instead, based on the policy-governance model (sometimes referred to as the "Carver model").[136]

This compensation reform lasted until 2006, when the Liberals replaced the statutory, fixed cap with ministerial authority to limit trustee honoraria by regulation.[137] The minister's regulation increased the maximum honorarium according to an enrollment-based formula that easily allowed amounts of more than $20,000 to be paid in urban boards such as Toronto, York, and Peel.[138] Harris's reform drew attention to the compensation paid to school board politicians and, to this day, has affected payments by resetting the base upon which future increases would be built. (One-quarter century later, even the highest amounts paid to trustees are a fraction of the pre-Harris allowances.[139]) His reform did not, however, affect any structural change to the compensation model.

While Mike Harris is not commonly associated with conflict-of-interest reform and the topic rated only secondary mention in his 1995 campaign platform, his government's conflict rules are probably Harris's most significant accountability initiative. At the same time, ironically, three signature accountability measures expressly promised by the PCs were never implemented.

During its seven years, the Harris government privatized very few assets: an obscure, government-owned savings bank, a handful of tree nurseries, and the ETR portion of the 407 highway.[140] No one expected that the most enduring legacy of the privatization initiative would be the conflict rules originally conceived as a defensive, political shield intended to blunt controversy over selling assets to the private sector.

The *CSR* had said little about conflict-of-interest rules, and only in the context of privatization:

> When a [privatization] deal is made, it will be independently reviewed. A rigorous conflict of interest policy will be enforced and the entire process will be open to scrutiny by the Legislature and the public.[141]

Harris became directly involved in government decision-making on implementation of this slender pledge. He wanted the conflict rules to apply to all government activities, not just privatization. In his view, all public servants who were able to make or influence a decision that affected the private sector should be subject to the new conflict-of-interest rules; also, because such officials were susceptible to lobbying, the new lobbyist registration law should cover attempts to influence them. In response to a suggestion that rules were necessary only for elected officials and their political staffs, Harris was adamant that civil servants be included, too.

Harris also championed a lifetime, post-employment ban on switching sides. A public servant who had advised the government on a specific proceeding, transaction, negotiation or case would forever be prohibited from acting on behalf of any business or entity, in connection with that same proceeding, transaction, negotiation or case, unless the government were no longer involved in it.[142] That rule still exists.[143]

In June 1997, the Harris cabinet approved the first conflict of interest and post-service directive. The directive, which applied to all public servants, prohibited the use of public office for personal or familial benefit or to favour any entity; the disclosure and improper use of confidential information; acceptance of most gifts and benefits; granting preferential treatment; nepotism; taking improper advantage of past office; and, as previously noted, switching sides.[144] The directive immediately affected the terms and conditions of employment; to facilitate enforcement by giving them the force of law, a few months later, key provisions of the directive, excluding the post-employment restrictions, were incorporated into a new regulation, the first Rules of Conduct for Public Servants.[145] It was understood and anticipated that the directive's post-employment rules, that, is, rules that applied after an individual was no longer in the service of the crown, would eventually need to be incorporated into law, presumably through statutory amendment.

These conflict-of-interest rules endure. Today, Ontario law includes all the Harris government's 1997 conduct rules, including both the rules that had been included in regulation and those originally implemented by directive.[146]

Harris's government also established a new, independent office, the conflict-of-interest commissioner, to administer the rules for senior public servants and the political staff.[147] An initial thought that oversight could be provided by the integrity commissioner appointed under the *Members' Integrity Act*, 1994,[148] was incompatible with the separation between parliament and the government that is a fundamental element of our constitutional system. It was ultimately agreed that an officer of the legislative assembly (integrity commissioner) should not be giving direction to government employees. The separate office of the conflict-of-interest commissioner lasted until 2018 when a new legislature, presumably less sensitive to the distinction between the government and the assembly, abolished the position and transferred all functions to the integrity commissioner.[149]

The significant legacy of Harris's conflict-of-interest rules stands in contrast to the fate of accountability measures that were promised but never implemented. A Declaration of Taxpayers Rights was promised in both the 1999 campaign platform[150] and the 1999 provincial Budget,[151] but no action was taken. Also unimplemented were 1999 campaign pledges to base public servants' promotions and bonuses partly on customer satisfaction,[152] and to create a permanent red tape watchdog.[153] The *CSR* commitment to legislate a sunset clause (that is, a fixed, automatic termination date) for each new program was similarly never fulfilled.[154]

As early as 1992, Mike Harris had argued that agencies funded by the provincial government needed to be more accountable and, among other things, should be subject to audit by the provincial auditor (now auditor general).[155] Consistent with this position, the PC Party's unpublished 1995 policy binder said the provincial auditor's review function would be extended to the "entire public sector."[156] Legislation to impose accountability measures on broader public sector institutions such as hospitals and universities was promised in the 1997 Budget[157] and again in the 2001 Throne Speech,[158] and finally introduced May 9, 2001 as the *Public Sector Accountability Act*.[159] The PCs then abandoned the bill; it was never called for second reading debate, and was not re-introduced during subsequent sessions of the 37th Legislature. Ultimately, Liberal legislative majorities would enact significant BPS accountability reforms. In 2004, the auditor general (formerly provincial auditor) was given authority to audit any entity that receives funding from the Consolidated Revenue Fund, a crown agency or a crown controlled corporation.[160] Six years later, the sweeping *Broader Public Sector Accountability Act, 2010* was enacted.[161]

* * *

Harris's transparency initiatives have survived for more than two decades and are a significant part of his legacy. The *CSR* promised, "Senior civil servant salaries and benefits will be disclosed to encourage greater accountability and restraint."[162] The scope of the *Public Sector Salary Disclosure Act*,[163] enacted in January 1996, exceeds that commitment. First, the law applies not just to the provincial civil service but also to municipalities, school boards, hospitals, provincial crown corporations and agencies, and universities and community colleges, as well as any entities (including not-for-profit organizations) that receive a defined amount of funding from the Government of Ontario.[164] Second, instead of attempting to define who is a "senior" employee, the act uses a monetary threshold; it requires disclosure of the name, title, and the amount paid to anyone whose salary, wages, bonus, severance and other remuneration from office or employment amount to at least $100,000 in a year.[165] The value of benefits paid to that individual is also disclosed.

While employers are required to make their salary disclosures available for public inspection,[166] they are also required to report them to the province no later than the fifth business day of March.[167]

The province posts the information online, and also maintains a permanent web record dating back to the first disclosures for 1996. These disclosures, often referred to as the "sunshine list" are widely reported by the news media when they are released each year in late March. Whether or not the public happens to associate Harris with the sunshine law, the fact of salary disclosures is common knowledge.

The public sector salary disclosure act was well constructed with transparency in mind. It declares that there is no copyright in the salary disclosures, and that anyone may publish the information.[168] The act is enforceable through a provision that allows the government to withhold funding from any employer that fails to comply with the disclosure requirements.[169]

Harris's legacy extends beyond Ontario. His sunshine law was the first in Canada. Manitoba quickly followed with its own legislation.[170] Eventually all provinces, save one, followed the Harris-Ontario example by adopting some form of public-sector salary transparency.[171] Only Prince Edward Island and the Parliament of Canada have declined to enact salary disclosure for government institutions and public-sector agencies within their jurisdictions.

Ontario's choice of a relatively high initial disclosure threshold ($100,000 in 1996 is equivalent to $170,680 in 2022 dollars and was twice the $50,000 threshold for compensation disclosure in Ontario's old public accounts) has been mitigated by the decision not to include an automatic inflation adjustment. In 2022, the province's disclosure threshold was middle of the pack, tied with that of Newfoundland and Labrador and Nova Scotia and higher than the thresholds of Saskatchewan ($50,000), New Brunswick ($60,000), Manitoba ($75,000), and Quebec (none, for holders of full-time senior positions in public bodies).

There is no evidence that salary disclosure had the effect of reducing public sector compensation, but cost-saving was never a realistic objective. Granted, the *CSR* claimed that the policy's purposes were both "accountability and restraint," but the latter was surely rhetorical excess.

The public benefit of a transparency measure is transparency in its own right, not the vain promise the particular conduct will be incentivized or deterred.

* * *

One of the most significant and lasting Harris transparency measures was not explicitly promised; instead, it was introduced as a companion to the conflict-of-interest rules discussed above. The *CSR* had expressly mentioned a conflict-of-interest policy for privatizations. Lobbyist registration was not mentioned as part of that package until two years later, in Eves's first budget speech.[172] While the initiative was at first communicated in the context of possible asset sales, Harris personally decided that the legislation would apply broadly to lobbying on all types of government decisions, and not just privatization.

Ontario's lobbyists registration act was the first provincial lobbying law in the country and more rigorous than the Mulroney-era federal legislation of the same name.[173] The Harris government's law included an integrity rule that the federal legislation lacked: it was an offense for a lobbyist to place a public office holder in a conflict of interest.[174] That prohibition is still on the books and, nowadays, is interpreted to restrict individuals who help candidates get elected from subsequently lobbying those politicians and their staffs.[175]

Implementation was remarkably fast, considering that an entire registration system had to be built from scratch. Cabinet proclaimed the act in force just 28 days after it received royal assent—to this day, the fastest implementation of lobbying legislation in Canadian history.[176]

By the end of its second year of operation, the registry included the names of seventy-six in-house lobbyists for businesses, 401 in-house lobbyists for non-profit organizations, and 193 consultants.[177] At the end of the 2021–2022 fiscal year, the comparable figures were 1,268,

1,560, and 573.[178] Harris's decision to cover lobbying on all government decisions, and not restrict the registry to lobbying on asset sales, was prescient, as most attempts to influence government had nothing to do with privatization.[179]

All the other provinces (and, in 2018, Yukon[180]) have followed Ontario's example, enacting their own laws on lobbyist registration and, in most cases, strengthening the Ontario model. The legislation of some provinces, notably Quebec and Newfoundland and Labrador, created numerous lobbyist conduct offences,[181] while the four Western provinces provided in their lobbying statutes for administrative monetary penalties.[182] Ontario's bipartisan unwillingness to catch up is beyond the scope of this chapter.[183] By giving birth to provincial regulation of lobbying, the Harris government has profoundly affected government relations across Canada.

Freedom of information was a third area in which the Harris government introduced significant and lasting legislative reforms. Enacted during Harris's first year, these amendments did not increase transparency; instead, they clarified the boundaries of the transparency laws (*Freedom of Information and Protection of Privacy Act* and *Municipal Freedom of Information and Protection of Privacy Act*) already in place. One set of amendments allowed institutions to deny access requests that were frivolous and vexatious. This was a legislative response to an IPC decision involving a series of requests to police forces for random information including washroom cleaning schedules and UFO sightings; the IPC found that the requester had abused the right of access but that institutions were nonetheless required to respond to frivolous and vexatious requests.[184]

Other amendments were intended to deter frivolous appeals to the commissioner. Consistent with the legislation's user-pay principle, a modest appeal fee was introduced.[185] The acts were also amended to address groundless appeals of decisions that no responsive records exist. As a result of the Harris government amendments, the IPC may dismiss an appeal that does not present a reasonable basis for concluding that the record exists.[186]

Further amendments clarified that various labor relations and employment records were excluded from the legislation.[187] The purpose was to give public-sector employers the same ability as private-sector employers to prepare for labour arbitrations, employment litigation, and negotiations, and more generally to manage labour relations and employment relationships, in a confidential manner. The provisions were intended to be, not an exemption, subject to review by the Information and Privacy Commissioner, but a complete exclusion from the act. Despite the intention, the IPC took the position that its jurisdiction includes the ability to determine whether a record is excluded, and that the institution must establish that the exclusion applies.[188] As a result, appeals from institutions' decisions on excluded records are still processed by the IPC and still require institutions to defend their positions, just as when institutions rely on exemptions.

None of these Harris-era amendments to FIPPA and MFIPPA have been altered or repealed by subsequent legislatures. They have been accepted as part of the ordinary fabric of freedom of information in the province.

* * *

Elements of successful democratic reform are unquestionably part of Harris's legacy. His openness initiatives, notably the salary-disclosure "sunshine" law, lobbyist registration, and simplified, transparent compensation for legislators, not only are entrenched but have been emulated by other provinces. His conflict-of-interest rules, intended to set ethical standards in privatizations that never occurred, are housed in new legal instruments, but remain in effect. Meanwhile, his symbolic attacks on the position and privilege of politicians (smaller legislature, capping school board trustees' compensation) had a transitory effect, rolling back to new starting points for inexorable growth; in this category, only the "scrapping" of MPP pensions appears to be permanent.

On the other hand, the failure to effect any type of direct democracy leaves an obvious hole in the legacy. After a decade on the opposition benches promising that voter approval would be sought and required for various public policy decisions, not to mention embracing citizen-initiated ballots; Harris and his cabinet, once in office, soon found that they much preferred the conventional system in which government, not the people, decided. Despite a refreshing pledge to make future constitutional amendments subject to referendum approval and the fact that by holding fast to that conviction Harris spared Canadians from a third constitutional imbroglio in less than a decade, provincial legislation to provide a framework for such a referendum was never even introduced.

Overall, the Harris government's democratic reform accomplishments are best described by half of the campaign brand. There certainly was no democratic "revolution." At the same time, the many meaningful "common sense" accountability and transparency reforms constitute an enduring legacy.

Notes

1   I am grateful for the research contributions of my Fasken colleagues Philippe Lefebvre Desrosiers and Mackenzie van den Berg.
2   Mike Harris, *The Common Sense Revolution*, 4th printing, 1994, p. 8.
3   *The Common Sense Revolution*, p. 16.
4   *The Common Sense Revolution*, p. 17.
5   *Blueprint: Mike Harris' Plan to Keep Ontario on the Right Track*, 1999.
6   According to *Blueprint*, referendums on tax increases were a component of cutting taxes (p. 12), a permanent red-tape watchdog would help strengthen the economy (p. 14), and a declaration of taxpayer rights was part of making government work smarter, faster, and better (p. 19).
7   *The Common Sense Revolution*, pp. 1–2.
8   The term "Big Blue Machine" has no universally agreed definition. Steve Paikin points out that the expression was first used by George Drew (Premier, 1943–1958).

During the 1970s and 1980s, some used the term to refer to the entire Progressive Conservative Party during its forty-two-year hold on the Government of Ontario. Others employed the term narrowly, and often pejoratively, to denote the advisors and strategists who ran the party's election campaigns.

9   Roy McMurtry, *Memoirs and Reflections*, University of Toronto Press, 2013, p.150.

10   Harris was sworn in February 8, 1995, and served until the resignation of the Miller ministry, June 26. From May 17 to June 26, he also served as minister of energy.

11   Prior to the 1989 amendments, party leaders were chosen by delegates in convention: These included eight delegates elected by each riding association, two youth delegates from each recognized riding youth association, or, absent a youth association, two youth delegates elected by the riding association, three delegates from each campus club, all Progressive Conservative MPs and Senators from Ontario, all PC MPPs, federal and provincial candidates nominated for the next election (or, where a candidate had not yet been nominated for the next election in a federal or provincial riding, the candidate in the last election), ten officers from each of the provincial youth association, campus association, and women's association, and five officers from each district youth association and women's association. A party member could vote multiple times: once in every association, club and executive of which the individual was a member.

12   The party's constitution committee recommended that the first objective of any new method of leadership selection should be "To open up the selection process at the riding level in order to give as many party members as possible a direct say in the selection of the party leader." Ontario PC Association, Constitution Committee, "Constitution Report: Working Paper" (April 29, 1988), p. 18.

13   Wayne Roberts, "New Tory leader appeals to party's right wing," *NOW Magazine* (May 17, 1990), p. 15.

14   Led by Miller, the Ontario PCs won a plurality (52 of 125 seats) in the May 2, 1985, election, but not a majority, and very soon lost a confidence vote in the legislature. "We won the election, we just lost the government" was a common PC defence, and young PCs sported "We'll be right back" buttons produced by the party. The outcome of the September 10, 1987, general election made clear that the party's relegation to opposition was neither accidental nor brief. Under leader Larry Grossman, the PCs won just 12 per cent of the seats (16 of 130) in the legislature, the party's worst-ever result and only its second third-place finish (the other occurring in 1919).

15   Led by Brian Mulroney, the federal Progressive Conservatives had won 211 of 282 House of Commons seats in the September 4, 1984, general election, and 169 of 295 seats in the November 21, 1988, general election.

16   At the time of the 1990 leadership election, party membership was approximately 33,000.

17   In his account of the 1990 Ontario PC Youth Association convention, Wayne Robertson accurately captures the iconoclast spirit of the provincial PC youth, and Harris's genuine connection to their anti-establishment fervour: "Young Tories charge ahead on rightward joyride," *NOW Magazine* (March 22, 1990), p. 15.

18 Harris received 8661 raw votes. His sole opponent, Dianne Cunningham, who had been elected to the legislature in a March 31, 1988, by-election, and whose campaign was organized by remnants of the Big Blue Machine, won 7189 raw votes. Paragraph 23.2 of the party's 1989 constitution provided that each of the 130 electoral districts was to have equal weighting when the votes were tabulated; the weighted (and official) results gave Harris 55.2 per cent and Cunningham 44.8 per cent.

19 The Meech Lake Accord was a package of proposed constitutional amendments privately negotiated by Prime Minister Brian Mulroney and all provincial premiers, announced to the public as an agreement in principle on April 30, 1987. The legal text of the amendments was then formulated in secret and unveiled on June 3 of that year.

20 Ontario, Legislative Assembly, online Hansard Transcript (June 20, 1990).

21 Harris voted to ratify the Meech Lake amendments, albeit with reservations: online Hansard Transcript (June 28, 1988). He supported the "Yes" side in the Charlottetown Accord referendum, but made clear that "this is not the deal I would've sought to negotiate": online Hansard Transcript (September 30, 1992).

22 Ontario Legislative Assembly, Select Committee on Constitutional Reform, "Report on the Constitution Amendment 1987" (June 23, 1988), p. 5.

23 Select Committee on Constitutional Reform, "Report on the Constitution Amendment 1987" (June 23, 1988), Progressive Conservative Minority Opinion, pp. 2–3.

24 The 31 Annual Premiers' Conference took place August 13–14, 1990. See Canadian Intergovernmental Conference Secretariat, "Premiers' Conferences: 1887–2002" (2002).

25 Mike Harris, Statement at Queen's Park (August 13, 1990), p. 2.

26 Ibid., p. 3.

27 Mike Harris, "Reforming the Constitutional Process" (August 22, 1990), speech delivered at National Arts Centre, Ottawa, p. 2.

28 Ibid., p. 4.

29 Ibid., p. 5.

30 Online Hansard Transcripts (March 27, 1991), (September 26, 1991), (April 13, 1992), (May 25, 1992), (June 1, 1992), (July 8, 1992).

31 Online Hansard Transcript (October 27, 1992).

32 Ibid.

33 On October 24, 1995, near the end of the 1995 Quebec referendum campaign, Prime Minister Chrétien announced in Verdun that he would attempt further constitutional change in the event of a "non" vote. Jean Chrétien, "An Exceptional Situation," Televised Speech, October 25, 1995.

34 The author was present during the Chrétien-Harris meeting of November 2, 1995. The account of Greenspon and Wilson-Smith in *Double Vision: The Inside Story of the Liberals in Power* (1997) is correct in most details, but does not include the central role of a referendum in that discussion. The prime minister seemed unaware

that Ontario's legislative approval would depend on the result of a referendum, presuming that if the Premier were onside, Ontario's ratification would follow. Harris explained the need for a province-wide vote, and advised that, in his view, the amendments would not be approved. It was in that context that he said Chrétien was making a "mistake." For more detail of the meeting, see Giorno, "The Man who stopped Meech III," *National Post* (October 27, 2005), p. A27.

35   In 1993, Harris introduced Bill 54, *An Act requiring Referendums on the Budgetary Policy of the Government of Ontario* (short title: *Budget Referendum Act, 1993*). His legislation would have allowed 5 per cent of the electorate to trigger a referendum on the provincial budget; if voter turnout were 50 per cent or higher, and at least 60 per cent of votes were cast against the budget, then the provincial government would have been required to present a new budget to the legislature: online Hansard Transcript (June 17, 1993). Previously, Harris had proposed Bill 138, the *Provincial Budget and Fiscal Policies Referendum Act, 1991*, that he said would "authorize a municipality to hold a referendum on provincial budgets and fiscal policies": online Hansard Transcript (September 25, 1991).

36   Online Hansard Transcript (June 26, 1990).

37   Online Hansard Transcript (May 17, 1993).

38   Ontario PC Party, news release, "Harris: A Pledge to Roll Back 'The Debt Clock'" (May 30, 1995).

39   On June 25, 1992, Harris voted in favour of second reading (approval in principle) of Bill 30, *An Act to Obtain the Opinion of the Public on Questions of Provincial Interest* (short title: *Provincial Public Consultation Act, 1992*).

40   At the June 11, 1987, second reading vote, Harris voted for Bill 75, *An Act to provide an Opportunity for the Electorate to Express its Views by Means of Referenda in Ontario* (short title: *Referendum Act*).

41   On July 22, 1993, all four PC MPPs present for the vote supported Bill 59, *An Act to provide for Petitions requiring the Premier to request the Calling of an Election* (short title: *Recall Election Request Act, 1993*), at second reading. On May 19, 1994, ten PC MPPs voted in favour of the motion of MPP Don Cousens that a committee "be required to develop a recall process for consideration by the Legislature and to present their recommendations and options to the Legislative Assembly by the spring session in 1995."

42   Ontario PC Party, *A Common Sense Blueprint for Ontario*, 1995 [printed but not publicly released]. The title of this unreleased policy book is not to be confused with the 1999 platform, named *Blueprint: Mike Harris' Plan to Keep Ontario on the Right Track*.

43   *A Common Sense Blueprint for Ontario*, Part 7 (Bringing Common Sense to Government Reform), p. 6.

44   Online Hansard Transcripts (October 18, 1993), (November 29, 1993).

45   Ontario PC Party, issue note, "Casinos" (1995).

46   "Feature Interview: Mike Harris, Leader, Progressive Conservative Party of Ontario," *Canadian Casino News*, Vol. 1, Issue 11 (March 1995), p. 2.

47   Online Hansard Transcript (November 29, 1995).

48 Ibid.

49 Hon. Ernie Eves, Budget Speech, 1996 Ontario Budget (May 7, 1996), p. 12.

50 While Ontario's opposition parties almost immediately described the sites as casinos, the Harris government initially avoided this terminology. The 1996 Budget called them "permanent charity event sites." The 1997 Budget called them "charity gaming clubs." The 1998 Budget acknowledged them as "charity casinos" and in the same year backbench Progressive Conservative MPPs started to use that name in the Legislature. Not until November 30, 1999, did a cabinet minister acknowledge, in the assembly, that these were casinos.

51 Revenue from racetrack slot machines would eventually be shared as follows: Province, 75 per cent; racing industry, 20 per cent; host municipality, 5 per cent: Ontario Racing, fact sheet, "Long Term Funding" (2017).

52 Management Board Secretariat, Fact Sheet, "Status of Gaming Premises in Ontario" (June 19, 2000). See also Management Board Secretariat, News Release, "Ontario Restricts Expansion of Gaming in Ontario [*sic*]" (June 19, 2000).

53 O. Reg 347/00, revoked June 1, 2012.

54 The amounts paid by the Ontario Casino Corporation to the Consolidated Revenue Fund (including the so-called "win tax," which the OCC booked as an expenditure) were $213 million in 1994–1995, the fiscal year ending three months before Harris took office, and $1.126 billion in 1998–1999, the fiscal year ending shortly before his second general election victory. Source: Public Accounts of Ontario: Financial Statements, 1994–1995 and 1998–1999.

55 Based on gross revenue. Ontario Lottery and Gaming Corporation, "Quarterly Performance Figures," Fiscal 2002/2003 and Fiscal 2003/2004.

56 *Re The Initiative and Referendum Act* (1919), 48 D.L.R. 18 (P.C.), at 25.

57 Standing Committee on the Legislative Assembly, Final Report on Referenda (June 1997).

58 Final Report on Referenda, p. 3.

59 Bill 103, the *City of Toronto Act, 1997*, was introduced December 17, 1996, and received Royal Assent April 21, 1997. The amalgamation took effect January 1, 1998.

60 The same question, with only the local municipality's name changed, was asked everywhere: "Are you in favour of eliminating [name of local municipality] and all other existing municipalities in Metropolitan Toronto and amalgamating them into a MegaCity?" The results were as follows: Borough of East York, No, 25,930, Yes, 5,879; City of Etobicoke, No, 28,486, Yes, 12,166; City of North York, No, 121,475, Yes, 31,433; City of Scarborough, No, 60,520, Yes, 17,861; City of Toronto, No, 121,475, Yes, 43,759; City of York, No 26,405, Yes 10,700.

61 *Municipal Elections Act, 1996*, s. 8, enacted by *Better Local Government Act, 1996*, S.O. 1996, c. 32.

62 See, in particular, the comments of the Hon. Al Leach in online Hansard Transcripts (October 30, 1995), (December 12, 1995, Vol. A), (December 19, 1996).

63 The Policy and Priorities Board of Cabinet, commonly known as P&P, functioned as the inner Cabinet, and was chaired by Harris.

64   Ontario PC Party, news release, "Harris: A Pledge to Roll Back 'The Debt Clock'" (May 30, 1995).

65   "I, Mike Harris, Leader of the Progressive Conservative Party of Ontario, pledge, if elected, to support immediate passage of Taxpayer Protection Legislation that will: One, make any increase in existing tax rates subject to approval by the voters of Ontario in a binding referendum; Two, require the elimination of Ontario's operating and capital deficits within at least five years, along with interim deficit targets for each of the years; and Three, contain 'pay for performance' ministerial salary penalties for the premier and cabinet ministers if interim deficit targets are not met." Source: Canadian Taxpayers Federation, Letter to the Premier (April 30, 1999).

66   Bill 99 (36th Legislature, 2nd Session).

67   Bill 99 was introduced December 14, 1998, during the last days of the legislative session and did not proceed beyond First Reading. Reintroduced during the 3rd Session, on May 3, 1999, as Bill 24, it again did not proceed beyond First Reading. Two days later, the Legislature was dissolved.

68   Ontario Liberal Party, news release, May 13, 1999.

69   Canadian Taxpayers' Federation, "CTF Demands Taxpayer Protection and Balanced Budget Legislation Now, Election Promises Are Not Good Enough," News Release (April 30, 1999).

70   On October 26, 1999, following the general election, the taxpayer protection and balanced budget legislation (in slightly revised form) was introduced a third time, as Bill 7 of the 1st Session of the 37th Legislature. As S.O. 1999, c. 7, Sched. A, it eventually passed and received Royal Assent on December 14, 1999. Dalton McGuinty and the Liberals voted in favour of the legislation.

71   Ontario's law (S.O. 1999, c. 7, Sched. A, s. 1) applied to increases in nine "designated tax statutes." The Manitoba legislation (S.M. 1997, c. 7, subs. 10(1)) covered four tax statues, while the Alberta law (S.A. 1995, c. A-37.8, s. 1) applied only to introduction of a provincial sales tax. British Columbia had brief experience with a *Taxpayer Protection Act* (S.B.C. 1991, c. 6, repealed S.B.C. 1992, c. 23), but its law merely froze certain taxes for three years and had nothing to do with referendum approval. The Canadian Taxpayers' Federation observed, "Ontario's Taxpayer Protection Act is now the most comprehensive in Canada surpassing the measures of similar legislation in effect in Manitoba and Alberta": Canadian Taxpayers' Federation, "After Two Strikes . . . Harris Hits Home Run for Taxpayers," News Release (November 23, 2020).

72   Claiming a need based on "the short-term fiscal situation," the minister of finance introduced legislation to postpone already-legislated reductions in personal income tax, corporate income tax, and education property tax, and to postpone the next phase of the Equity in Education Tax Credit. The original wording of the *Taxpayer Protection Act* made these postponements subject to referendum approval.

73   *Taxpayer Protection Act*, subs. 2(6), as enacted by S.O. 2002, c. 8, Sched. L, s. 1.

74 *Canadian Taxpayers Federation v. Ontario (Minister of Finance)* (2004), 73 O.R (3d) 621 (S.C.J.). It should be noted that the circumvention requires that each exemption be enacted before the corresponding tax-increase bill receives First Reading—a minor inconvenience, especially considering that finance ministers routinely introduce two budget measures bills annually.

75 S.O. 2002, c. 8, Sched. L, s. 1; S.O. 2004, c. 7, s. 17; S.O. 2004, c. 16, subs. 2(3); S.O. 2012, c. 8, Sched. 57, s. 1; S.O. 2014, c. 7, Sched. 30, s. 1; S.O. 2015, c. 20, Sched. 41, s. 1; S.O. 2017, c. 8, Sched. 31, s. 1; S.O. 2017, c. 34, Sched. 41, s. 1; S.O. 2018, c. 8, Sched. 33, s. 1.

76 In 2007, the office was renamed Chief Electoral Officer, to match the federal nomenclature.

77 *Taxpayer Protection Act, 1999*, S.O. 1999, c. 7, Sched. A, s. 4.

78 Government of Ontario, *Municipal Referendum Framework: A Consultation Paper*, 1998, p. 7.

79 Bill 62 (37th Legislature, 1st Session), introduced April 13, 2000.

80 S.O. 2000, c. 5.

81 *Municipal Elections Act*, ss. 8.1, 8.2, 8.3. 39.1, 82.1.

82 *Reference re Prov. Electoral Boundaries (Sask.)*, [1991] 2 S.C.R. 158.

83 O. Reg. 191/00 under the *City of Toronto Act, 1997*; *City of Toronto Act, 2006*, S.O. 2006, c. 11, Sched. A, s. 127.

84 City of Toronto Act, 2006, s. 128, enacted by *Better Local Government Act, 2018*, S.O. 2018, c. 11, Sched. 1, s. 5.

85 *Representation Act, 2005*, S.O. 2005, c. 35, Sched. 1.

86 *Representation Statute Law Amendment Act, 2017*, S.O. 2017, c. 18.

87 On May 6, 1997, Leach told the legislature, "So far in 1997, there are 134 fewer municipalities and over 600 fewer politicians." He also repeatedly explained that Toronto amalgamation would result in "fewer politicians": online Hansard Transcripts (January 14, 1997), (January 15, 1997), (April 21, 1997).

88 S.O. 1999, c. 14. This act also dissolved the Regional Municipality of Haldimand-Norfolk.

89 S.O. 1997, c. 3.

90 Ministry of Education, Backgrounder, "Less bureaucracy, fewer politicians" (January 13, 1997). The minister's original announcement said the number of school boards (called "district school boards") would be reduced to 66; in May 1997, the Ministry released boundary maps for its revised "72 Board Model." Using round figures, the Ministry claimed that the number of school trustees would drop from 1900 to 700, and summarized, "Number of politicians cut by two-thirds."

91 Speech from the Throne (April 19, 2001).

92 Subsection 60(2) of the *Legislative Assembly Act*, re-enacted by S.O. 1991, c. 57, s. 1, called it "An allowance for expenses," but the act separately provided for transportation and accommodation expenses (s. 67), staff salaries (subs. 74(1)), and "office equipment, services and supplies in accordance with standards established by the Speaker" (subs. 74(2)). No one explained what additional "expenses" were

covered by the allowance, and it was commonly accepted that no MPP incurred
expenses to offset against it.

93 Manitoba's tax-free allowances were eliminated 11 months earlier, effective April
25, 1995, but that binding decision was made by the arm's-length Indemnities and
Allowances Commission, not by MLAs.

94 S.B.C. 1997, c. 29, s. 26.

95 The change was announced in federal Budget 2017 and took effect in the 2019 tax
year. In addition to Quebec MNAs, elected officials of the territories and numerous
municipalities and school boards also were receiving tax-free allowances.

96 R.S.O. 1990, c. L.11, retroactively repealed effective January 1, 1992, by S.O. 1996,
c. 6, s. 1.

97 The scheme described in this paragraph applies to an MPP who was first elected
after October, 1, 1973, and who left the Legislature after January 1, 1986.

98 Ontario Teachers' Pension Plan, "How Pension Benefits Have Evolved"
(undated).

99 The 7.3 per cent contribution rate applied up to the CPPs' Yearly Maximum
Pensionable Earnings; the 8.9-per-cent rate, thereafter. Ontario Teachers' Pension
Plan, "How Contribution Rates Have Evolved" (undated).

100 Ontario PC Party, news release, Leadership by Example: Savings Will Start at the
Top" (April 29, 1995).

101 Canadian Press, "MPPs pensions got quiet boost (in Ontario)" (March 3, 1995).

102 Ministry of Finance, News Release, "Government Gets Rid of Gold-Plated
Pensions, Eliminates Hidden Tax-Free Allowances, and Cuts MPP Compensation"
(April 10, 1996).

103 Bill 42, *MPPs Pension and Compensation Reform Act*, 1996, S.O. 1996, c. 6.

104 A portion of the commuted value would be paid out as a lump sum. Essentially
this portion corresponded to the amount of LARAA payments that would have
exceeded the defined benefit limit under the *Income Tax Act* (Canada).

105 Over the years, the ad hoc adjustments were approximately 75 per cent of the rate
of inflation. Ontario MPP Compensation Commission, Setting the benchmark:
Reforming Ontario MPP pensions and compensation (November 1995), p. 42.

106 Ontario, Integrity Commissioner, *Re Ernie Eves* (May 6, 2002), p. 9, para. 21.

107 Ontario, Integrity Commissioner, *Re Ernie Eves*, pp. 11–12, para. 27.

108 Richard Mackie, "Mistake in MPP pensions to cost millions," *The Globe and Mail*
(January 26, 2002).

109 Ontario, Integrity Commissioner, *Re Ernie Eves*, p. 24, paras. 52–53.

110 Mackie, note 119.

111 Bill 173, *Legislative Assembly Statute Law Amendment Act, 2006*. The bill was time
allocated on December 20, and received third reading and Royal Assent on
December 21, 2006.

112 S.O. 1996, c. 6, ss. 7. 9.

113 S.O. 2001, c. 15.

114 One Liberal MPP, Gerard Kennedy, joined the NDP in opposing the legislation.

115   Office of the Integrity Commissioner, *Report pursuant to section 1 of the MPP Compensation Reform Act (Arm's Length Process), 2001* (August 27, 2001), p. 11.

116   Office of the Integrity Commissioner, *Report re MPP Compensation Reform Act (Arm's Length Process), 2001*, (September 5, 2003), p. 4.

117   S.O. 2004, c. 2, s. 1.

118   Office of the Integrity Commissioner, *Report re MPP Compensation Reform Act (Arm's Length Process), 2001*, (December 7, 2006), pp. 12–14, paras. 32, 39.

119   S.O. 2006, c. 36, s. 1.

120   S.O. 2009, c. 18, Sched. 15, s. 1.

121   S.O. 2014, c. 7, Sched. 17, s. 1; S.O. 2022, c. 23, Sched. 5, s. 1.

122   S.O. 1999, c. 7, Sched. B.

123   Ibid.

124   S.O. 2004, c. 27, s. 16.

125   S.O. 2004, c. 27.

126   S.O. 2019, c. 7, Sched. 30, s. 20.

127   S.O. 2019, c. 7, Sched. 30.

128   S.O. 1996, c. 6, s. 19.

129   S.O. 2014, c. 7, Sched. 17, s. 1.

130   *Education Act*, R.S.O. 1980, c. 129, s. 167.

131   S.O. 1982, c. 32, s. 47.

132   Duncan MacLellan, "The Fewer Schools Boards Act and the Toronto District School Board: Educational Restructuring 1997–2003," unpublished paper (June 1, 2007), p. 2; Stephen E. Anderson and Sonia Ben Jaafar, Ontario Institute for Studies in Education, "Policy Trends in Ontario Education 1990–2006" (December 2006), p. 12.

133   Standing Committee on Social Development, Transcript (February 24, 1997).

134   The 1997 *Education Act* amendments used the plural "honorariums" but the 2006 amendments substituted "honoraria."

135   S.O. 1997, c. 31, s. 97, re-enacting *Education Act*, s. 191. A board was permitted to pay its chair and vice-chair an honorarium of up to twice the amount paid to other trustees.

136   Ontario, Education Improvement Commission, *The Road Ahead II: A Report on the Role of School Boards and Trustees* (December 1997), pp. 10–11.

137   S.O. 2006, c. 10, s. 16, re-enacting *Education Act*, s. 191.

138   O. Reg. 357/06. The base amount was $5900 in 2006 dollars (inflation adjusted in subsequent years) plus a maximum enrollment adjustment based in the formula: average daily enrolment × $1.75 ÷ number of trustees.

139   The allowance paid to Toronto trustees in 1996 was more than $86,400 in 2022 dollars. For the 12-month period starting November 15, 2022, the honorarium paid to Toronto District School Board trustees is $24,917: Toronto District School Board, "Honoraria for Trustees," Policy P074 (revised September 28, 2022), section 6.4.

140   The long-term lease of Bruce Nuclear Generating Station, though not an asset sale, is considered by some to be a privatization.

141 *The Common Sense Revolution*, p. 17.

142 Ontario, Management Board Secretariat, Conflict of Interest and Post-Service Directive (June 25, 1997), s. 22.

143 O. Reg. 381/07, s. 20; O. Reg. 382/07, s. 20.

144 Conflict of Interest and Post-Service Directive (June 25, 1997), ss. 11–17, 21–22.

145 O. Reg. 435/97.

146 O. Reg. 381/07; O. Reg. 382/07.

147 S.O. 1999, c. 12, Sched. K, s. 2, enacting s. 4.1 of the *Public Service Act*, R.S.O. 1990, c. p.47.

148 Originally, the directive and the regulation identified the Integrity Commissioner as the "designated official" responsible for application of the rules to employees of the premier's office, ministers' offices and the privatization secretariat.

149 S.O. 2018, c. 17, Sched. 35.

150 *Blueprint: Mike Harris' Plan to Keep Ontario on the Right Track*, p. 19. "We'll also introduce a *Declaration of Taxpayer Rights*, including: The right to be treated with courtesy and respect, the right to be treated as an honest and law-abiding citizen, unless proven otherwise, the right to know why your business is being contacted, audited or inspected, and the right to timely response to your communications with government."

151 Ministry of Finance, 1999 Ontario Budget: Budget Papers: Foundations for Prosperity (May 4, 1999), p. 103: "Declaration of Taxpayer Rights: A Charter of Taxpayer Rights will be developed in response to the recommendation of the Canadian Federation of Independent Business. The declaration will demonstrate Ontario's commitment to administering tax laws with fairness, courtesy and common sense."

152 *Blueprint: Mike Harris' Plan to Keep Ontario on the Right Track*, p. 19.

153 *Blueprint*, p. 14.

154 *The Common Sense Revolution*, p. 16.

155 Ontario Progressive Conservative Caucus, *New Directions Volume Two: A Blueprint for Learning in Ontario* (October 1992), p. 18.

156 *A Common Sense Blueprint for Ontario*, Part 7 (Bringing Common Sense to Government Reform), p. 7.

157 Ministry of Finance, 1997 Ontario Budget: Budget Speech: Investing in the Future (May 6, 1997), p. 8: "To improve accountability in the public sector, the Government will introduce the Public Sector Accountability Act. This act will require that public sector organizations: report their financial activities in accordance with the recommendations of the Canadian Institute of Chartered Accountants; adopt policies that ensure that the private sector has an open opportunity to compete to provide services to their organizations; and adopt and publicly report on organizational performance using private and public sector benchmarks."

158 Speech from the Throne (April 19, 2001).

159 Bill 46, *Public Sector Accountability Act, 2001*. More information on the delay in acting on the 1997 commitment is found in the Provincial Auditor's 2000 special report:

Office of the Provincial Auditor, *Special Report: Accountability and Value for Money* (2000), Chapter 2 (Towards Better Accountability), pp. 17–20.

160 S.O. 2004, c. 17.

161 S.O. 2010, c. 25.

162 *The Common Sense Revolution*, p. 16.

163 S.O. 1996, c. 1, Sched. A. The salary disclosure law was included in the Harris government's first and most controversial omnibus bill, Bill 26, the *Savings and Restructuring Act, 1996*. The 17 schedules of Bill 26 enacted three new Acts, repealed two Acts, and amended 43 others.

164 The threshold was, and still is, funding received by an entity from the Government of Ontario that is, in a year, at least (a) $1 million or (b) 10 per cent of entity's gross revenues for the year if that percentage is $120,000 or more.

165 S.O. 1996, c. 1, Sched. A, s. 1, subs. 2(1), "salary" definition.

166 Ibid., s. 3.

167 O. Reg. 85/96, s. 2.

168 Note 201, subs. 4(3).

169 Note 201, s. 5.

170 *The Public Sector Compensation Disclosure Act*, S.M. 1996, c. 60.

171 *Public Sector Compensation Transparency Act* (Alberta), S.A. 2015, c. P-40.5; *Public Sector Employers Amendment Act, 2002* (British Columbia), S.B.C. 2002, c. 64, s. 5; New Brunswick, Public Accounts, Volume 2, Supplementary Information, "Salary Payments to Employees" (until 2007; starting in 2008 replaced with disclosure of salary ranges);*Public Sector Compensation Transparency Act* (Newfoundland and Labrador), S.N.L. 2016, c. P-41.02; *Public Sector Compensation Disclosure Act* (Nova Scotia), S.N.S. 2010, c. 43; *Regulation respecting the distribution of information and the protection of personal information* (Quebec), A-2.1, r. 2, subs 4(28); Saskatchewan, Legislative Assembly, 24th Legislature, 4th Session, *Fifth Report of the Standing Committee on Crown Corporations*, concurred in June 18, 2003.

172 Ministry of Finance, 1996 Ontario Budget: Budget Speech (May 7, 1996), p. 8."

173 From its passage in 1989 until 2008, the federal lobbying law's title was the *Lobbyists Registration Act*. It is now the *Lobbying Act* (S.C. 2006, c. 9, s. 66, proclaimed in force July 2, 2008).

174 S.O. 1998, c. 27., Sched., subss. 18(5) and 18(6). Effective 2016 (S.O. 2014, c. 13, Sched. 8, s. 5, proclaimed in force July 1, 2016) these provisions were re-enacted in a new location in the act (they are now subsections 3.4(1) and 3.4(2)) but otherwise they are the same as the Harris government's version.

175 Office of the Integrity Commissioner, Interpretation Bulletin #11, "What is a conflict of interest and how does it affect my lobbying?" (June 1, 2020).

176 By comparison, the federal act was proclaimed in force one year, 17 days, after Royal Assent.

177 Office of the Integrity Commissioner, *Lobbyists Registration Act, 1998*, Annual Report April 1, 2000, to March 31, 2001, p. 6.

178 Office of the Integrity Commissioner, Annual Report 2021–2022, p. 53.

179 In the first year of the registry's operation, privatization ranked 14 among topics of lobbying, immediately behind agriculture; the next two years, it ranked 13. The top five subjects of lobbying were the same, and in the same order, all three years: economic development and trade (1), health (2), taxation and finance (3), environment (4), industry (5): Office of the Integrity Commissioner, *Lobbyists Registration Act, 1998*, Annual Report January 15, 1999, to March 31, 2000, p. 9; Office of the Integrity Commissioner, *Lobbyists Registration Act, 1998*, Annual Report April 1, 2000, to March 31, 2001, p. 7; Lobbyist Registration Office, Annual Report April 1, 2001, to March 31, 2002, p. 8.

180 The *Lobbyists Registration Act* (Yukon) received Royal Assent November 22, 2018, and came into force October 15, 2020.

181 *Lobbying Transparency and Ethics Act*, C.Q.L.R., c. T-11.011; *Lobbyist Registration Act*, S.N.L. 2004, c. L-24.1.

182 In Alberta, British Columbia, Manitoba and Saskatchewan, lobbying enforcement may involve either prosecution in the courts or an administrative proceeding before the registrar of lobbyists. In British Columbia, administrative monetary penalties are routinely imposed.

183 During the spread of lobbying law to other provinces starting in 2001, Ontario's legislature has been controlled by Liberal majorities and PC majorities, with the exception of a Liberal plurality between 2011 and 2014. Lobbying conduct rules were strengthened only twice (once to limit consultant lobbying on behalf of publicly-funded entities, S.O. 2010, c. 25, s. 25, and later to prohibit success fees and prohibit lobbying by paid government advisors, S.O. 2014, c. 13, Sched. 8, ss. 4–5), and a conscious decision was made not to introduce administrative monetary penalties. (Instead, the Act was amended to provide for administrative *non-monetary* penalties: S.O. 2014, c. 13, Sched. 8, s. 14.)

184 Information and Privacy Commissioner, *Re London Services Board*, Order M-618 (October 18, 1995).

185 S.O. 1996, c. 1, Sched. K, s. 8, enacting FIPPA, subs. 50(1.1); O. Reg. 21/96, s. 1; S.O. 1996, c. 1, Sched. K, s. 20, enacting MFIPPA, subs. 39(1.1), O. Reg. 22/96, s. 1.

186 S.O. 1996, c. 1, Sched. K, s. 8, enacting FIPPA, subs. 50(2.1); S.O. 1996, c. 1, Sched. K, s. 20, enacting MFIPPA, subs. 39(2.1)

187 S.O. 1995, c. 1, s. 82, enacting FIPPA, subs. 65(6); S.O. 1995, c. 1, s. 83, enacting MFIPPA, subs. 52(3).

188 Information and Privacy Commissioner, *Re Ministry of Agriculture, Food and Rural Affairs*, Order P-1223 (July 10, 1996).

CHAPTER 13

"Common-Sense" Federal-
Provincial Relations

Craig McFadyen

W HILE FEDERAL-PROVINCIAL RELATIONS IN
ONTARIO and Canada have long been characterized
by a tension between intergovernmental collaboration
and intergovernmental competition, there were critical developments
in the 1990s that compelled Premier Mike Harris and his government
to respond—developments that continue to shape intergovernmental
relations to this day. In the next chapter, Hugh Segal provides
an excellent survey of some of the more collaborative aspects of
Ontario-federal relations during the Harris era, highlighting the cases
of the reform of the Canada Pension Plan and the development of
the National Child Benefit. This chapter will look at some of the
tensions that developed around the federal-provincial fiscal relationship,
as well as efforts to achieve "non-constitutional reforms" to the
Canadian federation in the aftermath of the 1995 Quebec secession
referendum.[1]

While there were some grounds for close federal-provincial
collaboration following the Harris election victory in June 1995, there

were early fissures in the federal-provincial relationship that became more strained over the course of the first mandate, especially as the provincial government approached the 1999 election. The clear intent of the *CSR* was to focus on a province-specific agenda in Ontario. However, subsequent events would compel Mike Harris as the Premier of Ontario to take a leadership role in the federation. His approach has been characterized as "leading from the middle."[2] And, in this sense, Premier Harris responded in a manner entirely consistent with those who held the office before him, seeking to maintain the integrity of the federation while protecting the evolving interests of Ontarians.

Throughout Mike Harris's tenure as Premier, Liberal Party Leader Jean Chrétien was the prime minister of Canada. The federal Liberal Party had won strong pluralities of the popular vote, and significant majorities of the seats in Ontario, in both 1993 and 1997. When Mike Harris was elected in 1995, ninety-eight of the ninety-nine federal members of parliament (MPs) from Ontario were Liberal, representing more than half the entire federal Liberal caucus. Two years into the implementation of the *CSR*, the Chrétien Liberals won reelection, taking 101 out of the 103 federal seats in Ontario with 49.5 per cent of the popular vote. The combined Progressive Conservative and Reform Party share of the popular vote in the province was 37.8 per cent but yielded only one seat.

These electoral results and partisan realities conditioned Ontario's approach to intergovernmental relations. Premier Harris and his ministers had to respect the fact that the federal Liberals under Jean Chrétien were popular in Ontario. Despite the big political changes taking place in the province (including the near decimation of the federal Progressive Conservatives in 1993), Ontarians seemed to have reverted to their traditional model of electing a government of one partisan persuasion at the federal level, while electing a government of a different partisan stripe at the provincial level, as if to keep each order of government in check. In this case, both governments were committed to expenditure control and fiscal discipline. However, while Harris had committed to and would implement a significant personal income tax reduction, the federal government found it difficult to honour its commitment to eliminate the Goods and Services Tax (GST) and temporarily lost one of its Ontario MPs to resignation as a consequence.

Ideological differences certainly existed, including in the realm of intergovernmental relations. Provincial Conservatives wanted a clarification of roles and responsibilities among orders of government, including getting the federal government out of the province's business, while federal Liberal MPs from Ontario generally believed the federal government had an important role to play in maintaining national standards and expanding health and social programs, which were primarily areas of provincial jurisdiction. This difference in perspectives was aggravated by the fact that the Harris government saw Liberal MPs from Ontario as ineffective representatives of the interests of Ontarians in Ottawa rather than as potential allies, in contrast to MPs from other parts of the country who would more regularly represent regional perspectives or provincial interests in Ottawa.[3]

The period leading up to the June 8, 1995, provincial election in Ontario was conditioned by two major intergovernmental issues. First, in February 1995, federal Finance Minister Paul Martin introduced a budget that committed to cut federal health and social cash transfers to provinces by 35 per cent over two years.[4] In response to this and previous federal constraints on provincial transfers, Premier Bob Rae's NDP government in Ontario had launched a "fiscal fairness" campaign, which would constitute a major plank in his party's 1995 provincial election platform. Second, in Quebec, the Parti Québecois (PQ) government had been elected in 1994 with a commitment to hold a sovereignty referendum within one year of its election. The referendum campaign was not officially launched until October 2, 1995, with the vote being held on October 30. In the run up to the 1995 Ontario election, "separation" was not deemed a serious threat given public opinion polls in Quebec on the sovereignty issue. However, this all changed with developments in Quebec, including the June 12 partnership agreement among Premier Parizeau, Mario Dumont, leader of the Official Opposition Action démocratique du Québec, and Lucien Bouchard, who had left former Conservative Prime Minister Brian Mulroney's cabinet to form the Bloc Québecois in Ottawa following the demise of the Meech Lake Accord. As public opinion moved more favourably toward the "Yes" side following after the partnership agreement, the federal government as well as the business community and federalists in Quebec and the rest of Canada began to take the existential threat of secession much more seriously.

Notwithstanding this context, the 1995 Harris platform was, almost exclusively, provincially focused. The *CSR* did not stake out a position on federal transfers, or Quebec sovereignty. The Canada Health and Social Transfer (CHST) cuts announced in the 1995 federal budget were not something that candidate Harris was going to join then Premier Rae in criticizing the federal government for having imposed. Indeed, on the campaign trail, Mike Harris was dismissive in response to Premier Rae's fixation on "fairness" in fiscal federalism, suggesting that the premier look somewhere else to find a culprit for the province's fiscal difficulties.[5] The significant cut to provincial transfers in the 1995 federal budget did require a reworking of the economic and fiscal assumptions in the *CSR* (first released in May 1994), as Ontario was anticipating a revenue decline of about $3.6 billion over two years as a result of the unilateral federal announcement.[6] And the Harris campaign team did release an updated version of the *CSR*, reaffirming their balanced budget and tax cuts objectives despite the federal transfer cuts.[7]

Beyond this, however, the only mention of inter-governmental relations in the provincial PC Party's platform document was in reference to internal trade. In this regard, the party was concerned about the number of barriers to interprovincial trade and was critical of the lack of federal leadership, as well as the lack of progress in reducing these barriers.[8] While tonally, this commitment may have intimated what was to come in areas where the new Ontario government parted ways with the federal government on policy issues, clearly the platform did not put intergovernmental relations at the centre of the province's policy agenda. Instead, the Harris revolution was almost singularly focused on what it could do in areas of provincial jurisdiction, possibly reflecting a preference to govern in a way that avoided or reduced intergovernmental entanglement.

* * *

With the June 12, 1995 signing of the agreement by Parizeau, Dumont and Bouchard, committing to negotiations for a partnership agreement with the rest of Canada in the event of a "yes" victory in the October referendum and, by implication, meaning no unilateral declaration of independence, as Premier Parizeau had preferred, the fortunes of the "yes" side began to turn, as evidenced in opinion polls.[9] In Ontario, Mike Harris and his Progressive Conservative Party won the provincial election on June 8, 1995 and were sworn-in eighteen days later on June 26. Right out of the gate, the new Ontario government was focused on keeping its election commitments and wanted to move its agenda forward quickly, as has been well-documented elsewhere in this volume. Premier Harris and his government were certainly not planning on being distracted by the actions of the federal government or developments in Quebec.

But as the summer wore on, and some early wins were chalked up in relation to the implementation of the *CSR*'s province-specific agenda, the premier and some of his key advisors began to consider what role Ontario and the premier might play in responding to what was becoming a more ominous secessionist threat in Quebec, one to which business and other key stakeholders in Ontario were beginning to direct considerable concern. Premier Harris well understood the role he might be expected to play. He had been a member of the Ontario Legislative

Committee that examined the Meech Lake and Charlottetown Accords and had considerable familiarity with the issues driving the national unity debate in Canada and the secessionist agenda in Quebec. He was also well aware of the roles previous Ontario premiers had played in these historical constitutional debates and developments.[10] This experience took on greater importance as the referendum campaign progressed, and it became increasingly apparent that the vote would be closer than initially thought by the federalist forces.

By virtue of the size of the province and its long, historic relationship with neighbouring Quebec, it was assumed that the premier of Ontario would be a very significant and important voice to appeal to Quebecers from the rest of Canada. Premier Harris's office commissioned a major speech for delivery before the referendum was held. Demonstrating that national unity was a non-partisan issue, the Premier himself reached out to his recent electoral rival, former Premier Rae for advice on the content of the speech. Advice was proffered and accepted.[11] On October 12, two weeks and two days before the October 30 referendum, Premier Harris delivered the speech to the Canadian Club, with former Premier Rae and Lynn McLeod, the Liberal Leader of the official opposition, on the podium beside him. The speech was important as a message, not from the federal government, but from a provincial leader speaking to Quebec. The purpose of the speech was to signal to Quebecers that Ontario wanted them to vote to stay within confederation and work with Ontario to reform the federation. Premier Harris, recently elected on a platform of significant change, was able to use his change-agent status to articulate a need and a willingness to work with Quebec for change within confederation.[12]

Further demonstrating that national unity was an issue that goes "beyond party and beyond partisanship in Ontario," Premier Harris brought forward an all-party resolution in the Legislature on October 26, seconded by the two opposition leaders. On October 27, just three days before the referendum vote, a Unity Rally was held in downtown

Montreal where an estimated 100,000 Canadians, from within and outside Quebec, came to celebrate a united Canada and urge Quebecers to vote "no" in the referendum. The rally was controversial insofar as the referendum rules did not permit for the interference or support (financial or otherwise), for one side or the other, beyond the officially sanctioned "yes" and "no" campaigns. Premier Harris attended the rally with his son as a private citizen and concerned Canadian.

When the final tally came in the night of October 30, 1995, the PQ had lost the referendum by a slim margin. Premier Parizeau saw fit to resign after having made some impolitic comments in his concession speech following the announcement of final results. Lucien Bouchard was soon installed as the leader of the PQ and premier of Quebec, unopposed. Premier Bouchard was committed to a "sovereignty-partnership agenda" but signaled readiness to hold another referendum as soon as "the winning conditions" permitted. It was a wake-up call for Prime Minister Chrétien, but in the immediate aftermath of the referendum, the federal government and the other provinces and territories were at a loss for what to do next. The Harris team at Queen's Park thought this confluence of circumstances and events might provide an opening to advance an intergovernmental agenda consistent with its philosophy of government and its perspective on federalism.

* * *

In the aftermath of the referendum, Prime Minister Chrétien decided to try to appeal to Quebecers by offering whatever he could in response to the province's traditional constitutional demands, including recognition of Quebec as a "distinct society" and extending a "Quebec veto" over future constitutional amendments, as well as the devolution of skills training through what became labour market development agreements.[13] To begin this process of constitutional renewal, the prime minister reached out to Premier Harris, just days after the referendum vote, but was

met by a complete refusal to discuss any constitutional matters. Premier
Harris did not think another run at constitutional accommodation of
Quebec was advisable and it was his perception that these matters had
dominated the country's intergovernmental agenda for too long. By all
reports, the prime minister was taken aback by the premier's resolve to
pursue a different path in convincing Quebecers of the merits of the
Canadian federation.[14] The premier's office was convinced that the prime
minister's office (PMO) leaked the details of the meeting to the media to
pressure and embarrass Premier Harris. The *Toronto Star* coverage was
not flattering, and suggested Ontario was taking a partisan approach
to the issue left officials in the premier's office wondering if they could
work with the prime minister's office in a way that was not tainted by
political opportunism.[15] But the Harris response to the prime minister's
overtures was not partisan obstinance. Coming out of the 1995 Annual
Premier's Conference (APC) in late August, Premier Harris recognized
that he could work with other premiers to advance an agenda on social
policy renewal and reform that might also address some of Quebec's
more practical and long-standing concerns with federal encroachment
in areas of provincial jurisdiction without further efforts to amend the
constitution.

Premier Harris and his advisors felt that the Canadian federation
needed "non-constitutional renewal." This would include an exercise
in clarifying roles and responsibilities, especially as it pertained to
health, education, and social programs, the so-called "social union."
This was something Premiers could agree on.[16] But for Premier Harris,
"renewal" would also involve an examination and disciplining of the
federal spending power. This was something his Quebec counterpart
and several other premiers could agree on, but had not yet achieved full
consensus at the premiers' table. Instead of seeking this "renewal" with
and through a federally led exercise, Premier Harris was convinced that
it was something that should be led by the provinces and territories in the
first instance. For many of the premiers, the federal government had lost

credibility as the unifying force in the federation, both in relation to events around the sovereignty referendum, but also following its significant reduction in transfers to provinces and territories with the introduction of the CHST.

At the August 1995 APC in St. John's, premiers had their first opportunity to collectively lament and respond to the transfer cuts announced in the 1995 federal budget. In response, all premiers except Premier Parizeau, agreed on the need to show leadership in the reform and renewal of social policy and to work together to develop common standards for health and social programs. But premiers believed that national standards did not have to be federal standards. This commitment led premiers to create a Provincial-Territorial Ministerial Council to undertake this work. With separatist Premier Parizeau's resignation, Premier Harris saw an opportunity to show leadership among premiers and in the federation by personally reaching out to Lucien Bouchard, the new premier of Quebec. While committed to achieving a "sovereignty-partnership" with the rest of Canada, Bouchard's stipulation that the next referendum be called only if the "winning conditions" obtained was, from Ontario's perspective, an opening for non-constitutional renewal of the federation. The thinking was that, if the federation could be renewed in a way that satisfied most of Quebecers' expectations and desires within a united Canada, then the "winning conditions" might never obtain.

Premier Harris and his team understood that the Ontario government's politics and approach to province-specific issues were not universally applauded in Canada, including in Quebec. As such, they adopted a "lead from the middle" approach, seeing the premiers' meetings as a vehicle through which this approach could be implemented. The 1996 APC was to be held in Jasper, Alberta, and premiers would hold their first session on the train transporting them collectively from Edmonton to the conference site. In advance of the conference, Ontario commissioned a paper from Professor Thomas J. Courchene, entitled "ACCESS: A Convention on the Canadian Economic and Social Systems," which envisioned a greater role for provinces and territories in the determination of both the social and economic unions within confederation. Notably, Courchene accepted the use of the federal spending power in areas of provincial jurisdiction, provided provinces and territories were given the opportunity to opt out of federal programs with full compensation. As well, Courchene envisioned the conversion of ongoing federal cash transfers, like the CHST, to tax point transfers over time (Courchene, 1996).

Opting-out with full compensation and a preference for tax room transfers over cash transfers was an established position taken by Quebec whenever the federal government sought to act in areas of provincial jurisdiction and one the new premier of Quebec would have a hard time disagreeing with. However, the conversion of cash to tax point transfers was not a position most other premiers of equalization-receiving provinces could abide, as the value of these tax points would grow more slowly in their provinces because of slower relative economic growth and thus were not viewed as equitable, notwithstanding the greater fiscal certainty they provided to provincial treasuries.[17] Brian Tobin, a former federal cabinet minister in the Chrétien government, now premier of Newfoundland and Labrador and outgoing chair of the premiers forum, took particular umbrage at the ACCESS proposal sponsored by Ontario. While the paper was not formally on the conference agenda, Premier Tobin made a public display of his position, stating "Courchene was thrown from the train" (Savage, 1996). To be sure, the ACCESS paper was more assertive in terms of embracing provincial autonomy and disciplining the federal spending power than the mandate and work of the ministerial council created at the previous year's APC and formally reporting into premiers with an update at the 1996 conference.

Certainly, the ACCESS episode had the effect of putting Premier Harris's intergovernmental agenda more out front than a "lead from the middle" strategy may have suggested. Nonetheless, Ontario's efforts did help drive a consensus among Premiers to issue a paper, entitled

"Social Policy Reform and Renewal: Next Steps," prepared by a provincial-territorial working group and to give a somewhat sharper edge to the work of this body going forward as it began to engage with the federal government. As we shall see, the direction from premiers was advanced by the ministerial working group on social policy renewal and ultimately set the stage for the first ministers' accord, called the Social Union Framework Agreement, in February 1999.

* * *

Premier Harris, and his colleagues from outside Quebec, were not finished on the theme of non-constitutional renewal. It was felt that a statement still needed to be made from the rest of Canada to reach out to Quebecers, but there remained divisions among premiers in terms of what that statement might look like and how far it might go in addressing Quebec's traditional concerns. Some premiers had not given up completely on constitutional change, while others were convinced otherwise.[18] Indeed, Alberta Premier Ralph Klein was reluctant to acknowledge Quebec's uniqueness in any way fearing that it would confer special status on the province which he knew was overwhelmingly rejected in Alberta during the Charlottetown process. The premiers agreed to work on a joint statement of principles that were aimed at addressing Quebecers' interests and that would serve as a framework for consulting Canadians. On September 17, 1997, the premiers met in Calgary. Premier Klein arrived at the meeting with his own revised statement of principles, still concerned about special recognition for Quebec. Premier Harris led the premiers to a more balanced statement, in part, by advancing a principle that acknowledged "all provinces, while diverse in their characteristics, have equality of status."[19] This allowed Premier Klein to accept the principle that spoke to the "unique character of Quebec," and the role the Legislature and government of Quebec have in protecting that unique character within Canada. In the end, the premiers outside Quebec agreed to a statement of principles and an approach to consulting with Canadians that came to be known as "the Calgary Declaration." Each premier undertook consultations on the framework. For the government of Quebec, although not a party to the Calgary Declaration, the principle of "equality of status" seemed to undercut any practical recognition of Quebec's uniqueness. While the declaration received strong support, including in Quebec, the inability of the premiers outside Quebec to get Premier Bouchard's concurrence limited its impact. On May 26, 1998, following consultations in Ontario, Premier Harris brought forward a resolution in the Legislature confirming support for the framework. The motion was passed with only one member of the Legislature dissenting.[20]

Perhaps the most important contribution of the declaration was in the enhanced working relationships and mutual understanding it cultivated among premiers. It confirmed a path forward for non-constitutional renewal of the federation. From Ontario's perspective, it was constructive insofar as it asserted the need for governments in Canada, including the federal government, to "respect each other's jurisdictions," and to work cooperatively "to ensure the efficiency and effectiveness of the federation."[21] For Premier Harris, this also helped bring him closer to Premier Bouchard, finding some shared interests in clarifying roles and responsibilities in the federation and, in this regard, seeing the role of the federal government in the areas of health, education, and social policy as being primarily restricted to funding, not policymaking and the creation of "national standards." An excellent example of this thinking was already embedded in the premiers' 1995 agreement that "national standards" do not need to be "federal standards." Premier Harris and his colleagues continued to encourage the ministerial council to advance its work in these areas, as a means of demonstrating provincial resolve to the federal government.

The last piece of the non-constitutional renewal puzzle, from Ontario's perspective, was getting the federal government to agree to respect provincial jurisdiction and constrain its use of the federal spending power. The vehicle for this would be the Social Union Framework Agreement (SUFA). There was already a provincial-territorial process initiated by premiers at the 1995 APC. Its first report, calling for the restoration of federal transfers and the clarification of roles and responsibilities in the federation, had been made available to Prime Minister Chrétien in advance of the June 1996 first ministers' meeting. First ministers agreed that a committee of ministers should be created to review the report, and the prime minister assigned his ministers of Health and Human Resources Development to the committee. This committee became the Federal-Provincial-Territorial Council on Social Policy Renewal and was ultimately charged with making recommendations to first ministers. Initially, however, the federal government was intent on using the council to develop and implement its commitment to a National Child Benefit. In the provincial-territorial process, Ontario took a leadership role in doing the staff work by virtue of its size and capacity, but also in terms of moving a consensus position forward on broader social policy renewal. The PQ government in Quebec chose not to formally engage, reiterating its traditional position that the federal government had no role in areas of provincial jurisdiction other than transferring cash, but Quebec would remain a keen official observer so long as provinces continued to seek to use the process as a means of disciplining the federal spending power.

As the negotiations ground on among the federal government and the other provinces and territories, more distance was created, and less urgency was assigned to this process as a means of responding to the 1995 referendum. At the same time, Bouchard's government appeared to be putting less effort into creating the "winning conditions" and more effort into managing the challenges of governing. The secessionist threat in Quebec came to be seen as less menacing. The federal government had begun to devolve labour market programs, including an agreement with Quebec in April 1997. In June 1997, Jean Chrétien's government won its second mandate, albeit with a somewhat reduced majority. The federal government was also moving into a period of sustained fiscal surpluses. In 1998, pursuant to its 1997 pre-election budget commitment, the federal government got agreement with provinces and territories on the creation of a National Child Benefit, better integrating federal and provincial supports in this area. The federal government was now keen on "reconnecting with Canadians," including through the exercise of its spending power in areas of provincial jurisdiction. As such, the federal government was considerably more assertive in the SUFA negotiations than it might otherwise have been, had they occurred earlier in the post-referendum period and had Quebec been a party to the social union negotiations.

For his part, Premier Harris was becoming more concerned with the upcoming provincial election. To that end, Premier Harris was prepared to avail himself of whatever opportunities presented themselves to advance his electoral interests, including those in the realm of federal-provincial relations. Compensation for Hepatitis C victims was one such opportunity.[22] An agreement had been reached among federal-provincial and territorial Health Ministers, in March 1998, to cost-share the compensation of victims infected by tainted blood through the Canadian blood supply after 1986. Following the announcement of this agreement there was considerable stakeholder and public reaction to the non-inclusion of persons infected through the blood supply prior to 1986. After a statement by Quebec on April 29, 1998, that the federal government should extend full compensation to victims infected prior to 1986 and the federal government's subsequent refusal to do so, Premier Harris seized the opportunity and offered to compensate such victims in Ontario unilaterally, to great political effect. Premier Harris was able to get a consensus position, agreed to by all provinces and territories, at the 1998 Annual Premiers' Conference in Saskatoon following the appearance of a young victim and compensation advocate at the meeting.[23] The episode ended up embarrassing both the prime minister and his health minister and helped cultivate a more compassionate political persona for Premier Harris going into the 1999 provincial election.

In this context, and without Quebec at the table, the Social Union Framework Agreement was eventually finalized at the February 4, 1999, first ministers' meeting. It went further in compromising provincial-territorial interests than Ontario and some other provinces may have preferred. For example, it included provisions requiring provinces and territories to consult with the federal government before they took actions in areas of their own jurisdiction, if it could be argued that these actions would somehow "substantially affect" the federal government.[24] The agreement did not confirm or advance the issue of opting-out of federal programs in provincial jurisdiction with full compensation. But SUFA did add some discipline to the exercise of the federal spending power, by requiring the federal government to

- not introduce any new national social programs without the agreement of a majority of provincial governments;
- consult with provincial and territorial governments at least one year in advance of the renewal or significant funding changes in existing social transfers to provinces/territories, unless otherwise agreed;
- build due notice provisions into any new social transfers to provincial/territorial governments.[25]

As one careful commentator subsequently noted, federal and provincial-territorial governments weighed the individual commitments differently and had the scope to interpret the agreement differently.[26] Moreover, SUFA was a political agreement, not a legal one, and had no formal sanctions in the event a signatory government did not respect its provisions. While SUFA could be deployed to embarrass the federal government if it contravened provisions of the agreement, negotiation with the federal government had not resulted in the substantive outcome Ontario and other provinces had sought with respect to constraining the federal spending power. Non-constitutional renewal of the federation was very quickly being reduced to the restoration of federal transfers, and advocacy was seen as the best remaining option for advancing this agenda.

* * *

If Mike Harris's Progressive Conservative government appeared unconcerned with federal transfer cuts in its first provincial budget in 1996, this benign view was not to last. Informed by the principle of subsidiarity and provincial autonomy advanced in the ACCESS paper and embraced by colleagues in Quebec and Alberta, as well as having learned from his experience at the premiers' table and the deliberations around the social union and the Calgary Framework, Premier Harris began increasingly to focus on and question the fiscal relationship in the federation. The ACCESS paper had provided some early speaking points on the issue of "over-equalization" in the federation, arguing that equalization should be restricted to the federal equalization program and not brought in through the backdoor in other federal programs like employment insurance, labour market training, and infrastructure funding. However, correcting "over-equalization" could mean reallocating federal funding away from the equalization-receiving provinces that benefited from existing funding arrangements. To maintain a provincial-territorial consensus on the larger question of the overall adequacy of federal transfers and the broader fiscal imbalance in the federation, Premier Harris focused his critique of the fiscal arrangements on the need for restoration of federal cuts to provincial transfers. This positioning at the premiers' table did not stop his government from raising its other concern with the fairness of federal transfers with a domestic Ontario audience.

In its second budget on May 6, 1997, the Ontario government was prepared to be much more direct and assertive in its criticism of reductions in federal transfers and the fundamental unfairness of federal support for provincial health care systems. In his budget speech, Finance Minister Ernie Eves stated: "Unlike the federal government, we have made support for health care our highest priority. The federal government has cut funding for people in Ontario from the program that supports health care by $2.1 billion since 1995–1996."[27] The minister went on to document the unfairness of the new CHST by outlining the differences in cash transfers among provinces, noting federal support on a per capita cash basis was second lowest in Ontario, only Alberta received less federal per capita cash support for health care (Ontario, 1997, p. 19). This inequity in cash transfers under the CHST was the legacy of fiscal arrangements dating back to 1977, and Ontario viewed it as wholly unacceptable that it should persist under the current and much different federal transfer programs.[28]

In the 1998 provincial budget, this lament over the inadequacy of federal transfers went further, beginning to make an argument around the balance sheet of confederation not working for the province:

> Despite the fact that the federal government reduced funding for the program that supports health care by $2.4 billion over the last three years, this year Ontario will spend $18.5 billion on health, up $300 million from the 1998–1999 spending announced in the December 1997 Economic Outlook and Fiscal Review.
>
> Despite the fact that the federal government now spends only $125 for health care for each person in Ontario, this year the Ontario Government is spending $1,639 to meet the health needs of each Ontarian.
>
> Despite the fact that the federal government collects twice as much in personal income tax revenue from each taxpayer in Ontario than the provincial government collects, it provides less than eight cents of every dollar spent on health care, while Ontario pays the rest.

> While the federal government has all but abandoned the health care needs of Ontarians, our Government is improving the services people have now, and expanding those that they will need in the future.[29]

The Harris government was beginning to echo the Rae government in terms of its concerns with fiscal federalism being fundamentally unfair to Ontarians. Ontario commissioned work to update its calculations of Ontarians' net contribution to the federation, using the same methodology as work that had been done for the previous government and based on Statistics Canada's Provincial Economic Accounts.[30] This research showed that Ontario residents made a net contribution to the federation of $15 billion or more each year between 1992 and 1997, or about 5 per cent of provincial GDP per year on average. Equitable treatment or "fairness" in fiscal federalism had now crossed the partisan divide as a central concern in Ontario's intergovernmental relations.[31] But, in working with other premiers, Premier Harris, kept his focus on the adequacy of federal transfers to all provinces and territories and the overall structural fiscal imbalance in the federation.[32] In their 1998 APC news release on healthcare funding, premiers observed "that every government in Canada but one—the federal government—has increased its funding to health care."[33]

By 1999, under pressure from all premiers, but perhaps none more vigorously than Mike Harris in Ontario, and no longer able to justify its mounting annual surpluses at the same time as it had not fully restored previous transfer cuts to provinces and territories, the federal government committed to restoring funding in support of provincial health care. While the Social Union Framework Agreement reached at the February 1999 first ministers' meeting did not deliver the results Ontario was seeking on the use of the federal spending power, it did create the conditions and impetus for the federal government to reinvest in social programs in its budget just two weeks later. The February 16, 1999, federal budget announced that Ottawa would be investing $11.5 billion more in the CHST over five years. This included $8 billion over four years that would be added to the CHST base beginning in 2000–2001 and a one-time payment of $3.5 billion through a CHST "trust" funded out of the surplus from the 1998–1999 fiscal year that could be drawn down by provinces and territories as they chose over the next three fiscal years.[34]

A key development in the 1999 federal budget from Ontario's perspective was a federal commitment to eliminate the disparities across provinces resulting from the cap-on-CAP being rolled into the CHST allocation formula. The formula would still be based on the value of tax points transferred under the 1977 Established Programs Financing (EPF) agreement and a residual cash transfer, but the vestigial unfairness from the cap-on-CAP would be eliminated over the next three years. These federal investments and changes in the allocation formula were noted in the 1999 Ontario budget speech as "a good first step, but it is only a first step."[35] One of the next steps for Ontario was getting the EPF tax points out of the CHST allocation formula, but this would have to wait until after a fuller restoration of federal health transfers.

At the same time as Ontario budgets advocated for greater fairness in federal transfers, Premier Harris continued to work with his colleagues to maintain pressure on the federal government to increase the quantum of federal transfers beyond those announced in the 1999 federal budget. Many equalization-receiving provinces continued to see their interests as better served through enhancements to the equalization program, rather than through enhancements to the CHST. Moreover, eliminating the inequity in the CHST allocation formula created by the cap-on-CAP, meant that Ontario, British Columbia, and Alberta (the only provinces impacted by the cap-on-CAP) would benefit proportionately more from the federal CHST investments in the 1999 budget. While the 1999 federal budget also renewed the equalization program on the five-year schedule required by federal legislation, these enhancements were viewed as modest by the equalization-receiving provinces, especially in relation to the federal investments in CHST.[36] Premier Klein, reflecting what had now become axiomatic for Alberta in its approach to fiscal federalism, was strongly opposed to any further equalization enhancements. Premier Harris recognized that he could play a key role in brokering a consensus among premiers, that addressed the interests of both equalization-receiving and non-receiving provinces, by keeping the focus on restoration of the CHST. This consensus was maintained in both the 1999 and 2000 annual premiers' conference communiques, which advocated for further federal investments in health care through the CHST and the inclusion of an annual escalator to ensure federal provincial expenditure growth in the related areas.[37] Premiers' communiques also became more explicit about the restoration of federal transfers as a means of addressing the growing fiscal imbalance in the federation as the federal government's fiscal position continued to improve.[38]

Throughout this period, premiers were building support among Canadians, including engaging with health stakeholders at their annual meetings, and undertook aggressive advocacy in their own jurisdictions. As the nature and extent of federal surpluses became clearer, and as this confirmed the structural nature of the fiscal imbalance in the federation, pressure on the federal government to restore its transfers for health care became overwhelming.[39] In Ontario, having learned from the Hepatitis C compensation episode, Premier Harris recognized that he could put additional pressure on the prime minister by differentiating Ontario's enhanced support for health care from the reduced level of federal support. In March 2000, the premier launched an advertising campaign doing just that, claiming the federal government was only contributing 11 cents on the dollar to provincial health care spending and describing the federal government as the missing partner in health care reform and sustainability. This ad campaign incensed Prime Minister Chrétien and his health minister, Allan Rock, who were left trying to explain to a confused public how tax points transferred in 1977 were an important part of the federal government's current contribution to provincial health care.[40]

The pressure on the federal government was unrelenting, from stakeholders and provincial-territorial governments alike, and Ottawa was losing the public relations battle. The prime minister and Minister Rock continued to insist that additional health funding would follow provincial health reforms but did not identify exactly what reforms were required.[41] At their 2000 annual conference Premiers released a provincial-territorial health ministers' paper on cost drivers and continued to press for a first ministers' meeting on health funding and health sustainability.[42] Following that APC, Ontario launched another round of radio advertisements that again vexed the prime minister and his government.[43] Finally, at a first ministers' meeting set by the prime minister for September 11, 2000, the federal government committed to restore an additional $21 billion to the CHST over five years.[44] The health funding agreement reached at the first ministers' meeting helped inoculate Prime Minister Chrétien and his government from the unrelenting criticism from health stakeholders concerning the federal health and social cuts from 1995. Shortly thereafter, Prime Minister Chrétien called an early election for November 27, 2000, and was reelected with a third straight (and enhanced) majority.

Until he left office in April 2002, Premier Harris and his government would continue pushing the federal government on its contribution to provincial health spending and the fundamental unfairness of the CHST allocation to Ontarians. Premier Harris's role in maintaining the provincial consensus remained important throughout the period and into the next round of federal investment. Taking their lead from the success that Ontario had with its advertising campaign in 2000, the premiers collectively initiated a paid advertising campaign in 2002 that put new pressure on the federal government to invest in health care as its structural surpluses continued to grow. The federal Royal Commission on the Future of Health Care in Canada, under former Saskatchewan Premier Roy Romanow, reported in November 2002. In 2003, Paul Martin became prime minister following the engineered resignation of Jean Chrétien. Based on a recommendation in Romanow's report, the Martin government's first budget split the CHST into two separate transfers, the Canada Health Transfer and the Canada Social Transfer and committed to additional investments in health care through a year-end "trust" if its fiscal position permitted.[45]

In the June 2004 election, Paul Martin saw his Liberal government reduced to a minority while still running significant surpluses and facing unrelenting criticism from premiers for under-investing in health care. In September, refusing the premiers' suggestion that the federal government simply take over responsibility for pharmacare as a permanent rebalancing of roles and responsibilities in health care, Prime Minister Martin convened a first ministers' meeting at which agreement was reached on a ten-year plan for health funding, including a 6 per cent annual escalator to ensure federal health transfers kept pace with healthcare inflation. Premier Harris's approach to focusing pressure on the federal government and his efforts to maintain a provincial consensus on the health funding issue for the seven years he was premier of Ontario should not be underestimated as a key factor in helping to set the stage for this landmark agreement.[46]

Both through provincial budgets and in bilateral engagements, Premier Harris let the federal government know that fairness in federal transfers was also an issue of principled concern for Ontario. On this he had more limited success during his years in office, notably the phasing out of vestiges of the cap-on-CAP under the CHST allocation formula. Arguably, this was the price to pay to keep a provincial consensus together on the restoration of health transfers. However, the principle of equity and fairness in federal transfers was picked up by each of his successors and received support from other non-equalization receiving provinces, principally Alberta. Stephen Harper's Conservatives were elected to a minority government in 2006 and agreed that it was no longer appropriate to include the tax points transferred under the 1977 EPF arrangements, as part of the allocation formula for the CST and the CHT. In 2007, federal Finance Minister Jim Flaherty, a former provincial finance minister under Premier Harris, put the allocation of the Canada Social Transfer on an equal per capita cash basis, addressing one of Ontario's long-standing fairness concerns.[47] In 2014, once the 2004 first ministers' agreement on health funding had expired, the Canada Health Transfer allocation formula was also put on an equal per capita cash basis.[48] This too can be understood as part of Premier Harris's intergovernmental legacy.

* * *

In an April 2002 interview, on the eve of the convention to choose his successor, Premier Harris stated:

> I disagreed with Bob Rae, I disagreed with David Peterson, I disagreed with Jean Chrétien on many issues. But never for a second do I doubt that they are doing what they think is in the best interests of the province or of the country. . . . And I am the same. And so, I hope the history books and those writers will understand that—that I came to try to make this a better place for my children, for their children, for the next generation, and I believe I have accomplished that in a very significant way.[49]

But was Harris right? Let's take stock of his intergovernmental accomplishments.

While candidate Harris and his team were not initially interested in focusing on intergovernmental issues, in opposition or on the election trail, this changed quickly following their election to government in June 1995. Premier Harris gave a major speech, specifically directed at Quebec on the potential for "non-constitutional reform" of the federation, just weeks before the October 30 referendum and personally attended the Montreal Unity Rally just days before. Premier Harris played a key role in advancing the non-constitutional renewal of the federation following the "near miss" in the 1995 Quebec sovereignty referendum. And these efforts at renewal had a lasting impact. While Quebec remains ever vigilant in protecting its jurisdiction from incursions by federal governments intent on using the spending power to condition transfers intended to support policy and programs in the provincial domain, there has been no serious existential threat to the federation since 1995.

Premier Harris was a strong advocate for the restoration of federal transfers beginning in 1997, effectively linking action on this to the non-constitutional renewal of the federation. He was successful in cultivating a special relationship with Premier Bouchard of Quebec, but also worked to cultivate the trust of other premiers, so that they could show a united front to the federal government and advance their common interest in the restoration of federal transfers. This had long-term positive fiscal impacts for all provinces, including Ontario. Federal transfers under the CHT now represent about 25 per cent of Ontario health spending, up from closer to 10 per cent following the full implementation of the CHST reductions in 1997–1998. At the same time, Premier Harris re-ignited the debate on the fairness of federal transfers to Ontarians and was able to position the province well for subsequent changes in this aspect of the fiscal arrangements. These changes making the major federal transfers equitable were, perhaps not coincidentally, delivered at the federal level by one of Premier Harris's former Ontario finance ministers. Major transfers are now allocated to all provinces on an equal per capita cash basis, returning billions of tax dollars to Ontarians each year. Based on this assessment of the evidence and historical record, it can only be concluded that in terms of effectively advancing the interests of Ontarians in the realm of federal-provincial relations and playing an effective role as Premier of Ontario within the Canadian federation, Premier Harris leaves a lasting and highly consequential legacy.

References

Canada, Department of Finance (1995). "Building Today for a Better Tomorrow." *The Budget Plan 1999: Including Supplementary Information and Notices of Ways and Means Motions.* February 27, 1995. Retrieved at: https://www.budget.canada.ca/pdfarch/budget95/binb/budget 1995-eng.pdf

Canada, Department of Finance (1999). "Building Today for a Better Tomorrow." *The Budget Plan 1999: Including Supplementary Information and Notices of Ways and Means Motions.* February 16, 1999. Retrieved at: https://www.budget.canada.ca/pdfarch/budget99/bp/bp99e.pdf

Canada, Department of Finance (2007). "Aspire to a Stronger, Better, Safer Canada." *The Budget Plan 2007.* March 16, 2007. Retrieved at: https://www.budget.canada.ca/2007/pdf/bp2007e.pdf

Canada, Employment and Social Development (2023). *About the Labour Market Development Programs.* On-line information for reference. Retrieved at: https://www.canada.ca/en/employment-social-development/programs/training-agreements/lmda.html

Canadian Intergovernmental Conference Secretariat (CICS) (1997). "Premiers Agree to Consult Canadians on Unity," *News Release,* Calgary, Alberta, September 14,1997. Retrieved at: https://scics.ca/en/product-produit/news-release-premiers-agree-to-consult-canadians-on-unity/

Canadian Intergovernmental Conference Secretariat (CICS) (1998a). "Health Care Funding: News Release," *39th Annual Premiers' Conference,* August 7, 1998. Retrieved at: https://scics.ca/en/product-produit/news-release-24736/#85007016e

Canadian Intergovernmental Conference Secretariat (CICS) (1998b). "News Release: Hepatitis C," *39th Annual Premiers' Conference,* August 7, 1998. Retrieved at: https://scics.ca/en/product-produit/news-release-hepatitis-c/

Canadian Intergovernmental Conference Secretariat (CICS) (1999a). *A Framework to Improve the Social Union for Canadians: An Agreement Between the Government of Canada and the Governments of the Provinces and Territories.* First ministers' meeting, February 4, 1999. Retrieved at: https://scics.ca/en/product-produit/agreement-a-framework-to-improve-the-social-union-for-canadians/

Canadian Intergovernmental Conference Secretariat (CICS) (1999b). "News Release: Priority Health Sector Issues." *40th Annual Premiers' Conference,* August 11, 1999. Retrieved at: https://scics.ca/en/product-produit/news-releases-index-of-news-releases-issued-on-august-11-1999/

Canadian Intergovernmental Conference Secretariat (CICS) (1999c). "News Release: F/P/T Health Ministers Take Action on Key Health Issues." *Annual Conference of Federal-Provincial-Territorial Ministers of Health,* September 16, 1999. Retrieved at: https://scics.ca/en/product-produit/news-release-fpt-health-ministers-take-action-on-key-health-issues/

Canadian Intergovernmental Conference Secretariat (CICS) (2000). "News Release: understanding Canada's Health Care Costs." *41st Annual Premiers' Conference,* August 10, 2000. Retrieved at: https://scics.ca/en/product-produit/news-release-understanding-canadas-health-care-costs/

Canadian Intergovernmental Conference Secretariat (CICS) (2000b). "News Release: New Federal Investments to Accompany the Agreements on Health Renewal and Early Childhood Development." *First Ministers' Meeting,* September 11, 2000. Retrieved at: https://scics.ca/en/product-produit/news-release-new-federal-investments-to-accompany-the-agreements-on-health-renewal-and-early-childhood-development/

Canadian Intergovernmental Conference Secretariat (CICS) (2000b). "News Release: Fiscal Imbalance in Canada." *41st Annual Premiers' Conference,* August 11, 2000. Retrieved at: https://scics.ca/en/product-produit/news-release-fiscal-imbalance-in-canada/

Canadian Intergovernmental Conference Secretariat (CICS) (2016). Premiers Conferences 1887–2002. Retrieved at: https://scics.ca/wp-content/uploads/2016/10/premiers_report_e.pdf

CBC News (2000). "Feds Unhappy with Ontario Health Ads." CBC. ca posted on August 29, 2000. Retrieved at: https://cbc.ca/news/canada/feds-unhappy-with-ontario-health-ads-1.243305

Courchene, Thomas J. (1996). "ACCESS: A Convention on the Canadian Economic and Social Systems" (Toronto: Ministry of Intergovernmental Affairs), reprinted in *Canadian Business Economics*. 4, no. 4 (Summer 1998), pp. 3–26.

Editorial (1995). "Harris' Opportunity to Lead on Quebec." *The Toronto Star*. November 3, 1995. P. A24. Retrieved at: https://www.proquest.com/hnptorontostar/docview/1357027101/DC0C873359F74C3FPQ/3?accountid=14369

Fox, J., Andersen, R. and Dubonnet, J. (1999). "The Polls and the 1995 Quebec Referendum," *The Canadian Journal of Sociology*. Vol. 24, No. 3 (Summer, 1999). pp. 411–424.

Gwynn, Richard (1995). "Petty, Parochial Premiers Can't Speak for Canada." *The Toronto Star*. November 3, 1995. P. A25. Retrieved at: https://www.proquest.com/hnptorontostar/docview/1356974240/DC0C873359F74C3FPQ/4?accountid=14369

Harris, Mike (1995). *Notes for an Address by The Honourable Mike Harris Premier of Ontario The Canadian Club Toronto*, Ontario October 12. (mimeo provided by David Lindsay).

Hébert, Chantal (With Jean Lapierre) (2014). *The Morning After: The 1995 Referendum and the Day that Almost Was*. Toronto: Alfred A Knopf Canada.

Ibbitson, John (2001). *Loyal No More: Ontario's Struggle for a Separate Destiny*. Toronto: Harper Collins.

Lazar, Harvey (2000). The Social Union Framework Agreement: Lost Opportunity or New Beginning. Institute of Intergovernmental Relations, Queen's University. Retrieved from: https://www.queensu.ca/iigr/sites/iirwww/files/uploaded_files/LazarSocialUnion.pdf

Legislative Assembly of Ontario (1998). "Orders of the Day: National Unity." *Hansard* Tuesday, May 26, 1998. Retrieved at: https://www.

ola.org/en/legislative-business/house-documents/parliament-36/session-2/1998-05-26/hansard-1

McIlroy, Anne (2000). "Health Care Fight Heats up as Chrétien Blasts Harris." *The Globe and Mail.* March 29, 2000. Retrieved at: https://www.theglobeandmail.com/news/national/health-care-fight-heats-up-as-chretien-blasts-harris/article4162071/

Ontario (1990). *1990 Ontario Budget.* Queen's Printer for Ontario.

Ontario (1995). *1995 Ontario Budget Plan.* Queen's Printer for Ontario.

Ontario (1997). "Investing in the Future." *1997 Ontario Budget: Budget Speech.* Queen's Printer for Ontario.

Ontario (1998). "Jobs for the Future Today." *1998 Ontario Budget: Budget Speech.* Queen's Printer for Ontario.

Ontario (1999). "Foundations for Prosperity." *1999 Ontario Budget: Budget Speech.* Queen's Printer for Ontario.

Paikin, Steve (2013). *Paikin and the Premiers: Personal Reflections on a Half Century of Ontario Leaders.* Toronto: Dundurn.

Provincial-Territorial Council on Social Policy Renewal (1997). *Progress Report to Premiers, Report No. 2.* July 1997. Retrieved at: http://www.scics.gc.ca/CMFiles/conferences/85006109_2e.pdf

Tobin, Brian (1996). "Premiers Release Report of the Ministerial Council on Social Policy Reform and Renewal. *News Release.* Executive Council Office, Government of Newfoundland and Labrador, March 26, 1996. Retrieved at: https://www.releases.gov.nl.ca/releases/1996/exec/0328n03.htm

TVO Today (2020). *Transcript: Mike Harris: "The Common Sense Revolution at 25,"* June 26, 2020. Transcript retrieved at: https://www.tvo.org/transcript/2619770/mike-harris-the-common-sense-revolution-at-25

Progressive Conservative Party of Ontario (1995). *The Common Sense Revolution,* 5th Printing.

Speirs, Rosemary, "Leaders Sound Dissenting Note." *The Toronto Star.* November 4, 1995. pp. C1 and C5. Retrieved from: https://

www.proquest.com/hnptorontostar/docview/1356976395/
DC0C873359F74C3FPQ/1?accountid=14369

Savage, John (1996), *Speech by Premier John Savage to the Empire Club*, October
15, 1996. Retrieved at: https://novascotia.ca/news/archive/viewRel.
asp?relID=/cmns/msrv/nr-1996/nr96- 10/96101506.htm

Walker, William (1995). "Heed Warning from Quebec, Bourassa
Urges." The Toronto Star. November 3, 1995. P. A4. Retrieved at:
https://www.proquest.com/hnptorontostar/docview/1357026836/
DC0C873359F74C3FPQ/5?accountid=14369

Walkom, Thomas (1995). "Canny Harris is Balking at Push for Quebec
Offer." *The Toronto Star.* November 4, 1995. p. C4. Retrieved
at: https://www.proquest.com/hnptorontostar/docview/1357026836/
3BD1921419674439PQ/10?accountid=14369

Notes

1   This chapter has benefitted enormously from the insights and comments of David
Lindsay and Bill Forward, who were both central to the development of Ontario's
intergovernmental relations and the provision of advice to Premier Harris during
the period under review. While this chapter has sought to use primary sources
where possible, the author would like to acknowledge John Ibbitson's book *Loyal No
More*. Written near the end of the Harris years, it provides historical context which
has become increasingly difficult to recreate through the (non-digital) historical
record. Finally, the author would also like to thank Alister Campbell, Kim Pearson,
and Colleen Mahoney for very helpful editorial advice, noting that any errors or
omissions are of his own doing.

2   There is some debate over the original ascription of this approach to leadership in
Ontario, but it was clearly being used in official government circles as a shorthand
for Premier Harris's style in intergovernmental relations. David Lindsay claims he
first heard the phrase used by Hugh Segal who, in turn, may well have evolved the
approach under his boss in the 1970s and early 1980s, Premier Bill Davis.

3   It is useful to remember in this context that the Bloc Québecois was the Official
Opposition from 1993 to 1997 and the Western based Reform Party became the
Official Opposition following the 1997 election. In the Queen's Park precinct, the
101 Ontario Liberal MPs elected in the 1997 were often referred to, somewhat
pejoratively, as the "101 Dalmatians" in reference to their tendency to be more
concerned with the interests and dictates of the Prime Minister's Office than the
interests of their constituents and province.

4   Canada, 1995, p. 51.

5   Ibbitson, 2001, p. 166. As Ibbitson suggests, Mike Harris's own commitment to fiscal restraint and deficit reduction In the CSR likely made it difficult for him to be too critical of the federal government in this regard (Ibbitson, 2001. p. 151).

6   Ontario, 1995, p. 5.

7   CSR, 5th Edition, pp. 1 and 21.

8   The CSR stated: "It has been estimated that barriers to trade within Canada cost each Ontario family as much as $1000 a year in lost income. For years, federal efforts to end these job-killing barriers have failed. Ontario cannot afford to wait for the glacial reform efforts of the federal government and certain other provinces. We will initiate bilateral trade negotiations with any interested province immediately after the next election. We will break the current log-jam by offering to work with any other government that is willing to co-operate in driving down costs. For example, we might share the costs of administration for transportation. We will actively work to initiate such cost-effective transactions at all levels of government" (CSR, p. 15).

9   Fox et al., 1999, suggest that the referendum was always closer than opinion polls suggested, because early opinion polls may have been disguising a higher propensity among undecided voters to tend towards sovereignty based on traditional approaches to apportioning the undecided vote in early polls. It is nonetheless the case that it was the changes in the decided vote in the opinion polls, that galvanized reaction in the rest of Canada, including Premier Harris's actions in relation to the Quebec referendum.

10 Mike Harris watched from outside of Queen's Park and government, as Premier Davis was able to help navigate rough waters in the debates around the patriation of the Constitution. The Premier's role was central and it is generally believed that Ontarians supported his approach to patriation. Premier Davis did not, however, stand for re-election following the patriation of the constitution in 1982, so there is no electoral outcome by which to measure Ontarians' appetite for constitutional renewal at that time. Mike Harris had a front row seat as an MPP in the provincial legislature and member of the legislative committee that reviewed and watched the ignominious defeat of the Meech Lake Accord, notwithstanding Premier Peterson's offer to forgo Senate seats in order to get a deal (something that many believe contributed to Premier Peterson's defeat in the 1990 provincial election). As leader of the third party at Queen's Park, Mike Harris observed Premier Rae pour considerable energy into the negotiations around the Charlottetown Accord, only to see it defeated in a national referendum. Even though the vote on Charlottetown showed that, by the narrowest of majorities (50.1 per cent), Ontarians that voted in the referendum supported the Accord, Mike Harris did not see his political base as interested in or supportive of constitutional reform, and he was not inclined to get distracted by issues that did not appeal to his base.

11 Paikin, 2013, p. 357

12 See "*Notes for an Address by The Honourable Mike Harris Premier of Ontario The Canadian Club Toronto*" (1995 mimeo).

13 Alberta and New Brunswick were the first to avail themselves of labour market development agreements (LMDAs) with the federal government that devolved both funding from the EI account and employment services to provinces and territories. Quebec signed its LMDA in April 1997. Ontario, concerned with the inequitable funding it was offered, as well as the logistics of integrating a large number of federal civil servants and programs into provincial programming, did not sign an LMDA until 2005 (see Canada, 2023).

14 *Hébert*, 2014, pp. 213–214. In the end, the prime minister introduced legislation in the House of Commons which required permission from the provinces of Quebec, Ontario and British Columbia for federal approval to be granted to any constitutional amendment, granting Quebec a *de facto* veto over any future constitutional amendments. The prime minister also introduced a motion in the House of Commons to "recognize Quebec as a distinct society within Canada." During the referendum, he also committed his government to "undertake changes to bring services and the decision-making process closer to citizens," which was in part addressed through the subsequent devolution of labour market training and federal engagement in negotiations around the social union.

15 The *Toronto Star* ran a series of articles and editorials chastising Premier Harris for opposing Prime Minister Chrétien's approach to post-referendum accommodation of Quebec, especially in relation to the adoption of a distinct society clause. See for example Walker (1995. p. A4), Speirs (1995. Pp. C1 and C5), Gwynn (1995. p. A 25), Walkom (1995. P. C4), *Toronto Star* (1995. P. A24) referenced in full below. Also see Ibbitson (2001, pp. 157–159) for an account of this meeting and its impact on Ontario–Canada relations.

16 Indeed, this was built into the mandate of the provincial-territorial ministerial council established by oremiers at the 1995 annual premiers' conference and was explicitly referenced in the release accompanying the council's first report to premiers: "In this context, premiers agree that clarifying the respective roles and responsibilities of both orders of government is crucial to effectively reforming Canada's social safety system." (Tobin, 1996).

17 Quebec was and remains a consistent exception on this point, preferring the transfer of tax points to federal cash transfers in most circumstances. It is, of course, also possible for the federal government to "equalize" tax points to ensure the value of a tax point transfer was made more equitable in this regard. For equalization-receiving provinces, however, the question was always what standard transferred tax points would be equalized to—that of the highest province, or some other average of provinces.

18 The Atlantic Premiers and Premier Romanow from Saskatchewan were of the view that constitutional renewal may yet be possible. British Columbia Premier Clark, Alberta Premier Klein and Ontario Premier Harris were not open to anything that might re-ignite what they believed to be a process aimed at unachievable constitutional amendments.

19 CICS, 1997.

20 Legislative Assembly of Ontario, "Orders of the Day: National Unity," *Hansard*, Tuesday May 26, 1998. On the issue of public opinion elsewhere in the country, an Angus Reid Poll conducted at the time showed 59 per cent of Quebecers "strongly" or "moderately" in support of the principles contained in the Premiers' Framework for Consultation. This compared favourably to the 62 per cent of Canadians overall in support of the principles.

21 CICS, 1997.

22 Ibbitson (2001, pp. 172–176) provides an excellent and fuller account of these developments.

23 CICS, 1998b.

24 CICS, 1999a.

25 CICS, 1999.

26 Lazar, 2000. p. 5.

27 Ontario, 1997, p. 18.

28 The 1977 Established Programs Financing (EPF) arrangement had been arrived at through intergovernmental negotiation and was an agreement between the federal government and the provinces. It replaced previous arrangements for providing financial support to provincial expenditures on health care and post-secondary education. The federal government's primary motivation for creating the EPF was to eliminate open-ended cost-shared programs in health and post-secondary education. The EPF arrangement was comprised of a tax point transfer and a cash component.

> The tax point transfer was an arrangement made whereby the federal government reduced its personal and corporate income tax rates so that provinces could move into the vacated tax room. That is, the provinces began to collect a higher portion of these taxes. The cash component began as a straight cash payment. Initially the cash payment was determined independently of the value of the tax point transfer. It was escalated each year by the growth rate of GNP per capita.

> Shortly after introducing EPF, the federal government began constraining the cash component of the transfer without provincial agreement. First, the federal government changed the GNP escalator so that, beginning in 1982, the total entitlement (cash plus tax points) rather than just the cash component of the transfer was escalated by the rate of per capita GNP growth. This meant that if the value of the tax-point transfer grew at a rate that was faster than the growth rate of GNP, the cash transfer would grow at a slower rate than that of GNP. The value of the tax point transfer was then subtracted from a calculated equal per capita total entitlement. In effect, the cash component became a residual. Throughout the remainder of the 1980s and into the 1990s, the federal government continued to make unilateral changes to constrain the growth of the cash portion of EPF transfers.

Provinces and territories expressed concern over the unilateral federal decisions to change the EPF and, with the creation of the CHST in 1995, argued that the fiscal arrangements had been changed so much that it was disingenuous of the federal government to continue to count the 1977 tax point transfer as part of its contribution to provincial health and social programs. In 2004, with the severing of the CHST into two separate transfers, the CHT and the CST, and the reapportionment of shares of the previous transfers, Ontario and other provinces were of the view that the federal government's continued inclusion of the 1977 tax points in the allocation formula for the CHT and the CST lacked transparency, was confusing and, therefore, untenable. As discussed in what follows, it was not until 2007, that the CST allocation formula was changed to equal per capita cash, and in 2014 that CHT allocations were put on an equal per capita cash basis.

29 Ontario, 1998, p. 21.

30 The net contribution to the federation of an individual province is calculated by totaling all federal revenues collected from a province (taxes, employment insurance premiums, fees etc.) and subtracting federal expenditures made in that province (direct program expenditures, transfers to individuals, transfers to the province or municipalities etc.), with some allocation of the federal surplus or deficit for that year. This is also sometimes referred to as "the balance sheet of confederation." Updated versions of these calculations later became the basis for the "gap" campaign deployed by Premier McGuinty and his Liberal government, confirming "fairness" in fiscal federalism advocacy as a fully non-denominational pursuit of the provincial interest in Ontario.

31 In fact, David Peterson's Liberal government had begun expressing concerns about the fairness of federal transfers when the Mulroney government introduced the "cap on CAP" in 1990. Under the Canada Assistance Plan (CAP), the federal government agreed to cost share "eligible" provincial expenditures on social assistance and related programs. In its 1990 budget, the federal government put a 5 per cent growth limit on CAP transfers to non-Equalization-receiving provinces (at the time this included British Columbia, Alberta and Ontario). This "cap on CAP" impacted Ontario most as the province's social assistance rates and caseload were growing at a rate faster than that of either BC or Alberta. The "cap on CAP" had such bite that in its 1990 Budget Ontario, otherwise known for its federal friendly approach to intergovernmental relations and constitutional renewal, called out the federal government for "not participating as a full partner in social assistance reform," noted the overall decline in federal transfers and began advocating for the renewal of the fiscal arrangements and "in the process contribute to the strengthening of Canadian federalism" (Ontario, 1990, pp. 9 and 11).

32 Fiscal imbalance in the federation refers to the imbalance between the revenue-raising capacity of each order of government compared to its expenditure responsibilities in areas of its own jurisdiction. The provincial argument is that

the federal government raises more revenue than it requires for its expenditure responsibilities in areas of its jurisdiction. Major transfers to provinces and territories, such as the CHST and now the CHT and CST, as well as other more conditional transfers, such as those for infrastructure and labour market training, are held up as evidence of the structural fiscal imbalance in the federation. There is much debate around the extent of this imbalance and how to fix it, and whether it even exists, especially when both orders of government are running deficits or surpluses. In the late 1990s, the federal surplus was significantly larger than the collective surpluses of the provinces and territories (which were, in fact, when aggregated in deficit for much of this period).

33 CICS, 1998.

34 Canada, 1999. pp. 83–84.

35 Ontario, 1999, p. 11.

36 In fact, while the formula changes based on the legislated renewal were relatively modest, amounting to an additional $700 million over five years, the overall equalization envelope increased by more than $2 billion as a result of stronger than forecast economic growth and per capita fiscal capacity in Ontario (Canada, 1999. p. 86).

37 See CICS (1999b). The healthcare communique states: "Funding is the key issue for health sustainability. Premiers and Territorial Leaders therefore request that the federal government fully restore Canada Health and Social Transfer (CHST) funding to 1994/95 levels with an appropriate escalator for the CHST cash transfer that keeps pace with cost and particular demand pressures."

38 See CICS (2000b). The fiscal imbalance communique states: "Premiers noted that the immediate and full restoration of the Canada Health and Social Transfer to 1994/95 levels, together with an escalator, is a modest step, and one that would still leave the federal government with substantial surpluses. Indeed, this proposal for the CHST would only partially address the fiscal imbalance that exists between the two orders of government."

39 On the structural fiscal imbalance in the federation, see the federal government's own estimates of the relative federal versus provincial-territorial fiscal positions and operating balances in the 1999 federal budget (Canada, 1999, p. 156).

40 See McIroy, 2000. Minister Rock insisted that, when the tax points were included, the federal contribution was closer to 33 per cent of provincial health spending. Under pressure from his Ontario caucus, the Prime Minister authorized print ads explaining the tax point transfer as a response to the provincial campaign, but the federal message was complex and lost on the Ontario public.

41 At the September 1999 meeting of federal-provincial-territorial ministers of health, Minister Rock found himself settling for vague commitments to "collaborate" on health human resources planning, population health, and the "effective use of information technology." In terms of the all-important reforms deemed necessary to provide greater access especially in primary care, each province or territory was "considering improvements" within its own jurisdiction (see CICS, 1999c).

42   See CICS, 2000.

43   See CBC, 2000.

44   See CICS, 2000b. In addition to the largely unconditional funding invested through the CHST, the federal government made additional funding available, including $1 billion over two years for medical equipment, $800 million over four years to support primary care reform, and $500 million in information technology. First ministers agreed to report publicly on a list of health indicators, outcomes, and quality of service, but there were no definitive targets and, critically from the premiers' perspective, "federal funding provided to any jurisdiction will not depend on achieving a given level of performance."

45   The split apportioned 62 per cent of the CHST to the CHT and 38 per cent to the CST. The federal government stated the split reflected provincial spending patterns on health and other social spending supported by the CHST at that time.

46   It is worth noting the equalization-receiving provinces also obtained an agreement with the prime minister in October 2004 to enhance the federal equalization program, just six months after the program had been changed under its five-year legislated renewal.

47   On this point, Minister Flaherty accepted the findings of the federal Expert Panel on Equalization led by former Alberta Deputy Treasurer Al O'Brien. "Accordingly, Budget 2007 proposes to legislate an equal per capita cash allocation for both major transfers, the Canada Social Transfer (CST) and the Canada Health Transfer (CHT), as they are renewed. By doing so, Budget 2007 will eliminate what the O'Brien report referred to as 'back door' equalization in these programs and make the federal contribution more transparent" (Canada, 2007, p. 114).

48   The strong and consistent advocacy of Alberta and its alignment of interests with Ontario on the issue of the inclusion of tax points in the CHT and CST allocation formulas undoubtedly contributed to the Harper government's decision to address this long-standing grievance of the two provinces. Given his experience as finance minister in Ontario under Premier Harris from 2001 to 2002, Finance Minister Flaherty was also well aware of the issue from the province's perspective. Minister Flaherty died April 10, 2014, just ten days after the allocation of the CHT was finally put on an equal per capita cash basis, ending the largest of Ontario's equitable treatment concerns. Notwithstanding the elimination of the inclusion of the 1979 EPF tax points from the CST and then CHT allocation formula, the federal government continues to include the value of the EPF tax points in its calculation of its contribution to provincial-territorial health spending.

49   Paikin, 2013, p. 180.

CHAPTER 14

Mike Harris and Ottawa

Hugh Segal

T HE PRIVILEGE OF BEING ASKED to submit a chapter on
federal-provincial relations for a book that analyses the impact
and operation of the Mike Harris government at Queen's Park
in the 1990s is made more precious by the rare privilege I had in serving
as the premier's "dollar-a-year constitutional advisor" during the
somewhat challenging months of the second Quebec referendum on
sovereignty ordered and managed by a Parti Quebecois government.
That window afforded me a rare opportunity to see the premier up close
and assess for myself his deep appreciation for Canada, his determination
not to let partisan excess get in the way of his duty as Ontario's Premier
to Canada, and his clear fidelity to the tradition of Ontario Premiers for
over forty-five years. . . to always be there for the national interest.

My prior role between 1979 and 1983, as associate cabinet secretary
for federal- provincial relations under Premier Davis afforded me a
rare and privileged role among many others in the negotiation of the
repatriation of the *British North America Act* from Westminster, the creation
of the Charter of Rights and Freedoms, the lobbying of members of the

Thatcher Government to facilitate the passage of the repatriation act through the UK Parliament and the many months of interprovincial discussions that led to the ultimate negotiations in the 1981–1983 period.

Readers will note in the following analysis, strong biases I am delighted to own and share, created by these fortunate and fascinating experiences. As I had no role, whatever, in any of the key negotiations referenced below, my biases are only thematically discernible in my analysis. The actual important federal provincial achievements I offer as evidence for my analytical conclusions re the Harris government record are not in any way impacted by my own biases cited here.

Over my time in federal and provincial politics and government, I have never been of the view that government is usually the first and best answer to any challenge faced by society. In fact, my bias is very much with those who prefer smaller government, that uses intelligent and evidence-based analysis to either array choices before parliament or the public or decide on negotiation strategies regarding other levels of government at home or abroad. While some on the extremes of the left or the right view Canadian federalism as too flexible and somewhat unpredictable, I would view those attributes as essential strengths of the Canadian idea. I have always recoiled from governments or politicians who sought to limit that inherent flexibility or choose to operate outside the constitutional rules—those rules requiring flexibility and a supple reflection of the regional and demographic diversity of the country.

I also believe very much in the planning doctrine of there being only one taxpayer who, for better or worse, pays all levels of taxation: federal, provincial and municipal, and whose core tax burden must always be kept on the lowest possible side of reasonable.

Both biases very much shape my view of, and involvement in federal provincial relations in Canada.

It would have been hard to imagine during the surprising majority outcome of the 1995 Progressive Conservative electoral victory, that federal provincial relations would have been an area of significant focus, let alone meaningful achievement, in the following two terms of government.

The campaign itself was about the *CSR*, which focused on tax cuts, a more streamlined provincial government, reducing the welfare burden on taxpayers, a general move back to the centre from the deemed excesses of the NDP administration and the core thematic of an anti-spending and anti-big-government Progressive Conservative tide.

The confluence of a Chretien-Martin Liberal administration in Ottawa focused on diminishing the deficit inherited from the Mulroney administration and the Mike Harris administration at Queen's Park seemed to suggest a period of intense federal provincial wrangling over issues like transfer payments and the general fiscal engagement zone of federal provincial relations. This broad political and economic context also renders the successes of the Harris government in federal provincial relations even more surprising on a host of fronts. Readers will remember that Finance Minister Martin had slashed transfer payments to the provinces by a third, along with national defence expenditures to meet his budgetary goals in his 1995 federal budget.

Yet, Ontario and Ottawa, Finance Minister Ernie Eves and Finance Minister Martin, found valuable ways to cooperate on the Canada Pension Plan and, through Ministers Pettigrew (federal) and Ecker (provincial), a National Child Benefit aimed at reducing child poverty.

Those areas of progress which enhanced the fiscal solvency, both of the Canada Pension Plan and, as a result, of the federal government and helped put in place a federal-provincial agreement on a National Child Benefit that meaningfully served low-income families nation-wide, facilitated not only gains for Ottawa and Queen's Park, but also for the entire country.

These two steps forward for the Canadian federation occurred because of a lack of any narrow ideology on the part of the Harris government in its dealings with Finance Minister Martin in Ottawa and a concurrent pragmatic approach to federal provincial relations on the part of Ottawa. This was despite the political differences between the centre-left Liberal Chretien government and the clearly centre-right Harris administration.

* * *

In this analysis of federal-provincial relations during the Harris years in Ontario, the case will be made that the substantial achievements for Ontario during this era were due to

- the traditional political and policy allure of constructive political outcomes between federal Liberals and provincial Conservatives in Ontario when both are in government due to the cross-over of federal and provincial voters (who are the same people, after all) between Conservative choices at one level and Liberal choices at the other;

- the specific benefits of a relationship shaped by two finance ministers, Minister Eves of Ontario and Minister Martin of Ottawa, for whom pragmatic joint progress toward shared fiscal goals superseded any narrow benefit for partisan gain at each other's expense;

- the inherited reduction in transfer payments made by the Chretien government which had preceded the election of the Harris government, providing the Harris government the opportunity to attribute program expenditure restraint at the provincial level in part to the revenue constraints inherited from another provincial government of another time;

- the negotiating premise of the Eves finance ministry which was, as was the case with the Martin department of finance, more about "win-win" than the partisan domination by either side of the section 91/section 92 division of powers framework by Ottawa or Queen's Park;

- the positive connection between Queens Park and Ottawa when the Mike Harris government supported the Chretien government's stance, despite misgivings regarding specific federal tactics during the very close Quebec independence referendum in 1995;

- the solid personal relationship between Mike Harris and Jean Chretien built during various "Team Canada" sojourns to different parts of the world in support of enhanced trade flows that had a serious upside for Ontario's economy and reflected the Chretien "Team Canada" approach to economic growth and foreign investment;

- the reduction both of contrived and ritualized irritants caused, under previous federal and provincial governments, by too many first ministers' meetings, where the political dynamics and incentives of the events often required the generation of areas of disagreement (especially for a sovereigntist government in Quebec) for local consumption; the Chretien government broke away from what it perceived as the excessive federal-provincial first minister meeting cycle associated with the Mulroney government, preferring one-on-one federal-provincial discussions with less drama;

- the constructive and creative role of the Hon. Janet Ecker, MPP, both as Ontario Minister of Community and Social Services and then as Ontario Finance Minister in seeking solutions for child poverty in Ontario as well as embracing joint federal provincial fiscal cooperation with Minister Martin in Ottawa on an integrated National Child Benefit that ended up serving Ontario and the rest of Canada. This initiative focused on the children of lower income families in a way that, by flowing cash to the neediest families with children, became the precursor of the Canada Child Benefit now operating nation-wide.

Whatever the other areas of disagreement between the Harris and Chretien administrations (for example, Ontario bristled, justifiably, at the lack of consultation by the federal government relative to the strategy and tactics re the Quebec referendum, which, was very nearly lost to the sovereigntist side), federal provincial fiscal relations and federal provincial generic cooperation on the core federal-provincial functions were not, in any way, contaminated by partisan or ideological excess on either side.

This mixture of both restraint and pragmatism characterized a unique period of federal provincial relations between the Harris and Chretien administrations, which conferred meaningful and measurable benefits on the country and on the taxpayers of Ontario.

This record of achievement differs markedly from the wildly partisan and rhetorically overheated critiques about allegedly extreme ideological positions often leveled at the Harris administration and reflecting the hostile intensity of anti-Harris media and concurrent institutional bias in many of the organizations, such as public sector unions and their media supporters, resulting from policy disagreements with the province on labour relations, public sector salaries, and the attendant welfare cuts and other "tightening" reforms consistent with the electorally successful *CSR* platform. Whatever the merits of the positions on either side of those disagreements, which are covered in other sections of this book, they cannot obscure the hard truth that there was no contamination of the federal provincial relations cooperative framework.

* * *

When Bob Rae and the NDP defeated David Peterson's majority Liberal Government in the election of September of 1990, few Ontarians were more surprised than Bob Rae. Whatever the somewhat myopic and "the time is ripe for an election" mindset that drove the Peterson decision to dissolve the Legislature before the normative four-year end of term, what is most relevant to the dynamic that shaped federal provincial relations during the Harris era were the scope and tenure of federal-provincial relations under the Rae government (1990–1995) and how that would shape the federal provincial context for the subsequent Ontario and Harris Conservative administration.

Paul Martin's budget speech of February 27, 1995 was the most radically apparent reduction of both federal expenditures and federal provincial transfers in the post-war years. (Beyond defence and provincial transfers, few federal spending cuts were substantial.) This was done to address the high budget deficit and accumulated debt inherited from the Mulroney administration, elected in 1984, and defeated under the leadership of Prime Minister Kim Campbell in 1993. The Mulroney administration argued that it had curbed and reduced year-to-year operational expenditures while in office and that its accumulated debt was driven by the interest costs inherited from the cascading deficits and debt from the previous Trudeau administration (1968–1984). The interest payments required to service the inherited Trudeau government debt were identified by the Mulroney administration as material contributors to the ballooning accumulated Conservative debt inherited by the Chretien administration.

In the context of federal provincial relations and Ontario, it is important to note that the Mulroney administration did not cut federal-provincial transfers or other transfers to the provinces under the federal-provincial fiscal relations regime in place in 1984. Much of this reticence was based on a strong bias within the Mulroney administration about sustaining the provincial financial capacity relative to (Section 92) powers in areas like education, health, and social services. The roots of the Mulroney landslide victory in 1984 encompassed strong support from entrenched provincial Progressive Conservative governments (Newfoundland and Labrador, New Brunswick, Nova Scotia, Ontario, and Alberta, with Social Credit in BC) which would have made finding a cabinet or caucus consensus on slashing payments to the provinces very difficult.

This provincial sensitivity was enhanced by the need Prime Minister Mulroney had for significant measures of provincial support on heroic efforts to produce, on two separate occasions, a signed constitutional agreement that brought Quebec back into the Constitutional accord of 1982 and the wish to have as much provincial support as possible during the free trade negotiations with both the United States and the United States and Mexico between 1986 and 1993. The two federal provincial agreements (Meech Lake and Charlottetown) both set aside by subsequent failures to ratify by individual provinces or a failed referendum, do not diminish the historic level of provincial consensus the Mulroney administration had achieved. Similarly, the important role the provinces played in sector specific consultations with Ottawa and with industry in the build-up to the free trade agreement finally enacted in 1989, was also uninterrupted by slash and burn federal transfer cuts, for good and substantial political and confederal cohesion reasons.

The size of the provincial debt and deficit inherited by the Harris administration, with the attendant federal provincial dynamics, was facilitated through the confluence of several inescapable fiscal pressures on the newly elected Rae government and the traditional tendency of NDP governments to invest in social and community programs especially during recessionary periods.

The Rae government came in during a difficult recessionary period[1] and, unsurprisingly, the NDP government undertook, with clarity and precision, "to fight the recession and not the deficit" as Premier Rae announced clearly in his first months of government. Depleted economic returns from the tax base, plus increased expenditures and reduced transfer payments from Ottawa, served to increase the provincial deficit. The fact that Ontario's economy and provincial tax base were hit harder than that of neighbouring American states and the NDP government's decision to tilt the labour relations rules in Ontario toward the labour side of the equation, allowed for an opposition and business lobby taunt that implied that Rae's taxation and pro-organized labour policies were driving jobs to the south.

The combination of these factors, with the substantial growth of both the deficit and the debt, forced the Rae government, after two years, to consider and implement relatively radical cost reduction initiatives before the end of its term. These included a Social Contract wage freeze (without meaningful labour leader consultation) for the public sector, plus mandatory days off without pay for public employees earning more than thirty thousand dollars annually. Public sector and other unions were infuriated with the Rae government. The plan did succeed in curbing provincial expenditures which, in Ontario and most provinces, are 70 per cent composed of public sector salaries.

The divisions in the 1990 NDP voter coalition, the defection of swing voters who had elected Rae in response to dissatisfaction at the Peterson Liberal government's electoral cynicism and the ineffectiveness of Liberal Leader Lyn McLeod facilitated a meaningful opportunity for the Harris-led Progressive Conservatives, producing an eighty-two-seat majority government in the 1995 election.

The core script of the Harris campaign, the *CSR*, was silent on federal-provincial relations. It proposed to cut provincial income taxes, imposing a "fair share health care levy" on Ontarians earning $50,000 a year or more, with the highest income earners carrying the largest part of the burden. They set a realistic goal for balancing the budget and reflected normative "small C" conservative values on small government, reducing the cost of welfare, law and order, less politicians, etc.

It left the Harris government a clear runway on federal-provincial relations.

* * *

During the Harris government's two terms in office (1995–2002), relations with Ottawa were largely even-tempered, pragmatic, and productive. And, despite the impact on Ontario of previous transfer payment cuts by Ottawa and the tax cuts introduced by the Harris government, a balanced budget in terms of annual expenditure was achieved by 1999.

That the overall federal provincial record on mainstream issues of wide import was essentially constructive reflected the genuinely collaborative approach to federal provincial relations between Messrs. Harris and Chretien and Eves and Martin.

While there were agreements on reform of the Canada Pension Plan and the National Child Benefit (discussed below), there was one area where, despite Martin's sincere efforts and a powerful lobby effort by national financial institutions and investment houses, Ontario would, in the end, not acquiesce to Ottawa's desire to create a national jurisdiction on securities regulation.[2]

Up until the advent of the Chretien Martin administration in 1993 in Ottawa, the regular proceeds from Canada Pension Plan contributions from employed Canadians were used by the Canada Pension Plan to make long term loans to the provinces. While these loans (via bonds) were at relatively modest rates of interest, they had been deemed in the public interest to facilitate what the provincial finance ministers referred to as "internal borrowing" for their own fiscal and liquidity needs. While, for the millions of CPP beneficiaries present and future, the loans were essentially secured by the taxing capacity of the provinces, in terms of the revenue flows essential to service and roll-over the loans from the Canada Pension Plan. They were seen as secured low risk loans.

The Canada Pension Plan reform proposed by Finance Minister Martin[3] had two key elements: it allowed the CPP to invest in something other than long term loans to the provinces so as to diversify its investment portfolio and long term rate of return on CPP contributions by Canadians; and, in the face of the unfunded liability that the Canada Pension Plan had acquired over time (contributions plus provincial loan yields did not produce a solvent fund going forward), there had to be an agreement on increasing the rate of individual contributions, plus a reduction of some of the benefit payment outflows. The contributions were too low to sustain the fund's balance and some of the benefits were too high to be sustainable on the existing income and earnings base of the CPP.

Ensuring that CPP Funds would be invested independently in financial markets would require an independent board for a new body, The Canada Pension Plan Investment Fund. This required an expert independent board of directors to oversee investment activity. That innovation plus a requirement that any future change in the structure of CPP Investment pools would require a two thirds majority of provincial governments to approve, assured the provinces that new flows into the CPP funds from increased contributions and enhanced revenues could not be siphoned off from the fund by any federal government in the future.

Because of the size of the Ontario workforce, both private and public, failure of Ontario to agree would have sunk the entire reform project. Ontario's support was seminal. The initial CPP Investment Fund was established at $121 billion, one of the more prominent sovereign investment funds in the world. And unlike the previous CPP loan portfolio which had to be invested in the treasuries of Canadian provinces, the new CPP Investment Fund could invest in financial markets world-wide to achieve the best possible returns for Canadian pensioners, present and future. Paul Martin, himself, in a speech in 1997, reflecting on the changes that took place in the CPP structure, fund, legislation and investment framework said, "Ernie Eves could have killed the reform, because Ontario had an effective veto. But when the time came to get the deal done, he got it through Queen's Park."[4]

In his address to the joint meeting of the Toronto Empire Club and Canadian Club on May 9, 1997, an event which followed every provincial budget, Finance Minister Eves listed the initiatives taken during his first months in office and his budget of the previous week, of which he was most proud.[5] Listing the investments in social justice his government had made, at the top of his list was "a new forty-million-dollar Child Tax Credit which will assist lower income working families who are not benefitting from the current system. This will assist some 90,000 families and some 125,000 children." Ottawa's proposal was to create an enhanced

National Child Benefit for low-income working families, providing the provinces agreed to spend what they might save through reduced welfare costs and investing those savings investing in further programs for needy low-income families with children in their own jurisdiction. Minister Eves' reference in his Empire Club speech was one example of provincial initiatives taken in support of the agreement with Ottawa.

Ken Battle, a distinguished social scientist who was the founder of the Caledon Institute of Social Policy in 1992 with philanthropist Alan Broadbent and who was an advisor to the federal cabinet and Finance Minister Martin on the National Child Benefit, described the context in this way:

> . . .in a rare act of cooperative federalism, Ottawa and the provinces and territories launched the National Child Benefit initiative in 1998.[6]

As this more generous child benefit was not targeted on those already living on welfare, it had the effect of being an incentive for parents to join, or stay in the work force, responsive to provincial government policy preferences. It was also observed in a retrospective on Paul Martin's achievements while finance minister some years later, that this Child Benefit creation was "one of the most far reaching" because "the benefit worked through the tax system to encourage low-income parents to get off welfare and into the work force."[7]

This was the work not only of Finance Minister Martin, but of the joint federal provincial table on child benefits co-chaired by Minister of Community and Social Services Janet Ecker.

In the ultimate design of the program, it is noteworthy the extent to which the very strong Ontario preference for encouraging people to enter or stay in the workforce became a guiding principle for the National Child Benefit overall.

* * *

The intricate nature of federal-provincial negotiations especially around joint program design challenges or sustaining provincial support for complex national programs is often too complex for detailed media coverage. The level of detail involved requires long-read journalism or uni-focus broadcast specials that the competitive media environment in Canada can rarely accommodate. It is far easier to cover picketers on a strike line, labour leaders issuing statements or ministers under attack in a legislature.

A famous media analyst and historian once reflected on how the thousands of airplanes that land safely every day are not newsworthy, while the one plane that veers off the runway or worse will lead the news. This is not about media bias or unfairness. It is about the nature of news in open and free societies. However imperfect, it is far better than the authoritarian news that flow out of the state supported media in places like Russia or China or Hungary or North Korea or Syria where all news about government is good and no genuine news about things that do not work for average citizens is ever permitted.

One of the anomalies faced by those who pine for a well-informed public who are better able to make thoughtful political choices is the absence of the kind of detailed plain-language explanations behind the programs that not only work in any society for the common good, but actually work well.

Both federal-provincial instruments examined in this retrospective on federal provincial relations within the time frame of Harris years in government actually connect directly with the quality of life and intrinsic fairness of Ontario and its people.

So, the Canada Pension Plan and the Child Benefit have entered the non-newsworthy world of aircraft that land safely every day.

It would be important for citizens and taxpayers to know how these programs were improved and adjusted to stay solvent, as is the case with the CPP, or were created through federal provincial innovation and design to help more low-income households as was the case with the National Child Benefit.

The cynicism and hostility toward government, sometimes unfair and, on occasion, justified, should never be allowed to obscure clarity about the good that government can do and how that good comes about. This contribution on federal-provincial relations during the Harris era is, hopefully, a step in that direction.

Notes

1   Walsh, Mary Williams, "The Hard Times Are Even Harder North of the Border," *Los Angeles Times*, 24 February, 1991.
2   CBC News, "Canada Needs National Security Regulation," June 19, 2007.
3   Little, Bruce, "The Deal Is Done," University of Toronto Press, Toronto 2008.
4   Martin, Rt Hon. Paul, Opening Address; CD Howe Institute Conference: "Ten Years after the CPP Changes"; Toronto, December 12, 2007.
5   Eves, Hon. Ernie, minister of finance; joint meeting of the Empire and Canadian Clubs, Toronto, May 9, 1997.
6   Battle, Kenneth, "Child Benefits: Policy and Politics," June 2017, p. 7.
7   Geddes, John; *Macleans*, August, 2003.

CHAPTER 15

The Harris Elections of 1995 and 1999

David Herle

OR DECADES, THE OUTCOME OF Ontario elections was as predictable as death and taxes: The Progressive Conservatives would win. Icons of Ontario politics, such as John Robarts and Bill Davis, were part of that Progressive Conservative (PC) dynasty, and that seemingly immortal dynasty seemed to define Ontario. The provincial Liberals were only a rural voice, and the NDP pushed from the left, but both were clearly minority parties. The PCs defined and owned the centre of Ontario politics.

Then, starting in 1985, Ontario had a series of very weird elections, by any standard, but particularly Ontario's. In the 1985 election, the PCs were held to a minority. Not the first time that had happened, but the first time the other two parties joined forces and threw the PCs out of office after forty-two consecutive years in power.

In the subsequent election, two years later, the PCs were absolutely smashed. The Liberals under David Peterson won an enormous majority after just two years in charge of a minority government. The NDP paid the price junior partners in coalitions usually pay and lost seats. Still, the

NDP emerged as the official opposition due to the complete collapse of the PCs, who now looked nowhere near as dynastic as they had just a few years before.

Peterson called an "early election" in 1990, and the results represented another dramatic reversal of fortune. His claim to government collapsed over the course of the campaign. But rather than returning the tried-and-true PCs to their "rightful" perch in office, the voters elected instead the first New Democratic Party government in Ontario history. So unexpected was the result that new Premier Bob Rae had never met many of his new MPPs. The PCs finished a distant third for the second election in a row. Ontario politics seemed to have rotated on its axis.

Yet within five years the PCs were back in office in the weirdest of these weird elections. In 1995, the incumbent NDP finished a bad third. The presumptive victor at the outset, the Liberals, lost badly despite the federal party holding every seat in the province and the provincial party holding a thirty-point polling lead at the outset of the campaign. The third-place PCs, despite their complete drubbing just five years prior, surged to a decisive victory. All in the course of just five weeks.

As do all winning campaigns, Harris 1995 had help from significant forces beyond its control: a clear change environment; ineffective campaigns from the other parties; and a political and economic system so broken that there was willingness to accept great policy change.

However, victory was not simply the result of those factors. It was also the result of an unusually insightful, strategic, and patient campaign that took advantage of those factors and created others. As one of their Liberal opponents said afterward, "they had more smart people thinking for a longer time than we did."

The recession of the early 1990s had been scarring for Ontario. The government's annual deficits had soared to unprecedented levels, largely because of the recession. Tax revenues fell, expenditures on social programs rose, and interest costs on the debt started to eat up an increasing proportion of total revenue. The NDP initially allowed the deficit to rise largely uncontrolled and then later brought in radical (for them) austerity measures. Both alienated voters and, in the latter case, the party's core vote.

Unemployment peaked at 11.9 per cent, which was the highest since the Great Depression, partly because of the recession and partly because Ontario was losing manufacturing jobs in the aftermath of the free-trade agreement with the United States (and later Mexico). Reliance on social assistance had become widespread.

This first "made in Canada" recession had led many, if not most, to believe the status quo to be broken and to conclude that radical changes were required to return to a stable and prosperous environment. For that rare time in politics, people would accept something that normally seemed radical and risky.

The first public demand in fixing Ontario was a steely-eyed determination to get public finances under control. Balanced even. For the first time in some time, it was accepted that reductions in the size of government were necessary and that sacrifices would have to be made, but not personally—the public was not looking to absorb large tax increases. It was this environment that allowed the Jean Chretien federal Liberal government and Finance Minister Paul Martin to initiate unprecedented spending cuts in Ottawa in the two years leading up to the 1995 Ontario election.

Unlike the federal Liberals, who seemed to approach the task of cutting government spending with reluctance, the Harris team and the *CSR* platform approached the task with relish and an expressed desire to reconfigure government. Unlike the federal Liberals, who attempted to portray their cuts as hitting everyone equally, the *CSR* was looking to significantly redefine the role and size of government. Unlike the federal Liberals, who described a period of sacrifice as necessary to long-term success, the *CSR* promised immediate personal and macroeconomic benefits.

This economic context is important to understanding the results of the 1995 Harris campaign for two reasons. First, it made the conditions almost impossible for the incumbent NDP to be reelected. The first NDP government in history had coincided with the worst economy in Ontario history. Point finale. But the context is equally important to understanding the success of the PC campaign. Much better than the other parties, it understood the mood. They understood the depth of unhappiness and worry among the public. And they understood that people really wanted to change. The winner would be the party that was most convincing that it would bring change. To that fight the Liberals brought a Swiss Army Knife, while Mike Harris brought a bazooka.

* * *

The PC platform was called the *CSR* and represented an entirely new form of political innovation in Canadian campaigning. Most party platforms are limited in scope and general in their prescriptions. The *CSR* was wide-ranging and precise. Most party platforms are released during the election campaign to avoid serious examination and scrutiny. The *CSR* was released more than a year in advance and invited scrutiny. The Liberal platform was designed to mollify all interests and stakeholders and not cost the Liberals an election they were destined to win. The *CSR* was the tool by which the PCs would seek to win the election. And the *CSR* platform expressed, in clear terms, exactly what voters could expect if Mike Harris became premier. This included balancing the budget, sharply cutting personal taxes, significant spending cuts (especially to welfare), and a tougher approach to crime.

This chapter is focused more on the "what" and "why" rather than the "who." For those interested in the personalities involved, I encourage readers to find a copy of John Ibbitson's *Promised Land* or Christina Blizzard's *Right Turn*. Suffice it to say that a handful of "tiny Tories" (Tom Long, Leslie Noble, Alister Campbell, Mitch Patten, David Lindsay, Deb Hutton, etc.), trained in the PC youth wing and attuned to evolving "neoconservative" policies in the United States and elsewhere, were intimately involved in the development of both the platform *and* the strategy to use it to win.

This cadre of true believers ensured that the *CSR* was rooted in both policy and public opinion. The policy was designed to be practically implementable, so as to make the platform a true governing blueprint. At the same time, every one of those proposals was rigorously tested in surveys and focus groups to ensure that each created a "wedge" between them and the other parties that worked in the PCs favour. This was not a new tactic. Parties design proposals that their opponents will feel compelled to oppose for ideological or other reasons and have the support of a large enough portion of the electorate to propel you to victory.

In this instance, the tactic was particularly successful due to the sharpness of the *CSR* proposals, the opinion research that informed the *CSR*, and the flabby Liberal platform.

The content of the *CSR* was central to the PC strategy, yet such a document was difficult to communicate through the media, especially when one is the third-place party in the Legislature. As a result, the "revolutionaries" used the resources they had. They ensured that every PC candidate and their teams were briefed in detail so that they could not only defend the *CSR*, but sell its virtues door to door. They printed more than 2.5 million copies (in a province with barely 11 million citizens). And the party threw valuable resources behind what was then a state-of-the-art VHS tape and hand-delivered videos of Harris talking about the platform directly to the homes of swing voters in target ridings.

Despite those efforts, the Harris campaign leaders knew that few people would know much about the PC platform until the crucible of an election, with its sustained media coverage, advertising, and the televised leader's debate. From that, they concluded that a Harris breakthrough would happen in the writ period and perhaps even late in the writ period. That conviction allowed them to be patient with their strategy and not question that strategy when it was not yielding early results as the writ approached. And, indeed, as the writ approached, the Liberals remained well in the lead. Much internal second-guessing normally occurs in such a situation.

However, campaign chair Tom Long and campaign manager Leslie Noble's polling analysis gave the PCs an insight that seemed to escape the Liberals. They knew that Rae was finished ("irrelevant," as Long famously described the Premier at an early press conference) and would simply not be a factor in the campaign. Despite often performing brilliantly on the campaign trail, Rae was never anything but a sideshow to voters who had already decided to move on. The Liberals were, in the Legislature and on the hustings, performing as the official opposition and acting as the "government in waiting." They assumed that if people decided to defeat the NDP, they would automatically elect the Liberals. The PCs, knowing people had already decided to change the government, spent their time differentiating from the Lyn McLeod Liberals, while the Liberals focused on differentiating from Rae (but not so much as to offend anybody).

Both Noble and Long had been around the party for some time, but neither had ever been in charge of a campaign before. Similarly, neither "Message Guy" Alister Campbell nor the head of advertising, Jaime Watt, had ever played their roles in a provincial campaign. Watt is now one of Canada's best-known public affairs professionals, but then he was running a one-room agency in London, Ontario. Looking at this group, it was clearly a clean break from the fabled "Big Blue Machine" of the forty-two-year dynasty. It's no surprise that it took a very different approach to the 1995 election than had recent PC campaigns.

While supremely confident people, the Harris team decided to augment themselves with advice from two other key individuals. Hugh Segal is the "happy warrior" of Conservative politics. Top advisor to both Ontario Premier Bill Davis and Prime Minister Brian Mulroney, Segal was steeped in the party and helpfully associated with the "progressive" wing. As such, he represented the kind of PC who might have felt alienated by the new team or its policies. His decision to engage with the Harris brain trust and help with his wise counsel was an important internal signal and helped to hold elements of the party together and provide "elite" validation to the neophyte Harris team.

The other addition came from further afield. Mike Murphy is now a legend in Republican circles in the United States, co-hosting a podcast with his Democratic equivalent David Axelrod. He's also now a "NeverTrumper" alienated in his own party. Back in the early 1990s, he was just taking off. He has already worked on George H. W. Bush's campaigns and was about to become the senior strategist to John McCain. He brought to the Harris campaign's advertising and communications the same edge, aggression, and directness that were already embedded in the *CSR* platform. The substance lent itself to the tactics Murphy employed.

Murphy brought a tactic that Watt and the PCs used in 1995 and has since become the conventional approach (for better or worse) for conservative parties in Canada: ugly ads. Murphy believed in the merits of simplicity of messaging in political advertising and did not think one needed fancy ad agencies winning Cannes awards to do it. He eschewed high production values and put that saved money into the media buy instead. This meant that the PCs were able to run their ads with more frequency than their opponents could.

PC advertising in that campaign hit harder than most Canadian campaigns did at that time. All political advertising is tougher and more personal now. Back then, so-called "negative advertising" was rarer and most well-known for when it failed. The Ontario PCs went in this hard-hitting direction just two years after the backlash against a personal and negative spot targeting Jean Chretien had been widely credited, likely erroneously, with the collapse of the federal PC Party in 1993. It was not without risk for the neophyte team running the Harris campaign. But, having finished third two elections in a row and not given much chance in 1995, it was probably time to take some chances. The debate over negative ads would now seem quaint as today they are used by all parties, but in 1995 the political class was far from certain one could graft Mike Murthy's American ad concepts onto sensible Ontario.

By the end of the campaign, the verdict was in. The ads produced by Murphy and Watt went right at the Liberals and their leader Lyn McLeod. After the surprise defeat in 1990, David Peterson had resigned as Liberal leader, and the Liberals scheduled a leadership convention for 1992. Lyn McLeod had won by nine out of 2,300 votes on the fifth ballot, having trailed on all previous ballots, a recipe for party division. From Thunder Bay, McLeod had been a respected minister in the Peterson government. However, she was not a natural performer. Nor was she armed with the type of clear vision Mike Harris was running on. Prior to the election, she had focused mostly on opposing the Rae government without putting much forward herself. The PCs had surprised the Liberals by winning a by-election (Victoria-Haliburton), and in response McLeod reversed her position on benefits for same-sex couples. This reversal looked craven and did more damage than the original position had. Entering the campaign, she had a very low public profile, which is not unusual for Ontario opposition politicians. However, her personal blank slate combined with the blank slate of her platform to create the perfect space for Harris and the PCs to write on.

Liberals have done so much winning in Canada, particularly at the federal level, that they have come to see themselves as they were once described: the "natural governing party." Despite having lost every provincial election for over forty years leading up to 1985, by 1995, the provincial Liberals had convinced themselves that they were the natural government of Ontario. If nothing went wrong, they would win the election. And so, they went about creating a platform and a narrative that were designed not to lose, rather than designed to win. While the *CSR* was edgy and looking for arguments, the Liberal platform sought to avoid conflict and offer something to everybody. The Liberals overall positioning was middle of the road, suggesting change from Rae but nothing that might be upsetting to anybody. More problematically, the

Liberal strategy viewed the NDP as the main opponent. They did not see Mike Harris and the PCs coming until far too late in the campaign.

This calculation really matters, because with the Liberals focused on running against the NDP and ignoring Harris, the *CSR* was not examined and litigated as it might have been had the Liberals made it their target from the outset. The PC platform contained many controversial ideas that might not have fared well in a campaign if the ultimate framing off those issues was not as the *CSR* architects intended. As it was, they had a pretty free run to present their ideas without substantial pushback from the Liberals.

As do all losing campaigns, the 1995 Liberals have good excuses. The federal Liberals were enacting big spending cuts and tax increases to balance the budget in Ottawa. While the federal Liberals were very popular relative to their opponents in Ontario in 1995 and the budgets they were introducing were, in general, popular, many of the individual items in those budgets were not popular and likely acted as some drag on provincial Liberal fortunes. Both the NDP and the PCs viewed the Liberals as their primary opponent and directed their resources and attacks against them. That is unusual when you are not the incumbent and left McLeod's Liberals fighting a two-front war while the other parties only had one. Rae didn't change his focus from McLeod to Harris until late in the campaign, seeing Liberal votes as easier to poach.

However, there was another factor, and it is a less comfortable one to talk about. Leadership is decisive to the outcome of elections. If the people of Ontario had decided, in 1995, that they did not like or respect Mike Harris, then all the "long thinking by smart people" would likely not have mattered. In 2023, we still have a lot to learn about leadership archetypes and gender stereotypes and how they interact when people form a judgment of a woman leader. Lyn McLeod was (and is) smart, experienced, and extremely well motivated. But in the aftermath of the leaders' debate, opinion about who would make the best premier moved decisively in

Harris's favour. He had been seen as strong and confident, calmly articulating a plan he believed in. This was in no small part due to the entire year prior to the campaign which he had spent speaking about and answering questions about his *CSR* plan for big change. Ms. McLeod by contrast was armed with no such plan and, advised to be aggressive, came off as pointlessly argumentative and without a vision for the province. It remains a question mark, despite the campaign's underperformance, just how Lyn McLeod's "plus/minus" rating (net of "favourables" versus "unfavourables" in pollster's lingo) could fall to as low as minus 48 per cent. Hard to not see some fundamental gender archetype issue in this extraordinarily low level of support.

Post-debate, there were still three weeks left to go in the campaign, but the trajectory had been set and neither the NDP nor the Liberals could seemingly affect it. People had tuned Rae out and the Liberals never produced a sustained attack or coherent ad against any element of the *CSR*. PC strategists had withheld a substantial portion of their media budget to counter a last-minute barrage from the Liberal Party. That barrage never came. By this time the Liberal campaign was too divided and dispirited to even respond.

That media budgeting decision takes us back to the intensive planning behind the PC campaign. Looking back, the principals involved in that campaign talk confidently about knowing at the outset how the campaign would unfold. They had polled extensively and knew how each argument, for or against an idea, would move opinion. They had conducted war game exercises, where they anticipated how the other parties would conduct their campaigns and how those parties would react to PC tactics. As a consequence, whenever the NDP or the Liberals made a move, the Harris team normally had anticipated it and had already thought through their response. They claim to have known not just that Harris was going to win, but how he was going to win.

It is easy to be skeptical of such claims. Not everything can be anticipated. The Liberals could have stumbled across a killer negative ad right after the debate. Harris could have made a bad mistake on the campaign trail. Some major event could have taken the leaders' debate out of the news. The permutations are endless. But this team in charge of the third-place campaign put aside extra money for the last week in anticipation that it would be leading and under attack. Maybe you've got to be lucky to be good, but the Harris team did broadly anticipate almost everything about the campaign except their opponents' inability to live up to their expectations.

The level of preparation and the utilization of Republican campaign tactics introduced by the Harris team has become an enduring feature of Canadian politics. The conservatives have more people interested in campaigns and elections as a profession. The other two parties tend to pull in people from their day jobs to take on key aspects of campaign management. Harris's team made conservatives excited about the professional practice of politics.

All things considered, the 1995 Harris campaign is one of the more impressive in modern Canadian politics. Going from third place in the Legislature to government is rarely accomplished. Overcoming a thirty-point deficit in the polls in even more rarely done, much less in just five weeks. Not the product of fortune alone, the PC win was carefully thought through and designed. It was built on a platform that was constructed to be both the heart of the PC campaign and the blueprint they would use in government. There is an adage in politics, when people assume the outcome of the election will resemble the polls of the day, that "campaigns matter." Never truer than in Ontario in 1995.

Final Results

Mike Harris/PCs: 45 per cent of the vote, 82 seats.

Lyn McLeod/Liberals: 31 per cent of the vote, 30 seats.

Bob Rae/NDP: 21 per cent of the vote, 17 seats.

* * *

The second election Mike Harris won, in 1999, was also a triumph. He was returned with a second straight majority government, the first time that had happened in Ontario since the 1960s. He received the same percentage of the popular vote as he had in 1995, despite four years of intense controversy over his policies.

In many ways, the 1999 campaign was 1995 redux—a validation of 1995. The fact that they had hewed in government so closely to the *CSR* they had campaigned on had given Harris an aura of character, a rare commodity in politics. He, like it or hate it, "did what he said he was going to do." This brand perhaps also stood in contrast to the federal Liberals who had discarded their biggest promises to eliminate the GST and scrap the Free Trade Agreement, and who's governing agenda bore little resemblance to their 1993 campaign.

The PCs in 1999 fundamentally ran on their record, not always the best move for an incumbent. They promised no change in approach, but more of what they had already done. They had balanced the budget and would keep the budget balanced. They had reduced taxes and would continue to reduce taxes. They would be even tougher on crime. And they would continue to shrink the overall size of government and introduce the private sector wherever possible. The *CSR*, grounded in public opinion research, had delivered and held the voter support it had promised.

This was greatly aided by the strong economic recovery underway. The mid-to-late 1990s were a time of very strong economic growth in both Canada and the United States.[1] Governments that were implementing the conventional neoliberal economic plan were generally being given credit for having induced that economic growth.

Of course, a platform like the *CSR* creates a lot of opponents. Spending cuts and policy change, particularly to healthcare and education, had galvanized the left in opposition. That opposition coalesced around the Liberal Party, because it was widely considered that the NDP (battered and divided after the Rae years in power) had no chance of winning.

For many voters and stakeholder groups, even unions, defeating Mike Harris was more important than their normal affiliation with the NDP. The stirrings of what would become the Working Families Coalition, a group of unions who funded anti-PC advertising in subsequent elections, could be found in the 1999 campaign.

Coalescing of the anti-Harris vote made this a closer run thing than 1995 had been when the non-PC vote had been more evenly split between Liberal and NDP. Tactically, the PC campaign was even more challenging than it had been in 1995. Still working with Mike Murphy and adding Canadian advertising executive Perry Miele, the PCs decided that the Liberal leader was the weak link in the chain of the opposition and he was targeted fiercely.

The Liberals were on their third leader in three elections in 1999. Dalton McGuinty emerged from yet another long, multi-ballot leadership convention as few people's choice but most peoples "could live with" option. Among his own caucus, many thought themselves to have been a better choice. An Ottawa MP, McGuinty's late father was more prominent than Dalton prior to his winning the leadership. McGuinty hadn't just stumbled his way down the middle though. He had stubbornly insisted on holding to a centrist positioning and refused to move left to capture the anger of anti-Harris activists. Over time, this would stand him in good stead politically. He also had a "Mr. Smith Goes to Washington" earnestness that made him very strong on character grounds.

However, he was not yet ready for the spotlight he had walked into. The PCs had a lot of money to spend on reelecting Mike Harris. Way more than the Liberals or NDP. In the year before the election, in advertisement after advertisement, Murphy and Watt told the people of Ontario that McGuinty was "not up to the job." Not that he was a bad person. Not that he held crazy ideas. But that he wasn't personally up to the job of premier. Too wish washy. Too lacking in charisma. No plan.

There is risk in building a campaign around something that your opponents could disprove. In 1993, the federal PCs tried to portray

Kim Campbell as the person who would slay the budget deficit. But the campaign revealed that she had little expertise or interest in the budget deficit and the campaign floundered. The Harper CPC spent millions leading up to the 2015 federal election persuading Canadians that Justin Trudeau was "just not ready." Not that he wasn't good enough, just not ready. The Justin Trudeau that showed up to campaign and debate in 2015 looked very ready indeed and the CPC no longer had an effective message.

That's the risk the Harris team took by making McGuinty's competence a key test. The televised debate among the leaders would be McGuinty's chance to prove his mettle. Dalton McGuinty would ultimately prove he was up to the job, but only years later and against a different PC Leader. On debate night in 1999, face-to-face against Harris, he showed that he was "just not ready." Evidently nervous and rattled by the confidence of the premier, McGuinty came off as just that: nervous and rattled. He was not able to clearly articulate his own proposals, nor match Harris's manifestation of leadership. NDP leader Howard Hampton made his one impact on the campaign when he compared Dalton's look to Norman Bates from the Hitchcock move *Psycho*.

It was a bad election night for McGuinty and a good night for Harris. The PC lead widened substantially in the aftermath of the debate. For the second straight election the Liberal leader had performed badly in the debate. In 1999 however, unlike in 1995, the Liberal campaign did not simply collapse after the debate. In fact, it showed surprising resilience and gained some support back in the last ten days, but the election was never close.

The PC victory of 1999 had three core components. First, a policy argument, both prospective and retrospective, that polarized the electorate in a way that left the PCs with the lion's share. The Harris team point to one particular example of this from campaign: "mandatory teacher testing." This policy proposal drove the teacher's unions to distraction and thus forced both the Liberal's and NDP to highlight their opposition to it.

The Tories knew that every day "teacher testing" was on the campaign agenda they were winning, with 75 per cent plus support for the policy in all their target markets.

The second component is always a blessing: the Harris Tories had a well-funded, well-targeted campaign operating at a high level. And the third component was no surprise: Premier Harris had a decisive advantage on leadership. "He did what he said he was going to do."

Final Results

Mike Harris/PCs: 45 per cent of the vote, 59 seats

Dalton McGuinty/Liberal: 40 per cent of the vote, 35 seats

Howard Hampton/NDP: 13 per cent of the vote, 9 seats

* * *

It is interesting that despite its success, the *CSR* represents the high-water mark for election platforms that are grounded in an analysis of the problems a jurisdiction faces and propose a coherent set of policies to address those problems. Most platforms since then have devolved into lists of five ideas or, in some instances, no platform at all. Political parties do not tell you nearly as much about what they are thinking and what they want to do as the *CSR* told the people of Ontario. Perhaps inevitable in a world in which TikTok is the primary vehicle for political communications.

It is also worth noting that the links and affinity between Canadian conservatives and the Republican Party in the United States have endured since 1995, at both the provincial and federal level. As the Republican Party gets stranger, that affinity is of increasingly dubious value to the electoral prospects of conservatives in Canada.

One last idea very much on my mind as I reflect on the Harris Legacy: the tax cut philosophy at the heart of the *CSR* has had an enduring impact in Ontario and across the country. Tax increases are seen as politically fatal. In order to win election in 2003, Dalton McGuinty had to publicly sign a declaration he would not raise personal taxes. There is no member of the Trudeau Liberal government today who does not believe that Stephen Harper's reduction of the GST rate was, and is, bad public policy, but there has been no consideration of restoring it to its previous level. Canadian governments in 2023 have less money at their disposal because of Mike Harris in 1995.

Note

1   Readers may be interested in Professor Eugene Beulieu's chapter elsewhere in this book, which shows Ontario's economy outperforming other provinces, Canada as a whole, and all neighbouring US states during the Harris years.

CHAPTER 16

The Intuitive Mike Harris

Jaime Watt

UCH OF THIS BOOK IS dedicated to explaining, framing, and providing context for the signature achievements of the Harris government.

My task is one that's not like the others. The editor asked me to consider the idea of the "counterintuitive" Mike Harris. The premier who did things we did not expect him to do. Things that were counterintuitive to the strong, powerful, consonant brand he had established of "promises made, promises kept"—counterintuitive given the continuing widespread perception of Harris as a "golf pro from North Bay," a stony-faced cost-cutter with limited empathy or compassion for those different or less fortunate. A man who obviously hated Toronto.

As I contemplated the assignment, I came to realize that this initial premise was flawed. It turns out that there isn't a counterintuitive Mike Harris. There is only one, single, and genuinely *intuitive* Mike Harris. That becomes clear when you understand that everything you need to know about Mike Harris and how he made decisions as premier arises from where he came from. From the values forged in small town Northern

Ontario where, after family, community means everything—where the challenges of day-to-day life breed lifelong characteristics of resiliency, respect for the individual, a belief in the power of equality of opportunity, and a level playing field for all.

When you understand this, you begin to understand his north star, and when you understand his north star, you truly understand the man.

Life for Mike Harris in his hometown of North Bay was very much like life for many Ontarians in small towns right across the province. People worked hard. Helped each other out. Joined the Rotary Club. Operated small businesses. Dealt with the intrusive insanity of government regulations. Marched in the Canada Day Parade while proudly waving the flag. And from this place, Mike Harris developed a profound sense of not just community but the power of development to grow and strengthen the community.

Nestled between two lakes, North Bay derives its name from its position on the northern shores of Lake Nipissing. Just as it was for the Voyageurs, who sheltered there along their journeys further into the interior, North Bay's downtown waterfront has always been a cherished asset.

In the 1990s, the city seized the opportunity to reimagine this space by purchasing rail lands along the lakefront. Doing so, they transformed the area into a thriving hub, fully connected to the downtown core, complete with pedestrian walkways and scenic parks.

Mike Harris supported this transformation and began to witness its transformative power as a community-building tool. And, so, it is unsurprising that, when presented with an opportunity to do the same for Toronto's waterfront, he leapt at the chance.

To fully appreciate just how visionary this decision was for Ontario's capital city, a little history is required. As Toronto departed from its traditional manufacturing roots in the latter stages of the twentieth century, its waterfront was left underutilized and, frankly, derelict.[1] But Premier Harris understood there was another way to look at that large swath of over 2,000 untouched acres: an unprecedented opportunity to rebuild for a post-industrial future.

Starting with Toronto's pitch to host the 2008 Summer Olympics in the late 1990s, Premier Harris, alongside Prime Minister Jean Chrétien and Toronto Mayor Mel Lastman (aka "the three amigos") came together to announce the formation of a task force to develop the waterfront as part of the city's bid. Although that bid ultimately failed, the task force's work would not be for nothing, as it found, Olympics or no Olympics, that the business case for redeveloping Toronto's waterfront was overwhelming. Fortunately, so was the political one.

On a bright October day in 2000, the three amigos reconnected, committing $1.5 billion in seed capital to a tripartite agency to oversee the planning and development of government-owned waterfront lands. That agency became known as Waterfront Toronto. Today, Toronto's waterfront is home to much-needed development and revitalization. Affordable housing is now mixed with commercial buildings, green spaces, public art, award-winning architecture, playgrounds, and new cycling paths.[2] Deeply necessary conservation work is being carried out. And abundant economic opportunity has more than doubled the value of government investments.[3]

The decision to participate in Waterfront Toronto, which may have, at first blush, seemed antithetical to the Harris brand, is actually emblematic of everything he stood for: the power of community to come together, to invest together, and to drive transformative, durable change together.

That belief in the power of infrastructure to not just define a community but to provide it with the tools necessary to prosper extended to another seemingly counterintuitive decision: to participate in the funding of the largest expansion of arts infrastructure in Toronto's history.

A small-town teacher and businessman who hated Toronto would never invest in projects like opera houses, museums, and art galleries, or so the narrative went. But again, Premier Harris proved them wrong. Not because he decided to be something he was not, but rather because he always moved forward based on what he knew and believed in.

Suffice it to say, Mike Harris and the City of Toronto have a complex relationship. But here is another territory where misunderstandings and careless assumptions disguise what is actually thoughtful and coherent policy.

In truth, the premier's attitude toward Toronto comes back, again, to his deep affection for his own hometown. The premier would often remark, "If North Bay is in tough straits, Toronto's there to help. But if Toronto's in trouble, there's not much North Bay can do." There is no small-town sentimentality here, no wishful thinking. Rather, we have a window into his appreciation for Toronto's pre-eminence and conviction that its success was crucial not just for the future of Ontario but for the entire country.

For Ontario to be competitive, Premier Harris understood that Toronto needed to be competitive. And for Toronto to be competitive on the global stage, it needed to offer all the attractions and amenities of any other "world-class" city. And that meant more than sports stadiums—it also meant first-rate arts facilities. The Royal Ontario Museum. The Art Gallery of Ontario. The National Ballet School. The Royal Conservatory of Music. The Gardiner Museum of Ceramic Art. The Four Seasons Centre for the Performing Arts.

These remarkable structures and the organizations they house define Toronto's identity as a prosperous cultural hub. When passing by them or stepping inside to enjoy their programming, the mind does not wander to the circumstances of either their creation or renewal. Cultural institutions, after all, betray an illusion of permanence, a feeling that they always have been and will be *here*, representing who we are and what we care about. But each of the ones listed above stands today in its fully modernized way because of the inspired decisions Harris made.

In 2002, as one of his very final acts in office, Mike Harris announced a historic collective investment of more than $118 million in support of the organizations on that list.[4] Today, they are known as "the houses that Mike built."[5] Beneath this seemingly surprising announcement lay years of complex negotiation and squabbles with the federal government. But once the deal was finalized, a sense of cooperation took hold, with both orders of government working together with philanthropic interests to rebuild and revitalize the province's capital.

At the time, the premier's motivations were called into question by naysayers, as is the custom of those with nothing better to do. He was accused of leaving office a different man than the one who arrived, one who had come to crave acceptance in the living rooms of Binscarth Road in Rosedale. He was accused of throwing a last minute "Hail Mary pass" to, if not save, at least burnish his legacy.[6]

But those who leveled this charge simply don't understand Mike Harris. In a 2006 interview with *The Globe and Mail*, at a time when shovels had broken ground in reconstruction sites across the city, he reflected: "When I went abroad as premier of Ontario, people didn't know Ontario. They knew Toronto, it was apparent to me that Toronto had to be a world-class city."[7] Indeed, at the outset of his second term, the premier focused his energies on securing greater global investment. He understood that if Toronto was to be considered a "world-class city," it demanded a strategic reorientation. Revealingly, the premier explained in the same interview: "Within the Toronto community, there was the will and the wherewithal. We just had to get off the little projects and into the keystone projects."[8]

After the difficult decision to cut arts and culture spending in the early years of his premiership as part of an urgent mission to restore fiscal sanity to the province, by 2002 the time was finally right to make major investments that would have a lasting effect on both Ontario's civic and economic wellbeing. All in all, SuperBuild, a creation of the Harris government, invested approximately $300 million in tourism and cultural attractions, not only in Toronto but throughout the province.[9] Far from being the philistine he is often made out to be, Mike Harris understood the catalytic role that arts and culture could play in Ontario's long-term economic viability and resilience.

Under a Mike Harris-led government, the "artscape" of the City of Toronto was fundamentally transformed to the benefit of generations of Ontarians to come.

* * *

At the core of Mike's understanding of the power of community was his belief in the power of the individual. And within that understanding was his absolute belief in fundamental fairness for everyone and equality of opportunity for all. That belief in fairness and equality of opportunity led him to make many decisions that, on reflection, were not particularly surprising.

His distaste for governments picking winners and losers stemmed, at least in part, from his experience running a ski hill with his dad. A tourist camp near the Harris' business got a government grant to add a ski lift to their property, while Mike's Dad had to take out a mortgage to improve their hill to compete. Hardly a level playing field.

And his belief that it was fundamentally unfair to the individual who owned a bungalow in Scarborough to have to pay more municipal taxes than the owner of a mansion in Forest Hill led him to reform the municipal tax assessment system in the province.

It was that same idea of individual fairness through which he saw issues of equality for gay and lesbian people. To say that times were different for gay men and women before and during the Mike Harris era would be a gross understatement. On the evidence, we were, at best, second-class citizens. And if there were a few rays of hope in the 1960s and 70s, with gradual progress being made on the march to inevitable equality, the HIV/AIDS crisis brought it all to a screeching halt.

Like all catastrophes, the epidemic served as an education in the appalling injustices of inferior citizenship. The farthest reaches of inhumanity were put on display. The brutal, corrosive power of hate was reinforced. And the pain of those around us, our fellow citizens and neighbours, turning a blind eye to the deaths, to the heartbreak, and to the devastation of our community was almost too much to bear. We can't, therefore, skirt this issue as we recite the story of the Mike Harris government. As with all truthful stories about Mike Harris and his government, it is not a simplistic one. But it does serve as yet another powerful portal to probe incorrect assumptions.

When I was asked to write about this subject, I was initially reluctant. It is my view, one I share with countless gay people who lived through this era in both this province and country that all our governments should and could have done so much more. That much is obvious.

But that much does not get us very far down the road of coming to an appreciable understanding of the matter. And that's why it is also wrong to try and comprehend this period and topic through a partisan lens. Sadly, this was much deeper than party loyalties. It was a deep, societal issue. And while partisanship and partisan history contribute to a culture of credit and discredit, demons and saints, that lens simply will not do, because that lens simply does not reflect reality.

Regardless of their political stripe, as every activist knows, there was more than enough blame to go around. The treachery of that terrain was exposed in the spring of 1994, with the failure of the NDP's Bill 167, the *Equality Rights Statute Amendment Act*. If passed, this legislation would have afforded gay couples rights and obligations equal to those of opposite-sex common-law couples by amending the definition of "spouse" in seventy-nine provincial statutes. Regrettably, it was not to be.

After the bill narrowly made it through first reading, Premier Rae, caving to opposition, proposed to water it down by omitting provisions for adoption rights and the redefinition of the word "spouse." Such maneuvers might be excused as an exercise in *realpolitik*, but the bill's true deathblow was the very reason the legislation barely made it through first reading: Rae conceded to a free vote within his own party, surrendering vital tactical terrain. Twelve members of his caucus, still known by some today as the "Dirty Dozen," exercised that freedom. They voted against their party's platform, their leader's entreaties, and the cries for equality from so many of their constituents. Bill 167 failed by a vote of fifty-nine to sixty-eight.

Premier Rae is far from alone in his culpability for this failure. Official opposition leader Lyn McLeod flip-flopped on the issue after promising her support to secure a by-election victory. And to be quite blunt and clear about this sad time in our province's history, Mike Harris, then leader of the third party, never once entertained supporting the bill, while some members of his own caucus decried the proposed legislation with disgusting hate speech on call-in radio programs across the province.

As painful as this development was, it drilled into me a cold truth that has remained with me all my life: a belief in the possibility and value of incremental change. Bill 167's defeat illustrated the folly of trying to lead those who were not willing to be led. It demonstrated that for durable change to take hold, you first need incremental change. And this Mike Harris intuitively understood. He had a built-in sense of how far he could push certain issues and when it was best to make that push. And it is this sense that allowed him to make remarkably clear-eyed decisions, often against the advice of some of his close advisors.

Two examples come to mind.

The first is when a family court judge ruled in favour of a lesbian mother in a custody case. While many around him urged the premier to appeal this decision for political reasons, he asked a simple question: Is this in the best interests of the child? Is this decision fair to the child? And when the answer was "yes," any idea that the decision would be appealed was abandoned. It was a decision that surprised many of those who made up the premier's political base. But it shouldn't have.

Another decision that shouldn't have surprised anyone was Harris's response to a decision by the Supreme Court of Canada to declare parts of the *Family Law Act* unconstitutional in *M v H*.

THE INTUITIVE MIKE HARRIS

It is easy to forget that the case of *M v H* arose from the heartbreak and pain of a failed relationship. The case involved a dispute between a lesbian couple, identified as M and H (the initials belong to their lawyers). After their breakup, M was denied the right to claim alimony. When it was brought before the Supreme Court, the majority decision found that the exclusion of same-sex partners from the benefits in the *Ontario Family Law Act* was unconstitutional.

What is also easy to forget is that although the court directed the provincial government to amend just one piece of legislation, the Harris government instead decided to amend more than sixty and embed individual rights for the gay community across the entire legislative framework of the province (with the exception of marriage). Viewed through the lens of fairness to individuals, it is not hard to understand why Harris personally instructed his attorney general, Jim Flaherty, to take this—at first blush—counterintuitive approach.

The Harris government's work to pass Bill 5, updating the *Family Law Act* and amending all those other provincial laws, to ensure that the rights and responsibilities of same-sex couples mirrored those of common-law couples, made a meaningful and material difference in the lives of gay men and women across the province and their families, including their children. Significantly, it was also the lynchpin in the inevitable march to full equality in all the other provinces. (We'd get marriage in the end.)

In every sense, the real equality that lesbian and gay people have today in Canada can be directly traced to that firm decision by Mike Harris and his government.

That said, the sausage-making was far from ideal. The act itself was inelegantly titled "An Act to Amend Certain Statutes to Ensure Their Constitutionality Because of the Supreme Court of Canada Decision In M Versus H." Accordingly, it was nicknamed by the opposition parties as "The Devil Made Me Do It" act (I have little doubt it felt that way for some Conservative caucus members). But perfection was not the order of the day. As is always the case, real progress is messy, complicated, and imperfect. And yet the decision to embark on that road was not a difficult one for the premier, because he only had to look to his north star and to embrace one of its foundational principles: fairness to the individual and equality of opportunity for all.

* * *

I attended the former Premier's portrait unveiling at Queen's Park in 2007. On that afternoon, I remember standing in the great hall. It was a political version of old-home week. People were renewing acquaintances. Everyone was looking a bit older than each of us would have hoped.

Eleven years later, I came across a photo on Twitter of Harris' son, Mike Harris Jr., standing in front of that great portrait of his dad on Mike Jr.'s first day in the Legislature as an MPP. It's a lovely shot. The image speaks of lineage, of course, but more importantly it expresses the kind of things you pass along, your values. For Mike Harris, his values were those of respect for the individual, fairness, and strength of community.

What made him a truly remarkable leader was that as he moved through government and gained experience from both incredible triumphs and humbling defeats, he stayed true to those values.

And, so, in the end, the premise of the "counterintuitive premier" proves to be dead wrong.

There is instead simply the intuitive one. And once you understand that, you understand not only Mike Harris but all that his government accomplished.

Notes

1 https://www.waterfrontoronto.ca/news/waterfront-toronto-legacy-achievement-exciting-future
2 https://www.waterfrontoronto.ca/our-purpose/inclusive-growth
3 Ibid.
4 The Roy Thomson Hall SuperBuild renovation bid additionally having been approved in 2001.

5   Ross, Val, "The Billion Dollar Baby," *The Globe and Mail*, April 15, 2006. https://www.theglobeandmail.com/arts/the-billion-dollar-baby/article1097561/
6   "Mike Harris and the Power of Negative Thinking," *The Globe and Mail*, March 29, 2002.
7   Ross, Val. "The Billion Dollar Baby," *The Globe and Mail*, April 15, 2006.
8   Ibid.
9   Ibid.

INDEX

North American Free Trade
  Agreement (NAFTA), 20–21
North Bay-Mattawa Conservation
  Authority (NBMCA), 303–304

O

Oak Ridges Moraine (ORM), 209,
  308
  conservation plan, 311–312
  ecological connectivity, 309–310
  environmental integrity, 310
  issues, 239
  protected as landform, 319–320
  south-facing slope, 309
Oak Ridges Moraine Conservation Act,
  240, 311
O'Connor Commission Report,
  306–307
O'Connor, Dennis, 69
  2002 *Report of the Walkerton Inquiry,*
  67–68
OECD's Programme for
  International Student
  Assessment, 137
One Member, One Vote, 6–7
Ontario
  ACCESS proposal sponsored by,
  373
  alternate financing partnerships
  (AFPs), 111
  amalgamation period, 210–211
  bipartisan unwillingness, 350
  budget, 44, 379–380
  CHST allocation to, 384
  civic and economic wellbeing, 433
  civil servant earning, 179
  CPP reform, 56–57

curriculum, 128
cut expenditures and, 30
day-to-day life, 430
debt/GDP ratio, 30
decreasing employment during
  Rae's term, 249
drug benefit reforms, 109
economic viability and resilience,
  433
economy, xx, 16
  fortunes, 16
  growth, 31, 238
  performance, 34–35
  power, 231
  provincial tax base, and, 406
  trajectory during Harris era, 12
education system, 241–242
election platform, 241
electrical system, 273, 289–290
  air quality in, 291–292
  challenges, 285
  coal out of energy mix in,
  290–291
  complexities, 275
  electricity policy in, 295
  private hydro, 294
  retail market, 287–288
employment
  growth, 33
  per cent change from pre-
  recession peak, 185
English- and French-language
  students, 134
environment
  area of undertaking (AOU),
  317
  auto emissions, 314